A Sacred Trust

A Sacred Trust

Nelson Poynter and
the *St. Petersburg Times*

Robert N. Pierce

University Press of Florida
Gainesville
Tallahassee
Tampa
Boca Raton
Pensacola
Orlando
Miami
Jacksonville

Library of Congress Cataloging-in-
Publication Data appear on the last
printed page of the book.

Frontispiece: Nelson Poynter in
1978, shortly before his death. *St.
Petersburg Times.*

The University Press of Florida is
the scholarly publishing agency
for the State University System of
Florida, comprised of Florida
A & M University, Florida Atlantic
University, Florida International
University, Florida State
University, University of Central
Florida, University of Florida,
University of North Florida,
University of South Florida, and
University of West Florida.

University Press of Florida
15 Northwest 15th Street
Gainesville, FL 32611

To Douglas and Diana,
with love and admiration

Contents

Illustrations

Prologue

—————

Why This Book

When I was twenty-eight, I decided there was no such thing as an honest newspaper. I had been working for daily papers nearly half my life, and perhaps it was partly burnout.

Somewhere, perhaps in college, I had acquired the notion that journalism was a profession, but I had since come to believe it was a profession chained inside a depredation. Young journalists also like to believe that they work for the public and that the publisher's function is to pay the light bill. This proved to be a fantasy. My job at a succession of newspapers was to make the owner feel important.

So if I were to sell out my dreams, I would do so dearly. I took a public relations job at higher pay in St. Petersburg, Florida. I had heard that the morning paper there, the *Times,* was remarkably good. But the Diogenes in me had blown out his lantern.

Try as I might, I could not fit the *Times* into the mold of moral corruption. Although as aggressively news-hungry as other papers, it was different. Its reporters were not satisfied with a grab at a headline but were willing to take the time to get the truth behind the facts. They were better educated, had good table manners, and, in the main, did not mask insecurity with arrogance. And unlike most papers, the *Times* looked like it had really been touched by human hand before going to press. Staff members, even in bar conversation, spoke of the paper's owner, Nelson Poynter, in hushed tones. They saw him not as an obstacle to their efforts but as someone who made all good things possible.

Over the following three decades, the miracle on a sandy Florida subpeninsula has attracted attention around the world. One by one, writers for national media have rediscovered the *Times*, always amazed that avant-garde journalism could come out of a county believed to be an elephants' graveyard where Lawrence Welk fans made their final trek.

These writers' recurring amazement also grew out of the conventional wisdom that outstanding newspapers could exist only in the largest cities. Furthermore, the *St. Petersburg Times* itself was continually making news. The first Pulitzer arrived in 1964, followed by two more in the 1980s. Other national prizes were added in profusion. The paper pushed past long-famous papers to gain a niche in *Time* magazine's "ten best" list.

But alert observers knew the most remarkable things about the *Times* occurred backstage. One was Poynter's dogged effort to give the paper away. He did not want his descendants to inherit it, because none had the qualifications he demanded of his executives. And he did not want one of the chains that now own 76 percent of American dailies to gobble it up; that would cost the paper its independence.

Laws make it almost impossible to give away a business, because this tactic often has been a tax dodge. Poynter had no such motive, but it took his accountants and lawyers years to devise an IRS-proof educational institute that would inherit controlling stock in the *Times* and its subsidiaries.

The offspring of this corporate insemination came to be called the Poynter Institute. Housed in a gleaming palace by the bay, this combined think tank and training school is perhaps the world's most nimble scout on the frontier of journalistic knowledge. And it never has serious worries about expenses, as Poynter built the *Times* into a marvel of money-making aggressiveness long before he died in 1978.

Even more ingenious was Poynter's strategy for projecting his philosophy beyond the grave. He believed a newspaper should be run by one person with the authority but not the wealth of ownership, someone as dedicated to the *Times*'s mission as Poynter himself. He changed the company's bylaws to require that each succeeding chairman appoint his or her own successor in an inheritance of ideals if not of genes. So confident was he that he vested a monarchical power in these future occupants of his chair; the board of directors would advise but not overrule the chairman.

The typical reader knew little about these boardroom scenarios and cared less, even though they made the *Times* what it was. Sitting on the porch of a retirement cottage or scanning the headlines before dashing off to work, subscribers sensed that this paper was different from those they had read elsewhere. It avoided the breathless trivia then fashionable in American journalism. One observer described it as "sociologically" edited: "It does not offer bits and pieces aimed at readers like birdshot, but attempts to relate one event to another so that readers can grasp how their lives are being affected. The technique . . . makes the *Times* more than just a newspaper, but a FORCE."[1]

Most newspapers that aspire to be a force are dreadfully dull. But there was a fizz to reading the *Times*. It was one of the first publications to launch a crusade for good writing, even putting a coach in the newsroom for this purpose. It set a national standard in using color graphics and photos to tell complex stories, and it probed the outer reaches of printing technology to make the paper look as elegant as money could make it.

Perhaps the strangest paradox of many was the *Times*'s refusal to go along with majority opinion in its community. In Florida's largest bastion of Republicanism, the *Times* kept intact its reputation as the state's most liberal editorial voice. Its presidential endorsements continually departed from local voters' preferences, and it exhorted its readers to change their minds on gun control, Contra aid, and capital punishment.

Sometimes its idealism went against its own interests. Poynter always insisted newspapers should not wrap themselves in the First Amendment to avoid taxes, even though this embarrassed fellow publishers who used editorial power for their own benefit. When the *Times* supported an advertising tax, it had to watch its fellow dailies club the proposal to death.

And despite its aggressiveness in pursuit of news breaks, the *Times*'s reporters found they had to carry a heavy baggage of ethics with their assignments. People mourning loved ones at a disaster scene could not be harassed with ghoulish questions, and staff members could not conceal their identity to get inside a story. Management refused to adopt a written code of ethics on grounds that it was self-defeating, but the standards got around by word of mouth.

If the *Times* was well known for the brilliant staff it assembled, it was even better known for those who left. Over several decades the paper became an incubator for talent that ended up in leading jobs with the *New York Times,* the *Washington Post,* and other major dailies. The chairman of the Knight-Ridder chain, the presidents of United Press International and the *Los Angeles Times-Mirror,* the publisher of the *Detroit Free Press,* and the editor of the *Louisville Courier-Journal* graduated from the *Times* staff. Direction of the flow turned slowly, and not only did the paper begin to keep many of its stars, but other big-name journalists were attracted to it as well.

Because it was so prosperous, the *Times* figured high on chain owners' shopping lists. Near the end of the 1980s one leading brokerage firm estimated the company's total worth at $800 million, which would be a record price if it sold for that. Poynter and his successors, Eugene Patterson and Andrew Barnes, rebuffed all offers. "You can buy the *Times*—for a quarter at the corner news rack," Poynter would say.

Instead of cashing in on spiraling prices, management kept taking plunges to expand and put profits to use. Like Spanish explorers four centuries before, Patterson staked his flag in longtime rival Tampa and proclaimed it *Times* territory. In fact, he invented a new megalopolis embracing dozens of towns and gave it a name, Tampa Bay. As in many such brazen strokes, dominating the new realm remained only a plan.

Just as Patterson handed over the reins to Barnes, there arose the very threat to the *Times*'s independence that Poynter had feared. A Texas oil heir, who had acquired control of 6 percent of the stock from Poynter's nieces, moved to convert this stake into 40 percent. This could have severely reduced income for the Poynter Institute, and many feared it would make possible a hostile takeover. The suit was settled out of court for a sum reported variously between $50 and $150 million, and the *Times* entered the debilitating recession of the 1990s with this pound taken out of its flesh.

I watched this drama unfolding from the distance of several universities. For a year I had worked for the *Times*'s sister, the *Evening Independent.* Then I became a professor, and I often would assign students to analyze the St. Petersburg enterprise because I knew they would hone their skills and send out sparks of idealism as a by-product. But there was no book they could read about the *Times*. No long look at the paper's current realities and its past existed. The nearest thing to a history was staff member Robert Hooker's hundred-year survey, which ran as a supplement to the newspaper's centennial edition in 1984.

When Eugene Patterson invited me to undertake a book, I thought it would be relatively simple because much data had been assembled. I knew that the *Times*'s extraordinary story had taken on mythical dimensions as told by true believers among its executives. But as I probed into the essence of the story I realized it deserved to be told in much greater proportions and with subtler shadings than had been offered before. I found, for instance, that Poynter's death was as significant as his life, because it put in motion the experiment he had devised—the plan for perpetuating his unique style of management at the newspaper and his obsessive pursuit of ideas at the Poynter Institute. For that reason I have chosen to begin the book with the end of one odyssey and the beginning of another.

I also decided to concentrate the book on the period of Poynter's life, although I have summarized the paper's development before Poynter took charge of it. I also have dealt briefly with some events after his death—those that had most relationship with his life, such as the founding of the Poynter Institute and the ultimate settlement of the dispute over his sister's stock.

Beginning the book with the end of the principal subject's life may be a timeworn literary device, but I employed it to emphasize the fact that Poynter's death was as much a start as a finish. Not only did he create a great newspaper during his lifetime; he also conceived a schema for a totally unique journalistic institution—one that could in many ways be reborn with each new chief executive who succeeded to absolute control of it, albeit challenged with the ideals that Poynter maintained. Poynter designed this experiment to commence the day he died.

This book is the result of eight years' efforts. I have tried to confine my own reflections to this section and the final chapter. Of course, the book is not totally objective, because I have tried to interpret the major themes in the newspaper's evolution rather than recount a chronology of poorly related facts. Nor have I shrunk from the less flattering side. But this is a story of human beings, some brilliant, some obsessed, all with limitations. Somehow, they worked together to fashion a newspaper unlike any other.

Ownership or participation in ownership of a publication or broadcasting property is a sacred trust and a great privilege.

—Nelson Poynter,
"The Standards of Ownership," 1947

Chapter 1

_____

The Day It Started

First glints of dawn crept across Tampa Bay toward St. Petersburg. Sunrises there lacked the fiery strokes of sunsets on the Gulf of Mexico, west of the city. But now and then a rocket launching at Cape Canaveral, eastward across the state, added a bit of drama. And the *Times* switchboard would twinkle with calls reporting a strange new star in the east.

Bob Haiman's alarm went off at 5:15. It was his usual wake-up time, even though as executive editor of the *Times* he would work into the evening. Haiman slipped out of bed where his wife, Royce, slept on. He glanced into the room where their nine-year-old son, Robert, was enjoying the long sleep of a kid on summer vacation. Bob suited up for running, let the dog out, and checked the morning paper to make sure no major story had broken after he left the newsroom the night before.

A tall, brown-haired man of forty-two, he had kept the good looks of the partying bachelor he had been when he joined the *Times* in 1958. He was a native of Connecticut but had lived in Florida since he was a college sophomore. The *Times* had been his career. He had moved up swiftly, becoming the youngest member in the history of the board of directors. An ex-marine, he was outgoing and aggressive, unhampered by an occasional stutter.

Despite his fervor for the *Times,* Haiman spread himself widely. He was a Presbyterian elder and served on civic boards. The year before he had been a Pulitzer Prize juror, and in a few years he would become

1

national president of the Associated Press Managing Editors Association.

As he stretched his legs on the front porch, Haiman felt the hint of a hot, humid day that would rise into the low nineties by noon. Then he set off on a three-mile jog through the quietly elegant streets. His house was in northeast St. Petersburg, close by Tampa Bay. It was on the mainland, surrounded by shading oaks, but later that year the family was to move to a finger-fill house with pool and boat dock near Snell Isle, dowager queen of the city's elite neighborhoods.

Haiman sat down to a low-fat breakfast he hoped would ward off the heart trouble that would come five years later anyway. He and his wife traded sections of the bulging Thursday morning paper, crammed with grocery ads. It was June 15, 1978, and the *Times* editors had a busy but not exciting run of news to fill the issue.

H. R. Haldeman, serving time for Watergate crimes, was told he would have to wait six more months for parole. Vice-president Mondale was off on a trip to India, and when he returned President Carter would go to Panama to sign the newly agreed-upon canal treaty. Consumers Union had kicked off a spat with Chrysler by declaring its new subcompacts unsafe. The president of Italy had resigned, and King Hussein of Jordan announced he would marry an American twenty-two years his junior.

In sports, the Baltimore Orioles beat the California Angels to run their winning streak to thirteen. An ad for the new Chevrolet Impala offered it at $5,689 with air, and the stock market was down 10 to 844.8. *Grease* and *Harper Valley PTA* were playing at the movies. Haiman decided it would be a good weekend to stay home and finish a new book by Howell Raines, a brilliant reporter who had left the paper two months before to join the *New York Times*.

Fresh in a cord suit, button-down blue shirt, rep tie, and loafers, Haiman kissed his wife and told her he hoped to be home by 6 o'clock as he expected nothing unusual that day. He backed out of the garage in his green 1972 Datsun 240Z, successor to the sports cars he had raced in his youth.

Driving south along the bay, Haiman passed the huge buff-colored Vinoy Park Hotel, which for several years had stood vacant as a symbol of the downtown area's decay. He recalled recent talk about revitalizing the center and decided to check it out. The seven miles of

The first issue of the *St. Petersburg Times,* dated July 25, 1884, was printed on this Washington hand-operated press. Courtesy of the *St. Petersburg Times.*

public waterfront, which the *Times* had saved from commercial exploitation early in the century, had fallen into neglect.

Haiman nosed the Z car into its space in a bank parking garage. He noticed publisher Jack Lake's big Lincoln in its slot. He figured that Nelson Poynter, *Times* owner and board chairman, would be along soon, as would Gene Patterson, president and Poynter's designated successor.

Across the street stood the rambling plant of the *St. Petersburg Times,* actually three connected buildings. There was the eight-story yellow brick structure that Paul Poynter, Nelson's father, had put up during the 1920s boom. Next to it was a four-story wing built in 1951 to accommodate the production equipment that Nelson Poynter was continually buying to stay in the vanguard of newspaper technology. On the corner was a handsome five-story white-and-gray building finished in 1968 and paid for in cash, fruit of the company's growing prosperity.

Haiman greeted lobby receptionist Jean Gagyi and rode the elevator to the third-floor newsroom, vowing to start using the stairs like

Poynter did. After reading the *New York Times,* the *Wall Street Journal,* and the cross-bay rival *Tampa Tribune,* he talked with some desk editors about their own paper. He said a story about arrest of smugglers bringing in ten tons of marijuana up the coast had been underplayed. It appeared Florida's role as a drug funnel would continue to grow, and the *Times* should do more, he added.

Haiman was aware that later that morning Poynter was to be honored at a groundbreaking for the University of South Florida's St. Petersburg branch. But he had other commitments, and he knew the newspaper would be well represented by other executives.

Andy Barnes, managing editor and next in command to Haiman, had started the day by fixing breakfast for his family. Although trees shaded their rambling house, its lack of air conditioning obviously would be felt that day.

When Andy and Molly Barnes left Washington, D.C., in 1973 for St. Petersburg, they had bought a home in an even more traditional part of the city than the Haimans' house, southeastward along a bayou leading to Tampa Bay. Near a small park, the house had been built for the scion of a wealthy merchant family. Their sons Chris, eight, and Ben, six, had room to rove, and soon baby Elizabeth would join them. The encroaching racial integration did not faze them.

But the Barneses obviously never would fit the mold of old St. Petersburg. He had gone to Harvard, she to Pembroke. They had imbibed the liberal intellectualism of New York and New England and had helped start experimental "free schools" for their children in the Washington area. After they moved south, Molly started her own private school, combining a return to basics with a homelike atmosphere.

Andy was a fully formed New Yorker when he started his career, and, although he did not flaunt it, he saw no reason to change. He was intensely oriented to his home—a quiet family life and long hours for reading. He shared in the chores—gardening, cooking, laundry—and spent much time with his children. The clarinet he had played in school now was used occasionally in a jazz combo of news staffers. He jogged twenty miles a week.

Barnes had not joined the Yacht Club, a stronghold for the St. Petersburg establishment. He realized that not mingling with the social elite could pose difficulties for him, but he had always ignored such risks and was compelled by no new urge.[1]

Barnes was proving an adroit newsroom leader at the *Times*. When Haiman was promoted to executive editor two years before, Barnes succeeded him as managing editor. Considering the energy and talent of both men, some observers were beginning to wonder whether there was room for the two of them in the paper's leadership.

Usually Barnes did more than an hour of paperwork at home before coming to the office. But this morning, June 15, he read the newspaper hurriedly, as he wanted to attend the USF groundbreaking. The campus site was on his route to the office, so he left his brown Toyota at home and made the three-mile trip on his bicycle. As he locked his bike to a sign, he noticed construction rubble in front of the dignitaries' stage. He wondered how they would get the ceremonial gold-painted shovels into the soil.

———

Snell Isle had little of the vulgar showiness often found on Florida's Gold Coast, the fortune-littered strip from Palm Beach to Key Biscayne. It was old rich, mostly dating to the 1920s when a developer who loved Mediterranean opulence transplanted some of it to the Tampa Bay shore of Pinellas County. An Atlantis in reverse, Snell Isle had emerged from the water of Tampa Bay, pumped from the bay bottom and buttressed into strips of land that allowed the wealthy to have docks behind their houses and a street in front.

Gene Patterson lived on the prime street, Brightwaters Boulevard. His home was a stately but unpretentious bi-level tucked into a small lot, as most Brightwaters mansions were. Reclinata palms softened the white stucco walls and barrel-tile roof. From the house or the pool one could just see the skyline of Tampa, and jets whispered across the horizon into the international airport. Out front usually stood Sue Patterson's Cadillac Seville and Gene's dark-green 1965 Mustang. The sports car recalled his younger days, when he held motion in his hands as a World War II tank commander and cavalry officer.

It was nothing like the hardscrabble Georgia farm where Patterson had grown up during the depression. His passion to achieve had brought him national note as a Pulitzer Prize–winning battler for racial justice. Most colleagues thought it fitting when, six years before, he climaxed his career by becoming Nelson Poynter's heir apparent to control the *St. Petersburg Times.* But they wondered how long Patterson's aging boss would keep the reins. Certainly Patterson had proved his mettle. A paper known as one of the nation's best "small" dailies was outgrowing its reputation. It now was the largest-circulation paper between Miami and Washington, and before long its quality would receive national ranking.

Patterson's eighty-eight-year-old mother was visiting him and Sue. Annabel Patterson had been the driving force in her family and Gene's inspiration. She had taught school for four decades, picking up a master's at age sixty-five. A carotid blockage was threatening her life, and a doctor back home wanted to operate. Gene had brought her down, hopeful that Nelson Poynter's physician could dissuade her from surgery. That evening he planned to drive her across the bay to Bradenton for dinner with an old friend whom she had not seen for nearly fifty years.

Short and redheaded, Patterson was losing his youthful wiriness to an expanding waistline. He kept to his habit of rising at 6:30, even though he usually worked until seven or eight at night.

Having prepared a light breakfast, he knew he had a full day ahead. After the 9:30 editorial conference there would be little time before he accompanied Poynter to the groundbreaking ceremonies. He strode out to the Mustang and set off on the ten-minute trip to the office.

———

Two executives more different than Jack Lake and Andy Barnes could scarcely be found. As publisher of the *Times,* Lake was an aggressive, impatient, outspoken manager. His silver hair set off his elegant clothes, but his hard-edged speech suggested the streetwise school of advertising through which he had come up. He was the paper's outside man, heading innumerable civic drives and shoving the city toward big-time sports.

Under his firm hand the *Times* had shaken out many of its business problems and turned from a moneymaker into a golden goose. He liked to say he was a eunuch in matters of editorial policy, but his loud disagreements with Gene Patterson sometimes had to be arbitrated by Poynter.

This week in mid-June was special for the Lakes. Cynthia, second of their three daughters, was to be married, and days of festivities were planned at the Boca Raton Hotel and Club, an architectural landmark. Its 920 units rented for up to $325 a day in the winter. Wedding guests were coming from all over the country, and they were even to have their own golf and tennis tournaments.

The Lakes enjoyed life at the clubs, and Cynthia had been Sun Goddess, the queen of the Festival of States Suncoasters' Ball. Her father would be Mr. Sun, the male honoree, a few years later.

Nelson and Marion Poynter had given a party for Cynthia and her fiancé, and their gift was a Lalique crystal bowl. As Jack was close to many baseball greats, Stan Musial and his wife were to cohost another wedding event the next day. Katharine Ann Lake already was in Boca helping with her daughter's wedding. Jack was to join her that afternoon by chartered airplane.

The view of Brightwaters Inlet from the Lakes' terrace was exquisite that morning, the pelicans and gulls already busy and the boats gently rolling at dock. But Lake quickly ate the breakfast the maid had served and headed for the office. He too would be attending the groundbreaking.

A Different Drummer

Unlike most of his executives, Nelson Poynter lived on the west coast of the Pinellas subpeninsula. Although his house was on Park, a street of expensive homes, the area was less fashionable than Snell Isle. It too had been developed in the boom of the twenties, but it was a jungle-like frontier and attracted the more adventurous.

Poynter was indifferent to most things money could buy. It was not until 1959, when he was fifty-five, that he and his second wife, Henrietta, had moved from a modest beach house to 900 Park Street. The serene one-story home was hidden in the spacious grounds and overlooked Boca Ciega Bay.

Poynter never had known want. He had grown up in a small Indiana town amid an extended family that had lived there since pioneer days. The Poynters were moderately well off, but liberal politics, community service, newspaper building, and buoyant individualism were more important than possessions. They adored each other while often scrapping over who was to be in charge.

Nelson had gained control of the *Times* after twenty years of financial upheaval. Ever since, he had jealously guarded the paper against any interference he thought might divert it from becoming the best newspaper in Florida and one of the best in the nation. He had a chivalric obsession for the grail of professional perfection, although there always was one more dragon to slay.

His wife, Marion, was twenty-two years younger than he. It was his third marriage. The first, to a local society girl, had ended in divorce after fourteen years, and their two adopted daughters went with their mother. The second was to Henrietta Malkiel, a New Yorker of towering intellect and newspaper skill. Their love-partnership was cut short when a stroke killed her. The match with Marion had come just eight years before in 1970, and she brought him a companionship of music, gentle wit, and support—without rough edges.

Marion had been having a heart irregularity. That morning she was to go to their doctor's office to be fitted with a Holter monitor, which logged a person's heartbeat over a day or so. They were planning a vacation that fall, a sentimental return to a rented cottage at Martha's Vineyard.

Nelson was elated about the groundbreaking. He dressed in a favorite summer combination, a tan linen suit with brown-and-white shoes and the habitual bow tie. His neglect of style had always exasperated the women around him. At least today his outfit projected good cheer.

It was a seven-mile trip eastward across the peninsula to the *Times* office. Poynter drove in a small gray six-cylinder Buick he had ordered to replace his old silver Cadillac because he wanted to set an example in fuel economy. The new car had taken months to arrive, as an eight-cylinder one was delivered by mistake. When Patterson had asked him why he didn't really save gas with a foreign car, Poynter, a friend of American labor, had recoiled at the idea.

Gene Patterson left his office off the third-floor newsroom about 11 A.M. and went to the executive suite one floor up. He invited Poynter to ride with him to the groundbreaking. When they got there, Poynter mounted the covered platform. From it he could see the raw patch of ground the city government had put together as an inducement for the state to build the university branch. A jumble of boat repair shacks and shell mounds had been cleared from the site. A library was to be one of the first of nine buildings; later it would be named after Poynter.

The whole project was expected to cost $25 million. More than a million that the city spent to acquire the land was private money contributed by local businesses. Poynter liked to use his benevolences to prime pumps. The *Times* had underwritten the first $500,000, and it shook the other donations loose.

Although he had never taught, his close associates considered Poynter a frustrated schoolmaster. He ran his newspaper that way, preferring to guide readers into choosing the high road rather than pampering them with entertainment or devil-theory exposés. He had set up a journalism training institute and bequeathed his properties, worth hundreds of millions, to it. He had established fellowships and study programs at Indiana and Yale, where he earned degrees. And for decades he had yearned to see a university built in St. Petersburg.

Poynter sat on a steel folding chair with seven other dignitaries who were to turn the first shovelfuls. He listened to the oratory, most of it from Chester Ferguson, Tampa's powerful strategist for the Lykes Brothers shipping and agricultural empire. Ferguson had married Louise Lykes, but he became one of Florida's two or three most influential men on his own. He had chaired the university system's regents and held financial sway over its highly competitive expansion into nine institutions.

Ferguson was as extroverted as Poynter was reserved, and the *Times* owner admired what the other man had achieved with his buccaneering ways. Both had combined pragmatism with idealism in a passionate pursuit of the public good. Poynter had badgered Ferguson repeatedly to have a branch campus of Tampa's University of South Florida built in St. Petersburg, and the magnate had delivered.

Now Ferguson was heaping praise on Poynter for all he had done for education. As he listened, Patterson realized Ferguson was going far beyond his usual courtliness. He seemed to have been saving this sincere tribute for a long time to deliver before Poynter's home folks. Poynter normally despised public attention. What with the *Times*'s unpopular editorial stands, he was accustomed to being called a Communist or, at best, a foolish dreamer. So he beamed at Ferguson's salute.

Then the honorees stepped down to the line of spades and stirred up the soil while photographers fired away. Poynter handled the shovel awkwardly. His small frame was not built for manual labor, and his shyness stiffened him in front of cameras.

A luncheon at the Yacht Club for about a hundred leading citizens was to conclude the festivities. It had been hot and uncomfortable at the groundbreaking. But as they made the short drive to the club, Poynter told Patterson how flattered he felt to get such kind words from Ferguson. Poynter was in good form at the luncheon. During a reception, he cornered Bill Bond, Sr., owner of a string of downtown retirement hotels. The Princess Martha, largest hotel in the section and a sentimental totem, was going into one of many sales or receiverships to come.

"Bill, it's up to you to save the Princess Martha," Poynter told him in dead seriousness, as he never shied away from telling leaders what they should do for the city. Bond squirmed away with embarrassed nods.

As the biggest contributor, Poynter was to give the luncheon's main talk. He usually was a poor public speaker, but this time he was notably effective—brief and entertaining. He recalled how the military presence in the city had wound down after World War II, leaving empty a sturdily built maritime base on the waterfront. The *Times* had supported a drive to convert it into a university. Now it was to be joined with handsome new buildings on the newly bought land.

The fact that St. Petersburg had to accept a satellite relationship with a Tampa institution to get its branch campus underlay all the day's polite orations but went unspoken. Poynter concluded by touching on both the rivalry between the cities and the unity that time was pressing upon them. Patterson was delighted to see Poynter's puckish humor emerging toward the end. Deadpan but with a twinkle, he intoned, "I want to thank our Tampa friends for all they've done for us in St. Petersburg. You built a beautiful new airport"—he paused—"and we use it." A few people snickered. "You built a great new stadium—we go to games there." Laughter rose as he warmed to his theme of how the cities were benefiting by competing.

As the two men rode back to the office, Poynter fell silent. Suddenly he blurted out that he had never, in this town, heard so many nice things said about him. Then he smiled: "They must think I'm going to die."

Instants later the Mustang pulled into the garage space. Patterson got out and noticed Poynter was still seated. He assumed the older man was fumbling for the door handle, as mechanical matters gave him trouble. The wait became too long. Patterson bent and saw that Poynter was just getting the door open, but he was having difficulty swinging his legs out.

At first Patterson did not touch him. Poynter was a private man, Christian Scientist by upbringing and stoic by inclination. One did not offer help to such a man lightly. But Poynter was holding on to the car and dragging a leg. Jack Lake had just stepped out of his car thirty feet away, and Patterson beckoned him. A startled look on Lake's face turned to alarm as he saw Poynter.

There followed a scene that was strange but logical, given how aware the younger men were of their boss's fierce independence. He obviously could not walk unaided, so each lifted one of Poynter's forearms and walked him down the ramp onto the sunny sidewalk of First Avenue South. As he stumbled between them he kept up a superficial conversation to look normal and avoid being noticed. They waited out a traffic light and inched into the tall glass doors of the newer five-story building. Jean Gagyi stared with alarm.

Patterson and Lake kept up the charade as they rode the elevator but exchanged anxious looks. They got Poynter into a chair in his office before Patterson said, "Nelson, I think I ought to call Charles Donegan to take a look at you." Donegan was the Poynters' physician and close friend.

This annoyed Poynter. "No, I'm all right. You and Lake go on to your offices. Somebody needs to get some work done around here." Patterson could see that he was adamant.

Poynter called in Rita Estrada, his secretary, and asked her to take dictation. She noticed his jacket was tossed on the couch, contrary to his usual neatness. Leaving to get her pad, the secretary heard Patterson call her from Lake's nearby office. He asked her to keep an eye on Poynter. As she was going back, she heard a thud. She found Poynter on the floor in front of his desk. He had been trying to walk.

Estrada and Lake got him onto the couch, and Patterson and Haiman rushed in. One side of Poynter's face was swollen and sagging, and they realized he was having a stroke. Poynter said he wanted to go home. But Patterson had sent a message to Marion Poynter, and she insisted that her husband be taken to an emergency room. He acceded to her wish but refused to ride in an ambulance. Lake went down to get Poynter's car out of the garage. Dr. Donegan was notified.

Patterson and Haiman started helping Poynter out of the office, but Poynter would not leave in his shirtsleeves, despite the heat outside. Patterson urged him to forget the jacket, but Poynter glared back. "I feel undressed without my coat," he said. They wrestled him into it like a sack of potatoes.

On the trip to the hospital, Poynter could not sit up but refused to lay his head in Patterson's lap, propping himself half-lying on an elbow. Poynter kept up the banter, talking about everything except his health. Patterson had heard Poynter do this countless times before—covering other people's awkward moments with incessant if inane conversation. He had patched over shouting matches between Patterson and Lake with it.

Patterson also realized Poynter was coping with a challenge. "I like pressure," he had often said. "Some men try to avoid it. The higher the pressure on me, the better I do." If he feared he had been beaten this time, he concealed it well. He recalled the day's events. He wanted the others' opinion of the new USF branch dean. Patterson praised the dean. "One great guy," Lake said, hitting the accelerator.

Dr. Donegan arrived a few minutes after Poynter was installed on a gurney. After some quick checks, Patterson saw in the physician's eyes that the situation was bad.

Poynter was making jokes. "I'll bet you Charles is going to try to give me the operation he wouldn't give your mother," he chortled at Patterson. Then, for the second time that day, he told Patterson to get back to work and take Lake with him. When he got to the office, Patterson wrote a notice for all bulletin boards telling the news.

Marion had lunch at the Donegan home after getting her monitor at the doctor's office. She was still there when the call came from the *Times* office, and at Donegan's request she had delayed going to the hospital. When she got there Nelson was in good spirits, and they joked and chatted.

"You're the one who should be in the hospital!" he laughed, pointing at the monitor.

Then they grew more serious, and Nelson took off his wedding band.

"You gave this to me, and I'm going to give it back now," he said.

Marion refused it: "No, this is for keeps."

Marion was in and out of his room as tests were made. About 7 P.M., Nelson lapsed into what seemed to her a deep sleep with heavy snoring. She left to go home and thought little of the fact that she heard Dr. Donegan's name being paged.

Final Edition

It was a day for catching up at the Modern Media Institute, housed then in a converted bank building on Central Avenue that looked like a miniature Ft. Knox. None of the seminars that pulled journalists from all over the country was in progress. Director Don Baldwin and his staff of two were getting ready for future sessions.

Keystone of a project intended to ensure the *Times*'s independence, the institute had been founded three years before to give journalists the kind of training in short supply elsewhere, such as management skills, ethics, graphics, and the fine art of writing. The institute still was in its infancy, but its full mission was programmed to start at some unknown point in the future—the day Nelson Poynter died. That was because he had willed nearly all his stock in *Times* enterprises, worth hundreds of millions of dollars, to the institute.

The plan would prevent inheritance taxes, the death sting that had forced heirs of so many fine old independent papers to sell out to the chain operations that were binding the nation's journalism into a few bundles. Despite years of fine-tuning by lawyers all the way to Washington, the plan had its risk. The Internal Revenue Service had never been faced with just such a plan, and there was no assurance the government would approve it.

Poynter had chosen Don Baldwin to launch the institute. Baldwin had been president and heir apparent to control of the *Times* company until their relations had gone bad and exploded during a confrontation in Poynter's office. That was six years earlier, and their friendship had resumed. Baldwin was a tall, lanky man from Idaho who had won success as an Associated Press editor in the Far East. Possessed of a generous spirit and quick temper, he was agile and quick-minded at sixty.

Early that afternoon Baldwin got a phone call from Bob Pittman, in his office at the *Times* plant two blocks away. He said Poynter was in the hospital with what appeared to be a minor stroke. It did not appear life-threatening, and they chatted about the weather, the groundbreaking, and other small matters. As chief of the editorial page, Pittman was another pillar of the newspaper. A soft-spoken North Carolinian, he had shouldered the attempt to bring the community closer to Poynter's way of thinking, even though that meant being liberal in Florida's strongest Republican bastion.

After hanging up from Pittman's call, Baldwin called his wife, Pat, and told her the news. That evening the Baldwins went over to 900 Park Street, resolved to spend what time was needed to keep Marion company. Pittman and his wife, Ruth, joined them. About dark Dr.

Donegan called Patterson at the *Times* and said he'd better get an obituary ready.

"He's not going to make it?" Patterson asked.

"His condition doesn't look good."

Bleeding in Poynter's brain had stopped for a moment but started again at a rate that ruled out surgery. Poynter had finally admitted his head ached.

Newspapers keep obituaries ready for prominent people, but they never seem to be in final shape. Patterson pulled out clippings and files and reread instructions Poynter had written three years before. He had specified a one-column headline and vetoed any commentary or "silly tributes by those who want to get their names in the paper." And there must be no follow-ups after the first day.

> You know, of course, there will be cremation—no funeral or memorial service of any kind—no requests "in lieu of flowers."
>
> You might include . . . that I have observed no one really likes to go to a funeral. I am trying to be considerate of any friends who might come to my funeral—by having none.
>
> Important in the story is emphasis no change whatsoever in TPC [Times Publishing Co.] as result of death. I'll haunt you like the devil if the above is not carried out. . . . Just live up to the Standards of Ownership thereafter.[2]

The standards were a unique set of demands he had laid down for himself and his successors when he bought control of the paper from his family in 1947. He had pledged not to sell out to a chain or form a chain, to leave power over the paper in one person's hands, not to let stock ownership scatter, and to share profits with employees and pay them above average.

Patterson wrote a mostly straightforward obit, letting facts and quotes carry the tribute. He marked it for the top of the front page under a one-column color photo. Jumping to an inside page, the story ended up more than two columns long with four other pictures.

Charles Donegan and his wife went by the Poynter home about 8:30. The doctor said his friend's temperature was rising, but as Nelson had earlier vetoed heroic measures, nothing was being done to prolong life. Later, when the hospital called to report the fever was 104, he prescribed a heavy dose of aspirin. The little group stayed at the house, chatting about vacations and an upcoming dinner party; even Marion took part. They had a drink or two.

About 10:30 P.M. Haiman was in Patterson's office when the phone rang. He saw the editor's face blanch. "He's gone? Oh, Lord!" Standing behind his desk, he bent over to write something on a pad. Patterson carried the obit into the newsroom and said Poynter had died. Some staffers wept, others struggled with tears. Sandy Stiles, the paper's longtime trouble-shooter, came by wearing the sweatsuit he had been jogging in.

It was decided that none of the thousand full-time employees should have to get the word by reading it in the paper first. Moving downward through the pyramid, one level after another of supervisors called their staffers. Many came back to the office near midnight. The story moved on the national wires, and calls poured in.

Patterson realized he would have to call a meeting of the board of directors the next morning so he could entertain a motion making him new chief executive officer. "Forget the dead hand," Poynter had said. "Do not miss a step."

After writing a memorial to be adopted by the board, Patterson left for 900 Park to sit for a while with Marion, who was going to spend the night with the Donegans. In the dark privacy of his car, he let the tears fall.

Chapter 2

———

The End of the Line

Steamboat *Mary Disston,* the soot-belching "Dirty Mary" that linked the Pinellas subpeninsula with the outside world, chugged northward on a Monday in May 1887. The craft was not making its usual eighty-mile supply run to the railhead at Cedar Key. It was nosing along the coast loaded with excursionists.

Sunlight jeweled the breeze-rippled bay. The trip took half a day to cover a dozen miles, and passengers enjoyed picking out landmarks from the virgin shoreline and peering at fish in the transparent blue water. When the ship tied up at the Tarpon Springs wharf, local residents greeted the sightseers with a feast under the trees.

Afterward everyone gathered in a new church building for the era's main form of small-town entertainment—oratory. A local dignitary climbed scales of rhetoric until he reached his point: Railroads would soon bring all the advantages of booming America to their secluded nook. He warned against the social evils—particularly alcohol—that modernity would engender. More than 100 miles of the gulf coast were free of "grog shops," he noted with pride.[1]

A local newspaper's enthusiastic coverage of the speech betokened the economic revolution sweeping through Florida, although somewhat later than it enveloped other southeastern states. Journalists, eager to share in the wealth that would come with the movement, were among its chief boosters.

Florida's population in 1880 was dwarfed by that of other south-

eastern states; Georgia's was six times as large. Most Floridians lived in the northern part even though Key West, with its strategic location, was the largest city, with 9,890 inhabitants.[2] Jacksonville, the north-eastern gateway, soon would zoom past Key West to hold the dominant position for decades. Dominance by the central and southern sections was far in the future.

Newspapering followed the same pattern. Jacksonville had the only three dailies in the state. (Georgia had eighteen.) The other forty-two papers published less frequently.

But Florida's boom started in the next decade, thanks largely to arrival of railroads, and the population rose 45 percent by 1890. Newspapers increased far more rapidly, almost tripling to 122.[3]

The Pioneer

Now that railroads were inching down the state, the sky was the limit, and Florida's heavens were attracting settlers from the older, colder states. Newcomers had to be ready for dangers such as were faced by the wife of Pinellas's first editor, who reached into a chicken coop to get eggs and was bitten by a water moccasin. She ran screaming into the house with the snake still attached and died the next day.[4]

The man who brought journalism to the Pinellas subpeninsula was Cooley Sumner Reynolds, who switched between editing and preaching. A native of upstate New York, he had studied for the Baptist ministry but was told by his doctor to go to a warmer climate.[5] After several journalistic ventures elsewhere in Florida, Reynolds moved to what was then known as Clear Water Harbor (later Clearwater), in the so-called Neck or narrowest part of the subpeninsula. A gaunt man with a flowing beard, he still was looking for relief from his asthma, and his wife needed a change of scene after the loss of their first three children.[6]

Always the restless innovator, Reynolds founded a four-page weekly measuring about seven by nine inches. He called it the *Clear Water Times,* as the symmetry of the three five-letter words pleased him, and its first issue was dated July 12, 1873. Reynolds told his readers he had invested $25 in a press and $75 in type and other supplies. As soon as he saw his paper was "appreciated," he wrote, he would spend another $50 and enlarge it.[7] Readers apparently thought

it worth the fifty-cents annual subscription price, as within a year the pages were nine by thirteen inches.[8]

Reynolds's first issue struck a chord that would become a dominant motif of Pinellas journalism—promotion of the area's merits to attract new residents. He wrote that "we" had been getting letters from all over the United States asking for information about the area, although he did not explain why the inquiries had come to him before the paper started. So he devoted his entire front page to an essay extolling the natural wonders of Clear Water Harbor. Its greatest appeal, the frail-chested editor said, was healthfulness: "Other portions of the State have larger bodies of rich farming lands, and more of the conveniences found in sections of the country which have been longer settled; but we boldly challenge the world to furnish a locality more favorable to health."[9]

The paper is reputed to have died after several years, but it was distributed at least into October 1877. By then it had become newsier and larger and had acquired some display type for advertisements.[10]

A Time to Be Born

A railroad reached Tampa in 1884, and developers were booming their promise to build a model community, Disston City, at the southern tip of the Pinellas subpeninsula for at least 50,000 residents.[11] Despite this excitement, the commercial center of Pinellas remained in the Neck— in Clear Water and, five miles to the north, Dunedin. Cooley Reynolds had shown that a newspaper could survive there for at least four years, a remarkable span for a newspaper then.

So it was in Dunedin on Thursday, July 15, 1884, that the *West Hillsborough Times* was first published. The paper would become the *St. Petersburg Times* in a more or less direct line of name and location changes. But some argument could be made that Reynolds had laid its foundation in 1873 with his *Clear Water Times*.

All three founders of the *West Hillsborough Times* were newcomers to journalism, as having several lines of work was common at the time. The editor was James Montgomery Baggett, a dentist from Mississippi. The other two were Jason L. Edgar, a physician born in New York State, and M. Joel McMullen, a printer born in Georgia.

McMullen and his wife printed the four-page weekly on a hand-operated press not much different from Gutenberg's. The size of the

Emma and M. Joel McMullen hand-set the type for early issues of the *Times* in their kitchen because the printshop was too small. *St. Petersburg Times.*

paper's circulation put little strain on the press capacity. For at least a decade from its founding its weekly run was 480 sheets, or a ream of paper.

Two pages each week were "readyprints"—sheets printed on one side with two pages of editorial material and advertisements. These were sold by national suppliers and were an economical way to publish a small-town paper. By 1880, two-fifths of the nation's weeklies used them.[12] But the readyprints, with their news and features rewritten from big-city sources, provided a frontier reader with a crude equivalent of modern wire service and syndicate material. Contents ranged from White House events to features such as "Woman's World—Pleasant Perusal for Feminine Readers." One such column described "A Wife's Province" this way: "She is not expected to do any grand work; her province lies in a contrary direction—in gentleness, in cheerfulness, in contentment, in housewifery, in care and management of her children, in sweetening her husband's cup of life . . . —these are emphatically a 'woman's rights'; her heritage, her jewels, which help to make her crown of glory."[13]

Ethics accorded with the era's scant professionalism. An advertiser could buy space in news columns, and the "Local Items" section would alternate legitimate reports with ad paragraphs:

> Mr. Thomas Crichton, tobacco drummer was in town this week and made us a call.
>
> —A good assortment of groceries and dry goods, cheap for cash at Futrells.
>
> The schooner Falcon left the dock here at 10 o'clock Monday, and returned at 2 o'clock p.m. Wednesday.[14]

Baggett apparently was a better dentist than editor. The founders had expected help from Reynolds, the area's only experienced journalist, but he did not want to commute so far to work. His wife died that September of snakebite, leaving him with three young children.

So after four months the founders sold the paper to Arthur Campbell Turner, a forty-year-old Clearwater merchant. Unlike other early leaders of the *Times*, he was a native Floridian, born near the Georgia border. He fought for the South in the Civil War, and when he

John Donaldson, who came to the Pinellas subpeninsula in 1876, was the area's first black pioneer. He delivered its mail when only twenty-five families lived there. *St. Petersburg Times.*

came home on sick leave his mother did not recognize the poorly fed scarecrow. In his battle cap a hole marked how close a Yankee bullet came to him. When Turner trundled the *Times* printing gear five miles south to Clearwater, Preacher Reynolds was waiting to edit it. Joel McMullen also came along to run the printshop.

Reynolds had a courtly, verbose style. Unlike many frontier editors who delighted in harpooning rivals in other towns, he declared a benevolent policy for his paper. He forswore the partisan creeds that newspapers of that time fought over, and he opted for the role of community spokesman. He wrote that the *Times* would not advance any new dogma or pose as a "general instructor." Because the community was "speaking with a thousand tongues" and needed a translator, he added, the paper aimed "to become merely the telephone through which its inviting voice may be carried to many listening ears."[15]

When Reynolds left the paper after about a year, Turner took over the entire operation, billing himself as editor and proprietor. He had a feistier approach than the parson. Once when a reader asked how he earned his money, he replied in print: "The editor is writing this article at 1 o'clock a.m. His children who went to a temperance meeting at Dunedin, have been home and asleep two hours. That is how he earns his money; but how he gets it is a question about which he will write when he gets it!"[16]

Turner advertised his own store heavily in the *Times*. Even before he bought it, he placed a spirited appeal in a "reader" or news-column ad:

Oh Yes! Oh Yes! Oh Yes!

If you want to find where you can get the best goods, and the most goods for your money, just go to the store of A. C. Turner....

No trouble to show goods; in fact, he loves to do it—thinks it just the way to keep the dust off.

He wants everybody to come and see him, bring dinner and stay all day—and they needn't buy a thing if they can help it.[17]

Turner enthusiastically backed several causes. The first movement to separate Pinellas from Hillsborough County, which foreshadowed the *Times*'s successful campaign two decades later, was boosted prominently.[18] Turner never missed a chance to strike a blow against liquor, and he regularly ran a temperance column.

Black residents were almost nonexistent in the Neck at that time, so little occasion arose for comment on them. But Turner casually dealt out ethnic slurs now and then. One of his "reader" ads joked: "The fire-cracker and the boy, like the mule and the 'nigger,' belong together. Munnerlyn can furnish the crackers."[19]

Taking the Plunge

Despite much fanciful talk about coastal shipping, everyone knew that only a rail connection could exploit Pinellas's future. The person who knew it and had the fierce drive necessary to accomplish it was an immigrant freebooter in high finance, Peter A. Demens. He had arrived in the United States in 1880 at age thirty, spreading the story that he had been born into the Russian nobility as Piotr Alexeivich Dementief. He said he had become a captain of the Imperial Guard and was close to leaders of the government but had decided to throw over his inheritance of the family estates because he lusted after freedom and democracy.

Demens joined legions of exploiters who were stripping the nation of its virgin timber at the time, and he set up a sawmill in central Florida. He soon exhausted the timber around him and looked for new ideas. A tiny new railway company, the Orange Belt, had bought crossties from him and could not pay its bill. To salvage the $9,400 owed him, Demens took over the line's charter and raised $37,000 in working capital. He finished the line's first tracks—a thirty-four-mile stretch north of Orlando—and won instant local worship. This led him

Alligator hunters in St. Petersburg typified the frontier spirit that prevailed around 1900. *Heritage Park, Largo, Florida.*

to a grandiose dream—to extend the line nearly 100 miles to the Gulf of Mexico, at Pinellas Point. He set out to sell $700,000 in bonds but was turned down by New York brokers.

Just as he was about to give up, a Philadelphia heir named Hamilton Disston appeared in Demens's office. Disston had bailed the state of Florida out of its Civil War debts in exchange for huge tracts of land. He then set about developing them for farm use by draining swamps, building canals, and running steamboats.

Disston offered Demens 60,000 acres he owned along the Orange Belt route as a gift upon completion of the track. He also offered influence in Tallahassee to get state land grants for Demens. These promises turned the tide and won Demens the bond issue.

The next eighteen months were a nightmare for Demens. Lenders failed to send the money in time, shipments of rails were months late in arriving, creditors chained his engines to the tracks, torrential rain and a yellow fever epidemic prevented progress, and unpaid workmen threatened to lynch him. He lost 25,000 acres of the land grants because he could not meet a deadline. At one point he wrote his laggard lenders, "Everything and everybody is disorganized and disgusted."

Demens wanted to place his Pinellas terminus on a key off the Gulf side of the subpeninsula, which would require a bay causeway of several miles. He tried to get financing for this from the Disston company directors, who were planning a community development on the mainland nearby. They turned him down, figuring that wherever the railroad went in Pinellas it would benefit them, as they owned most of the area.

Then Demens discovered John Constantine Williams, a Detroit businessman and son of its first mayor. His flowing white beard and honorary title of general gave him the prestige needed to be a city founder. He also had asthma, and doctors of the time, lacking good medicines, prescribed for problem cases a cure few could afford—a trip to Florida. Williams could pay, and in 1875 he set off. He visited Tampa, Lake Okeechobee, Key West, and other places, but none suited him. Then he stumbled across Pinellas, liked it, and bought about 2,000 acres on the Tampa Bay side of the subpeninsula. He also decided the area must have a railroad.

Early in 1887 Williams made a deal with Demens for right of way ending at a fishing village called Paul's Landing. Demens quickly used this contract as leverage to get more capital from investors. One bothersome detail remained—the site had to have a more alluring name. Most historians agree that Demens had always wanted to name one of the many towns he helped found after his home city in Russia. Williams probably wanted to do the same, but, whether by a toss of a coin or by fiat, Demens finally got his chance and named the city St. Petersburg.

The Orange Belt tracks arrived at the edge of the Williams property on April 30, 1888; another five weeks and the first train, a rickety narrow-gauge, rolled into the town. A week later Demens himself arrived in his private car, conferred with Williams, and agreed to split the cost of a $10,000 hotel, to be named the Detroit as consolation for the general. By the next winter the hotel, a depot, and a 2,000-foot railroad pier running into Tampa Bay were finished. There was almost nothing else, but at last the way was clear to build a dream city for anyone who wanted to try.

With its emergence as a railhead and imposing new name, St. Petersburg soon generated the same kind of excitement Clear Water Harbor had, and it became the journalistic center of the Gulf Coast. When the Orange Belt rolled past Clear Water toward its terminus-to-be, time started running out for the paper printed in the Neck. The population of St. Petersburg was growing rapidly, reaching 273 in the 1890 census.

In 1892, the *Times* decamped to St. Petersburg. Turner sold it for $1,200 to a preacher, Richard James Morgan. A native of Alabama, he came to central Florida as a young man, started a family, and grew oranges. He operated a dry goods and millinery store in Clear Water for about six years before settling in St. Petersburg.

Morgan apparently was a restless man who achieved local fame delivering lectures at a time when "Chautauquas" were creating a mass appetite for them. When he addressed "the Chautauqua of the Tropics" on arts and monuments of antiquity, he held the capacity audience "spell bound from the beginning to the end," according to one report.[20] Something of a showman, he used a large painted canvas illustrating Africa for him when lecturing.[21]

Undecided what the paper's name should be, Morgan changed it several times. He was calling it the *West Hillsborough Times* as late as 1894, and an employee later recalled he tried out the *News,* the *Times* and *Once a Week* before settling on the *St. Petersburg Times.*[22]

Morgan built a newspaper shop next to a drugstore at the city's main intersection, Fourth Street and Central Avenue. It had a tar paper lean-to roof and leaked copiously.

The new publisher threw himself into the task. He wrote the news, helped with the printing and engraved his own wood-cut pictures.[23] Morgan also brought new technology to the *Times* by designing a homemade cylinder press whose roller came from the trunk of a large live oak tree. Morgan was ecstatic about his invention: "It's a world beater. There's not another like it!" Later he would build another press and try to patent it. The paper apparently got off to a good start; the *Tampa Tribune* reported a month afterward that it was "a cock-crowing success."[24]

After an abortive attempt to sell the paper to a young teacher, Morgan sold the paper to J. Ira Gore in 1894 or 1895 (the date is uncertain). Although little is known of his family background, Gore grew up in Ocala, where he became interested in politics and litera-ture.[25] He cofounded a paper called the *Artery* in a north Florida town, but the bloody resemblance to his name led to joking and a change to the *Florida State Journal*.

St. Petersburg was launching a boom that would send it bustling into the twentieth century. The town would more than quintuple in population during the 1890s. Electricity and telephones were coming in, streets were being laid out, and a public park with a bandstand was opened. During the Spanish-American War thousands of U.S. troops gathered in Tampa for transport to Cuba, and the economic benefits spread to St. Petersburg. Gore capitalized on this growth in September 1897 with a six-page special edition to be handed out at an exposition in Nashville. It hailed St. Petersburg as the "Ideal City by the Sea."[26] Nothing stirred the editor's enthusiasm more than fishing:

> Those who have visited St. Petersburg in the winter have seen the immense crowds which line the wharf fishing from morn to night, all jolly, all eager for the sport, all unmindful of the masses and classes around them, with negligee shirts, the men rigged in oil-cloth suits and rubber boots and slouched hats, and the ladies with home-made cracker-bonnets and calico wraps. The millionaire and the professional bait-catcher and fisherman are hail fellow well met, seemingly enjoying each other's company.[27]

There were indications that Gore did well with the business side. An 1898 issue shows the front page more than half filled with paid advertising. Some ads came from Tampa companies trying to attract trade from Pinellas, and professionals such as doctors, dentists and lawyers were well represented.[28]

Gore's two sons worked with him in the business. Will served as editor of the *Tarpon Springs Record* in 1900 when he was nineteen, but he died that May of typhoid. Four months later, on September 7, the father succumbed to Bright's disease. The other son, Ira, Jr., took over, but he was not to lead the *Times* far into the new century. That challenge fell to a brash young man from the Great Plains, William L. Straub.

Inventing a City

Bill Straub, a North Dakota journalist, was barely thirty years old when doctors in the North told him he would die if he did not have major surgery, and even if he did he had little chance to survive. They prescribed a rest cure at a Michigan sanitarium to strengthen him for the operation.

"I know a sanitarium that is better than any you have in the North," Straub told the doctors.

"And where is that?"

"It's a little fishing village down in Florida, on the Gulf of Mexico. I'm always better there, and I believe it beats any sanitarium."[29]

Straub had spent several winters in St. Petersburg, and his recurrent bronchitis always cleared up after several weeks there. So in December 1899 he moved there with his wife and baby daughter. His health returned so steadily that he never returned to the North or had the operation. He had used a cane and crutch since a childhood illness in Michigan left him with a withered leg, but he lived another four decades after arriving in Florida, robustly pursuing a career as the most flamboyant editor the *St. Petersburg Times* has ever had.

Straub typified many immigrants to Florida—people who wanted to start life anew in a land where opportunity awaited. One such prospect was escape from illness related to cold weather. The *Times* ran a column called "I Came Here to Die," written by local residents to whom the Florida sunshine had restored health.

More and more northern visitors, like Straub, became so captivated after several vacations they would return to live. Growth had quickened to the point that the 1900 census showed 1,575 persons in the city, nearly five times the population of a decade before. Most new-

Editor W. L. Straub, shown here with his wife, Sarah, and daughter, Blanche, built the *Times* into a significant force in the first decade of the 1900s. *St. Petersburg Times.*

comers were in the prime of life, and the undertaker in a single year buried only twenty-one persons, five of them infants. After a spell of relaxing, most newcomers set about making a living. They brought Yankee ways with them, and St. Petersburg's image as a fishing village faded rapidly. One visitor from Middletown, New York, wrote to his hometown paper that it was "more like a Northern town possibly than any other in the State, having enterprise and push."[30]

Straub and many other immigrants were drawn to farming a crop that had stirred excitement since it was introduced in 1896—pineapples. The first grower put in two acres and made $10,000 profit even after paying for the growing sheds. The rush was on, and by the turn of the century a score of growers with small plots were showing off fruit up to twenty pounds. But the boom died within a few years as Cuba and Puerto Rico recovered from the Spanish-American War; their exports made Pinellas pineapples unprofitable.

Even with his farming, Straub had plenty of time to read the two little weekly newspapers, the *St. Petersburg Times* and the *Sub-Penin-*

sula Sun. Both were in a sad state, and the widow of *Times* owner J. Ira Gore wanted to sell out.[31]

Straub got together with two friends and decided to buy the *Times.* The partners were A. H. Lindelie, whom Straub had known in North Dakota as editor of a Scandinavian newspaper, and A. P. Avery, a young real estate man who later would become the city's leading banker and politician. Together they paid $1,300, and Straub was to

W. L. Straub often illustrated the front page with cartoons. The nameplate resulted from a painting that he sketched by climbing a ship's mast, despite his crippled leg. This issue is dated April 6, 1907. *St. Petersburg Times.*

have editorial command.[32] The newly organized Times Publishing Company announced the deal in the edition of May 4, 1901. Management promised to expand the paper to eight pages by use of readyprint.

The introductory editorial dealt with something that was to dog Straub throughout his editorship—the fact that he had been a Republican activist up north and carried his affiliation with him to a state where this party was identified with the scandals of Reconstruction. The editorial did not refer to Straub directly but only noted that some were skeptical about whether the *Times* would remain nonpartisan: "Why should it be partisan? Every business man in St. Petersburg has his own political views, but which of them takes them into his place of business and does a partisan trade? . . . The *Times* is as strictly a business proposition as any mercantile concern in the city."[33]

Indeed, the *Times* avoided controversy in early months of the new regime. But before the year was out Straub had planted seeds of the great campaigns that he would be remembered for and that shaped the community's future:

1. Political independence from Tampa, forming Pinellas County from the larger Hillsborough.

2. Rescue of the downtown waterfront from commercial exploitation and visual ruin through parks, a pier, and marinas (part of Straub's passionate drive to make St. Petersburg "the City Beautiful").

3. Good roads and bridges to open the Pinellas subpeninsula to the north.

4. The commission form of city government and an end to vote-buying.

Straub had an opinion, pungently written and usually reinforced by a cartoon, on practically every issue that faced St. Petersburg. But he returned to these four repeatedly over the years, seizing upon any relevant news event to hammer his points home for the voters or for some governing body. In the end, he was successful in all. Looking back, a politician recalled that the city council "often gave in to his will to shut him up."

Straub clearly was affected by the so-called golden age of editorial writing during which he lived. He displayed the faith of E. L. Godkin of the *Nation* that America could be saved from excesses of free enterprise gone wild. His choices of editorials to reprint showed that, like most editors, he admired the penetrating elegance of Charles A. Dana's New York *Sun*.

The *Times* had one distinct advantage over other newspapers its size—Straub's cartooning pen. Sketch artists of his caliber usually were found only on large dailies, as was the technology of newspaper illustration. Making engravings from original drawings, as Straub had to do, was a tedious and messy process with "dragon's blood" acid used for etching. Straub did it on the back porch of his home.

Straub always described himself as the world's worst businessman. During his first decade he apparently did everything possible to rid himself of the responsibilities of publishing and distributing a newspaper. But they stuck to him like flypaper, and rather than meeting disaster the *Times* plodded through the years as a steadily improving product. Twice during the first decade of the century, the paper moved to larger buildings, both within a block or two of the main Central Avenue intersection. The second move brought two-story quarters. Straub retreated to an upstairs office, hopping nimbly on his crutch, and distanced himself from the staff. St. Petersburg was turning into a small city with a sturdy brick downtown, and these were the last wooden buildings the *Times* would occupy.

A new building fronting on the downtown railroad tracks was acquired by the *Times* in 1909 and served it until a brick structure was finished in 1921. *Heritage Park, Largo, Florida.*

Straub's efforts to bring stable management to the *Times* were constantly frustrated in his first decade. Less than a year after they bought the paper in January 1902, the names of partners Lindelie and Avery disappeared from the masthead. Straub formed a corporation in 1904 with two investors who did not join in the operation. After the weekly *Independent* was founded in 1906, the *Times* had a vigorous new competitor that would become daily the next year.

So in 1912 Straub took a step that would make the *Times* marketable to a new owner—he changed it into a daily. Then he advertised it nationally for sale.

Good Times, Bad Times

A trade journal about newspapers was unlikely reading for an Edwardian lady from Indiana, especially one on vacation in Colorado Springs escaping the Midwest summer with her family. But Alice Poynter was no bird in a cage. Her husband relied on her to run their newspaper while he roved about looking for new enterprises, and she had become a self-taught expert in her field of public service—penology. Just the year before she had been named a trustee of the Indiana women's prison by her husband's Democratic party ally, Governor Thomas R. Marshall, soon to become vice-president of the United States.

An advertisement for the sale of a new daily in St. Petersburg, Florida, caught her eye. It was a hundred miles from the central Florida orange grove her father owned, where she had enjoyed visiting as a girl. She had taken her daughter and son other places in the state for vacations, so the attraction to Florida was strong.

"You might want to look into this, Paul," she called out to her husband.

He read the ad. "I might just do that."

Making quick decisions came naturally to Paul Poynter. By age thirty-seven, he had merged a fierce business drive with populist politics to produce success as a newspaper owner.

His father had been a drummer boy in the Civil War and became a wagon maker in Cloverdale, Indiana.[34] Paul apprenticed to his father but decided he liked business when he made a big profit by cornering milkshake sales at a town picnic. He learned politics around the dinner table, as his father was a strong McKinley Republican. Paul rebelled in favor of William Jennings Bryan's liberalism. He had been named Saint

Paul, which he always shortened, and he early turned to the new Christian Science because of its appeal to turn-of-the-century idealists. The boy helped the Cloverdale Temperance Society raise money to buy out and close the town's only saloon.

As a teenager Paul became agent for farm accessories and made enough to enter DePauw University. There he fell under the spell of historians Charles and Mary Beard and economist Edward Mead. Paul turned twenty-one the year that Bryan, only thirty-six himself, made his "Cross of Gold" speech, and college students everywhere were swept up in the crusade for free silver and Henry George's single land tax. Some, like Paul, even went for Bryan's prohibitionism.

Paul managed the college yearbook and saved several hundred dollars. After graduation he looked for a way to put his newfound talents to work. He talked the father of a fellow student into bankrolling him to buy the *Sullivan Democrat*, a weekly in a small city near the Illinois border.

Sullivan County's cornfields were speckled with coal mining camps and rife with bare-knuckle politics. Saloonkeepers held political and economic power, and the young publisher threw himself into the fight to drive them out. The effort succeeded, and a local-option vote closed the saloons.

Married in 1900 to Alice Wilkey, daughter of a pioneer family, Paul soon was the father of two children—Eleanor, born in 1901, and Nelson Paul, born in 1903 and named for his father and his maternal grandfather.

The year his son was born, Paul Poynter made an important move. He bought a rival weekly, the *Sullivan Times,* and turned it into a daily. His name was getting around the state, and he became president of the Indiana Democratic Editorial Association. But he had no desire for political office, the logical next step. After his wife brought up the St. Petersburg advertisement, he faced pressure from her and the children, who loved their vacations in the state. He took the family back to Sullivan for the start of the school year and caught the train southward. All trains heading for the west coast of the Florida peninsula had to go first to Jacksonville in the northeast corner. It was Poynter's first trip to the state, and he saw the swamps and sawgrass Bill Straub had passed through fourteen years before. It was alien to anything he had known, as was the talk of the booming "tourist industry," so different from corn and coal as an economic base.

A sail car on tracks, seen here in 1912, carried ice out the St. Petersburg pier to fishing boats. It was deactivated when it ran over a tourist. *Heritage Park, Largo, Florida.*

The Atlantic Coast Line train whuffed down its tracks into midtown St. Petersburg like a trolley car hugging the middle of First Avenue South, parallel to Central Avenue a block away. It hauled up at the tacky little depot Straub had fulminated against so often in his editorials. The idea of having a depot in the middle of downtown made city planning a joke, but at least new arrivals could touch ground within sight of the bayfront and the hotels. When special trains came in, local boosters often greeted them with music and cheers.

Facing the depot at the corner of Third Street was a narrow white wooden building with two stories, into which the new *Daily Times* had just moved. It was Friday, August 30, 1912, when Poynter walked across the street to ask at the office for Straub. The editor and his wife were in Tampa and would return by the Saturday morning boat, he was told. Everyone who read the personals column that morning knew that.

Poynter, restless as ever, went out in the heat and roved around, pumping everyone who would talk about the city and its newspapers. Everything he heard appealed to his idealism. Here was a town on the move. The Board of Trade, led by rival editors Bill Straub and Major Lew B. Brown of the *Independent,* was stirring up excitement with its membership drive pushed by opposing red and blue teams. Pinellas was basking in its new importance as a separate county, which Straub was credited with masterminding. The waterfront park, also Straub's brainchild, was rising from rubble.

The city was experiencing an avalanche of tourists, with visitors outnumbering locals in the winter. And the very fact that a small, newly founded city could support two dailies impressed the Indianan. The *Independent* looked better than the *Times,* although it lagged the morning paper in news content.

By Saturday morning Poynter's mind was made up. He told Straub he was ready to do business. But weekends at Loafer's Lodge, Straub's beach cabin on Pass-a-Grille Island, were inviolate for the editor, so they agreed to resume their talks Monday.

Poynter went out first thing Monday morning and joined the Board of Trade blue team (which eventually won). Then the two sat down in Straub's office. Poynter knew that, whatever deal were made, the editor would be an invaluable asset. By St. Petersburg standards Straub was an old-timer, and he was a community institution as an editorial writer. He and Poynter shared their political views, discovering that both were prohibitionists.

What gave Poynter pause was the competition from the *Independent.* It seemed a resourceful, well-made newspaper. He wondered whether anyone else would have dared to take on the challenge. *The Times*'s equipment was in bad condition, and it seemed to him that the staff was hopelessly inefficient and riddled with hookworm.[35]

Although the main agreement came quickly, Poynter fretted because of the leisurely way Straub dealt with lesser details. He wrote his wife that "the principal advantage of the Times is the faith of Alice Poynter that her husband has remarkable qualities that the cold world fails to recognize in the full measure of merit."[36]

Terms of sale showed that, for a daily newspaper, the *Times* was financially weak. Poynter bought 51 percent of the stock from Straub for $3,000 and agreed to pay off company debts. It is estimated he put a total of $10,000 in the project. Straub would keep minority stock, title to the building, and the position of editor.

Newsboy Ray Shappard
sells copies of the *Times*
on Central Avenue
about 1912. *Heritage
Park, Largo, Florida.*

Poynter telegraphed the news to his wife. Word spread so fast
that the *Independent* beat the *Times* getting the story into print. By
Wednesday, Poynter was in charge. Writing from the Yacht Club,
he told his wife of the "bad mess . . . that I have jumped into with
my eyes open. . . . I am not discouraged however and I believe that I
can make the proposition pay me dividends and at the same time put
the property in condition that it could be sold to others if I choose
within a few months. . . . You are one of the directors and you are
to serve as President of the corporation. I am the Secretary and
Manager."[37]

In his letters, the only reference Poynter made to the editorial
operations is his admission that "I am at this time getting out a *sorry*
looking newspaper." But the Paul Poynter the people of St. Petersburg
came to know displayed none of the doubts and fears he poured out to

his wife. Everything about him was dynamic, optimistic, and energetic. They found kindliness and tolerance laced with firm convictions in this short, chunky, round-faced man with a crooked smile.

Christian Science played a large role in Poynter's life, as in his wife's. Besides loathing liquor he did not smoke until the era of Franklin Roosevelt, when he would occasionally puff a cigarette through an FDR-style long holder.

Daily Life

When Poynter bought control of the *Times,* it was still stumbling into its new role as a daily. Straub had committed himself to the change amid the excitement of Pinellas County's birth. On December 12, 1911, he promised his readers they would have a daily within ten days. But it did not come until January 14.

Preparing for the change, Straub had bought a secondhand double-cylinder press once used by the *Ladies' Home Journal.* It was a monster beside its predecessor, filling an entire boxcar when it was hauled into the depot. The new machine could print eight pages at a time and turn out 1,200 copies per hour but was primitive compared with new presses in large cities.

To set type, three new Linotypes were installed over the first six months. In the office, reporters could turn out copy on two Underwood typewriters, although Straub never stopped sending his own work to the printers in his flowing penciled script.

The greatest change was in scope of news. Worldwide news agencies, which had developed in Europe during the endemic wars of the mid-1800s, were just shaping up in the United States on a competitive basis. The Associated Press, junior partner of the European cartel, was a membership affair, still accessible only to a tight coterie of associates who guarded it from their competitors. But in the first decade of the century the Scripps-Howard chain had started its United Press and the Hearst group its International News Service.

Since the rival *Independent* had INS affiliation, the *Times* was able to get a supply of news—although not a membership at first—from the AP. It did secure the lowest-grade affiliation the AP had, its "pony" service. AP editors at a regional bureau would select top stories of the day, skeletonize them into a code and send them through Western

Union offices. The receiving newspaper would add a heavy dose of imagination and flesh out the telegrams.

Suddenly the *Times*'s page one was awash with global news. Headlines bristled larger, and all the diplomatic jolts and little wars leading up to World War I poured in for *Times* readers. Church socials and tourist picnics did not disappear from the front page, but they were being crowded out.

During the newsprint shortages of World War I the paper committed itself to an all-out effort to cut out "padding"—the rambling wordiness that had long afflicted news writing. "Every thing is 'boiled,'" the announcement said. "A word is saved here, a sentence there, a paragraph somewhere else with a result that on the whole it is probably more satisfactory to the average reader."[38]

Soon after war's end the *Times* adopted two policies that later would bring it distinction—investigative reporting and Latin American coverage. In 1919, when St. Petersburg merchants took advantage of a cigarette tax increase to raise their prices higher than those in Tampa, the *Times* exposed the ploy. The gougers promptly cut their prices. The same year an editorial bemoaned U.S. neglect of Latin America: "We shall come to see that South America is no backward little sister toward whom we exercise a sort of half-shamed tolerance, but a hitherto neglected member of the family who awaits only interest and fostering care to become the pride of the clan."[39]

Several killer hurricanes put the *Times* staff to the test. One such calamity devastated south Florida in 1928. The newspaper sent several staff members down, including a woman and the owner's twenty-four-year-old son, Nelson. Stories reported a community on a lake island being wiped out and sixty persons buried in one grave. Nelson Poynter, after traveling more than a thousand miles through the damaged area, reported that much of the region was normal and that the tourist season was not endangered. He noted that a small-town police chief tried to censor his story for fear of negative publicity, "but finally decided to leave the matter alone when I told him I was too busy to talk to him."[40]

Technology usually was late in getting to St. Petersburg relative to northern cities, but the newspapers capitalized on it. Long-distance telephone arrived in 1913, when the *Times* made a call to the *Clearwater News*. The big breakthrough came in 1920 when the *Times* began receiving the full leased AP wire, replacing the small-time pony service. Full-time telegraph operators worked around the clock, decoding the dot-dash signals just as at major newspapers elsewhere. This meant a far greater selection of news, plus the city's first ever complete stock-market report, filling up to two columns. The first dispatch read, "King Alexander of Greece is dead," and it ran in a box on the front page.[41] Five years later the paper introduced a Teletype machine, which automated some of the process, but an operator stayed on another nine years until the last telegraph line was taken out.

A Chicago financial publication called the *Economist* was perhaps the first major medium ever to "discover" the *Times*. In a long paean praising the paper's aggressive gathering of news and advertising, the *Economist* spoke of "a big paper with superb news service . . . the volume of which you would not find in any state outside of Florida." It said the editors "are the ablest that can be found and many of them have declined offers from the east and north."[42]

The event that marked the sharpest lurch into the news age was the departure of Straub to become St. Petersburg postmaster, an appointment gained as a favor from a congressman he had supported. Just why he left the *Times* editorship remains a mystery, explained only by the fact that his income from the newspaper was always skimpy.

The editor seems to have gotten along well with Poynter and the newly hired executives; in fact, he enjoyed the relative peace that liberation from business matters provided him. His place as editorial sage was almost universally conceded. The things for which he had fought long and exhaustively were beginning to be realized.

When Straub resigned, praise poured in from many neighboring editors. The *Sarasota Sun* called him "one of the most valuable members of the newspaper fraternity, not only to his city and county, but, in the sanity of his conclusions, to the whole state."[43]

Straub's successor was announced along with the resignation. He was Edwin E. Naugle, a tall, bulky man already balding at thirty-three, usually pleasant but with sharp eyes that burned in a florid face when his temper flared. A baseball addict and sometime golfer, he mingled well and soon was Ed to everyone. Even more than Straub, he had a taste for civic work and became involved in a maze of organizations, from Rotary to Elks. And he was from Indiana, having studied journalism at its state university. He had worked on every paper in Indianapolis before moving on to edit several in Florida. Naugle had brought his wife and four children to St. Petersburg from a cow-country weekly in Kissimmee.

Despite all the glowing predictions that Naugle would carry on where Straub left off, it was clear that he represented an entirely new approach to making a newspaper. He was no paladin of the editorial page. His writing style displayed none of Straub's fire-eating style, and he showed little taste for bitter controversy. (His first editorial dealt with shade trees and benches on Central Avenue.) But he was something Straub had never been or apparently wanted to be—a news executive. For about a year Straub continued in the masthead as editor with Naugle as managing editor. Then Straub appeared only as vice-president of the company and Naugle as editor. Throughout Naugle's seven years at the *Times,* however, Straub clearly contributed only occasional editorials, usually on issues about which he felt strongly.

Nothing demonstrated the difference between the men and their eras more than their tastes in sports. Straub had a passion for fishing, which symbolized the pioneer village of his youth. For Naugle, baseball—the obsession of the commercial class taking over the city—was everything. He loved nothing better than to call the telegraphed results of big-league games to the crowds huddling beneath the *Times*'s windows. He even had a ten-foot-high "Playograph" built on side of the building. It was like a huge board game showing each play on a diamond, with all the statistics. Naugle would stand beside it, bawling the moves through a megaphone.

Meanwhile the same drive that had led Poynter to buy the *Times* was propelling him into even newer business ventures. Over the more than five decades of his career, he would buy or found ten newspapers in Indiana, North Carolina, and Florida, although only the one in St. Petersburg grew large. In time, these would be eclipsed by ventures into Pinellas County real estate.

Needing someone to run the business side of the *Times,* Poynter again chose another young Indianan, Charles Carl Carr, the thirty-year-old manager and part owner of the *Sullivan Times.* Poynter arranged in 1914 for him to exchange both his job and stock for the same in St. Petersburg.

Slim and dapper with a small mustache, Carr became perhaps the most joining executive the *Times* has ever had, rivaled only by Jack Lake a half century later. Even more than Naugle, he fitted in well. Before finally leaving the *Times* two decades later, he filled a myriad of

C. C. Carr (*at desk*) steered the *Times* to temporary prosperity in the early 1920s as general manager. His assistant was Gertrude Reed (*background*), and Ed Naugle was editor. *St. Petersburg Times.*

civic and political roles, including stints as chairman of the school board and of the committee that solved the city's water problems. He also was Poynter's partner in some property purchases.

Carr's title was manager, and after Straub's departure that job included the editorial department. Carr did most of the hiring, brought in many news items, and kept a sharp eye on stories about school matters but otherwise interfered little with the news. His endless responsibilities put him under much pressure. Once a decrepit Oliver typewriter so enraged him that he threw it out the second-floor window onto the sidewalk. It sat there an hour before he asked a reporter to retrieve it. After a few keys were straightened, it worked almost as well as before.

One day in 1923 Carr showed up in the newsroom with a gangling fourteen-year-old wearing knickers and long black socks. He introduced the recruit as the new copy boy and deadpanned, "He says he wants to be editor of the *Times*."

The boy was Thomas C. Harris, born in Virginia but reared in St. Petersburg, where his father had an ice cream shop. The boy was so enthralled with journalism that he had started his own little magazine, making the type himself out of cork and printing adventure stories he had written. By the time he was seventeen, Tom had become city editor of the *Times*. Over the next four decades Harris would stairstep into the highest levels of management, becoming managing editor in 1933 and retiring as general manager in 1968.

When Carr decided to join the land boom and go into the advertising business in 1923, he sold his stock back to Poynter, who became almost sole owner except for a small block held by Straub. (Carr kept an interest in the *Times*'s real estate.)

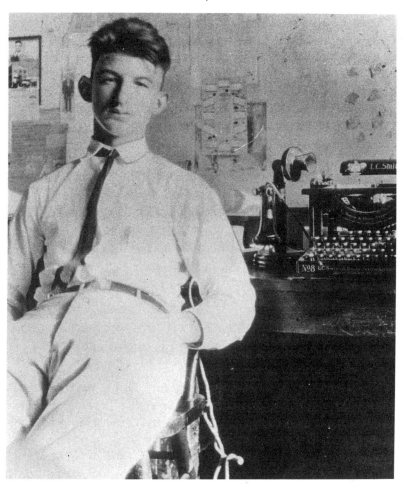

Tom C. Harris started as a fourteen-year-old *Times* copy boy in 1923 but soon became a well-known reporter in an era of splashy human-interest news. *St. Petersburg Times*.

Poynter announced that he would fill the void by spending more time on "his interests in St. Petersburg, which are quite extensive." But he soon persuaded another Indianan, David B. Lindsay, to take over Carr's stock and job. Lindsay was a tall, well-dressed man of thirty-five who had operated small papers in Indiana and North Carolina. He kept aloof from the news staff and spent most of his time dealing with the enormous production and business problems of the paper.

Apparently Poynter and Lindsay did not always coordinate their roles. The job of managing editor fell vacant in 1924, and Poynter brought in a new man whom he introduced to the staff as their new boss. Twenty minutes later a man whom Lindsay had hired for the job showed up. After a conference between Poynter and Lindsay, the owner's man stayed and the other left.

The partnership lasted until 1927, when Lindsay wanted out. He and Poynter shuffled the properties they owned together, with the result that Lindsay left the *Times*'s ownership and got full possession of a daily they had started in Sarasota. Poynter also ended up with principal ownership of the *Clearwater Sun*. Then, to bring things full circle, Carr returned to his old arrangement with the *Times*.

Straub returned to the editor's chair in 1923 after Warren G. Harding's election as president had brought patronage back to Republicans. It seemed like old times, and even Straub's trademark editorial paragraphs reappeared. But it was never the same; Straub kept more to his office, and editorials became increasingly irrelevant. Nevertheless, Poynter apparently made no move to inject new blood into the editorial page. Straub's health tumbled through a series of strokes until his death in 1939.

A World So New

The two decades after the *Times* went daily settled some important things for both the city and the newspaper. St. Petersburg would become the only large city on the west coast of Florida (other than Tampa, at the head of a bay). The city would depend on immigrants and visitors from up north and would not become an industrial and shipping giant like Tampa, with its cigar factories and warehouses. It also became clear that the *Times* would dominate the growing market, slowly making gains against the *Independent*. The paper achieved dominance not by the innovations that would make a national name

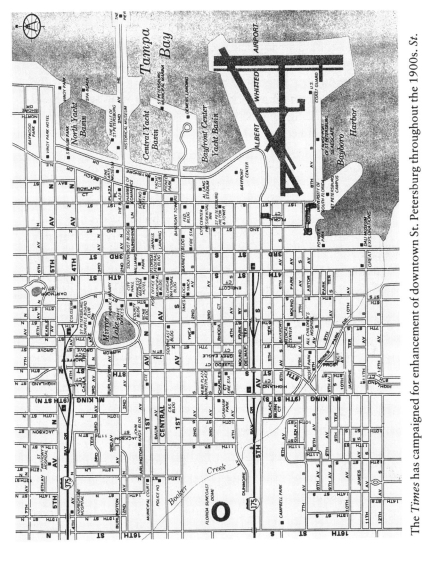

The *Times* has campaigned for enhancement of downtown St. Petersburg throughout the 1900s. *St. Petersburg Chamber of Commerce.*

for it later but rather by plying the trade of journalism along conventional lines and by doing it well.

For a company whose new mission was to take raw events and turn them into profitable images, the *Times* could not have asked for a better run of news than what happened during most of the twenty-year span. Life was a fireworks display, punctuated by brief lulls and, at last, by the sober necessity of facing economic reality.

St. Petersburg's orientation to Tampa Bay represented a fading era. True, the downtown center was booming as never before, and the 1920s saw it acquire a modest skyline. The *Times* itself would build two multistory buildings in this period, affirming a commitment to the downtown area that became permanent.

But the talisman of the twenties was land, and it existed westward, the direction to which early townspeople had turned their backs. Settlers had written off the barrier islands with their glistening beaches as a haven for mosquitoes, raccoons, and snakes. Now they took on a Cinderella aura. It may have been because Straub preached the glories of Pass-a-Grille for decades or because picnickers always delighted in boat excursions there. Perhaps it was that the new styles in swimsuits made seeing and being seen an attraction, unlike the days when beachgoers would be covered from neck to ankles. Or even because Florida's great equalizer, the automobile, was replacing coastal boats as the way to get around the peninsula. Finally, there was that miracle of modern science, mosquito control.

The city and its newspapers rode the rapids of two distinct economic booms before foundering in the slough of the Great Depression, preceded by the 1926 Florida Bust. The *Times* did more than its part in creating the booms and profited mightily from them.

After the prosperity of World War I, some thought peace would put an end to the surge of growth. But the fall of 1919 brought a sight St. Petersburg had never known. Factory workers and bank presidents alike invested in automobiles, and the start of the tourist season brought them bumping down the Pinellas subpeninsula by the thousands. They came the traditional way also. Trains were sold out weeks in advance, and railroads put on specials to meet demand.

At first visitors thought only of spending a short time vacationing. Then, well before cool weather signaled the start of the 1920–21 season, a historic event occurred. Two families, tourists just arrived,

Tourists found the sand roads leading to St. Petersburg a major hazard to their cars around 1918. *Heritage Park, Largo, Florida.*

pitched tents on city property because they could not find hotel space. This was on August 26, 1920, when normally there was so little demand that hotels almost gave away accommodations. Two days later there were twenty families, and two weeks later 125. It was a shabby scene of tarpaulins and lean-tos or of people living in vehicles. It was not that they were poor; they were just unable to spend their money. The National Guard loaned its tents, and suddenly Williams Park turned into a campground.

The first response was to build hotels. St. Petersburg always had been a resort of boardinghouses and small hotels. But now, within five years after the first tent was pitched, available room space nearly doubled, to 4,500, much of it in hotels of 300 rooms or more.

Finally, the Pinellas mainland was no longer the end of the line. A bridge and causeway had been built to Long Key, the island occupied by Pass-a-Grille and soon to be site of the town called St. Petersburg Beach. There another bigtime plunger, Thomas Rowe, had built a pink wedding cake hotel called the Don Ce-Sar after his favorite opera character. To save his guests' skins, Rowe had pushed through a program to largely rid the island of mosquitoes.

Green benches on Central Avenue became a metaphor for the languorous life sought by tourists after World War I. *Heritage Park, Largo, Florida.*

Invasion of the tin-can tourists, as the motorists called themselves, marked the end to the Pinellas subpeninsula's isolation. Within a two-year period, barriers that had made it so difficult to visit were overcome. The county agreed to bonds totaling nearly $3 million to build the first real system of good roads and bridges. Then, in 1924, the biggest excitement St. Petersburg had ever known came with the opening of Gandy Bridge across Tampa Bay. It was built by a flamboyant former executive of the Disston saw company in Philadelphia, George ("Dad") Gandy, whose bristling whiskers covered a face of rugged determination.

Despite the boom in tourism, anyone could buy a lot and build a house for a reasonable amount. For almost three years, 1921–23, the city's assessed valuations climbed briskly but not wildly at about 16 percent per year. People were buying property to live on.

But, almost as suddenly as the tent city's birth, this trend changed in the fall of 1923. Dad Gandy, frustrated over his years of trying to finance the bridge, brought in a high-pressure salesman named Eugene M. Elliott to raise the money. Within four months, Elliott had hit the $2 million mark, and local residents realized the bridge actually would be built. They also grasped that property values would skyrocket along the route out of the city to the bridge. People began buying land not with the idea of building on it but rather of reselling it for profit. Interest turned to appetite, then to obsession, and finally to frenzy.

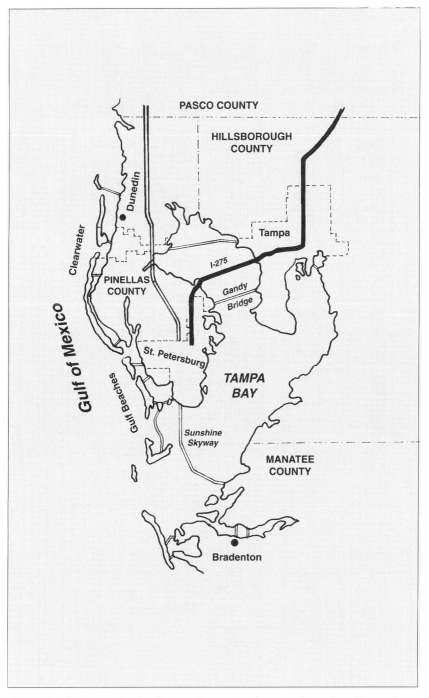

Because it is on a peninsula, St. Petersburg missed out on through traffic until bay bridges were built. *Tom Brady.*

Before bridge construction started, land north of the city on the access route was going for $50 an acre. When Elliott fanned the heat under the stock sale, it quickly doubled, tripled, and quintupled. By the time the bridge opened land was selling for as much as $5,000 an acre, a hundredfold increase.

Paul Poynter and all his executives were true boomers, but they had little idea what would happen to the *Times* after the encampment of tin can tourists in the 1920–21 season. Land salesmen and all their retail retinue were desperate to be heard above the mob, and the newspapers offered a way. The larger the ad, the louder the shout. The more advertising space, the larger the staff and the more news needed to fill the columns around the ads.

The advertising and subscription orders came in like a tidal wave. In the year ending October 1923, advertising went up 50 percent. Circulation averaged 4,522, about 50 percent higher than in 1920.

Population figures tell much of the story. The count in St. Petersburg had multiplied by two and a half in the decade before 1920. But it went up by the same proportion in half that time during the boom, rising to about 37,000.

The *Times*'s advertising went up even faster. After zooming to a new high in 1923, it tripled that figure two years later. In 1925 the paper was the nation's second in total advertising, trailing only the *Miami Herald*.

Hemmed in as it had been by shorelines and bad roads and competing with dailies in Tampa and Clearwater, the *Times* had found it difficult to sell copies over a wide area. But Poynter decided to break this barrier. He stepped up promotion of the paper, added reader magnets like a horoscope, and hired a seasoned circulation manager, W. R. Geisman. Poynter gave Geisman one order: "We want this field so completely covered by 6 in the morning that every householder within 25 miles can reach out on his front porch and pick up his morning newspaper." They added equipment, worked out a detailed plan, added dozens of employees, and ten months later announced the delivery system was working with a bare .0005 percent complaint rate.

Circulation figures responded. Sales rose at a slightly less dizzy pace than advertising but faster than population. They more than tripled from 1920 to 1927, when figures of 10,570 daily and 13,106 Sunday were listed. These figures were more reliable than earlier counts, because the *Times* had acquired the hallmark of certified honesty, membership in the Audit Bureau of Circulations.

Paul Poynter loved to deal in real estate almost as much as newspapering. He may well have sensed the fever of St. Petersburg's pre–World War I boomlet when he decided to buy the *Times,* because he began investing soon after his arrival, joined by C. C. Carr when he came onto the staff. In 1917 they bought a Central Avenue lot on which they made nearly a 20 percent profit by reselling it two years later. This was the forerunner of deals that grew in frequency and later nearly brought disaster to the newspaper.

An air of speculation even hung over plans for new quarters for the newspaper twice within a few years. With the end of World War I, inadequacy of the old frame building across from the train station became too evident to ignore. Poynter and Carr went to Chicago to see how big city newspapers were housed and to shop for a new press, which they needed and which usually is installed with a new building. They came home to find that Straub had decided to sell the old frame building across from the depot, which he had retained when he sold majority stock in the paper. Tampa interests were to buy the building for $15,000, and Poynter apparently did not want a new landlord.

In March 1920, Poynter announced the purchase of three lots totaling 100 by 120 feet two blocks west of the old building. The site still had the advantage of fronting on the train tracks for easy delivery of newsprint, and it was just as centrally located, only a block from Central Avenue.

Construction of a three-story brick building started right away, and the first issue that came out of it was published January 4, 1921 (although the facade always boldly said 1920). The building was a simple box in design, relieved on the front by arches and a few ornaments above. But it was a far cry from the narrow little frame structure across from the depot. Nestled in the new building was a twenty-four-page "monster" press, as an editorial called it. Although secondhand, the press was a rotary machine, which meant it could print much faster by using the superior technology of stereotyping.

A Castle Too Late

Poynter had grossly underestimated the boom with his 1921 expansion. The three-story building was bursting with people, as the payroll

The post–World War I boom led to a new brick building for the *Times,* occupied in January 1921. *St. Petersburg Times.*

had risen to two hundred. Employees were working in shifts around the clock.

No one quarreled with the idea that a new building was needed, although Poynter and Lindsay argued over where it should be. Both favored downtown sites and agreed to delay their selection until plans were drawn.

In a burst of boom-time exuberance, a local architect drew up an astounding edifice of twenty-one stories with two eight-story wings, resembling somewhat the Tribune Tower in Chicago. But wild architectural dreams were normal in 1925, and no one was surprised when, in a more sober moment, the *Times* took out a permit for a four-story building. This soon changed to eight floors as the idea of renting out unneeded office space developed. The site was in the same block as the 1921 building and also fronted on the railroad tracks. It occupied an 80-by-100-foot plot. As usual, the building went up around the presses. This time management bought two forty-eight-page machines, which went into use long before the rest of the structure was occupied in June 1926.

There seemed to be no end to the tales of how zany the boom-time real estate situation could become, such as the $100,000 lot sold while the principals were standing in a driving rainstorm. But even the heartiest boomer could not help having second thoughts. In an advertisement boosting sale of stock in a palatial movie theater, the salesman mused: "Is the boom too lively, too fast, too gamblesome? Can it be kept up, will purchasers this season be able to sell again next season at still higher prices? . . . This thing must stop. It is against reason. It can't go on. The prices are too high to realize sufficient income out of buildings placed upon such high priced land"[44]

Early in December 1925 it rained, turned cold, and was nasty for a week. A thousand investment bankers from all over the country were in St. Petersburg for a convention. Expecting a week of leisure in the Florida sun, they were miserable. Bad weather lingered through the end of January. October and November had set new records for land sales, but figures for December were down badly. A sour smell was in the air.

The *Times* moved into its new building just in time to report the collapse of the boom. Throughout the winter and spring of 1926 it seemed the good times were bound to stay. In the first three months the paper printed more advertising than it had in all of 1923, again ranking behind only the *Miami Herald* among the largest in the world.

In October 1926 *Times* management took a full-page house ad to express optimism, although admitting "we are not publishing as much advertising this year as we published last year although circulation is

The *Times* bought its first high-speed rotary presses in 1921. They made stereotype plates necessary. *St. Petersburg Times.*

50 per cent larger." The year-end total showed ad lineage one-sixth below 1925.

By January the last bubble of hope had burst. Just as every thinking person should have known two years before, an editorial said, "The exciting game of pyramiding and ballooning land prices . . . could not possibly go on indefinitely." In 1927 advertising lineage plummeted to less than a half the amount of the year before.

After growing accustomed to filling papers of a hundred pages or more, staffers learned to deal with a dozen pages, sometimes as few as eight. Employees foresaw the personnel cuts that were bound to come and began drifting away to cities up north, not to be replaced. Others were let go.

Those who remained faced an uncertain payroll. The paper began making deals with merchants to trade advertising space for goods. In lieu of part of salary, a staff member would receive a certificate from a store to be exchanged for groceries or clothes. One employee furnished his new home with this scrip.

But the greatest millstone dragging down the *Times* was its debts. Its financial statement at the beginning of 1927 showed it owing more than $500,000, much of it debts from the new building. Advertisers whose credit seemed rock solid suddenly could not pay their large overdue accounts to the *Times,* and others went bankrupt. Accounts receivable totaled nearly $200,000 by 1927, with another $100,000 added by year's end.

The paper's debts were dwarfed by Paul Poynter's personal obligations. He had plunged into land purchases and acquired newspapers in smaller Florida cities—Sarasota, Clearwater, Brooksville, and Perry. When the bust came he owed $1.3 million at 8 percent interest, a sky-high rate for those days.

It was small comfort that almost everyone else in St. Petersburg was in trouble. When banks closed on New Year's Eve of 1926, they had deposits that had fallen by nearly half in a year. And the first baby born in the city the next day was responsible for $802.06 of bonded city debt. This was one person's share of the bill for all the streets and sewers and bridges built during the boom, which was fun while it lasted.

Chapter 3

The Knight Errant

While the *St. Petersburg Times* twisted in the winds of the Florida land bust, the rest of the nation continued to enjoy prosperity. Al Smith would have it right with his 1928 presidential campaign song—happy days were here again—although the country saw that as all the more reason to stick with the Republicans. The American dream still seemed just around the corner.

This optimism ran deeply in Paul Poynter's second child and only son, Nelson. He was a bouncy twenty-three-year-old whose wiry five-foot-five frame was surmounted by a round face and broad grin like his father's but without Paul's bulldog homeliness. From one second to another the grin could shade to a shy smile or, less often, a penetrating stare.

Real estate salesmen and golfers were putting away their knickers as St. Petersburg sobered up, but flannel trousers and fraternity pranks remained a way of life for collegians like Nelson. He had become a Big Man on Campus at Indiana University, fifty miles from the Poynter home in Sullivan, and had gone on to study economics at Yale. Although the Poynters nearly always drove Cadillacs, the state of union labor troubled Nelson. Something terrible would happen unless the government paid attention to the needs of the masses, he felt.

The Poynters had maintained a zeal for reform despite the comfortable life they led. For Paul it had come out in his teenage crusade against saloons. For his wife, Alice, it meant a lifelong effort to

The Poynter children from Indiana—Eleanor and her brother, Nelson—delighted in Florida vacations before their father bought the *St. Petersburg Times* in 1912. *Poynter Library, University of South Florida, St. Petersburg, Florida.*

improve women's prisons. For their daughter, Eleanor, it was pushing women's clubs into social service. For all three it meant carrying the ideals of Bryan and Wilson into the ruling circles of Indiana Democratic politics and applying devout Christian Science to problems like alcoholism and criminality. To them, such vices were illnesses amenable to spiritual treatment. Nelson was like his family, but different—no clubs, no church, no party. He wanted to kill all the dragons they did, but with the editor's lance.

Most of all he wanted to please his mother. She had given him a childhood filled with wonder and delight at 302 West Washington Street in Sullivan. All his life he carried memories of her cooking strawberries in the sun, catching his pet rabbits when they got away, and helping him clean frogs he brought home in the depth of night. On vacations in Florida, she took him and Eleanor fishing, chased skittery fiddler crabs with him in the wash of waves, and carried on over the ugly shellfish he would present to her.[1] All his life, Nelson would write adoring letters to his "Minno," sometimes even when they were in the same city and he had seen her earlier in the day.

Nelson and his father cared for each other, but Paul was away from the family much of the time tending to his other newspapers. In apparently his earliest preserved letter, undated and scrawled in pencil, Nelson wrote Paul: "My dear dad, I want to see you. I want you to sell your barn and I want you to come down here and fish with me and I want you to buy a automobile before we get home. I love you and Mama does too."[2]

Though a loyal Hoosier, Nelson loved to go south with his mother to visit St. Petersburg. By the time he was eleven he already had made the train trip through Tennessee seven times, and it still excited him enough to write a school composition marveling at the twists and turns and grades the engine made. A hint of a later lust for travel appeared: "Far off you can see a little mist arownd a big dark mountain it is blue and as the sun shines on it looks as a rain bow were arown it. But the mountains that are right by you are very different. Their sids are covered with trees, (mainly furs) rocks and moss. A stream runs under bridge that passes over the valley. The rocks are gray and look very pretty against the dark dirt and among the trees."[3]

The essay also portended Nelson's lifelong enchantment with the written language and his awkwardness with it. His grades mostly were in the low A range, with Latin his biggest problem.

It is curious that although he later would be known as a poor public speaker, Nelson became a star orator at Sullivan High School. In his junior year he won the school's contest but lost at the district level. He won again in his senior year, gaining a four-dollar prize by besting four other students. Calling his original oration "The Boiling Pot of the World," he delved into his lifelong passion—economics. His main concern was labor-management conflict. He suggested a way out might be cooperative ownership between capital and labor. Flushed with this victory, he went on to win in the district meet by one point, only to be defeated in the state championship match.

Another lifelong trait was Nelson's insistence on financial independence. Paul urged the boy to work for pocket money, just as Paul's father had encouraged him. Nelson exulted in earning more than any other child on West Washington by cutting neighbors' grass, delivering newspapers, selling the *Saturday Evening Post,* and washing windows.[4]

In both St. Petersburg and Sullivan, Nelson's favorite pastime was hanging around his father's newspaper offices looking for things to do. Once, when he was eleven, he stumbled upon what was to be his first byline story—the crash of pioneer aviator Tony Jannus off the St.

Petersburg waterfront. In Sullivan, he wangled a news job when the paper's only reporter was drafted for World War I service. He covered the full range of basic news—courthouse, police, general news. As the paper had only 3,000 circulation, it was a chance to make an apprentice's mistakes before forgiving readers.

Nelson always knew he could find sympathy at home. Years later he would recall how his parents backed him up: "If I competed in an oratorical contest the judges were crooked if I didn't win. If I couldn't play baseball as well as other kids then baseball was a lousy game, and kids who do play baseball well grow up to be morons."[5]

His doting parents did not bar him from a boy's ultimate thrill of that era—going up in an airplane. Barnstorming pilots worked the small towns of America for any dollar they could pick up, and when one came to Sullivan the editor's son went with him on an eighteen-mile trip. According to the newspaper account: "After gaining an altitude of more than two thousand feet, the machine disappeared in the clouds to the south, and when the town of Carlisle was reached, it swooped down to within a very few feet of the ground and thrilled the townspeople, scores of whom were watching its maneuvers. . . . Lt. Force . . . drove back to Sullivan in a driving rain, and made a safe landing at the aviation farm."[6]

The boy's firecracker energy resulted in two "double promotions," putting him ahead of his classmates. So by midway through his senior year, with nothing else to do, he took the train south with a man who was joining the staff of the *St. Petersburg Times.* Then he went to Eau Gallie, a town on Florida's East Coast near where he had romped on the beach years earlier.

Kentucky Military Institute decamped to Eau Gallie every winter. Nelson checked himself into the academy and spent the rest of the school year there. Then he returned to Sullivan to pick up his high school diploma.

The Wine of Bloomington

Both of Nelson's parents had attended DePauw University, a small Methodist institution in western Indiana, but Nelson chose the larger and worldlier state university in Bloomington. At sixteen, he was publicized as the youngest student on campus. Indiana had one of the earliest journalism schools, but the publisher's son felt he knew enough about that field from his experience on the family newspapers, so he majored in economics. The decision may have been reinforced when he finished his sophomore year with his only grade below an A being a C in journalism.

Arriving at Bloomington in 1920, young Poynter plunged into the postwar giddiness that made campus life a metaphor for the Jazz Age. He pledged a prestige fraternity, Phi Gamma Delta, and became editor of the chapter newspaper. He went on to become president of two groups—the journalism society, Sigma Delta Chi, and the military honorary, Scabbard and Blade—as well as colonel of the cadet corps. He also was invited into groups such as the Garrick Club (drama) and two leadership honoraries.[7] But his dream was to be editor of the *Indiana Daily Student.* He slogged through the ranks as a reporter, city editor, and managing editor. Then, in January of his junior year, the magic title came to him.

One of Poynter's friends was Ernie Pyle, a poor farm boy who had studied journalism at Indiana and worked on the *Daily Student.* He quit after three years and was working on a small daily. Like Poynter he wrote stories embarrassing to the Ku Klux Klan, then riding high in Indiana.

A recruiter for the Scripps-Howard newspaper chain came to Indiana looking for talent. This group had been founded late in the nineteenth century by E. W. Scripps, a crusty individualist who developed a market for light, inconsequential newspapers that appealed to the working class and got along without much of the advertising that establishment dailies attracted. On the other hand, it shunned the worst of the sensationalism that marked the Hearst papers and the shameless New York tabloids. The chain favored midsized cities. It managed to make money on its low advertising revenue and relatively modest circulations by hiring bright young people willing to work for a pittance while aiming for bigger things. Scripps's successor was Roy Howard, a flamboyant salesman who wanted a higher visibility for the empire.

The recruiter, Earle Martin, had been editor of Scripps's *Indianapolis Star* and president of the country's largest feature syndicate, National Editorial Association. Now Howard wanted a voice in the nation's capital, and Martin took the lead in founding it. Its name, the *Washington Daily News,* brought it inevitable comparison with the dean of the tabloids, the *New York Daily News.*

Poynter, cocky at having reached his collegiate goal, considered himself a journeyman journalist. He thought well of Pyle also, and when Martin visited Bloomington he not only signed up Poynter to work on the *Daily News* but also hired Pyle at his friend's recommendation. Poynter immediately admired Martin both as a person and as a newsman.

The Big Time

The two youths left for Washington by train in early June 1923. Poynter felt at home right away. Their first day was a Sunday, and they went to a Washington Senators game with Francis Stevenson, the Associated Press White House correspondent and an Indianan. That night they dined at the National Press Club and met many of the reporters they had worshiped as bylines on big-city papers.

It was a summer of discoveries. Poynter and Pyle stayed together in a "dandy" room, as he wrote his mother. Social contacts with Hoosiers eased them into a steady round of shows, dancing, visits to country houses, golf, and beach parties. "I am feeling better than I have since last summer," he wrote his mother, "and I know I look it. I eat THREE meals a day, walk about 25 miles, learn a lot and am self supporting and saving money. What more could I ask?"[8] Despite the hard work, he felt a zest for the challenge:

> It is easy to see why Scripps makes money. This sheet is published at the very minimum of expense. All told it will not run much over the expenditures of the Kokomo Dispatch. For instance I covered an aerial circus yesterday and the Evening star [*sic*] had three men there with nothing else to do. I then went to a regatta where the other papers had one man assigned for the afternoon. In the mean time I had covered a death accident, rewritten some stuff, etc. It is a simple formulae [*sic*]. Everybody works—and likes it. The staff is fine. I like and respect practically every body on it.[9]

As a nineteen-year-old who had heard about politics since the cradle, Poynter reveled in the daily thrills of Washington. He bragged to his mother that he had glimpsed President Harding's wife leaving the White House. His journalistic hero was David Lawrence, who had come to Washington in the Wilson era and had founded a newspaper of record, the *U.S. News*. It foreshadowed the *Congressional Quarterly* service Poynter would inaugurate two decades later.

When the summer heat drove the Hardings and most of the elite from the city, Poynter lamented that he could almost feel the laziness getting into his bones: "I cannot stand for that and if necessary will move out rather than be touched by such a malady."[10]

Apparently Poynter's drift away from organized religion was yet to come, as he assured his mother he was going to church. He also was seeing a Christian Science practitioner about an itch, which his roommate had caught from him. Noting that an acquaintance had contracted tuberculosis, he wished that the man could be "interested in Science."[11]

Poynter apparently never thought of staying in Washington longer than the summer, although he did consider the idea of transferring to an eastern college. He soon felt the tug of Indiana—and a girlfriend back there—and wound up his stint with the *Daily News* after eight weeks. He took a vacation in the Northeast and was back in Bloomington to graduate with the class of 1924. As a crowning touch, he covered the Democratic national convention that summer in New York for the *Indianapolis Star*. He wrote his mother that he was having a "corking time" meeting famous journalists but that the Democratic party was a hopeless mess. Assuring Alice that all his entertainments were tame, he added, "I toured Greenwich Village in an innocent way."[12]

Even more than being a Washington reporter, Poynter yearned to be a foreign correspondent. The Bryan-Wilson dream of a world casting off shackles of oppression and inequality thrilled him. He had to see that world—and not just the glitter of Europe. Alice and Eleanor Poynter had done the grand tour of Europe the year before, and Nelson's friends were going abroad in the same style. But he decided to take as little money as possible from his parents. He scoured San Francisco for a shipboard job, being turned away at most docks before he wangled a union permit to be a bellboy. As a warning, his card was stamped "No Sea Experience."

Poynter first went to the Philippines, where family connections won him a visit with General Leonard Wood, the U.S. colonial governor. Wood had repressed the people, but Poynter met some young Filipino idealists who sought independence and would become leaders of the new nation after World War II.

Nelson Poynter worked
as a freighter's cabin boy
to start a trip around the
world in 1924, the year
he graduated from
college. *Poynter Library,*
University of South
Florida, St. Petersburg,
Florida.

The young Hoosier had gone to Asia to launch a career as a correspondent, and the only war at the time was in China—one of the endemic feuds among warlords of the 1920s. When he reached the Philippines he discovered the war was over, so he continued by Japanese liner to Tokyo. There he billed himself as a correspondent of the Scripps syndicate, the National Editorial Association (NEA), although he apparently was a stringer at best. An English-language daily felt he rated an interview, and in it he regaled the readers with his "several weeks in the Philippines investigating the customs and habits of the Igorottes."

Poynter told the reporter that while he was in the islands, there had been five headhunting incidents. He also went into gory detail about the illegal selling of dogs as food. Folks back in Sullivan read about their boy's adventures, as Alice Poynter published a letter from him in their daily. She also had a letter waiting for him in Japan expressing regret that Nelson thought it necessary to travel "in such an unpleasant way." She promised to send him money and urged him to keep up with his religious reading even if he couldn't go to church. "You are right," she commented on a letter of his, "it is important to keep the real ever before us."[13]

Poynter found there were no job openings for him in Tokyo, but he talked another English-language daily, the *Japan Times,* into taking him on for no pay. The paper was shorthanded, and soon he was put on the payroll. Before long he realized he would never go far internationally without speaking other languages, and he had no gift for them.

Poynter struggled to apply his college French to translating his paper's only wire service, the Paris agency Havas. Doing so, he felt the pull that many of his generation did—to know Paris. After all, he had gone nearly halfway around the globe, and it would cost little more to return home via Paris than to go back across the Pacific.

Leaving the job in Tokyo, Poynter went on to Beijing and shuddered at the rigors of crossing Siberia in midwinter via railroad. He found he could get the most mileage by freighters on the southern route. This also gave him a chance to tour many ports of call and get to know the polyglot young people traveling the same way.

Stretched out on a ship's deck or sitting around café tables, he found the youth of Asia excited about Wilson's Fourteen Points. They felt the plan promised independence for their homelands, most of which were colonies. This promise would shrivel as worldwide depression and dictatorship choked out idealism. But the dreamers would demand payment on the pledge for helping fight the next war. Besides their political ideals, Asians seemed to Poynter to want the same things Americans did—a better life for their children, a better opportunity to work. He felt that a common thread laced together all cultures.

Poynter's route ran through Singapore and Malaysia, then to the foothills of the Himalayas and across the subcontinent to Bombay. In a deck passage aboard a ship bound for Karachi, he found a bit of comfort when British soldiers invited him to share the hospital cabin and he paid two dollars a day extra to eat with the second-class passengers.

Poynter, the habitual listener, found his greatest delight in what people around him said. He decided the Tommies were a valuable source of information if not taken too literally. The piety of the Arabs impressed him as they spread their prayer rugs on deck to pray to Mecca. On through the Persian Gulf, Jerusalem, Cairo and a fifth-class passage from Alexandria to Naples. He looked forward to arriving in Paris and meeting his family, again touring Europe.

In Paris he tried vainly to master French, even hiring a tutor, who learned more English than Poynter did French. Because of this, and because it was hard to get away from Americans in Paris, he gravitated toward them.

Meanwhile, he sold freelance articles to NEA, the *Indianapolis Star,* and Scripps's *New York Telegram.* He found it relatively easy to make sales, as few American journalists were working abroad then. The Associated Press, largest supplier of foreign news to U.S. newspapers, was a junior member of a worldwide news cartel dominated by Europeans, and it was forced to take its news from them.

Poynter rounded out his year abroad among the Lost Generation of hedonistic young Americans, but that was enough for him. He fretted about all the chances for learning he had missed at Bloomington because of his immersion in the student paper. He decided to remedy this with a master's degree, and he chose Yale. He always would consider it one of his wisest moves.

Grazing in Academe

Yale's economics department was one of the strongest in the country, yet it had flexible requirements. For two years Poynter gorged on courses he had wanted to take as an undergraduate. Not burdened by the demands of an adviser, he shopped through the catalog.

One of his subjects was statistics, which he found to be sheer drudgery. But it unlocked the secrets of figures the government was spewing out, including indexes of all kinds, particularly the cost of living. Poynter wanted to know not only how to read them but also how they were developed.

Poynter found labor law far more exciting, as it involved most of the burning issues of the time. The fight for union rights that had risen and fallen since the 1880s was on the upturn again, but this time it carried the badge of respectability. Wilson had made it compatible with middle-American values and associated it with the vision of a fair and just world.

The Poynters—mother Alice, son Nelson, father Paul, and daughter Eleanor—were buoyed by their newspapers' success in the 1920s, but relationships became strained in later years. *Poynter Library, University of South Florida, St. Petersburg, Florida.*

The conservatism that had swept through American universities after Harding's election in 1920 made the Yale Law School's liberalism even more noticeable. Those who supported labor ran the risk of being called radicals or Bolsheviks, as the shock of the Russian Revolution was only a few years past. American socialists and laborites were trying to decide whether communism was the wave of the future and whether they must mount it.

A child of comfort, young Poynter was notable for his liberalism, but only to a degree. The kids who grew up on West Washington Street had an unusually strong political appetite; although a generation older, the next-door neighbor had been Will H. Hays, Republican strongman and Hollywood morals czar. The Poynter family's *Sullivan Times* had given low-key support to unions, but it avoided controversy. Nelson identified with "the people" against the "special interests" as so many liberals did while steering toward the safer moorings of pragmatism. He admired Wilson for having freed the country somewhat from the manipulators of Wall Street by founding the Federal Reserve System and moving money management to Washington.

Poynter thought the capitalistic system was worth saving, and the only way to prevent revolution was through reform. This would cost money, he reasoned, so income taxes would have to be expanded to a realistic scope. He drank deeply from the ideas of the *New York World* and *St. Louis Post-Dispatch,* which Joseph Pulitzer had built as avatars of practical liberalism.

Filled with all this social conscience, Poynter thought about becoming a teacher. But as an economist he was drawn by the challenge to make money—in the field he knew most about, newspapering. His Yale studies would prove crucial decades later when he devised pioneering cost-of-living bonuses for his staff and stood up to striking unions with law as a main weapon.

At New Haven, Poynter's grades were three honors, one high pass, and nine passes. His thesis was rated good.[14] He graduated with a master's degree in 1927.

The Real World

Finished with his education, Poynter got an offer to join the management of the *Cleveland Times* at $200 a week, a notably high salary. Earle Martin, his idol from the summer in Washington, had left Scripps-Howard and wanted Poynter's help.[15]

But while vacationing in North Carolina, Poynter received a visit from C. C. Carr, then general manager and part owner of the *St. Petersburg Times.* Carr said Paul Poynter wanted Nelson to join them.

The *Times* was in deep trouble. It was staggering because of the Florida land bust, its revenues falling 50 percent a month. Its executives were relying on $300,000 in accounts receivable to pay for the new eight-story building contracted just before the bust.

Paul Poynter and his partner David Lindsay had plunged deeply into real estate and newspapers, and Paul's liabilities totaled $1.3 million. After Carr bought out Lindsay's third of the *Times* company, he and Poynter started trying to solve the crisis.

So Nelson became assistant general manager of the *Times* in 1927 at $75 a week. He realized that loose management practices had emerged during the land boom; the paper almost was expelled from the Audit Bureau of Circulations. Nelson and Carr set out to tighten the operation, with the younger man reorganizing distribution and rates. Later he would credit this work with adding hundreds of thousands of dollars in revenue during the depression years.[16]

Nelson's moving to St. Petersburg brought into focus a conflict that would bedevil Poynter family relationships from then on. Nelson,

Eleanor, and both parents were flinty individualists who mingled almost cloying affection for each other with utter inability to get along in business matters. The friction varied with time and person, although it was least between Nelson and his father and most heated between Nelson and Eleanor.

Nelson always made clear to his relatives that he would not be a long-term partner with any of them. So when he joined the *Times* management he and Paul agreed he would buy the father's stock with earnings over an extended period.

Nelson also reached the point of starting his own nuclear family. He had descended on Pinellas County with an aura of romance, a world traveler who had met great people and polished himself with an Ivy League education. To many, he seemed a good catch as a husband. He dated Sarah Catherine Fergusson, daughter of a prominent St. Petersburg family and called by some the prettiest girl in the city. Nelson and Catherine had a surprise wedding at Sebring in central Florida three days after Christmas 1927 while his parents were in Indiana, where they still kept their main residence.

Alice could not have asked for better credentials for a daughter-in-law. Catherine was a Christian Scientist and had gone to prep school on Long Island and graduated from Principia, a Scientist college in St. Louis. She went on to DePauw, where she was a member of Kappa Alpha Theta, as Alice and Eleanor had been. Not only was it the oldest sorority in the country, but DePauw's was the founding chapter.

Eleanor and her parents did not arrive in St. Petersburg until spring, and the newlyweds invited them to dinner. There, for the first time, Paul mentioned to Alice and Eleanor the stock purchase agreement with Nelson. Both women erupted in anger, and Alice demanded that Eleanor be included in the agreement. Nelson felt this was out of the question because Eleanor had no journalism experience, and it also would mean they would be partners. To him, his mother and sister seemed obsessed with the fear that if he died Catherine would inherit his shares. Catherine was shocked mostly by the casual way her in-laws talked about the possible death of her twenty-four-year-old husband.[17]

A few weeks later Nelson found a chance to distance himself from the family squabble. One of the *Times* company's largest problems was the *Clearwater Sun*. The *Times* had bought two-thirds interest in its up-county competitor during the Florida boom. It proved to be a money loser, and Paul Poynter and Carr wanted to save their shirts.

Alice Poynter (*left*) spent much of her mature life moving from one resort to another in a chauffeured Cadillac, often with family members. *Poynter Library, University of South Florida, St. Petersburg, Florida.*

An executive of the *Sun* asked Nelson to buy his one-third interest in it. He agreed and also set out to buy his father's shares, although the paper had heavy debts. Nelson refinanced the paper and saw that it had to be sold, as it had more debts than assets. He found a buyer in less than a year. The process eased Paul's credit crisis and made it possible for him to pay off $125,000 in mortgages. Nelson took away from the deal a $20,000 profit in notes receivable.[18] Although the feat plainly resulted solely from his efforts, Alice insisted that Paul set up an equal amount of obligations to Eleanor.

Flushed with his success at Clearwater, Nelson made it clear that his world was much larger than Pinellas County, and according to one report he fell out with his father over politics.[19] He used the Clearwater profit to buy another of Paul's Indiana dailies, the *Kokomo Dispatch*, in 1929. He earned a reputation as the best journalist the town had ever seen. He tried out a concept that would fascinate him throughout his life and that finally caught on in the age of consumer journalism: He devoted regular news coverage to goods being advertised, with critical judgments. A half-century later the *St. Petersburg Times* would be a pioneer of hard-nosed restaurant reviews, merchandise testing, and shopping advice.

But Poynter had just arrived in Kokomo when the Wall Street crash brought the paper's debts down around his ears. This time he could not find an out-of-towner loaded with cash. He had to sell out in 1930 to the rival Kokomo newspaper to pay off his personal and corporate obligations. In the process, his $20,000 in notes, which he had invested in the enterprise, went down the drain. He was able to send Paul $100,000 in cash, however, averting a threat that the *Times* would be thrown into receivership because of its debts to a collapsing bank.[20] Ironically, Paul had never invested much in the *Dispatch,* having acquired it for its debts in 1920. He got operating capital from local bank loans.

The publisher who bought out the *Dispatch* was keenly aware of how Nelson had enhanced its value. He insisted that Nelson include in the deed a pledge not to enter the newspaper business within fifty miles of Kokomo, even though he was broke.

Retreating to the golden memories of his summer with Scripps-Howard, Nelson Poynter visited the chain's headquarters in New York to see Roy Howard about a job. He was received cordially, and soon he was sent to the *Cleveland Press,* in the heart of Scripps country. Although he had no idea what the job would be, he felt able to handle any newspaper assignment. He did not expect what he got—the lowly rank of advertising salesman. The relatively high pay of $100 a week salved his hurt pride. Besides, he knew the fact that he was overpaid meant a promotion was in store.

A Field for Conquest

Sure enough, by the end of the year Poynter was back on the newspaper of his adolescent initiation, the *Washington Daily News,* and he was advertising director with the same salary as in Cleveland. At twenty-seven, he was one of the youngest newspaper executives in the nation. The *News* had about 50,000 circulation and was the lowest-ranking of five Washington newspapers in every respect. Scripps-Howard was losing $100,000 a year to maintain its profile in the capital but was determined to cut this loss.

Indiana had furnished seven native sons to important positions on the *News.* One was Lowell Mellett. He was editor of the paper when Nelson arrived and served as the younger man's father figure for decades, even more so than Paul. Nelson had known Mellett's brother Don, who was Paul's partner in an Indiana paper before he went on to become a crusading editor in Canton, Ohio. Don was assassinated by bootleggers he had exposed.

Lowell Mellett realized that young Poynter was as dedicated to the editorial side as Mellett himself, and they became close friends and joined efforts to reduce the paper's red ink. It was the depth of the depression, and newspapers suffered even more than other businesses. The two men concentrated on tapping a source of revenue previously denied them, department stores. The plan worked, and soon the paper was slightly in the black. Circulation rose by 10 percent, to 55,000, and advertising linage nearly doubled.[21]

Poynter was the hero of the hour, both inside and outside Scripps-Howard, and he was rewarded with the job of business manager at $125 a week. He knew that his feat had been overrated. For one thing, the *News* was so small that the margin between profit and loss was narrow. Also, Washington was a far better market than other cities because the federal payroll had cushioned the city against the depression.

Poynter thrived on the Washington excitement when bad times defeated other men. With arrival of the New Dealers in 1933, Scripps-Howard's support of Roosevelt opened doors for Poynter. Mellett was close to many in the new regime, and through him Poynter made friends with brain trusters such as Thomas Corcoran and Ben Cohen.

It would have been easy for Poynter to fall into a stereotype. He could have been the enlightened businessman battling the depression or the eastern-educated heartlander dispensing shrewdness. But a lifelong trait began to surface: He was a practical visionary. He rarely made public statements, and he preferred working alongside employees to sending down lightning bolts from the mountaintop. "I really am working less strenuously than ever in my life," he reassured his mother, "but at the same time we seem to be accomplishing much in the building of this newspaper. I think that everyone but myself is fully satisfied with the progress we are showing."[22]

Although Poynter had shown little interest in his family's newspaper properties outside St. Petersburg in his twenties, he began to advise them from the perspective of his Washington success. Once he suggested to his mother how to handle Sullivan advertisers when they asked for discounts.

Nelson and Catherine, still without children, agreed to rent a house along with a couple they knew, Bert and Betty Garnett. It was a large structure across from Georgetown University, with room for both couples' possessions, even two pianos. Catherine cared much more for furnishings than Betty did, and the arrangement worked well for a year. Then the families bought houses near each other in Alexandria.

In a Mother's Day letter to Alice Poynter, Nelson wrote: "Mother, I love hell out of you, always have and always will—not because you are my mother, but because you are the swellest woman over 29 that I know." Referring to Catherine, he added, "You can guess who 'Alice Junior' is."[23]

One winter, when the Washington weather hung heavily, Poynter proposed a bachelor trip to three friends—Garnett, Pyle, and John O'Rourke. Paul Poynter, like most publishers, had a stack of "due bills" from resort hotels that insisted on paying for their advertising with coupons for board, liquor, and lodging. It was a common way for newspaper owners and favored employees to get luxury vacations.

The four piled into Poynter's car and headed south, arriving in Miami three days later. After enjoying the due-billed hospitality of the Everglades Hotel, they split up. Pyle had become the nation's foremost aviation columnist, and he found he could get free rides for two to Nassau. Garnett and O'Rourke took due bills earned from Havana hotels and went there, while Pyle and Poynter went to the Bahamas.

The four reunited in St. Petersburg, where Poynter and Pyle, both flyweights, bragged about surviving a barroom fight with British sailors. They put the car on a coastal ship at Savannah, and the highlight of the trip to Baltimore was Pyle's making movies of Garnett retching in the swells off Cape Hatteras. The trip came just after Poynter's thirtieth birthday, and it would his last youthful fling. Nearly to the end of his life he would be immersed in his work.

With entrepreneurial success under his belt, Poynter reasserted his earlier role as a newsman. In 1933, during a visit to St. Petersburg, he wrote four articles to be distributed by the Scripps-Howard chain. They were filled with research about how Florida had coped with the land bust, the hurricanes, and the depression of the previous decade. There was a heavy dose of consumer economics. He told of paying fifty cents for two slices of French toast in 1925, whereas now he could get a full breakfast for a dime.

Ernie Pyle was going about the country writing the story of the depression in elegant simplicity, a style that later would make him the most admired correspondent of World War II. He would tell of a sick child of sharecroppers needing to get into a hospital or of people trying to keep a scrap of dignity. Poynter deeply admired his friend's gifts, but his pieces had little resemblance to Pyle's.

Although Poynter had received job offers to manage other papers, he preferred to stay with Scripps. In December 1934 he told Roy Howard he wanted to start training a successor for his position with the *News*. The candidate he suggested would not be ready for a year or so, he said, but he wanted to eventually start over with Scripps on the editorial side, taking a salary cut if necessary. Howard told him he thought it was a mistake, but he acceded.[24]

A Dangerous Leap

Two months later a Scripps executive told Poynter that his replacement was coming and he was to be assigned elsewhere. Poynter was left in limbo until May. Mellett and Poynter went to New York to plead with Howard and his aides that Poynter remain in Washington, perhaps as managing editor of the *News*. Pyle had been filling this job, which he detested, and wanted to be cut loose to write his roving column full-time.

Management denied the request. Later that month Poynter was told to go to Ohio as publisher of the *Columbus Citizen*. The understanding was that the editor and the business manager would stay on until Poynter decided whether to let them go.[25]

En route to Columbus in June, however, Poynter learned that the editor was to be fired. The business manager was unhappy with the new arrangement, and the chain sent him to Pittsburgh within a few weeks. Poynter also was dissatisfied with the advertising manager and tried in vain to find a better one inside the chain. From his parents' paper in Sullivan, he hired away Warren Pierce, who later would serve as Poynter's editorial-writing right arm.

Poynter threw himself into Columbus's civic life, becoming a member of the Rotary Club, the Athletic Club, and the Columbus Club. One observer remembered him as "capable, intellectual, impulsive, a good conversationalist, only a social drinker." Poynter had the image of an energetic young man who "wants above everything else to succeed." He praised Catherine for getting them settled into a home quickly—"grand little sport that she is." They bought little in the local stores, although they had an excellent credit rating.[26]

Despite his staffing problems, Poynter kept up his abiding cheerfulness. "I never felt better in my life," he wrote to his mother. "I get plenty of sleep, eat, exercise, and am having a whale of a good time getting this paper geared up. It's true I am working hard, but when didn't I?"[27]

The picture of Poynter in Columbus that emerged from a routine FBI check four years later, based on interviews in the city, shows him as having been "very liberal in his views towards labor movements." Poynter editorially supported a strike against an auto parts maker, according to the report, and this upset many people because the city was not accustomed to strikes. He also advocated an innovation in local government, the city manager system, a position that drew "quite a lot of unfavorable comment from the citizens as a whole." The report concluded that there was "nothing pink or un-American about him at all."[28]

Poynter found a national platform for his liberal views during the Columbus period. He was invited to give an annual lecture in memory of the martyred Don Mellett at the University of Minnesota. *Editor & Publisher*, trade journal of newspapers, reported it extensively.[29]

"We cannot save democracy by denunciation, by red baiting and teachers' oaths," he told the university audience. "Therefore, the best way to protect democracy is to make it work. It will not work for the whole United States if it fails in the component parts of local government which make up the United States." Then he drove home his point: The press could be blamed for the wave of chaos and corruption that had swept across local governments in the previous few years.

In an age when sensation and superficiality had become a hallmark of American newspapers, Poynter pulled no punches: "We can't wise-crack ourselves out of the fact that democracy is not surviving in Europe. We cannot ignore the signs of indifference to democracy's survival here." If newspapers would expose abuses in government, he said, the people would use their political power to clean up the problems. He expressed faith that citizens "would not yield without a fight to a black shirt dictatorship of plug-uglies."

The speech provided the charter of what he would stand for in years to come—the responsibility of newspapers to take the difficult and unpopular path, the importance of local government, the power of information in reforming government, and the danger of both fascists and communists.

After a while the chain sent a new man to Columbus as business manager, and Poynter became editor. They were supposed to perform as a team, but it did not work as it had between Mellett and him. In May 1937 the chain management fired Poynter and put in Robert Brown as editor. (Brown later worked for Poynter in St. Petersburg.)

Several decades later, Poynter was to refer to his departure as resulting from his support of Roosevelt's Supreme Court packing plan, which the chain opposed. But two years after the incident he focused on his lack of preparation as an editor. Writing of himself in the third person, he declared: "Poynter did not represent himself as an editor. He wanted an opportunity to work his way up on the editorial side as he had done on the business side from the job of advertising solicitor."[30] In a letter to Roy Howard, he expanded on this:

> I don't mind being fired if you felt I was a lousy editor. I do think it is unfair to place the responsibility of my going to Columbus on me, and I would like to clear that up for the record. . . .
>
> I think you fellows share in this ghastly fumble. I have never ducked any of my responsibility in it, but I don't want it to haunt me the rest of my life and be branded as misrepresenting myself. On the basis of my publishership of the Kokomo Dispatch, I could hardly merchandise myself as a finished editor.[31]

Howard responded that Poynter "went out of our show not only with the affection, but with the very real respect, of every man in our outfit who came in contact" with him. He recalled that he had advised against "trying to switch from a number one on the business side to a lesser post on the editorial." But he said it was Poynter's right to try the change, "and to whatever extent it was a mistake we rode along with you and were also guilty of faulty judgment."[32]

Scripps-Howard offered Poynter another job elsewhere, but he declined, according to one report.[33] At any rate, Poynter never again had a formal relationship with the chain, which faded drastically in power and prestige later in his career.

After his firing, Poynter was approached by the publisher of the *Minneapolis Star*. This major regional paper was owned by two dynamic individualists, brothers John and Gardner Cowles, who also owned the *Des Moines Register*. He was hired at $1,000 a month to be business manager.

Again the young couple made a good impression. They moved into a fashionable apartment hotel, and Catherine was noticed for her charm. Nelson was described as "morally straight," a man who "makes an excellent appearance and possesses a magnetic personality . . . and was exceedingly courteous."[34]

As in Columbus, Poynter failed to strike managerial gold. The paper was in bad financial condition when he came. Six months after his arrival, an editor who would rise to greatness on the *Star,* Basil ("Stuffy") Walters, was brought in. No place was found for Poynter in the new organization.[35]

In a 1939 letter to John Cowles, Poynter recalled that "I replaced no one . . . and no one replaced me." Apparently explaining his lack of success, he noted that "while I was optimistic, I made no brave promises of miracles." He called it "idiotic" for anyone to enter a strange market and guarantee any specific amount of advertising. After six months in Minneapolis, he left the employ of the Cowleses. When Poynter asked John Cowles for comment on the episode, John Cowles averred that he had "the highest regard for your ability and energy and all around competence, wholly apart from my fondness for you personally." He said he had spoken "extremely favorably" about Poynter to several publishers looking for executives.[36] Gardner Cowles also assured Poynter that "we would be glad to have you associated with us again in any executive position."[37]

Poynter's apprenticeship—though not his roving—had ended. He was no longer the bright boy from Sullivan but rather the dynamic young man from St. Petersburg, veteran of failures and successes. Pinellas County, where he had found the winter sunlight of his childhood, where he had chased fiddler crabs and made his first success in publishing, now would be his base of operations.

Disaster in Slow Motion

The St. Petersburg to which Nelson Poynter returned showed little of the change a decade usually brings. The most notable fact about the city was that it had survived. The years after Poynter went off to Kokomo were filled with three-cent breakfasts, free hotel rooms, Santa Claus arriving by parachute and blimp, and prosaic feats like a new water supply, the reopening of banks, and the return of the tourists.

Even when the *Times* admitted that the land bubble had burst in

A devastating hurricane in 1921 tested the *Times*'s transition to big-city news gathering. *Heritage Park, Largo, Florida.*

1926, a dogged show of optimism remained. As the year closed the paper scraped together statistics showing a net gain in prosperity, disguising the fact that these advances came early in the year. Merchants staged a pep rally in Williams Park, and 250 residents watched the ceremonial burial of an effigy of "Old Man Gloom."

Aware of how fear of hurricanes can keep tourists away, the *Times* blazoned across the top of its 1928 season-opening edition an overline that read "St. Petersburg Has Never Experienced a Destructive Storm or an Epidemic." This was blatant hype. Killer storms had swept the settlement before the city was chartered, and a 1921 blow wreaked painful destruction. The *Times* stated that the wind then had been clocked then at only fifty-five miles an hour: "It lacked quite a bit of being even a baby hurricane."[38] This was the storm that ravaged the bayfront and dealt severely with the Gulf beaches.

Meanwhile, the paper indulged in a common vice of Florida newspapers—ridiculing the weather up north while glossing over the area's own embarrassments. The *Times* printed pictures of snowdrifts in Clifton, Ohio, with a headline that read, "Here's Why Clifton Folks Wished They Had Stayed Through June."[39] It also put on the best face when it promoted a civic celebration of 6,770 days of sunshine since the city's founding—not continuous, of course. The sun god Ra was supposed to rule on the festive day, which opened the summer season. No humor was seen, apparently, in the note that "if rain interrupts, the entire program will be postponed until Thursday."[40]

Although most of its boosterism was directed toward the community, the *Times* saved some ammunition for its own cause. It mailed a copy to the South Pole to cash in on Admiral Byrd's explorations, and motorists arriving via the Gandy Bridge were welcomed with free copies. When stripper Sally Rand visited the city fresh from her triumph with fan and bubble dances at the Chicago World's Fair, the *Times* got her to take subscription orders in its circulation office. The first ten subscribers got passes to her show.

No amount of public cheeriness could mask the fact that the 1926 land bust was a disaster for developers. But there was a bright side. The boom had driven consumer prices—particularly room and board—to levels that only the rich or fly-by-night plungers could afford. With the bust, it turned into a buyers' market. Tourists, many of whom had stopped coming, returned in droves. The Wall Street frenzy was getting hotter by the minute, and people up north had money to spend. The 1927–28 winter season provided St. Petersburg with a bumper crop of tourists, and the next year was even better. They were more frugal than the boomers, but they restored confidence in local residents that steady growth was ahead.

Clearly the man who most personified midcentury St. Petersburg was a pharmacist who had come south seeking his fortune. He embodied the resilience, opportunism, and quirkiness that had pulled Pinellas into the modern world.

This man was James Earl Webb, known universally as Doc. He was born three years before Nelson Poynter, and their careers were entwined, not because they wanted it but because Webb's advertising in the *Times* helped to make fortunes for both men. Although Doc had come up from poverty, in many other ways he was uncannily like Poynter. They even looked alike. Doc started peddling goods door to door in Nashville, Tennessee, when he was nine. He dropped out of school after the seventh grade and worked in drugstores. By age twenty-two he was running a store in Knoxville, having managed to get a pharmacist's license. He worked sixteen hours a day and concocted patent medicines, one of them touted as a cure for venereal disease. He sold it at a 1,000 percent markup.

One day, after Webb had saved $5,000, the grandest car he had ever seen pulled up in front of his store. It was driven by Eddie Rickenbacker, auto racer and flying ace. Webb started bargaining to buy it, Rickenbacker came up with a $7,000 price, and they closed the deal for $4,500.

Doc needed a warmer climate for his health, and he headed south in his new toy. He hoped to get to Miami, but the engine fell out near St. Petersburg. He looked around the town, decided it was the place for him, and opened a tiny drugstore with a partner. But Doc was too flamboyant for the other man, and they broke up after three months.

The store was in a bad location to attract "snowbirds"—winter residents from the North. It was seven blocks from the center of downtown, at the edge of the black section. But Doc knew most visitors were living on a tight budget. He used bargain prices to beat the established merchants. His advertising was lavish in both newspapers, promising prices "10 percent less than anybody." He flaunted his bargains, posting competitors' prices and his reductions, all long before discount stores had been created.

Webb had started in 1925, just in time for the next year's bust. While other merchants were going broke, he made a small profit the first year. Volume more than doubled the next year, and all through the depression and for decades afterward it soared. The store became known as Webb's City. In the 1960s, soon before it was sold and Doc died, the business had $30 million in annual sales volume and served an average of 60,000 customers a day.

Billed as "the World's Most Unusual Drug Store," Webb's City actually was the forerunner of the suburban shopping center. It became a complex of seventy-five stores scattered about eight city blocks and surrounded by parking for 2,000 cars. They sold everything from haircuts and high fashion to groceries and roofing materials.

Webb used creative pricing. To introduce a new cafeteria, Webb offered breakfasts—an egg, bacon, grits, gravy, and toast—for three cents. He made sure his customers felt like they were in a bargain store. His main building had the atmosphere of a Persian market, cramped, cluttered, dingy, noisy, tacky, and dark but somehow intimate and friendly. Doc literally kept an eye on the operation by maintaining his office in a mezzanine ten feet above the main floor and overlooking it.

Because a large number of his customers were snowbirds, Doc decided to turn his so-called drugstore into a tourist attraction. The operation itself was eye-popping enough, but Doc added elephants, flea circuses, and barely dressed models. The "mermaid show," which

Webb's City, forerunner of modern shopping centers, helped make the *Times* prosper with profuse advertising. *Heritage Park, Largo, Florida.*

consisted simply of a couple of girls wearing fish tails, lounging amid marine decor and waving at the gawkers, became something of a tourist shrine. People lined up to see it.

To be sure travelers heading south knew about his mecca, Doc hired away a young executive from the *Times,* Sanford ("Sandy") Stiles. Stiles stalked pastures all over Dixie to find sites for signs, and 147 went up. It competed with Rock City and Burma Shave for roadside fame.

The Owner's Curse

As the *Times* approached its fiftieth birthday in 1934, it seemed to lead a charmed existence. Despite ups and downs, it had flourished. Its editorials had done much to shape its community. Its news operation was aggressive and competent. It had the respect of the people, it had more room than it needed in a fine new building, and its circulation and advertising were ahead of its evening competitor.

But in one way it seemed cursed. Owning it rarely had been lucky for anyone. Its first owners sold it within four months of its birth,

Paul Poynter, Nelson's father, was principal owner of the *Times* for nearly thirty-five years. *St. Petersburg Times*.

and it changed hands six times in its first seventeen years. Bill Straub, who had put more of his heart into it than anyone else, held on to it only eleven years. Even Paul Poynter, who had remained principal owner for two decades, took in partners continually to raise money. And as his editors put together the edition celebrating the half-century mark, it seemed the curtain was falling on another owner-ship.

Like so many problems in St. Petersburg, it started with the land bust. At first things seemed to be taking a turn for the better. After David Lindsay left as general manager of the *Times* in 1927, C. C.

Carr quit the advertising agency business and brought back his sure touch to the newspaper's management as one-third owner.

Carr's first official act was to name Nelson Poynter his assistant. With Straub keeping a steady hand on the editorial page and Tom Harris a rising star in the newsroom, management seemed to be better than ever. Although Carr and Paul Poynter always addressed each other as "mister," they worked together well. Carr provided the drive and discipline the paper needed, and Poynter gave him free rein.[41]

Beneath the placid surface ran currents of trouble, however. The *Times* was trying to collect debts it was owed for advertising and had to go to court to win judgments. Paul Poynter formed a real estate holding company called Semit (*Times* spelled backwards) which he used to raise money for his own investments and debts. Two months before the stock market crash in 1929, Semit offered $50,000 in mortgage bonds at 8 percent interest—a breathtakingly high rate for those days. The bonds were secured by *Times* buildings but guaranteed by Poynter, Carr, and the newspaper.

Within a few weeks new money was evident in the *Times*. It came from two brothers who would play a crucial role in the newspaper's coming crisis. Frank G. and William J. Smith, newspaper proprietors from Waukegan, Illinois, were listed as holding securities. Nelson Poynter, having left for his venture in Kokomo, no longer was on record as either a staff member or a stockholder.

More key actors came on stage a year later. These changes—or at least the outward versions of them—were fully publicized.

The Ottaway family, owners of a newspaper in Port Huron, Michigan, had been making winter visits to St. Petersburg for three generations. In 1930, following the example of Straub and many other northern publishers who followed the sun to Florida, they bought into the newspaper that came along with their morning orange juice.

In what a news story called an "addition to the Times organization," the scion of the Ottaway interests became Carr's assistant. The young man was W. W. Ottaway, a graduate of the University of Michigan and a son of E. J. Ottaway, co-owner and publisher of the Port Huron *Times-Herald*. The story boasted that the *Times*'s "stability" as an institution had led the Ottaways to invest. They bought $100,000 worth of stock, all or most of it apparently coming from Carr's personal holdings.[42] The Smith brothers no longer were listed as holding securities, but Nelson Poynter returned as a stockholder.

Although the Ottaways apparently did not seek to control the paper, never having more than about 20 percent of the stock, bad feelings always existed between them and Paul Poynter. They disapproved of his high-rolling outside interests and his ethics. It seemed to them that he "skidded awfully close to the edge" and indulged in "chicanery."[43] When his father died in 1934, W. W. Ottaway went back to Michigan to run the paper there. His brother, James H., succeeded him at the *Times*.

A seed of controversy was sown in 1932 when the Smiths made a new loan, this time to Paul Poynter. As collateral, he used his *Times* stock—2,900 of the 4,688 total shares. The Smiths once more were listed as stockholders. Frank Smith soon died, and his wife inherited his shares.

That year Poynter took advantage of the bargain real estate prices in St. Petersburg. He invested in the Hall Building, a Central Avenue office structure. The building was to prove an albatross around his and his family's necks for years to come.

Meanwhile, the *Times* was sinking financially. After the land bust its operating revenues decreased steadily—down 31 percent from 1928 through 1933. Part of this shrinkage came through having to write off bad debts incurred when advertisers could not pay their bills. Management cut expenses to keep up with this shortfall, including a reduction for the newsroom. So the newspaper averted net losses throughout the period, although profits fell from $65,000 to $34,000.

Just as real estate holdings were Paul Poynter's downfall, so they were the *Times*'s. The eight-story temple of high hopes that Poynter and Carr had built during the land boom now became a liability. Expenses on it exceeded income throughout the period by a ratio of as much as six to one. So the deficit on the building ate up the newspaper's earnings, reducing profits of the parent company to paltry amounts. One year, 1932, saw a net loss of $1,192. It was in this era that Bill Straub suffered a stroke, lost his St. Petersburg home, and had to move to his beach cottage.

The company had begun to recover from the crisis when the fuse for a later explosion was lit: C. C. Carr, Paul Poynter's ally and right arm, again left the *Times*. Carr had been restless since he sold much of his stock to the Ottaways and was searching for something else to do. Nelson Poynter, with his wide contacts in northern power centers, came across what seemed like the perfect spot. He put Carr in contact with Aluminum Corporation of America, which hired Carr as a public relations executive. He needed the money, and he moved his family to a life of relative luxury in Pittsburgh.

When he left the *Times* in May 1934, Carr was described in the published announcement as having been "the active directing force" in the newspaper for twenty years except for his four-year absence during the land boom. He sold his remaining stock back to the corporation, and W. W. Ottaway took over as manager.

As Carr cleaned out his desk, he recalled Paul Poynter's warm message of farewell read at the testimonial banquet. He also thought of the perils that might lie ahead for his former partner, with his impulsiveness and unsystematic ways. He composed a final memo to Poynter, still with the formal "mister," in which Carr advised that Poynter "keep a tight rein" on all departments of the paper. "I hate to see you have to take on this burden, but from what I can observe, it will be necessary for you to do so." He said that if Poynter needed his help, "all you need is to call on me."[44]

Carr had to make good on this offer within little more than a year. At the height of the winter season in 1935, William Smith and his wife and son arrived for their accustomed visit to St. Petersburg. The *Times* flattered them with a picture and an interview of Smith. It identified him as a friend of the governor and reported his conservative opinions ranging from a golf club fee increase to old-age pensions, both of which he opposed.

Nelson Poynter, who was moving between jobs in Washington and Columbus, also was photographed when he and Catherine visited in June. Although he clearly was chagrined by his father's real estate activities, he had praised his operation of the newspaper in a letter the previous April: "The March statement of The Times thrilled me. If I had ever had any idea that I was any great shakes of a newspaper operator in comparison with my dad—that statement would have cooled me off. I recognize the tremendous improvement in the capital position in the last year since I have seen a statement."[45]

But on the following July 1 Paul Poynter's financial house of cards collapsed, and his son led the effort to put it together again. The newspaper's board of directors was meeting that morning. About noon Paul Poynter came by the office of Tom Harris, who had become managing editor. "They're trying to take my paper away," Poynter told his twenty-six-year-old executive. "Go ahead and run it like you always do."[46]

Smith called Harris to his office and gave him a news story and two photographs to run the next day. The pictures, of Smith and of James Ottaway, ran on the front page with the announcement that the two men were the new president-manager and vice-president/general manager, respectively. Straub was to continue as editor, which by then meant he was in charge of editorials.

Poynter marched out of the newspaper office and set up business in the Hall Building a block away. He lost no time preparing his counter-attack.

The 2,900 shares Paul Poynter had used in 1932 to secure a loan from the Smiths were at the heart of the dispute. Poynter contended they were still under his control. The Smiths maintained they had controlled and voted the stock since the loan three years before.[47] Poynter had defaulted on his repayments, so the entire debt came due.[48] On this basis they had voted Poynter out of office.

Eight days after the takeover Poynter got a circuit court order barring his opponents from doing anything with the stock. The judge also appointed a receiver to run the paper, and the dispute wended its way to the state supreme court.

Meanwhile, the *Times* editorialist, apparently Straub, brushed off the controversy as something of no concern to the public: "There is one institution which the public cares less about as to who owns or controls it than almost any other kind of semi-public business—it's the newspaper."[49] After all, it was the month Will Rogers was killed, a price war lowered milk to eight cents a quart, and Webb's City was selling neckties three for a dollar.

The public did not read about the battle being mounted by Paul Poynter's family and friends to save the newspaper for him. Nelson took time off from his new job to fly to St. Petersburg. He and Carr used all their ingenuity to shore up Paul's financial position. Many advertisers told Smith they would pull their business from the *Times* if he held out, and staff members threatened to quit.[50] Carr apparently reacquired some *Times* stock, as he returned to the shareholders' list.

Nelson borrowed money in Columbus, and friends made personal loans to Paul. Although Paul had put the *Sullivan Times* in Alice's name earlier, she let him mortgage it to a relative during the crisis.

Raising money from normal credit sources was made difficult by the fact that Florida, especially St. Petersburg, had a bad name with investors. Untold millions of dollars in public bonds had been defaulted upon. Paul borrowed all he could from Union Trust, a small new bank of which he was a director, but little was available.[51]

At one point the rescuers considered starting a new morning newspaper printed in the *Tampa Times* plant. They knew this would frighten the Smiths and Ottaways, as they also were in a financial bind, and new competition was the last thing they wanted.[52] Even while the matter was still in the courts Smith agreed to a deal giving the presidency of the company back to Paul Poynter while Smith stayed as chairman.

The dispute was over by August 22, when stock claimed by the Smiths was transferred to Paul. The supreme court ordered Ottaway and his lawyer not to interfere with the operation of the paper. Paul's wife and his secretary were added to the directors. For the first time in years he had full command.

Alice Poynter appears to have been a strong force behind her husband in the crisis. After Nelson returned north, he wrote her in praise of the courage, sportsmanship, and values she had shown while she chafed at staying backstage: "I have grieved that he would be subjected to such badgering and embarrassment, but it is you that my heart goes out to. . . . I have your same impatience, I know the torture of waiting, and yet how beautifully you yielded to it."[53]

Even though Nelson averred that "with all our imperfections I think we have a swell family," the question arose as to whether Paul had lost his grip. The Poynters entertained the idea of selling out to the Ottaways, but Nelson counseled against it on the grounds that his father was not ready to retire. He told his mother that Paul should sell out some of his other interests and "stick to the one good newspaper as a means of keeping his hand." Nelson, his training as an economist coming out, suggested that Paul refinance the newspaper with the Ottaways left out completely. Convert much of his father's debt into preferred stock, he advised, "so that come panic or hurricane, there will not be a huge debt payment to meet."[54]

The Ottaways ended up selling their stock back to the company. According to James Ottaway, they did so because they were "fed up with the whole kit and kaboodle." But Eleanor Poynter Jamison said her father decided to exercise an option to call in the Ottaway stock.[55]

So the leadership of the newspaper reverted to two old men, Paul Poynter and Bill Straub. The real question as the 1930s neared an end was whether either could provide the stimulus the *Times* needed. The ownership crisis of 1935 had shaken many people's confidence in the elder Poynter, and Straub's life was slowly slipping away. A vacuum was developing. Nelson Poynter, upon his return from Minneapolis, clearly was drawn into the void.

Chapter 4

Alarums and Excursions

The *Times* always saluted the new year with brassy boosterism, and to start 1938 it had two pages of classified ads voicing best wishes. It would soon print the name of every visitor then registered in the city.

But that year was special. There were plans to resurrect a wood-burning locomotive that would wheeze down First Avenue South to the midtown Atlantic Coast Line depot, marking the fifty years since Peter Demens's railroad had arrived and the city was born. A *Times* editorial saw St. Petersburg as standing on "the threshold of a new era" with "high hopes and good prospects."

The paper polled city leaders on what they thought would happen in the next half-century. Its forecast of the future of newspapers quoted from a speech: "It is not hard to believe the news story will enter your office, skip the cluttered desk of the rewrite man and the copy reader, not to mention the Linotype operator, the foundry, the mat department and instead land almost directly on the press."[1]

The *St. Petersburg Times* certainly was no closer to that dream than any other small daily in the country, and the likelihood that any newspaper would soon achieve such technological advances was fading. On March 12, Adolf Hitler's forces marched into Austria and annexed it, and France rushed troops to its border.

Less than two weeks later, however, the *Times* took the first step in a course of events that would result in its becoming one of the ten most highly rated newspapers in the country, the only one with a written covenant with its readers. That step put Nelson Poynter in charge.

Reading the announcement would lead to no high expectations. It said only that Paul Poynter's son had resigned in Minneapolis and arrived in St. Petersburg to "take an active part in the management and publishing" of the *Times*. Nelson Poynter bore the title of general manager, as Bill Straub was to be honored as nominal editor until he died. The thirty-five-year-old newcomer unmistakably was in charge of the whole operation.

Although news pages continued to give readers familiar fare—news that their favorite dance was the big apple and that they could see the local premiere of Lou Gehrig's first movie—they quickly found out things had changed. Two days after his appointment, Nelson Poynter wrote an editorial that quoted verbatim a memo he had sent to all *Times* employees:

> Let's practice what we preach.
>
> We have written numerous editorials, cartoons, and news stories calling attention to the dangerous traffic situation existing here. There are many remedies all of which deserve consideration. But the quickest, most effective is for all citizens and visitors to:
>
> Observe all traffic regulations, stop signs, etc.
>
> A copy of this will go to Chief Vaughn and municipal judges asking that they show no favors whatsoever to Times employees who are picked up for traffic violations.
>
> This is the least we can do to protect ourselves, our families, neighbors and visitors.[2]

Journalists at that time took for granted that they had to supplement their pitiful salaries with largesse from theaters, publicists, and all others who looked for breaks in news columns. Sports writers got free drinks and boat rentals, government reporters ate free at restaurants thanks to lobbyists, and those who covered airlines got vacations abroad. *Times* staffers had never been notably unethical, but from then on they would have to *look* ethical.

Other changes obviously were ahead. Poynter wanted to put out a great newspaper, but he knew he would have to build it on a far better financial basis. It would take almost two decades to put the paper on such sound footing. Meanwhile, the new broom would sweep away some longtime stalwarts on the staff.

Editorial crusades would equal or surpass those of Bill Straub in his prime. Although Poynter now used St. Petersburg as his base, he would make other sorties into the outside world. These would take him into the publishing cockpits of New York and Chicago, the inner circles of wartime Washington and the high life of Hollywood, and back to Washington to found an innovative national information service. Along the way he would acquire worldwide visibility as well as critics, who labeled him a Communist, and a new wife, who would adopt his obsession and help realize it.

The First Jousts

With his father and Charlie Carr over him, Nelson Poynter could do little tinkering during his brief stint with the *Times* in 1927–28, and in his jobs up north he also was cramped in influencing the paper's life. But when he returned to St. Petersburg he ran into no effective limit on what he could do, despite the fact he was not majority owner.

He deferred to editor Straub and managing editor Harris in his first year. Editorials continued at a temperate level as the old editor faded away. Some editorials, though, clearly were written by Nelson Poynter and turned up the fire.

When President Franklin Delano Roosevelt dangled a new basket of federal aid projects before local governments, Poynter brought out what would become one of his hallmarks, a set of goals for the community. Straub had done the same thing in his early years, keeping up a drumfire of demands so the public would never forget the agenda the *Times* had set for it.

Poynter's topics for reform resembled the traditional Straub plat-form. They were heavy on transportation, seeking to break bottlenecks that hampered travel into Pinellas, now including air routes. Emphasis remained on the "good place to live" theme—waterfront improvement to serve yachtsmen and fishermen, a municipal auditorium, enhance-ment of the gulf beaches.[3]

Another of Poynter's lifelong passions soon came to light—his devotion to local self-government as the only way to make democracy work and his determination to get good people to run for office. He believed that political sportsmanship constituted an essential ingredient of the process, and he set out to defuse the hard feelings that often came out of a tough campaign. This would lead to a Pinellas County institution—the "winners-losers" parties in the *Times* building on election night, when the two sides could listen to the vote count and make peace over punch and cookies.

In the years to come the *Times* would develop a unique twist to its editorials, taking the lead in doing what it urged others to do. Poynter continually put the *Times* first in line to donate to causes he advocated and to make sacrifices he espoused. A hint of this came when he praised the medical association for planning a clinic to serve low-income persons. He offered the group free office space in the *Times* building for a year.[4]

As feelings became inflamed over events leading to World War II, Poynter maintained Straub's habitual pacifism. Their position was summed up as the Munich conference between Hitler and Neville Chamberlain approached: "War can yet be averted. But whatever may happen, the guilt must rest squarely on Hitler and his aides. It is Nazi propaganda that has bred violence."[5]

Four days after he took on the title of editor in 1939, Nelson Poynter had a byline on an article from Europe. It was the first of four probing the prospects for war. "War Unlikely, Times Editor Finds on Tour of Europe," the first headline read, less than three months before Hitler invaded Poland. After touring central and southern Europe, Poynter concluded, "No one is itching for a fight." The other articles were closer to the mark, telling how Germans were sacrificing butter and eggs for tanks and planes. Both Hitler and Benito Mussolini would win in honest elections, he decided, and only the loss of a major war could overthrow them.

Poynter's passion for world affairs, which he would burnish throughout his life, stemmed from his postcollegiate year of wandering around the world. Mixed into it was the uncomplicated idealism of William Jennings Bryan, Poynter's boyhood hero. There also was the glow of friendships gained while lounging on the deck of a freighter with youths of various colors and the economist's contempt for the wastefulness of war.

So the *Times* began to take on an internationalist tinge. Partnership with Latin America, always a favorite subject of Straub and Harris, was pushed nearly to the level of a campaign. Authorities were urged to step up the teaching of Spanish, and the *Times* itself sponsored language lessons on radio and printed Spanish-language cartoons.

It would be decades before the paper's world view fully ripened, and Poynter's initial crusades aimed at closer targets. The first two were central to Poynter's philosophy—using economics to benefit the people and achieving racial justice at the local level.

Although commerce in St. Petersburg was recovering from the bad years, local government finances remained chaotic. The city, county, and school board had enormous debts left over from the land boom of the 1920s. The crisis had started when local banks failed in 1930, taking official bank accounts down with them. The city council was forced into its most dreaded recourse—default on its debts. Its credit disappeared overnight, and its bonds lost much of their market value. Civic leaders, including Paul Poynter, were appointed to a blue-ribbon committee that for years muddled through the difficulty, seeking the least possible harm. Toward the end of the decade taxes once again fed municipal coffers.

The biggest problem remained, however. Citizens were paying off their governments' debts at what were then absurdly high interest rates. Most leaders realized the solution lay in refinancing—borrowing new money at low rates to pay off the old high-interest bonds. Nelson Poynter had done just that with the burdensome debts his father had piled onto the newspaper. In the spring of 1939 he consolidated the loans into a new one for $250,000, drastically reducing interest at a low brokerage fee.

Poynter started a campaign encouraging local governments to refinance their debt. The project moved ahead, and brokers flocked around, eager to make hefty fees. Drawing on his Yale economics education, his knowledge of Wall Street, and his success in negotiating a low fee, Poynter took on the brokers, who included some prominent local citizens. He charged that they would get such a large slice of the new money, the public would be saddled with excessive debt again.

Not content with editorials, Poynter played an activist role in the controversy. He helped pay for one survey of the bond market and went to Washington twice at his own expense to get expert opinions. His most impressive editorial effort was a half-page signed editorial calling on the public to rise up and force the school board to drop an expensive refunding plan. It was a bombastic display reminiscent of Straub's broadsides for Pinellas independence. A banner headline read: "Your School Bonds May Gyp Your Child of a Full Term—It's a Long and Sorry Story—Important to You/ We Recommend You Read Every Word."[6]

The outcome was that the city and the school board laid down much stricter terms than the winning broker had originally asked. Poynter always considered it his greatest editorial campaign. He felt it led to legislation giving the St. Petersburg example statewide scope. On a local basis, it allowed the city to steadily reduce its debt at low interest and regain a good credit rating.

Much closer to citizens' everyday concerns was Poynter's other major campaign during his early years. It also had a more obvious linkage with his passion to make St. Petersburg a good place to live.

After much wrangling over sites, the city council finally had completed a federally financed slum clearance project named Jordan Park for black housing in 1940, one of the first in the nation. Far more housing was needed, though, and the local public housing authority proposed to nearly double the size of Jordan Park. Slum landlords dug in, claiming unfair competition and labeling the plan socialistic. The council went along, in effect killing the addition.

The *Times* mounted a campaign to overturn the decision, running a photo of a shabby outhouse in the slums alongside that of a bright new bathroom in Jordan Park. This set off a series of such pictures. Although Poynter offered a column of space per day to opponents, there were no takers.

A civic revolt welled up. The League of Women Voters, with Catherine Poynter as a leader, called for a public vote on the matter. Newspapers ran blank petitions demanding a referendum, and 225 volunteers turned out to gather signatures. Within two weeks the required number was obtained, and five weeks of bitter campaigning followed. When the vote was in, the project was approved by a four-to-three ratio.

Within less than a decade, the housing authority declared that Jordan Park had become a garden spot in an otherwise drab section, a new tradition. "The dwellings are known for their cleanliness; the well-kept lawns and shrubbery advertise the pride the tenants take in their new homes; the orderliness and community spirit of the people are evidences of better citizens."[7]

A Titan Falls

For several years Bill Straub had come to the office less and less. He spent most of his time at his beloved Loafer's Lodge, the beach house to which he and his wife had retreated after he had a stroke in 1932 and a bank foreclosed on their downtown home. He became a gray eminence to newer staffers who had never known him.

But many at City Hall remembered him, and some still felt the wounds of his editorial harpoon. By the spring of 1939 they knew they could no longer avoid paying him the tribute he deserved, at least if it was to come while he was alive. Partially acknowledging his role in saving the shoreline, the public waterfront north of Central Avenue—a five-block stretch—received the name of Straub Park. A bronze bust of him was placed in the park, paid for not by tax money but from a fee fund "in order that this shall not be a burden to the taxpayers." The resolution designating the park conceded Straub had been "more instrumental than any other individual in preserving the waterfront for the public."

Paul and Nelson Poynter jointly signed an editorial thanking the city council for the move. They noted that such tributes rarely were made to living persons, "especially by gentlemen who have disagreed at times" with the honoree. The whole community, they predicted, would appreciate the councilmen's concession.[8]

Straub tried his best to keep working, penciling his columns as usual. He wrote one admitting that newspapers were imperfect because their operators were imperfect. But, he concluded, newspapers represented the finest examples of free speech and the desire to serve.

Then he began his final drift. On a Sunday night, April 9, he whispered his last words—that Tom Harris should be notified so the *Times* could get the break on the obituary. Even so, he lingered into the morning, and the competing *Independent* ran the story first. The *Times* carried a lavish spread about Straub's life, with columns of comment from citizens, pictures from various eras, and a summation of his achievements. So many things he advocated had become reality, the notable exception being removal of the downtown railroad tracks. An editorial noted his singlemindedness: "Friends, gifts or threats could never dissuade him from a crusade in the interest of his readers." Because of his localism, it identified him with the great heartland editors such as William Allen White rather than the national thunderers like Joseph Pulitzer.

City Hall closed on the day of Straub's funeral. The family decided to hold it in First Congregational Church, although the editor had never taken part in organized religion. Two months later his widow died. The *Times* followed its penchant for constantly shuffling the masthead, and the space carried only Paul Poynter's name (as president and general manager) on April 11, 1939, the day of the obituary. Nelson Poynter and Tom Harris were omitted. By June, however, Nelson was listed as editor and general manager, without any other announcement. Harris again appeared in the masthead as managing editor that fall.

The *PM* Episode

After a year at the helm of the *Times*, Nelson Poynter was pleased with his results. He boasted that circulation had increased while that of the *Independent* had fallen, advertising potential had increased, and all nonunion employees' wages had risen. Most notably, after the dreary finances of the 1930s, profits had risen.[9]

The outside world still tempted Poynter, however. This time, he dreamed of inventing a newspaper unlike any seen before, on a stage much bigger than the Pinellas subpeninsula.

Poynter had given little evidence that he was a bold innovator. He had come up with clever, enlightened ideas in places such as Washington and Columbus, but he had never devised anything radically distinctive except for his vain effort to keep his Kokomo paper alive when the chain supermarkets denied him advertising. He knew that people often bought papers to get the information in some ads, so he ran grocery prices in the news columns at no charge.

But Poynter's ideas fermented during the 1930s. Success with the *Washington Daily News,* where he avoided head-to-head competition with the big dailies, convinced him that alternative newspapers could be profitable. Of course, E. W. Scripps had the same inspiration a half-century before when he started a chain of lightweight papers that eventually would include the *Daily News.*

Actually, it was hard for any bright young journalist not to be caught up in brainstorms. Magazines with daring concepts such as Harold Ross's *New Yorker,* the Wallaces' *Reader's Digest,* and later

Henry Luce's *Time, Fortune,* and *Life* were bursting onto the scene. Young newspaper people all over the country itched to try out some of these ideas.

Keystone of Poynter's ideal paper would be its coverage of news overlooked by standard dailies—news that touched on readers' own lives, such as what new taxes and laws would mean to them. It would take advantage of the new Wirephoto process, which sent pictures by telegraph. But Poynter wanted to exploit it to transmit word packages by photographic process, thus saving the cost of editing and type-setting, benefits that would come decades later with computerized transmission. And, most subversive to the American way of newspa-pering, his publication would close the door on advertising.

Poynter had become a friend of Thomas ("Tommy the Cork") Corcoran, a brilliant young aide to President Roosevelt. In the early spring of 1939, as Straub neared death in his seaside home, Corcoran was recovering from a heart ailment at Poynter's cottage on Madeira Beach. His host showed Corcoran a draft prospectus he had written for his paper of the future. It intrigued the sick man, partly because it reminded him of a project then being pushed in New York City.

"You ought to meet Ralph Ingersoll," Corcoran told Poynter. Ingersoll was an editorial genius who had provided the organizational drive to get the *New Yorker* and the Luce magazines started and now wanted to blaze his own trail by founding an experimental newspaper.

At that time Poynter was having another brainstorm. He wanted to buy the *New York Evening Post,* which had perennially provided highbrow liberal commentary while losing money. It was the creation of poet William Cullen Bryant and the vehicle for an intellectual giant of the late 1800s, E. L. Godkin. Poynter wanted to turn the *Post* gradually into an adless wonder, in accord with his prospectus. He made two trips to New York and conferred with the paper's owners. It could be bought, but at a price he could not afford. Meanwhile, he met Ed Stanley, a former Associated Press executive who had been Inger-soll's first hire for his New York project. Poynter was intrigued with the similarity of their ideas.

President Roosevelt had a keen interest in the power structure of the newspaper industry, and he was not above trying to influence it. He heard that Ingersoll was about to launch an innovative liberal paper— it soon would acquire the name *PM*—and decided to lend a hand. After all, the Democrats had a distinct minority of editors on their side.

Without warning, Ingersoll got a call from Washington summoning him to Corcoran's office.[10] "The President likes your newspaper idea," the aide told Ingersoll. "He wants to help raise the money. It's not really a problem. How much do you think you need?"

"Ten million dollars." Actually, Ingersoll had been talking about $1.5 to $3 million.

"Fine," Corcoran replied. The White House, he added, had even lined up an angel who could spring this amount. "Have you ever heard of Edward Noble?" he asked.

"No."

"But you have heard of Life Savers?"

"Life Savers?"

"Sure—candy Life Savers—the ones with the holes in them. That's Edward J. Noble." Ingersoll recalled Noble as a rich donor to the New Deal who had been thanked with the title of assistant secretary of commerce.

"When the right time comes, if we have to, we'll get the boss himself to give the word," Corcoran confided.

Roosevelt and Corcoran expected Ingersoll to woo the candy king, and thus began a furious campaign, with messages rocketing among Corcoran, Ingersoll, Noble and his lawyers. It went well, as Noble was delighted when Ingersoll showed him the prototype of the new paper. But Noble doubted Ingersoll's ability as a businessman. So Corcoran called Poynter and urged him to pay a visit Ingersoll immediately.

Ingersoll already had sent Poynter a copy of his prospectus for *PM,* a discourse that filled sixty-one pages in its early drafts and that has since become a classic of visionary journalism. It ranged from the lyrical to the technical. Perhaps the most quoted section—the one which stuck in Poynter's memory—was this:

> We are against people who push other people around, just for the
> fun of pushing, whether they flourish in their country or abroad. We are
> against fraud and deceit and greed and cruelty and we will seek to
> expose their practitioners. We are for people who are kindly and

courageous and honest. We respect intelligence, sound accomplishment, open-mindedness, religious tolerance. We do not believe all mankind's problems are soluble in any existing social order, certainly not our own, and we propose to applaud those who seek constructively to improve the way men live together. We are American and we prefer democracy to any other form of government.[11]

Poynter flew to Lakeville, Connecticut, where Ingersoll had a country estate. He found a man uncannily like himself. Both came from well-off families with backgrounds in politics. Both idolized their mothers and strived to measure up to their successful fathers. Like Poynter, Ingersoll had attended Yale and emerged trying to accommodate liberal idealism with hardheaded commercialism, and both liked to take risks. A crucial difference was their sense of place. Ingersoll, although he had worked in the gold mines of California and Mexico as a youth, was a deep-dyed New Yorker. Poynter never coped well in anything larger than middle-sized cities, and he was at least partly a man of the heartland.

The two men compared their proudest possessions—their prospectuses. Poynter later was to recall, "It was fantastic, really, how much they had in common except mine provided for a paper without advertising while in his the last eight pages (they were both tabloids) would carry classified advertising, but not in the want-ad sense. He wanted all the women's clothes to be in one classification, hardware in another and so on."[12]

The high points of Ingersoll's prospectus resembled what eight years later would become the cornerstone of the *St. Petersburg Times*—Poynter's "Standards of Ownership." According to the prospectus, the new paper should (1) have journalists, not investors, as proprietors. ("Its working management shall control its editorial policies, in perpetuity"); (2) own no real estate nor press equipment; (3) support itself without advertising; (4) be founded on "respect for talent"; (5) draw on a wide range of talents—established authors, underappreciated young journalists, and untrained but well educated graduates in the liberal arts; (6) use photographs of high artistic merit to tell stories, not just illustrate articles (the concept here is clearly that of *Life* magazine); (7) use—or create—new technology to bring the quality of the best magazines into newspaper production (involving everyday use of full-color, fine-screen reproduction of photographs, and neat, orderly design of pages); and (8) after the paper begins making a profit, pay its employees well and share with them its profits "above a stated reward to its capital investment."[13]

Just what agreement the two men reached is hazy in the records, as it apparently was between themselves. It is clear that Poynter committed himself to a rigorous work schedule split between New York and St. Petersburg. His mother seems to have objected to the idea, as he defended it to her at length. "I have certain reservations concerning the NY adventure. While I am not obliged to make investment there, it is desirable that I do so if I want to come into it almost on terms of equality with Ingersoll. Since I shoot only at the top I have had to ponder this."[14]

He predicted that the *Times* would operate successfully without him, but he did not want it to lose "the momentum that I have pumped into it during the last year." Addressing his mother's doubts as to whether Catherine could take the change, he replied, "There's no doubt we can take it physically, but unless the setup in NY is absolutely to our liking *I* don't think it is worth it." Commuting and other expenses would eat up additional income, he said, and only the prospect of a stock bonus would make it attractive.[15]

Despite his misgivings, Poynter went to work immediately as business manager of Publications Research, Inc., parent of the unborn and unnamed daily. He commuted almost weekly from St. Petersburg by the fledgling Eastern Airlines and paid all his expenses. As there still was no business to manage, Poynter shouldered the burdens worrying Ingersoll most—formulating an advertising policy, a budget, and a campaign to raise capital investment.

Poynter proved right away that he could play one of Ingersoll's favorite management games, memo writing, although not as well as the master. Where other executives would deal out two or three thoughts at a time, he would dispense a full deck in his voluminous but by no means verbose messages.

Within a few days after the Lakeville meeting, Poynter sent Ingersoll a four-page memo entitled "Arguments Against Advertising." It scampered through ten numbered sections relying more on ethics, common sense, hunches, audacity, and rhetorical questions than on hard facts.

In short, it looked much like an Ingersoll memo. The longest and strongest point of the Poynter memo was its proposal for giving the reader an unpaid summary of the ads in other papers. *PM* could promote itself as the "only newspaper in New York with all the ads." It would be the "paper with *complete* store news." After making a case against relying on ads, Poynter laid out a grander version of what he had tried in Kokomo:

> LET'S REVIEW ALL THE MOST INTERESTING ADS IN NEW YORK EVERY DAY—the ads in about 5,000,000 copies of our competitors' papers will be promoting our paper every day.
>
> Let us have on our reportorial staff gals with good stout feet who know their merchandise. Their job will be to report to Mrs. Reader what she would find out for herself if she devoted full time to shopping. The ads of the other papers would be their leads. They would critically pass judgment. If Gimbel's carry a sensational fur coat ad in the New York News this morning, "our fur specialist" would tell our readers that the fur coat advertised was lousy, if in her judgment it is lousy. If it is a shrieking bargain, she will say so.[16]

The memo also suggested a rating system for advertised goods, using stars or dollar marks, along with a "union made" label. The feature was to run on the back page, where "Mrs. Reader" could tear it out and file it, even to the point of keeping a "running catalog" in a folder for her shopping trips. The payoff, it said, would be a saving of "hundreds of millions of hours of shopping time."[17]

Ingersoll wired Poynter in St. Petersburg that he was happy to report himself "practically sold on your major point." He also was lining up appointments, presumably with potential donors, starting the day Poynter returned, August 25.

Ingersoll had no illusions that *PM* could get past its first year or two without heavy investments from outsiders. He preferred people who were so enamored of the concept that they were willing to risk losing their stakes—rich liberals, that is. A key question was whether to "go public" for part of the money—sell stock on the market and approach bankers.

Despite the pressure the two men put on themselves, they seemed unaware of how rapidly events were nearing a climax. On the Friday when Poynter arrived in New York, he gave Ingersoll another four-page memo, this time on financial projections for *PM*. This memo was much more businesslike than the one on advertising, although it still relied more on his own self-confidence than on specific data. It gave three options on how to survive the first year, all of them more frugal than Ingersoll had in mind.

The first plan, based on a $3 million capitalization, envisioned chopping $500,000 from expenses by using a form of letterpress printing rather than offset printing. This addressed Ingersoll's passion for a better-printed newspaper than ever before. Offset, for which Poynter was to win national attention in later decades, was then in its infancy as a high-quality process. Poynter knew it was not then feasible for a large daily.

Another $500,000 would be saved by scrapping the idea of going public, as Ingersoll expected to spend this much on the campaign to raise $1.5 million. Poynter used a humanitarian appeal: If the newspaper found an insufficient market after a year, it still could return some money to private investors with minimum suffering. "The idea of public issues with the inevitable high pressure salesmanship is distasteful to me. I don't want widow and orphan stockholders in a new newspaper." So the first plan envisioned ending the year with $2 million left in the till.

The other two plans involved even more thrifty approaches. They reflected Poynter's dread of his father's style of financing. He noted he was "ultra conservative as to newspaper debt whether it be in the form of preferred stock, mortgages or notes." The paper should try to live on its income and keep reserves, he argued.

Nevertheless, he thought the paper could start up, and the sooner the better, as *PM* had no monopoly on its concept. "I was within a few hundred thousand dollars and a few days of converting the N.Y. Post to approximately this kind of newspaper before I met you," he told Ingersoll.[18]

The advertising issue moved to a head. The two men spent a whole evening thrashing out the idea. The next day, over lunch, Ingersoll told him he had decided to forgo paid advertising.

Trouble with Angels

In the same period Ingersoll met with Poynter at the Yale Club, where the latter usually stayed. Sagging in spirits, Ingersoll confided that the

Wall Street public issue deal was off, but Poynter convinced him that a $1.5 million collection from private investors would work and that they could raise this at $100,000 each from fifteen persons. He even talked about putting in $100,000 of his own. Buoyed by Poynter's optimism, they went out together searching for angels.

Ingersoll had been working on Ed Noble (of Life Saver fame) for several weeks. Despite Corcoran's optimism and promises of presidential help, Noble had oscillated between excitement over the plan and a complete disenchantment. He agreed to come back in, but only as one of ten backers providing the $1.5 million total. Then Ingersoll tried to sell Noble again on being the sole backer, this time with half ownership and management control, investing the $1.5 million by himself. Noble resisted because of rumors that Ingersoll, though an editorial genius, was careless about financial matters. Ingersoll solicited endorsements from his former employers, Ross and Luce, but what seemed to impress Noble most was the business acumen of Nelson Poynter.

For three days at the end of August 1939, Ingersoll and Noble stayed at separate hotels in Washington and began a fervid exchange of memos seeking to effect the marriage. Noble's lawyers raised all manner of provisos, and Ingersoll agreed to them one by one, with Corcoran acting as middleman. At 11 P.M. on August 31, Corcoran called Ingersoll to say the deal was all "buttoned up" and the papers would be signed the next day. He told the editor he could get drunk: "Congratulations; you're a newspaper publisher now." Ingersoll just collapsed into bed.

The next morning at dawn, Corcoran was on the phone again. "Have you heard what's happened? At midnight last night Hitler invaded Poland. We've been too busy here for me to call you before." Corcoran predicted that Ingersoll would not hear from Noble that day. Sure enough, the investor sent a message that he could not think of taking such a chance when the world was in an uproar.[19]

Though his spirits plummeted again, Ingersoll asked Poynter to try again to coax $100,000 from Noble. He also began relying on Poynter in other ways. He boasted to the staff that Poynter's hiring was one of *PM's* major steps, and he announced that under Poynter's direction "all figures were re-scrutinized and a downward revision is currently being audited." Ingersoll was buying his business manager's argument that both expenses and capital could be cut to a half or perhaps a fourth of the $3 million anticipated earlier. He repeatedly urged

Poynter to spend longer periods in New York, and he put more responsibility in the other man's hands.

Poynter even entered a field totally outside his franchise—editorial matters. He composed a statement of policy, presumably for Ingersoll's approval, on how to help save democracy through innovative journalism. It was a three-page variation on a 1936 speech he gave at the University of Minnesota. The theme was his belief that "the best way to save democracy is to make it work," and the best place to do that was at the local level. He also cautioned against "those sincere patriots who see a communist or fascist behind every lamp post."

In an unusual twist on the anti-Roosevelt states' rights theme, Poynter argued that power had been centralized because local and state forces had abdicated it. He called this "an indictment against the American press" because it had not educated the citizenry to its stake in local government.

> We propose that PM would take on the most gigantic assignment ever assumed by an American newspaper. We propose that PM would actually translate to Joe Zilch what he pays for various governmental services so that he could understand it as well as his great-grandfather who could figure out how many days a year of his life the government cost. The stockholders in democracy at present can not read their own operating balance sheets. The American newspaper throws large sums at the readers which are absolutely meaningless.[20]

In the midst of all these crises, Ingersoll steered a sharp turn. He wrote Poynter a three-page business letter in which he set out "a definition of our relationship." No doubt it grew out of his years of frustrating work for Henry Luce, when he never knew what his boss and friend had up his sleeve.[21]

The letter to Poynter spoke of "the prospect of doing five years of intimate work together." But it made clear who was in charge: "I am the fellow who is going to define the relationship—for you to accept or reject." Actually, the letter never defined such a thing except indirectly. It contained mostly scathing criticism of Poynter, dredging up rumors about his job performance with Scripps-Howard and the Cowles brothers, accusing him of cheekiness in equating his authority with Ingersoll's, and reprimanding him for "beginning distribution" of a prospectus of his own.

Most cutting was the part that confronted Poynter with what Inger-soll supposedly had been told by "people you have worked for or with."

> You will be interested to know that the most striking thing about the reports I've gotten is the unanimity of opinion about you. You don't appear to be loved by some and hated by others. Your enemies, your friends and your associates agree on these characteristics:
>
> You are smart, able, aggressive. You are given to over-emphasis, over-statement, and have a tendency to over-step your authority. You have a tendency to talk too big—right up to, and sometimes into misrepresentation.
>
> No one accuses you of doing this maliciously. It appears rather to come out of your confidence in yourself and a certain carlessness [*sic*] with fact.
>
> The Scripps-Howard people said it was your over-confidence that misled them into making you publisher of their Columbus paper. You promised an editorial ability you could not deliver and they fired you for it.
>
> The Cowles boys tell me that you were at once over-ambitious and unable to deliver in your relations with important people in Minneapolis.[22]

After laying out all these reports, Ingersoll said his own observation confirmed them. Ingersoll recalled that Poynter had wanted "the publishing authority over the editorial operations" of *PM* but that limited authority over business operations was all he could offer. He also cited an earlier promise that, if *PM* should later found a sister publication in another city, Poynter "would have the first crack at publishing it." The letter had the patronizing tone of a big brother, concluding, "If you want to get along with me, . . . I will happily make the crucial bet that you're smart and aggressive and able enough to overcome the handicap of your ignorance of big city newspaper publishing."

It took only one day for Poynter to place in Ingersoll's hands an even longer and more detailed rebuttal. It was breezy but fired back with equal candor.[23] Ingersoll's more specific accusations were answered with concrete evidence. Poynter appended to the letter thorough accounts—from his viewpoint—of his stints with Scripps-Howard and Cowles.

Poynter also matched Ingersoll at gossip he had gathered before he joined the staff. "From your former associates and workers I learned that you are: erratic, hard to work for, get involved with trivia, too literary and academic to edit a newspaper, ruthless, self-centered and selfish, subject to opinion of last man seen." Even so, Poynter said, he put confidence in Ingersoll and "bet" his own money on *PM*. Then he mentioned some incidents that implied that Ingersoll had betrayed the confidence. One of these involved a pledge that his associates would not be given stock in the paper until after a one-year evaluation of their performance. Nevertheless, Ingersoll had promised stock to two other top aides but not to Poynter.

Poynter summed up by admitting that he did not know New York and citing their different geographical roots, which had led to different values. Ingersoll had violated his sense of values, Poynter charged. Furthermore, he alleged, Ingersoll had "a certain attractive lack of sense of reality." He said he had found an atmosphere of "Alice in Wonderland playing store" at *PM*. "I thought my role was to bring some reality to this charming scene," he added. "I see I was wrong."

So saying, he resigned, wished Ingersoll luck, and expressed gratitude that the conflict came up so soon. In a separate memo, he said that he had told Noble he was pulling out, giving the reasons. That night he returned to St. Petersburg.

To back up his arguments, Poynter sent the memos about his service with the newspaper chains to their leaders. Roy Howard and the Cowles brothers denied telling Ingersoll anything derogatory about Poynter, and in their messages they praised him highly.

A week after leaving Washington, Poynter sent Ingersoll a casual letter outlining "the story I am telling as to why I have withdrawn" from an active role in *PM:*

> Poynter was merely drawn-in to render some practical publishing advise [*sic*] and criticism in setting up the New York picture. It became obvious that, because there is no advertising, what Ingersoll needed was a production man whereas Poynter's talent, if any, is more on the promotional and editorial side.
>
> Poynter and Ingersoll therefore agreed that Poynter was to continue to render any assistence [*sic*] possible in getting the New York paper started but . . . are agreed that they will explore the possibility of a

New York and Chicago paper, cooperating on certain editorial
features. . . .[24]

Such a statement would be "satisfying to any morbid curiosity,"
Poynter predicted, and he asked that Ingersoll concur. Ingersoll
promptly did so and plunged into a long, chatty report on life at the *PM*
office as if nothing had happened. He urgently asked Poynter whether
he would have "a definite proposal" soon, apparently referring to the
idea of starting an adless paper in Chicago. Ingersoll tried to stir up the
coals of the Noble deal, quoting Poynter's explanation to the candy
magnate. But Noble had lost confidence upon Poynter's departure and
disappeared from the scene.

The next February, after Poynter's role with *PM* had in effect ended
forever, the stormy friendship took another turn. Ingersoll said he
wanted to show his appreciation for "your valuable advice on the
business aspects of this venture. . . , your championing of the cause of
our going into business without advertising at a time when we were
still debating that important question, and your shrewd advice on
costs—as well as your helpfulness in negotiating with our friend Ed
Noble in Washington." For this he gave Poynter two hundred shares of
PM common stock.[25]

The Chicago Bubble

Meanwhile, Poynter was off on his own quest of a journalistic grail, a
project to start a *PM*-type adless paper in Chicago. Little evidence
remains about this venture, and Poynter made scant mention of it to
interviewers late in his life. He clearly was using ideas he developed
before meeting Ingersoll, but the experience bore the imprint of his
weeks with his mercurial soulmate. Poynter also thrust his own image
forward in promoting the enterprise, just as Ingersoll had done. In
biographical sketches, which he apparently wrote, he indulged in
justified bragging mixed with exaggeration.[26] He noted that he had
been "born into the newspaper business" and possessed "rich business
experience," having been the youngest metropolitan business manager
in Scripps-Howard history.

He also wrote, however, that he had edited "everything from a
country weekly to a metropolitan daily" and that the *St. Petersburg
Times* was "one of the best and most successful dailies of its size in the

country." As for his two vacation stints as a neophyte journalist, he asserted that before he was twenty-one he had been a "reporter" in Washington and was news editor of the *Japan Times*. He also made sure that his former links with Ingersoll were widely known. The two men "seemed to talk the same language," he said, and their brainchildren were "conceived along similar lines."

Trouble with Ingersoll sprang up again briefly over three statements in Poynter's Chicago promotional pieces, in which he asserted that (1) "Poynter and Ingersoll worked out an arrangement whereby they would help one another in their respective enterprises if mutually advantageous"; (2) Poynter had "sold" Ingersoll on the idea that an adless newspaper would be more profitable than one with ads; and (3) he had assisted Ingersoll in setting up his budget.

The *PM* chief first objected to Poynter's suggestion of an "arrangement." Ingersoll said that when he had finally secured enough backers to start the paper, he became a minority stockholder and had to answer to a board of directors, which had ordered him not to make any such deals with anyone. Ironically, this episode was almost identical to one involving Luce and Ingersoll when the editor was trying to use Luce's name to secure support for *PM*.

No sooner had Poynter changed his prospectus to meet this objection than Ingersoll complained to him about the other points, claiming that others had done most of the work on the budgets, both before and after Poynter's tenure. Ingersoll also cited the many times he had pondered the adless format before Poynter's arrival. "Your counsel was good and I drew much comfort from your confidence, but for me to agree that you 'sold me on the idea' would be to do an injustice to a number of others on whose advice I set great store." He even claimed that Poynter's fondest creation, the idea of consumer news shoppers, had been born in the *New Yorker,* where he had helped Harold Ross work out the service called "On and Off the Avenue."

Conceding that these points might seem small, Ingersoll argued that many other people's feelings were involved. Poynter wrote back with counterarguments, concluding that his feelings should be considered also. "I spent a good many weeks on your show, paid all my expenses, and I know you don't want to be stingy on credit." The letters in both directions were cordial, unlike the bitter exchange the previous September. Poynter apparently met Ingersoll's objections, and they continued a voluminous and friendly correspondence.

Poynter left St. Petersburg for Chicago early in April 1940 and quickly decided he could start his morning paper there in competition with Colonel Robert R. McCormick's mighty *Tribune*. A friend of his, a newspaper broker named M. Smith Davis, indicated he could raise $500,000 within the newspaper industry, and Poynter stood ready to put in $100,000 of his own.

First he met with Barry Bingham, owner of the two dailies in Louisville, Kentucky. Poynter considered him one of the country's most liberal publishers. The Chicago plan excited Bingham, and Poynter had little doubt he would invest in it. Then he got an introduction to department store heir Marshall Field III, who was one of *PM*'s founding backers and who within a year would found the *Chicago Sun*. Field was interested in investing in Poynter's paper but wanted to wait and see how *PM* fared. Poynter argued that his venture would help *PM* because it would buy several thousand dollars worth of editorial matter from the New York paper each week. Besides, he said, each paper could learn shortcuts from the other.[27]

Poynter set his financial sights lower than Ingersoll had. He figured on a break-even circulation of 150,000 and found printing plants which would produce the paper below his budgeted cost.

Chicago was infamous for newspaper circulation wars, and Poynter expected McCormick to make it difficult to sell from corner newsstands. McCormick's cousin and partner, Joseph Patterson, had thrown the weight of his *New York Daily News* against *PM* to intimidate news dealers from carrying it. Poynter calculated he could make up for newsstand problems with home delivery profits. This was because Chicagoans were conditioned to pay more for the convenience of getting newspapers on their doorsteps than for street sales. Hearst's *American* already was getting the princely sum of thirty-five cents a week for home delivery.

Without a production staff to hire, since he would contract out the printing, Poynter could concentrate on the editorial side. His financial conservatism did not keep him from aiming high for personnel. He budgeted 109 persons at $442,000 annually, an average of $4,055, well above the going level. The managing editor would get $13,000 a year, 30 per cent more than Ingersoll was paying his top executive. Desk editors would range from $3,900 to $9,100, secretaries as low as $1,560. These figures were described as "absolutely outside," with "top-flight men in every position." They could be cut by 12 percent and still provide for salaries above the Chicago newspaper average, Poynter argued.

The Chicago paper clearly would be highly departmentalized, as *PM* was then and as the *St. Petersburg Times* would become. No reporters as such were listed, only combination reporters–rewrite men. Most staffers were editors or their assistants, assigned to areas ranging from the conventional sports and national news desks to labor, religion, and science, then rarely found on U.S. newspapers but standard in newsmagazines. Other hints of the future appeared. More than a fifth of the staff was in photography and graphics. The paper listed no society or women's department—a fixture in those times—but rather "domestic features," including a specialist on men's furnishings and goods. There was a business editor with three assistants, plus seven staff artists. To obtain letters to the editor—usually taken for granted—$100 a week was budgeted. The librarian would have a research assistant. Poynter's cherished idea of a shopping news section would be implemented by eight paid shoppers.

Poynter's prospectus took one more step toward defining his philosophy of public education via the newspaper, first voiced in the Minneapolis speech and later offered to Ingersoll. Much of the wording was the same as before, but the idea was more fully developed. It revolved around a method to explain to working people what the government was doing with their money. Instead of a one-shot story, Poynter suggested that every day's news be projected into the lives of four families of different incomes. He would hire a cost accountant to find out how much each family would have to work to pay for every government expenditure as it came into the news.

At first glance it seemed a typical conservative attack on official spending. But Poynter saw the relation between the taxpayer and his representatives as dynamic—a partnership in creative statesmanship. He felt the newspaper should show the readers what a bargain they got from some governmental services: "Let's sharpen their appreciation of government. We cannot ignore the world-wide trend whereby governments are assuming more and more social responsibility. Increased taxes for increasing services are inevitable. Our problem is to make some saving by eliminating some of the waste and duplication of local government."[28]

As the world moved closer to a conflict over ideologies, Poynter again touched on a favorite theme. He said that only by lightening the crush of local taxes could the country avoid the necessity of "the streamlined dictatorial economies of fascism or communism." Poynter predicted his Chicago newspaper would set the pace for others, as such a scheme had never been tried. He hoped it would be "the most vitalizing force in democracy in 100 years."

The paper never had a name. The budget jokingly called it "The Morning Brainstorm," and other documents referred to it as "The New Newspaper." But by summer there was no need for a name. Poynter failed to attract the necessary financing, and he abandoned the project. The bubble had burst.

Getting on the Air

Mingled with Nelson Poynter's New York and Chicago expansionism was a bold venture in St. Petersburg. It initiated him into the broadcasting field, where he was to pour out torrents of work and money over the next two decades. It was to repay him with disappointment and losses.

Like most smaller cities, St. Petersburg had toyed with radio for twenty years. The first signal it could hear came across the bay in 1922 from a Tampa station. Then a resort hotel operator in St. Petersburg set up a station in his ballroom but soon unloaded it on the Chamber of Commerce in lieu of a $5,000 pledge he had made. Chamber officials glowed with dreams of publicizing the city and renamed the station WSUN. The novelty soon wore off, and the chamber gave the station to the city government, which, in turn, found the project a burden and sold a half-interest to the City of Clearwater.

Fly-by-night local stations dealing in light entertainment dominated until the late 1930s, when radio began emerging as a major force throughout the country. Newspapers had worried little about it as competition. Small stations were content to read the newspaper over the air as an excuse for news gathering, and advertising was minimal.

In the 1940s, however, stations began hiring their own reporters, and network news suddenly became respectable. Gifted correspondents like Edward R. Murrow, Eric Sevareid, and H. V. Kaltenborn provided live commentary on the war in Europe. The industry won access to Associated Press news, previously reserved for newspapers. The intruders also began taking advertising away from papers. Publishers retaliated by buying stations, as Tampa's two dailies, the *Tribune* and the *Times,* did.

Poynter saw what many others did not—that all the cities of the Tampa Bay area could easily become one giant market for mass media. He felt secure in competing with homegrown newspapers and broadcasting stations, but he knew an entry from outside posed a real financial challenge to the *Times.* He particularly dreaded a radio investor who would team up with local forces such as Webb's City and the shopping papers.[29]

His solution was to set a backfire, getting his own station. A group of local businessmen had gone on the air November 30, 1939, with WTSP (Welcome to St. Petersburg). Its studio was thirty-five blocks north of Central Avenue, and it had a paltry power of only 100 watts at night and 250 in daytime. Frequency was in the unpopular upper range, 1370 kilocycles. The opening-night show was a high school football game between St. Petersburg and Clearwater.

Poynter bought the station seven weeks later. Announcing the deal on the *Times*'s front page, he said the founders had agreed on a price with him—apparently $80,000—and turned down a higher offer because of their respect for the newspaper. The station would have no editorial opinion and would operate separately from the paper, Poynter pledged.[30]

Despite his money-making ways with newspapers, Poynter never expected WTSP to produce notable profits. He saw it as a pro bono offering by the *Times,* carrying the idea of public service to the limits. His bounty continually appalled his bookkeepers. Three decades later, a local historian ventured that no broadcast station had ever matched the volume of public service that WTSP had under Poynter.[31] Practically any noncommercial operation that wanted free time could get it—local government, boy scouts, churches, lodges, political parties. Such liberality went far beyond federal requirements, and Poynter bragged about it in full-page advertisements in the *Times.*

Aside from winners-losers parties broadcast each election night, WTSP was a cornucopia of forums, talk programs, and symposia. Poynter sometimes would introduce speakers himself. When Sen. Robert A. Taft came to St. Petersburg to campaign for the presidency, *Life* magazine showed Poynter interviewing him at the microphone. Taft ventured that the climate was perhaps the best anywhere.

Exchanges with the *Times* were frequent both in news and features.

At one time a character called Old Pappy read the paper's comics over the air. The station gained some journalistic muscle in 1941 by joining the Mutual Broadcasting System, a major news organization at the time.

WTSP moved to the *Times* Building three years later, settling into spacious quarters on an upper floor. The show-business atmosphere upstairs added a circus air to a newspaper office already accustomed to hijinks.

Besides the outlay on WTSP, Poynter had to spend heavily on the *Times*'s equipment. It was a matter of catching up after a decade and a half of little such investment, when proceeds went into his father's real estate activity. Part of the presses acquired with the 1926 building were worn out; they could not even be sold secondhand and had to go for scrap metal. Four new units replaced them. Overall, Poynter spent about $120,000 on the physical plant in his first four years.

The War in Washington

Poynter's 1939 articles doubting the prospects of war were discredited even more when the European war started in earnest with the Germans' 1940 spring offensive. War jitters grew in the United States, particularly in Washington, a city that fascinated the *Times* chief.

As an honors student in military science, Poynter had been cadet colonel in both his high school and college years. He had edged toward pacifism and never kept up his martial bent. Now as war approached he was almost too old for active service, although he joined the U.S. Coast Guard Reserve as a hometown gesture.

St. Petersburg shared Washington's excitement when Poynter gave a beach house party for Thomas Corcoran. Several other officials from the capital attended, and Poynter had invited journalists from the Tampa Bay area to rub shoulders with the power brokers. One guest was Karl Bickel, a retiree from Sarasota, who as president of United Press had shown a flair like Corcoran's. The two instantly liked each other, and the White House aide was intrigued with Bickel's experiences in Latin America.

Just at that time, the U.S. government was worried about Axis attempts to sweep South America into a sphere of influence. The stalking horse was Francisco Franco, dictator of neutral Spain and a Nazi sympathizer, who was trying to pick up the banner of pan-

Hispanicism which had fallen in the wars of independence and had been tattered by Spain's weakness in recent decades. If Franco could nudge the Latin American countries into neutrality, valuable assets would be lost to the United States.

To wage a war for the minds of southern neighbors, President Roosevelt chose a scion of the Standard Oil fortune, Nelson Rockefeller. From boyhood Rockefeller had adored the region and had pushed vast outlays of Rockefeller Foundation money there. He was forming a staff in 1940, and Corcoran decided Bickel was just the man to bring professional know-how to its communications bureau. But Bickel was enjoying his retirement too much to give it all up for the war effort.

Poynter and Bickel felt a fraternal link because United Press was a part of the Scripps-Howard empire for which Poynter had worked in the 1930s. So they made a deal whereby Bickel and Poynter would run the press section on a tandem basis as dollar-a-year men. They would rotate every week or so in Washington. Both dailies in Tampa ran editorials congratulating Poynter. The *Tribune* intoned, "We applaud the selection," and the *Times* called it "an excellent appointment in every way."

This job gave Poynter a stage for his favorite role—that of an idea man. He drew on all his strengths—economics, politics, journalism, knowledge of the Washington scene. And he could pursue themes close to his heart—the need for openness in government, not censorship, and for the U.S. brand of enlightened capitalism.

He preached to the Commerce Department that if the country were to develop influence in Latin America as Hitler had in Europe, it must do so by treating neighboring nations as partners and not as neocolonial lackeys. He urged that the Latins must be convinced that U.S. trade goods and way of life were superior to those of the Axis.[32]

As he honed his facility at writing memos, Poynter tried to lay a philosophical basis for political persuasion. Josef Goebbels had stunned observers everywhere with his success at dirty propaganda. Many felt the United States should copy his methods. Poynter rejected this:

> The United States has more than a strategic stake in not choosing its opposition's weapons. If we choose his weapons we violate the very ideology we seek to protect in the Western Hemisphere, and the tradition of a free press which is vital to democracy.

We must courageously, and uncompromisingly decide and publicize that we shall not use the same sleazy, back-door, back-alley tactics that the opposition uses in dealing with the Latin American press.[33]

Poynter believed the United States had three "overwhelming advantages" in choosing clean weapons over corrupt ones—having an "honest story" to tell, being able to take criticism, and having the best press in the world, capable of getting out the truth. He elaborated the U.S. propaganda line—"Our Story" as he called it—in glowing terms in his prospectus, which also reflected his own view of the United States. The Latins were to be told about a land that had made magnificent progress with little bloodshed, possessed hidden cultural and scientific virtues, had ample living space and thus was not imperialistic, preferred not to fight wars, was vastly productive because free people work better than slaves, and was socially progressive.

The way Poynter proposed to put over this message grew out of his newspaper experience. It would be pictorial, and it would involve paid advertising. The idea of pictures was based on the Latins' severe shortage of graphic material from the United States through commercial channels. The idea that the United States should pay for insertions was argued in idealistic terms of the dignity of open trade, but it also accorded with the notorious tendency of the Latin American press to sell space—editorial or advertising—to anyone with cash in hand.

Dealing with Rockefeller frustrated Poynter because he felt that his boss failed to carry through on commitments he had made and was too conservative in his methods. This was the young heir's first big move in public affairs, and the family surrounded him with advisers who above all wanted to keep him from doing anything rash to embarrass the Rockefellers. So Poynter resigned.

By this time, the summer of 1941, Poynter was caught up in the excitement of Washington. Although Pearl Harbor was still months away, many thought U.S. involvement in the war was inevitable. And watching what Goebbels had done, they wanted to remake the world with the information weapon. Personal competition among instant bureaucrats was intense. In addition to droves of journalists, people from the arts like poet Archibald MacLeish and playwright Robert Sherwood wanted in.

Friends and patrons weighed heavily in the quest for power. Poynter always had counted on the help of Lowell Mellett, the Scripps-Howard editor who had been his longest-standing professional hero. Now Mellett had become one of Roosevelt's closest aides, and Poynter was seen as not only his protégé in the bureaucracy but also as his agent.

Named as the first "coordinator of information" was World War I hero William J. ("Wild Bill") Donovan, by then a successful lawyer. His was a loosely knit mélange of bureaus ranging from censorship and propaganda to espionage.

Poynter, in the latest of his frequent master plans, had drawn up a proposal for government information in wartime. He showed it to Mellett, who passed it on to one of Donovan's top aides, Robert Sherwood. He, in turn, submitted it to Donovan, who liked it and wanted to meet its author. It was a Sunday afternoon at Donovan's stately Georgetown home, and a law partner who had gone to Yale was on hand. The partner had known Poynter in college, and he phoned him in St. Petersburg, asking him to come immediately.

Poynter hit it off well with both Donovan and Sherwood. Donovan was more interested in the espionage side of the agency, and he turned over to Sherwood the Foreign Information Service (FIS), a radio operation that later became the Voice of America. Poynter was named Sherwood's deputy. He started with no pay, but when Donovan decreed he would have no dollar-a-year men around, Poynter went on a government payroll and stopped his salary from the *Times*.

Poynter's organizing abilities soon were put to the test. On the day after Pearl Harbor, he called a meeting in his office to decide how to censor international broadcasts beamed from the United States. Attending were officials from the State Department, Rockefeller's operation, the FBI, and the armed services. A secret report of the meeting by the FBI representative depicted it as a melee of distrust and profanity. A basic clash in viewpoints apparently was at issue. The civilians were concerned more with getting out propaganda with no more censorship than was necessary, and the military was interested only in censorship.

The navy claimed control of this field by law, and it was prepared to delegate some responsibility to Donovan's office. But the naval captain attending was aghast at what he called "chasing fairies" on the part of the civilians, who he felt did not realize the country was at war. The military officers were at the point of dismissing the whole idea of civilian control when Poynter suggested a plan. It prevailed, and he set about carrying it out.

The government had no shortwave transmitters, much less a staff to supply them with propaganda material. There were only a few experimental stations, owned mostly by radio set manufacturers.[34] Poynter advocated hooking together the private shortwave stations into a network, a plan that had to overcome the radio industry's resistance to a government "takeover" of a field that had long been left in private hands. Poynter also had to convince dozens of agencies, from the War Department to the FBI, that his plan for spreading "Our Story" would not duplicate or interfere with their handling of sensitive information. Within a few months Poynter succeeded. To mollify the owners of private stations, they were allowed to name a representative to give the final word on what went on the air.

Feeding more than 300 quarter-hour programs each week into FIS was an army of government journalists. Sherwood ran the New York headquarters—although he spent much time writing speeches for Roosevelt—and Poynter headed the Washington office. They beamed their programs over much of Europe and Asia, and Latin America remained Rockefeller's preserve.

FIS carefully avoided the methods of hard-core propaganda, but the results were the same, as it planted its messages with conventional news sources. During the British offensive into Libya, American-built tanks first were tested in desert fighting and came off splendidly. The FIS wanted to brag about it but first asked the army to provide a general to make the statement. This was quickly transformed into radio copy bolstered with background data about how the miraculous U.S. military production was spewing out high-quality tanks and planes. The FIS staff worked twenty-four hours a day, seven days a week. Soon after the stations on the Atlantic were mobilized, Poynter arranged for a shortwave network beaming from the West Coast to Asia.

Poynter endlessly drove home the conventional theme of the war—a struggle between democracy and fascism. But others in Washington already were more worried about the ideology of an American ally, the Soviet Union. Poynter had run-ins with investigators who wanted him to fire subordinates whom they claimed had "radical backgrounds" or were proven Communists. According to FBI records of the time, Poynter heatedly defended the loyalty of several of the accused.[35] However, when Poynter called the meeting on censorship the day after Pearl Harbor, he enlisted the FBI's help. He asked it to carry out security checks on people working at shortwave stations and to inspect the security precautions of the operations.[36]

A Parting of Ways

Although he returned to St. Petersburg for brief visits every few weeks, Poynter left much of the running of the paper to Tom Harris—"I wish I had a dozen of him," he would say. He also promoted Max Ulrich, a buddy from the Bloomington days, from circulation chief to business manager. When he was in town, he spent most of his time at the office, so Catherine saw little of him. This was nothing new. Poynter's work had steadily absorbed more and more of his time, and his wife intensely wanted to build a conventional home life. It seemed to her that she was continually moving the household to a new city, only to find that she had gotten no closer to her husband—he was off on business trips.[37]

Living in strange cities with little companionship from her husband took its toll, as did being surrounded by strange people at business parties. Sometimes Nelson entertained his associates at catered affairs, which left her feeling even more inadequate. When they discussed her feelings, he suggested that she develop more outside interests. Although she became prominent in the League of Women Voters, what she really wanted was to see more of her husband.

Household chores symbolized different things for each. Nelson pointed out that he could earn enough to pay people who knew how to do them better than he. To Catherine, this signaled indifference. One such incident involved replacing a very high light bulb. Catherine wanted her husband to get a ladder and fix it. Nelson called an electrician.

In 1937, nine years after their marriage, it appeared they finally would have a child, while Nelson was with the *Columbus Citizen*. But Catherine miscarried, then suffered blood poisoning and had a serious operation.

A week after Catherine left the hospital, Nelson was fired. He went off to New York on business, then to California. Desolate, Catherine drove by herself to St. Petersburg, a nervous wreck when she arrived at her mother's home.

She decided that children were the way to bring the couple together. They adopted two girls, only two months apart in age. They were

Sally and Nancy were the adopted daughters of Nelson Poynter and his first wife, Catherine. *Poynter Library, University of South Florida, St. Petersburg, Florida.*

named Sarah Catherine (Sally) and Nancy Alice. The stratagem failed to work. Nelson was interested in the children but not in the drudgery of changing diapers and other demands of infants.

When Poynter took the Donovan job in 1941 his wife asked him to decide whether he would be in New York or Washington for the summer so she could rent a house to be near him. She felt that she and the children needed to be there, and he needed some home life. He opted for Washington, and she took a house in Alexandria. His stays there were erratic, often only weekends. At one point he was writing a book and took his meals in his study. In her view, the summer was a total loss.

Catherine returned to St. Petersburg to stay with her mother. In October, Nelson called to say he could lease a house in Georgetown, but Catherine felt it was too small, particularly if they were to join him. He leased it anyway, as rentals were tight. Having driven up to Washington with a friend and the family cook, she arrived earlier than scheduled. The women had to go out to dinner without Nelson because he was having business friends over that night. He spent only two nights of her week there with her, and he was exhausted both times.

Finally, they talked seriously. Catherine asked him whether he would ever settle down and be happy with a normal home life. He replied that he had a one-track mind with an engine inside, and he hoped that if he was on his deathbed at eighty-five he would say, "Darn it, I can't die today. I have got to get up to New York to see a man."

Nelson accepted the blame for the situation. He said that as a young man he had thought he would never be married because of the engine inside him. After his marriage he had thought things would work out, but now he realized it was a great mistake. Nevertheless, he said he would leave his government work within two weeks. Catherine did not accept or reject the offer, as she wanted him to think about it. Within a few minutes he told her that he could not be home for Christmas, that he had to make a trip to San Francisco and another to the Soviet Union.

After Christmas of 1941, Catherine decided to act. She asked Nelson to meet her in an Atlanta hotel. She arrived first and took a room. The next morning she discovered he had arrived the night before and had registered in another room because he was exhausted and had to sleep.

They agreed to get a divorce. Nelson expressed profound regret. Catherine considered it necessary to save her health. The property settlement listed Poynter's "net" annual income as $12,000 and gave his wife $3,000 in alimony and the same amount in child support. Also, each daughter was to get 150 shares of preferred stock in the Times Publishing Company, and their mother was to hold it as trustee. Poynter would be able to visit the children.

Catherine soon married William Stephenson, a St. Petersburg economist active in Democratic party affairs. Poynter accepted him as her choice and showed an interest in his political aspirations. Stephenson frequented the *Times* newsroom, giving political news at times and getting publicity in return.[38]

The Hollywood Salient

Springtime of 1942 was a time of pressures from all sides for Poynter. His father's health was steadily failing, moving toward a severe stroke later in the year. Apparently his parents were worrying about debts and were thinking about selling the *Times* and leaving St. Petersburg. Nelson wrote that he saw no wisdom in this: "It is like burning down a house to cook a pig."[39] But his mind was mostly elsewhere. He was leaving Washington, this time for a place totally unfamiliar to him— Hollywood.

Both Donovan and Sherwood considered him as deputy, and although Poynter liked both of them he felt caught in a squeeze. Mellett had become head of the Bureau of Motion Pictures, and while he stayed in Washington he wanted a field man in Hollywood. Poynter jumped at the chance to solve his command dilemma.

He breezed into the job with his usual confidence. He told his mother the film capital was "a Helluva place to fight a war even tho I know it's important." He said the work was "down my alley—to relay to creative elements of Hollywood what the government would like to see on the screen—features, shorts, documentaries."[40]

In reality, it was a strange decision to send such a man. He cared little for moviegoing, and any film fan who read a newspaper's amusements page knew more about the empire of glitter than Poynter did. One legend had it that, seated next to superstar Greta Garbo, he tried to strike up conversation with "And what do you do, young lady?"

Poynter moved in a staff and on May 4, 1942, opened what the movie colony dubbed the Hollywood White House. In essence, he was political commissar to filmdom. A four-page list of duties included:

1. To tell Hollywood producers the government policy on films.

2. To cut the red tape of getting messages to and from the Washington bureaucracy.

3. To get government cooperation in making films—in particular, help from the military branches.

4. To let producers know when their proposed films would be "harmful to the war effort."

5. To tell them how to put "affirmative portions of the war information program" in their films.

6. To work with studios to produce "Victory Shorts"—propaganda blurbs to be shown in movie houses.[41]

Aware of the power-inflated egos of movie moguls, he assured them repeatedly that he was no censor. He told them they could make films saying the whole war was a mistake and Hitler was right, and they would not be touched. Freedom of information was that important, he said.

But given the all-for-one atmosphere of wartime, Poynter's word was virtual law. Patriotism ran rampant in the film colony. Aside from all the male stars and personnel who enlisted for regular service, producer Jack Warner wangled a colonel's uniform and proudly flashed it around the studios. Air raid wardens poked around, warning people to observe blackouts. Movie people lined up to give blood, get rationing stamps, and donate services at servicemen's centers such as the Hollywood Canteen.

Poynter's first big confrontation came at a meeting soon after he arrived. More than 800 persons—writers, actors, directors, producers—sat through pep talks from their own people and watched promotional skits presented by Henry Fonda and the Three Stooges. Finally, late in the program, Poynter sat down at a small table with a microphone and faced the tired and squirming audience. He spoke slowly and quietly for less than ten minutes.[42]

Variety described his words as "a polite spanking." He suggested that the studios be concerned more with the "causes" for which the country was fighting and less with "the spectacular and photogenic phases of the war." Hollywood had done little to explain why America was fighting, he said.[43] "It is easier to portray the gallant struggle of Great Britain than that of China and Russia—the two front lines of our war. . . . If someone could do a 'Mrs. Miniver' of Russia and China, it would go a long way in an effort to confuse our enemy and aid our allies."[44]

He suggested some propaganda themes. China should be shown not just as a country "where they make nice exotic dishes and do laundry very well" but also as a world power. Americans must be told about the sacrifices necessary to win the war, he added. But most of all he emphasized the need to build unity. The movies must combat "the innocent sabotage of patriotic people that are wedded too much to their own group—where farmer is suspicious of labor, labor of other groups."[45]

Poynter also liked to remind moviemakers that the war would not last forever and that dubbed versions of their wartime films would be shown in unexpected places after victory. When larded with racial and ethnic slurs, the products go over badly, he argued: "How is this picture going to look after the war when shown in Italy? Or in Japan?

Or Germany?" Dore Schary had just produced a film that depicted an American soldier struggling with a Japanese and growling, "You yellow-bellied bastard!" Poynter reminded him that America's Chinese allies might resent it.[46]

For many in Hollywood, Poynter was the only link with all-powerful Washington. A producer of B cowboy films came to him with a worried look. Would the government continue to let him have scarce film for such frivolity?

"Of course," Poynter replied. "You're making some of the most fundamental pictures there are, because it always turns out that law and order will prevail against the bad guys. That's all this war is about. We're fighting for law and order, based on consent." Bucked up, the producer went back to grinding out Westerns.[47]

True to his instincts as a social scientist, Poynter saw movies as a tool rather than art or tinsel. Gasoline rationing had cut off millions of Americans' sources of relaxation. Factories were turning out war materials around the clock, and workers needed a way to unwind after eight hours of boring labor. Theaters in industrial cities were staying open twenty-four hours a day to meet this demand, and they needed ammunition for their projectors.

Despite Poynter's disavowal of censorship, producers got a constant feedback on how far out of line they were going in their plans through a voluntary control called "script review." A report done by two of Poynter's staff members on a proposed RKO film called *Government Girl* typified the process. The story came from top-flight writers: The original was by Adela Rogers St. Johns, the screenplay by Budd Schulberg. The Poynter office classified it by themes—women at war (major) and conversion to war economy (minor).

The heroine of the film, according to the synopsis, was a young, good-looking, ambitious secretary who arrived in Washington for a war job. She was pursued by various dashing young men but fell for a ruthless young lawyer for a Senate committee. She was drawn into a swirl of corrupt back-stabbing indulged in by important Washington figures, all connected with war production. In the end, it all got sorted out and the pure at heart prevailed.

In a confidential summary, the reviewer called the film "a dangerous vehicle from the standpoint of this office" that was presented "in a manner which would delight the heart of Herr Goebbels." She saw in it every anti-administration propaganda theme then being used in the press and elsewhere. Some of them were (1) "love of power rather than love of one's country"; (2) disapproval of the administration point of view through "a typical Nazi 'Divide and Conquer' tactic"; (3) "there is never any identification of the people with the government"; (4) "insistence of the President's personal charm to the exclusion of any other quality"; (5) "a sly attack upon the Secretary of Labor"; and (6) depiction of the labor movement as irresponsible and influenced by Communists.

All of the main characterizations were shown to be subversive to the war effort. The reviewer winced at calling one of Roosevelt's sons the "Crown Prince" because such a term was undemocratic. She also objected to calling a black housemaid such things as "an Ethiopian jewel." Negroes were contributing to the war and deserved consideration, the report said. For the same reason, an oblique reflection on the Soviet Union was resented: "Russia is our ally. Her heroism in this war deserves our respect."[48]

After eight months of operation, Poynter issued a report saying his office had reviewed 219 scripts and all had been "taken up" with the studios. The staff had viewed 248 completed films and conferred with studios about them.

Despite all this intervention, Poynter remained on good public terms with the power structure. On one occasion he and the moviemakers took part in a banquet that was to haunt Poynter years later in the McCarthy Red-hunting era. It was called the Free Peoples Dinner, under auspices of the Joint Anti-Fascist Refugee Committee and the Council on African Affairs. Both groups later were to be cited by the U.S. attorney general as subversive organizations.

The banquet invitation list was a who's who of Hollywood. Among sponsors named in the printed program were the governor and lieutenant governor of California, the mayor of Los Angeles, a bishop, producers Louis B. Mayer and Gus Kahn, directors Alexander Korda and George Stephens, composers Jerome Kern and Ira Gershwin, and stars by the dozens—Tyrone Power, Katharine Hepburn, Ida Lupino, Sir Cedric Hardwicke, Basil Rathbone, Herbert Marshall, Claudette Colbert, Ronald Colman, and others.[49]

The dinner was at the Beverly Hills Hotel at the princely price of

$5.50 per person. Announcements of the event were vague as to its function. They said Hollywood had freed forty-seven anti-Axis leaders from the Gestapo the year before. Hundreds of film people were still in concentration camps and stood ready to aid the Allies, they added, and those who are free "must give these fighters the gift of life."

The guest of honor was Paul Robeson, the first black American operatic singer and actor to win a national reputation. At that time he was a proud symbol of black achievement for the whole nation, and he was singing with major symphony orchestras. The next year he would go on to the height of his acclaim, enacting the title role of Shakespeare's *Othello* in New York. It was not until eight years later that his passport would be lifted for his Communist associations.

The "guest speaker" was listed as Nelson P. Poynter, "associate coordinator of government films." When he had received the invitation to speak, he cleared it with Washington and was told to go ahead. Twelve other persons were on the program. Paul Lukas did a scene from his classic performance in *Watch on the Rhine,* and Robeson sang a solo. "Tributes to the free peoples" were given by Soviet, Chinese, and Mexican consuls. The dinner stirred no controversy at the time. But because Robeson and some of the groups involved later became identified with subversives, rumormongers would dredge up the incident even after Poynter's death as supposed evidence that he was a Communist.

The Epoch of Henrietta

Soon after arriving in Hollywood, Poynter earned the ultimate Hollywood recognition—mention in Hedda Hopper's gossip column. In its second item on August 6, 1942, she disclosed: "Nelson Poynter is as quiet about his private life as he is about what he's doing in Hollywood. Somewhere today, in either Arizona or New Mexico, he'll marry Henrietta Malkiel."[50] Actually, Hopper jumped the gun. Two days later Poynter and his bride were married in Williams, Arizona. They had not made their plans public.

The couple had worked together on the 1940 Roosevelt reelection campaign and later for the Rockefeller and Donovan offices. Henrietta

Henrietta Malkiel, daughter of immigrants, worked with the intellectual elites in New York and Europe before she became Nelson Poynter's second wife. *Poynter Library, University of South Florida, St. Petersburg, Florida.*

was two years older than Nelson and as great a contrast with Catherine as could be imagined. She was self-sufficient, intellectual, cosmopolitan, Jewish, and professional. And, although she had been agreeable to look at when young, as she approached middle age she was developing a striking homeliness. Although the marriage to Nelson was to be monumentally important to both of them, Henrietta was in most senses a finished woman when they met.

Nelson had written his family just five days before the wedding, enclosing a follow-up story for the *Times*. He predicted it would be "the most successful marriage in history" and described Henrietta as "this wonderful girl who up to now has found ideas, work and geography more interesting than marriage."

Their ideas on propaganda and the world in general matched from the start, he wrote, but not until the spring of 1942 did they get to "something much deeper." He regretted dragging her away from her work but deemed it "uncricket" for her to work for either the Office of War Information or movies while married to him.

Nelson sought his family's approval. He bragged about the "virile literary, political atmosphere" of Henrietta's upbringing, about her education, and about her "crusaditis." He shared with her the latter, he said, "inherited from radical democratic parents in Sullivan, Indiana."

Henrietta's parents were born in Russia but immigrated as children, Leon Malkiel to North Carolina and Theresa Serber to New York. Leon went to Columbia University for a law degree. When he met Theresa, she already was a political activist, and while their children were growing up she made cross-country tours speaking for women's suffrage. She wrote a book, *Diary of a Shirtmaker,* after the Triangle factory fire killed 148 people in 1911. It was credited as a factor in reforming New York state laws affecting factory safety. She also was a translator for two muckraking magazines, *Everybody's* and *McClure's.* Leon became a lawyer-politician who had the same enthusiasms as his wife. He was a Socialist candidate for mayor, and they joined in helping found a Socialist party newspaper, the *New York Daily Call.*

The Russian Revolution of 1917 threw American leftists into disarray, and a split between radicals and moderates resulted. The Malkiels pulled out of active politics and registered as Democrats. Theresa turned to the vocation she would pursue long past her husband's death in 1932, teaching and counseling immigrant women to adjust to the New World, just as she had done. She lived seven years after her daughter Henrietta's marriage.

New York recently had gotten its first journalism school, endowed at Columbia University by the old reformist editor Joseph Pulitzer as a pathway toward his ideal society. Henrietta had done so well at Hunter College High School that she won a regents' scholarship, and she used it to enter her father's alma mater. In 1922 she earned a bachelor's degree from the journalism school, which was then at the undergraduate level.

Despite learning the excitement of politics from her parents, Henrietta was more enthralled by the artists, musicians, and actors her father often represented. So she launched into the chic milieu of arts journalism. Shipping out to Europe about the time Nelson was starting his world trip, she wrote features for two music magazines.

She hit her stride at twenty-four by getting a job on the staff of two of Condé Nast's stylish publications, *Vogue* and *Vanity Fair*. This brought her to know big-name authors and critics, as her editing pencil was the key to publication for many. It was a time of theater parties and first nights for her. As radio became a sensation, she doubled as arts commentator on what was then the Gimbel's department store station, later WOR. In 1929 she was given the title of foreign editor of *Vogue,* which entailed going to Europe to liquidate the German edition of her magazine. After traveling in Morocco, she returned to New York to work on play and movie scripts and act as a literary agent.

At one point she went to Hollywood simply to earn money, decided it was not worth the unpleasantness, and used her savings for a trip to England just in time to run into the war. Then followed her work on the Rockefeller and Donovan projects. Her skill in languages helped her become assistant program chief of the shortwave radio operation. Just when the foreign broadcast service started, someone turned around and called out, "What'll we call it?" Henrietta Malkiel had an idea: "The Voice of America!" The title stuck.

After her marriage to Nelson, Henrietta swung into a new role as a housewife. Nelson boasted to his family that she had found "the most exquisite-charming house in Hollywood," not ostentatious but as luxurious as any house on Snell Isle, the elite suburb where his parents lived in St. Petersburg. She settled down to gardening and homemaking in general, appearing with her husband at Hollywood parties. When Olivia de Havilland invited them to dinner, they survived one of the many meatless days imposed by law by having California lobster. Nelson found it indigestible.

Their marriage was at first clouded by the possibility that Nelson would be drafted. As editor of the *Times* he had come around to advocating intervention in the war, and he felt honor-bound not to ask for a draft exemption. Soon before Nelson's thirty-ninth birthday, however, Roosevelt ruled out drafting men over thirty-eight.

Henrietta did not meet the Poynter family for nearly a year after the wedding, although the couple repeatedly urged Alice Poynter to pay a visit. Meanwhile, the new wife started writing her mother-in-law the charming, adoring letters that would go on for years. She carried on over gifts from Alice—"that kind of lace . . . doesn't happen any more and the candy topped off a party day."[51]

The newlyweds felt guilty to be so happy amid the tragedies of war.

While her husband was federal liaison to Hollywood in World War II, Henrietta Poynter helped christen a liberty ship. From left are Marc Connelly, a playwright; Mrs. Poynter; Mrs. Ira Gershwin and her husband, a lyricist; Mrs. Jesse Lasky and her husband, a movie producer; and Paul Whiteman, a band leader. *Poynter Library, University of South Florida, St. Petersburg, Florida.*

Life in Hollywood was pleasant, gasoline was more plentiful, and housing was delightful. But it soon came to an end. New OWI chief Elmer Davis consolidated some offices, and Poynter's patron, Lowell Mellett, was out of the picture. The Hollywood White House was closed as of July 15, 1943.

The Poynters spent a month returning to St. Petersburg. It was the first of their annual working vacations to all parts of the globe. This time they flew to Mexico City. They probed restlessly into the country-side, trying to understand the peasant way of life and how U.S. values and products were penetrating it. Then they returned via Cuba and Miami.

Nelson Poynter predicted that the war in Europe would end in late 1943 and the Pacific fighting would finish within a year after that. He felt that the war had broadened his life. His experiences in Washington and Hollywood certainly had been on a grander scale than whatever he could have expected in St. Petersburg, which he considered "a relatively small town, a relatively small paper."[52] But now he was going back—for at least part of his time—to resume trying to make it the best newspaper in Florida.

Chapter 5

Toward Higher Ground

It had been a horrible honeymoon as far as weather was concerned for Stan and Pat Witwer. They had been married one afternoon in Dayton, Ohio, and immediately started driving south. All along the Dixie Highway they struggled with snow and ice. Disabled cars marked the passing miles.[1]

On the fifth day they rolled into Clearwater. Sunlight danced in the soft winter air. "Y'know," Stan said, "it's silly to bust our tails fifty weeks a year just to save enough money to stay down here two weeks and enjoy ourselves. Why don't I look for a job here?"

Witwer had something to offer. Like Tom Harris, he had grown up in the business. He had joined the *Dayton Herald* staff at sixteen and now, thirteen years later, he was assistant sports editor there. He presented a tough exterior—tall, athletic, with a rasping voice. But his sincerity and openness easily won friends.

The *St. Petersburg Times* of 1937 seemed to him small-townish. A large part of the front page was filled with a list of the pairings for a tennis tournament it was sponsoring. But he went to see Harris, who promptly offered him the vacant sports editor's job. Witwer was not ready to move immediately because of prior commitments.

Two years later, in 1939, Harris again offered Witwer the job. It was to pay $35 a week, more than Witwer was getting on the *Herald*. But like most sports journalists he had been doubling his salary through payoffs from sports promoters, an above-board practice sanctioned by editors at the time.

Determined to move south, Witwer enthusiastically accepted. Nelson Poynter had taken over the *Times* the year before and had not met Witwer, so Harris asked the new employee to go to Columbus and have a proxy interview with Claud (Doc) Weimer, an old friend of Poynter's and a Scripps-Howard executive. "Nelson Poynter is an aggressive guy," Weimer told him, "and, mark my word, he's going to make one hell of a newspaper out of that St. Pete *Times*."

With Weimer's blessing, the Witwers moved down. The new boss, slight and mild-mannered, was not imposing. But Witwer told himself, "This is my kind of guy." He sensed electricity powering a lightning-fast brain.

Witwer took a tour of golf courses and shuffleboard courts. When the oldtimers there heard what job he was going to fill, they blew off steam about the liberalism Paul Poynter's son was bringing to the *Times*: "That paper sure isn't what it used to be, and that Nelson Poynter sure has some strange ideas."

Paul Poynter's easygoing affability also contrasted sharply with his

Nelson Poynter in the 1940s, when he divided his time between war-time government jobs and editorship of the *Times. Poynter Library, University of South Florida, St. Petersburg, Florida.*

son's feistiness. Whenever possible, Paul avoided unpleasantness and was widely loved by the staff, but he came to the office less often now that Nelson was there. Witwer, like most who joined the staff in this period, knew the father only from a distance.

The real dynamo was the younger Poynter. He always worked either through or alongside Tom Harris, but he inevitably overshadowed his managing editor, even when out of town. Nelson began hiring young professionals like Witwer from all over the country. They were fascinated with his burning zeal for three goals—to make St. Petersburg the best place in the world to live, to make the *Times* the best newspaper in Florida, and to make the *Times* the best possible place to work.

World War II seemed at first to portend disaster for St. Petersburg, with rationing of gasoline and tires, which reduced the usual flood of tourists to a trickle by winter of 1942. But that year the city became a basic training center for air force ground personnel, and by the fall 20,000 young servicemen had arrived at the resort hotels, which were leased as barracks.

If St. Petersburg had a boom in young men, the *Times* had a shortage. One after another, men—and in one case a woman—left the staff for the armed forces. Dick Bothwell, a young South Dakotan whose features and cartoons were in demand, left for the service but sent back rollicking accounts of life on an army post, which the newspaper always ran. Sandy Stiles stepped from the newsroom into the editorship of an air base newspaper near Tampa.

A recourse was to rely on older men. One who had been brought in from retirement was quietly editing his page when someone pointed out to Stan Witwer that he was not moving. They went over, shook him and discovered he had suffered a stroke and was still upright in his chair. He died later in a hospital.

Since the 1920s women had often filled what were considered the less-essential reporting jobs—society, features, entertainment, culture. With the war, however, they began moving into traditionally male positions such as politics, police, editing, even the fishing column, where they proved they could show as much flair as the men. One young woman photographer adopted a red slacks suit as her trademark.

Most of the news staff worked a six-day week to fill the gaps. Top executives—even Poynter when he was home—regularly did weekend duty on the copy desk.

The *Times*'s efforts during the war went largely toward local coverage, as the days when the paper could send correspondents abroad or even out of state remained far in the future. (Dick Bothwell's features from army posts were the nearest approximation.) Nor did the paper have any news sources other than the three leading wire services.

Harris and his team threw themselves into providing the best possible war report from wire services. Although the final edition normally closed about midnight, it was common practice for the desk staff to sit up until 6 A.M., playing cards and waiting for the military

Managing editor Tom Harris, an ardent typographer, prepared gigantic custom-made headline type for major World War II events. *St. Petersburg Times.*

communiqué issued each midday, European time. Then, if the news was big enough, they would put out an extra edition for street sales.

Harris had a knack for anticipating big news. When he expected a major story to break, he prepared the largest possible headline, even though this was a tactic usually reserved for big city papers competing hotly for street sales. Two weeks before Pearl Harbor he had a headline set in type, then photographed and enlarged to a zinc engraving seven inches tall, so that on the tragic Sunday the *Times* was ready for a quick extra. "WAR," the main word of the headline, covered a third of the page. It was the largest head the paper had ever run.

The *Times*, like many other newspapers, rushed to publish an AP story revealing in 1945 that Germany had surrendered. Then the wire service sent editors a message that the story was "unauthorized." An AP correspondent had broken an agreement among fifty-five reporters to withhold the news until the military released it. It was fairly obvious that the story was correct, but many saw it as an ethical matter. Witwer phoned Poynter in Washington. The press was rolling with the surrender story, but Poynter told Witwer to stop it and pull back all 13,000 copies.

On V-J Day there was no such confusion, and the *Times* put out five editions. Thousands of people jammed the street in front of the plant, buying copies as fast as they came out. The Atlantic Coast Line tracks still ran there, and a train had to meet its schedule by shoving through the crowd. The engineer caught the spirit by tying down the whistle and blowing it all the way to Clearwater.

Late in the war Poynter sought to create a statewide Florida news weekly, which he envisioned as a Sunday supplement he would sell to the state's newspapers. He thought *The Floridian* was the perfect title, so he bought the rights to this name from an obscure publication and set several editors to clipping and rewriting newspapers from all over the state. The project lasted only a short time, and the title later was used for the *Times*'s Sunday magazine.

The *Times* as an opinion leader followed a pacifist course before Pearl Harbor and in the waning days of the war, but while the fighting was thickest it cheered stridently for the war effort. It reached this point gradually, having opposed U.S. involvement repeatedly after Hitler's invasion of Poland, partly because it doubted American will to fight: "Are we willing to make economic sacrifices in advance, rather than pay a still higher price for a blind, futile involvement? The hope of the world lies in our ability to stay out."[2]

It is notable that a poll taken in May 1941 showed Florida was the most interventionist state in the union, with 35 percent of respondents favoring war.[3] By then the *Times* was well launched on a hard line. It criticized Charles Lindbergh for advocating a negotiated peace with Hitler, saying that "you can't do business with an outlaw, a pirate and you can't depend on a liar."[4]

As the country's concern over internal security grew feverish, an editorial said the government had been too soft on spies, saboteurs, and traitors. The solution, it said, was to execute them.[5] Another editorial glowed about Hollywood's production of films boosting the war effort, calling cinema "now a force for community good." It did not mention that this was the goal of Poynter's mission to Hollywood.[6]

Nelson Poynter's fertile brain was coming up with novel ideas as usual. One of them led to the birth of the frozen juice industry, and it saved Florida's citrus farming, which usually staggered between boom and bust. Poynter was intrigued with the economic concept of an "ever-normal granary" as applied to citrus. He got together with two Pinellas citrus growers, and they decided that the solution to the irregularity of supply lay in concentrating juice so it could be stored and marketed when the price was best. Later one of the citrus men, J. J. R. Bristow, recalled that Poynter badgered them until they saw that the process had been perfected by a chemist. Poynter also used his connections with Secretary of Agriculture Henry A. Wallace to get a loan for the project through the Reconstruction Finance Corporation. Bristow felt Poynter and the *Times* should get "a full measure of the credit."[7]

Another idea did not get as far. An editorial suggested that, because of the housing shortage in the District of Columbia, the government should resettle the capital's civilians in St. Petersburg to free up housing.[8]

Poynter's war work also led to another frequent editorial thrust against censorship. Time and again Poynter returned to the theme that censorship would not aid the war effort and would destroy American traditions.

Returning to Tomorrow

For much of its life St. Petersburg had dwelled in the future. Recently founded and flooded with newcomers, it had little concept of the past. Besides, its stock in trade was not manufactured goods or farm produce but rather a dream of a bountiful life ahead—mild weather, beautiful scenery, outdoor fun, the prospect of a good job.

To realize this dream meant buying a lot and building a house or getting one ready-built. This dream had brought Bill Straub to his $600 nest at the turn of the century and later to his beach cottage. It had brought Paul Poynter to his sunny place on Brightwaters Boulevard. And it had brought a horde of charlatans and bargain hunters in the land boom of the 1920s.

First the land bust of 1926, then the Great Depression of the 1930s, and then World War II had put a brake on real estate sales. But the people were there, and they needed homes. Although the breakneck population growth of the early 1900s had slowed in the 1930s, population still rose 50 percent during that decade, and a special census in 1945 showed that in only five years the count had risen another 40 percent. All told, 44,000 people had been added in fifteen years, with practically no building of homes.

But this growth was nothing compared with what was to come. Population more than doubled in the next fifteen years, and even that growth was obscured by the suburban sprawl that made Pinellas County a swath of buildings from one end to the other. The second-smallest Florida county in land area, it was on its way to becoming the most heavily populated.

The Vinoy Park Hotel, symbol of St. Petersburg's downtown elegance between the wars, has had several failures and revivals. *Heritage Park, Largo, Florida.*

St. Petersburg always had been a city without a smokestack, except, of course, for the old power plants on the waterfront. In the 1950s it began to attract manufacturing companies whose professionals wanted to live in just such a city. Their own operations were so-called clean industry, supported largely by a new demand for military electronics.

Lured by civic boosters, mid-Pinellas began transforming into an earlier version of Silicon Valley. Four big electronics companies moved into sprawling, windowless cubes. Their major work force consisted of hundreds of highly trained engineers, the first wave of post-Sputnik heroes. Satellite industries also popped up.

These highly paid and educated workers created an upscale market for everything from houses to pleasure boats and night spots. Providing homes for the burgeoning population required a massive effort. The search for building sites ran into a stumbling block. Thousands of lots had been abandoned after the land bust when owners could not afford mortgage payments or taxes. Because the tax liability kept mounting and improvement bonds had placed liens against them, these parcels came to be city and county property. So governments auctioned off the land, and a carnival for bargain hunters resulted. At sales on the courthouse steps, bidders could pick up lots in posh neighborhoods for as little as $10 each.

Nelson Poynter's prediction that veterans who had trained in St. Petersburg would come back to live proved true. At war's end they began arriving by the thousands. To show appreciation, the city held a special auction for them.

Most homes sprung up in totally new subdivisions. For a while it seemed that the fastest vehicle in the county was a bulldozer. A jungle of signboards appeared, with names enticing buyers to escape to luxury—Eaglecrest, Leslee Heights, Seminole Gardens, Orange Estates, Meadowlawn, Bahama Shores, Broadwaters, Maximo Moorings.

Canny developers realized that tastes had changed since Straub's day. Lots were narrow and long when the town was first platted— about 50 by 135 feet. The typical house was multistory and built of wood. There had to be a deep back yard to accommodate a horse, a cow, an outdoor toilet, a woodpile, a barn, a water cistern, and a well and pump.

Modern conveniences swept all these away; in fact, most became illegal. People began putting up sprawling ranch houses with glass-

A Florida boom after
World War II suffused
downtown St. Peters-
burg with optimism,
soon to be deflated by
flight to the suburbs.
Shown here is a Festival
of States parade on
Central Avenue, about
1950. *Heritage Park,
Largo, Florida.*

enclosed "Florida rooms." The dwindling lumber supply led to concrete block structures. Buyers wanted broad but not deep yards in front
and back to show off a patch of lawn and provide a barbecue space and
patio. So lots became wider and shallower—more like 75 by 100 feet.

This expansiveness put shoppers farther from stores and ended the
easy stroll to the grocery. Nearly everyone had a car now, and it was
fun to take a spin to make purchases. Thirty shopping centers erupted
in rapid succession, steadily drawing the younger suburbanites from
downtown merchants. As developers competed for the jackpot, newspapers reaped an advertising bonanza.

Despite this boom in young families, St. Petersburg held on to its
reputation as retiree capital of the country, having a proportion of
oldsters nearly three times that of Florida in general. The flight to the
suburbs merely opened up the downtown area as the senior citizens'
special preserve, and the green-bench crowd along Central Avenue
thrived as never before. Retirees feuded with motorists who blocked
crosswalks while waiting for traffic lights. One septuagenarian would
whack offending cars with his cane.

The city government, which had profited on utilities during the military training period, had a million-dollar surplus when the war ended. It set off on a spree of capital improvements—new parks, streets, waterfront structures, even a completely new sewer plan.

Aside from attractions that appealed to everyone, St. Petersburg catered to what was an addiction for many—baseball. As spring-training ground for two major-league teams, it needed and built a baseball field with covered stands overlooking Tampa Bay. The stadium was finished in 1947.

The steady flow of well-educated immigrants had kept St. Petersburg from becoming an intellectual Sahara, but it was the only major city in Florida lacking a four-year college. When the state legislature decided to build a fourth state university, in the Tampa Bay area, St. Petersburg went after it feverishly, but Tampa used its superior political power to get what opened in 1960 as the University of South Florida. All was not lost. The Presbyterian church in Florida decided to build a four-year liberal arts college in the Bay Area. This led to a second flurry of competitive courtship, which St. Petersburg won, and Florida Presbyterian (later Eckerd) College opened the same year as USF.

A Newsroom Full of Stars

Just as St. Petersburg had reflected the ups and downs of the two decades ending in 1945, so had the *Times* staff. With the end of World War II it nearly exploded with pent-up energy and resources. Soldier-journalists returned home to reclaim the jobs they had left. Tom Harris terminated fourteen women employees ranging from typists to reporters in one day. All had known their jobs would end with peace. But women had proven they could cope in their own right, not just as substitutes for men. Slowly they began regaining the lost ground in the 1950s, but it would take three more decades before they would rise to higher ranks on their proven merit.

Colorful stars and eccentric characters had always brightened the newsroom, but after World War II they became the rule rather than the exception. Most of these standouts of the 1940s and 1950s still were not stamped with the professional mark of later years—journalism and liberal-arts educations. They came from all backgrounds, from Dakota ranches to private European schools. They were the last generation that could make it to the top with grit and bravado.

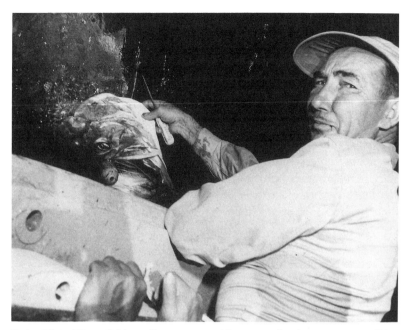

Rube Allyn, *Times* fishing editor, was notable among flamboyant personalities on the paper's news staff in the 1950s. *St. Petersburg Times.*

Most flamboyant of these was Rubert ("Rube") Allyn, the *Times*'s outdoor writer for twenty-five years. His father was a minstrel singer turned printer who set the pattern for his son's eccentricity. Once, when the elder Allyn operated a newspaper plant on a Sarasota Bay pier, he attempted to escape a warrant server by running a barge under the pier, waiting for high tide to lift it off its foundations, towing the barge into the middle of the bay, and mooring it.

The son started as a Linotype operator for the *Times* and rose to authorship of a daily column. He became noted not only for giving uncannily accurate tips on fishing spots but also for his conservation crusade, a losing battle in an era when developers dredged bay bottoms into miles of expensive home sites.

Equally famous were Allyn's stunts. He and *Times* photographer Bob Moreland were the first persons to cross the Skyway Bridge. Long before the floor was complete, the two men teetered across an eight-inch steel beam 155 feet above the water, with Moreland's camera snapping away.

Allyn's column was populated with unique characters, real and imagined. He invented a philosopher of the fishing docks, Johns Pass Sadie. But his best-known promotion was a real Indian he called Stingaree Joe, a former carnival worker with as much flair as Allyn. He was put in front of numerous civic clubs to teach the white men Indian-style conservation ("Kill only what your squaw and papooses need"). Joe liked the attention so much he staked a tribal land claim and put up his tepee in Straub Park, near the posh Soreno Hotel.

Allyn put a twist on tarpon fishing tournaments by capturing some specimens and attaching metal tags to them. Then he released the fish and offered prizes for catching them. None was ever recaptured.

Allyn eventually was fired from the *Times* for spending too much time on his booming sideline—publishing outdoor material, notably his *Dictionary of Fishes*. At age sixty-six he died in a bicycle accident. He was buried at sea, wrapped in sailcloth, at a spot where he had decreed the kingfishing was best. Swarms of mourners went along in pleasure boats, and a Coast Guard chaplain did the honors.

No less a public figure than Allyn was a woman who had been born Hildegarde Fisher but changed her name to Lorna Carroll on her way to stardom on the Broadway stage. She switched to journalism while young and became an elegant version of an old-time newspaper fixture—the sob sister, a woman who made news out of human foibles.

Carroll was the daughter of a wealthy New England leathermaker,

Lorna Carroll, a well-known *Times* human-interest writer, came to the paper after a career as a Broadway musical star. *St. Petersburg Times*.

attending exclusive schools in Europe and America. While a student at Chevy Chase Seminary she eloped with a young naval officer but threw him over to become a chorus girl at New York's Earl Carroll Theater. Climbing rapidly, she climaxed her career playing the lead in *Abie's Irish Rose* for two years. The *New York Times* called her "the darling of the Broadway stage."

During the depression, Carroll moved to St. Petersburg with her second husband to establish a theater. It failed, and she wangled a job at the *Independent,* joining the *Times* when Nelson Poynter arrived. She was soon drafted to be fishing editor, replacing Rube Allyn when he went off to war. Carroll proved enormously popular with fishermen. One of them duped her into running a fake story about his catching a 1,000-pound sea bass. When Carroll's admirers found out she had been played for a sucker, they cornered the offender and beat him up.

Carroll lived down the disgrace and after the war switched back to more general topics. She was known for penetrating, carefully researched feature articles on highly original topics. Although they glowed with emotion, they were understated and relied on Carroll's sharp eye for detail and knack for getting people to talk. Year after year she harvested prizes at state press contests.

One of her more riveting works grew out of her curiosity about what it meant to live as a senior citizen in the downtown retiree ghetto. For eight days she masqueraded as a gray-haired widow from upstate New York. At first she moved in the most indigent circles, then in moderate comfort, and finally in dizzy wealth. Carroll spent hours researching the series on the fabled green benches, she jitterbugged at free dances and took on the passion of the older set, shuffleboard. Her last act was as a bejeweled, fur-draped denizen of an elegant and expensive hotel. The series' main conclusion was that loneliness was the common hazard of all levels of retired life. Letters to the editor poured in, praising her acuteness.

Neither Allyn nor Carroll could approach the popularity of their contemporary, John Richard ("Dick") Bothwell, best known as a columnist of humor, human interest, and whimsy. He worked at the *Times* forty-two years before unexpectedly dying of a heart attack in 1981. One of his editors described him in retrospect as the most loved and respected man in St. Petersburg.[9] Bothwell belonged to a traditional class of newspaper writers, as Carroll did, but like her he was

Dick Bothwell, humor
writer and cartoonist
who liked to show off
his roping tricks,
was much in demand as
club speaker. *St. Petersburg Times.*

unique. There was no one thing he did surprisingly well. His jokes
could be painfully low-level ("Worst gas guzzler of all is the power
mower. You get only one yard per gallon"). His cartoons were clever
but unremarkable. His reporting range usually was limited to lightweight matters such as weather, personalities, and civic celebrations.

Bothwell somehow skated the thin ice over sentimentality, silliness,
and shallowness. His personality invested his words—both in person
and in writing—with magic. Managing to spoof himself more than
others, Bothwell avoided the tedious egotism of standup comedians.
He was plain-looking at best, but he liked to claim that women pursued
him because of his resemblance to Robert Redford as well as to
Redford's father: "Women will look me boldly in the eye and say
suggestive things like, 'Have a nice day,' which is obviously a come-
on."

Bothwell was drafted in World War II, and he started sent back humor pieces to the newspaper. He had basic training at "Camp Croft School for Boys," as he called it. After his postwar return to the *Times,* Bothwell shifted from cartooning to writing a weather column to general reporting. He always treated the weather with a flair, sprinkling it with cartoon characters such as J. Thundersquall Drip.

In 1962 Bothwell capitalized on his booming popularity by starting a column called "Of All Things." His material usually was mundane—chitchat about winter visitors, civic events, and the rhythms of daily life—but he never lapsed into being maudlin, even when he collected money to buy a piano for an eighty-seven-year-old musician.

The paper's average reader could identify with Bothwell, and he was the paper's public personality, much more than Nelson Poynter. He often cited a young reporter's story that ranked the amount of class that things and people had. Bothwell fell behind the Gideon Bible and just ahead of Dolly Parton. Late in life, Bothwell told an interviewer, "I love newspaper work, and it has made me rich. We have our own swimming pool, although it takes me half an hour to blow it up."

One Thursday he was posing for pictures twirling a lasso and wearing a cowboy suit; it was among his favorite put-ons. The next day, when news of his death swept the newsroom, tough editors wept openly.

A Time of Beginnings

Three years after the war, the Florida Press Association voted the *St. Petersburg Times* and the *Miami Herald* the two best newspapers in the state. It was a small victory, but a telling one. The *Herald* itself was still a second-rate provincial entity, but both papers were beginning a competition in quality. (They were outside each other's circulation area.) This competition laid the basis for national reputation that both attained in the 1960s.

Competing with the *Independent* or even the *Tampa Tribune* across the bay no longer seemed relevant at the *Times.* Editors at the *Times* and the *Herald* would anxiously flip through each other's product every day to see which had shone brighter. And as they raised newspaper standards for other cities, Florida as a journalistic arena became the envy of much of the nation.

As far back as the early 1940s Poynter and Harris had set the direction for all later reforms—departmentalization. The idea of displaying material in the paper by category ran counter to the concepts of popular journalism developed around the turn of the century. Journalists believed that, except for a few sections such as sports and society, each news item competed with all others. The front page was supposed to sum up the most important items of all kinds, the second page the next most urgent, and so on, to the end. Related to this policy was the tyranny of printers over newsrooms. Makeup men—grizzled autocrats who placed type into page forms—chose where to position stories, usually with poor results. Dummies—diagrams of what stories and pictures should be put where on each page—were anathema to most composing rooms. At most, innovative editors dummied the front page.

Despite stabs at breaking out of this bind, no departmentalization of any note endured until *Time* magazine showed it could work in 1923. Stories in each field, from international news to books, had an allotted space. Furthermore, journalists were allowed to specialize in areas in which they were happy and most qualified.

Embedded in the departmental concept was a step that would become a cornerstone of the *St. Petersburg Times's* success—intense processing by editors. *Time* magazine concentrated its desk efforts on detailed manipulation of story texts. Newspapers usually had restricted deskmen to catching obvious errors, smoothing out a few phrases, and writing headlines. But departmental reform offered them the chance to do far more. They could plan attractive combinations of type, photography, and art work. Concern for the beauty of the page, dimmed by the industrial revolution, returned to a place of pride.

The new concept meant giving editors control of sections. Advertising departments liked to sell front pages of sections and charge premium rates, so a paper that handed section pages over to the news side was believed to sacrifice revenues, which inhibited many publishers from taking the plunge.

For the *Times,* the change did not come easily or quickly. Poynter and Harris toured the nation studying how a few other newspapers were trying to work out a format. The *Times* started by departmentalizing local news. As in all dailies, this consumed the most news space. Most city editors and reporters considered state, national, and foreign news to be filler material and felt local news deserved top spots on the front page. Yet when the city desk got its own space, it invariably was the second section of the paper. It took years, even decades, to convince journalists and readers that it was no comedown for a story to be on the front of the second section.

The *Times* was not content to enlarge its scope to a few kinds of news broken up into departments. Once the movement started, new categories followed in rapid succession during the 1940s and 1950s. Each was provided its own separate space and staffing.

The obverse side of Poynter's interest in labor was his belief that business also should receive far better coverage. This too went beyond the demands of the community, as St. Petersburg was not a commercial center like Tampa or Jacksonville.

A clearly identified business reporter, Frederick R. Barkley, appeared in bylines by 1949. He rose above the spot news and free advertising that so often marked newspaper business coverage of the time. Instead he took an analytical view, such as sizing up the city's first department store, Maas Brothers, after its inaugural year. Three decades later this policy led to a business news emphasis that gave the *Times* perhaps its strongest department beyond local and sports.

Another field in which the *Times* broke the mold was religion. Even more than business, this coverage traditionally had celebrated the trivial. Other than Paul Poynter's reprinting of Christian Science lectures in the 1930s, the *Times* had followed the general practice of having a "church page" in which the most notable news was next Sunday's sermon titles.

While not liberal on religion, St. Petersburg always had been relatively tolerant. Socially conscious young people, along with some ministers who sent out ripples of change, infiltrated the suburban churches. The new arrivals welcomed journalism that tried to find new meanings in religion and dared to be objective or even critical. Before long, church people would be making news by leading civil rights demonstrations, taking the side of migrant workers, and protesting the Vietnam conflict. The *Times* identified with these new waves at least indirectly by reporting them. In 1956 it started a weekly religious tabloid.

In the 1950s the *Times* turned toward depth reporting, often aimed at a basic reform. There was a probing look into juvenile delinquency. Dick Bothwell did a series targeted at getting the waterfront cleaned up, and a team turned out a series on why St. Petersburg needed a four-year university. "For a Better Florida" became the theme of a recurrent series, notably including John Gardner's study of state prisons. When St. Petersburg was considering plans for a city auditorium, Harris toured cities in other regions and told what they offered.

This surge of energy led to a plan adopted decades later by innovative news media, called the enterprise writer system. Poynter had long bemoaned the fact that on the typical newspaper a reporter had no way to rise in prestige and pay other than becoming an editor. When this happened the paper often lost a good reporter and gained a bad editor, he said. He felt that top reporters' pay and prestige should rival that of editors. Henry Luce had founded *Time* and *Fortune* on this tenet, and Ingersoll and Poynter preached it at *PM*.

Star reporter Lowell Brandle, who had an intellectual bent, returned from a stint with British newspapers in 1957, agog over the autonomy of reporters he had seen there. None of the typical American clamor and chaos in the newsroom, he recalled. Reporters even had their own offices. Treated that way, he argued, they could turn out models of depth and originality.

Poynter and Harris liked the idea, and they adopted it with flourishes of their own. Five initial enterprise writers were named, each with his own bailiwick. Brandle dealt with "human needs"—societal and intellectual matters. Jerry Blizin had police and city government matters, John Gardner state government, Douglas Doubleday ecology and real estate and Bothwell his usual province of the lighter side.

Not only did the elite five receive their own offices, they were elevated from the third-floor newsroom to the fourth-floor executive suite. They were put on salary instead of hourly wages, given leased cars, and taken out of the city editor's control. How they spent their time was up to them. Much stock was put on sharing ideas in brainstorming sessions. No handbooks existed on this new reporting style, and there were no good examples elsewhere. The nearest cognate was editorial-writing staffs on a few rich newspapers such as the *New York Times,* so the *Times* developed its own techniques by guesswork. When the reporters began to be invited to address national workshops, they were astonished to find they were so far ahead of the largest papers.

A Place for Blacks

Soon after Nelson Poynter came to the *Times* in 1938, editors ran a feature photograph of a cute, tearful black baby on the front page. The headline revealed that an open safety pin was threatening the life of the fifteen-month-old child, named Leonora; she had swallowed it and it was working itself through her system. The head carried an overline that read "PICKANINNY TROUBLE."

Decades later the paper would have been inundated by protests against such a racist label. But what the *Times* experienced then was just the opposite: Readers complained that a black's picture had been run at all. Some advertisers were so incensed that they switched their ads to the *Independent*.

Yet the coverage of little Leonora ushered in a new era for blacks, and the *Times* was to set the pace of reform for most other papers. The change did not result from blacks' demands for fair treatment; editors did it without pressure. Certainly it was not a money-making stratagem.

In the 1940s many southern newspapers discovered a clever way to satisfy the news needs of black readers and still appear lily-white. This was the "Negro makeover." For the relatively few copies sold in the black community, editors would clear out one page of news that had reached white readers and substitute a page of news about blacks. No one saw a need for blacks to read movie ads (they could not attend white-owned theaters) or stock quotations (they had no such funds), so these usually were thrown out to make room. As the blacks seldom saw the whites' edition and vice versa, each group was unfamiliar with what the other was reading. Many blacks even thought the whites were reading about them when they saw their news in the paper.

The *Times* started a Negro makeover relatively early, in October 1939. It was crowded with small-town chitchat of the kind the *Times* had provided white readers in its early days—social events such as weddings, births, and funerals and doings of organizations like churches, schools, and clubs.

Harris always had believed the maxim that names make news. This resulted in long lists of people who had scant claim to distinction and pictures showing rows of smiling faces celebrating such things as ribbon-cuttings, presentations of awards, and school honor assemblies. It was standard newspaper fare, it was boring to anyone not involved with the event, and it was considered tacky by professional journalists.

As the *Times* began to outgrow this content on its general news pages, it seemed incongruous to have it on the makeover. But blacks made little news in politics and public affairs then, and their involvement in police news ran on the general pages. Because there was nothing to replace the "chicken dinner news" on the black page, by default it contained the ego items that were disappearing on the other pages. The page also legitimized a black establishment. Those who emerged as newsmakers—leading clergymen, educators, and businessmen, rulers of the nascent black high society—became spokespersons. From their ranks would come many civil rights leaders of the 1960s, and also some of the conformists who would be called Uncle Toms.

Thus, blacks achieved on their special page a dignity denied them elsewhere. White norms of the time held that blacks had no claim to honorifics such as Mr., Mrs., and Miss, then routinely used for white persons, particularly women. So a black woman who appeared in the general news pages would be called Mary Jones on first reference and Jones, the Jones woman or just Mary on second reference, never Mrs. Jones. But on the Negro makeover she was accorded the same respect as a white woman.

To produce copy for the page, the *Times* hired bright young people from the local black community as part-time correspondents. They usually had no training or experience in journalism and learned on the job.

The page ran weekly for its first decade, but in 1948 it became daily. This led to the hiring in 1951 of Calvin Adams, the first full-time black reporter. Less than a year went by before Adams was given an assistant, Mamie Brown, who concentrated on society items. Unlike some other papers that had black workers, the *Times* did not segregate their desks. They were placed conspicuously in the newsroom, startling white groups touring the offices. Restrooms and water fountains also were not segregated, contrary to the norm. Brown was delighted that most fellow staffers tried hard to be helpful.

Although the makeover was a device to segregate the news, it carried the seeds of its own destruction. The very presence of the black journalists and the talents they developed made change seem inevitable to their white colleagues. With change came introduction of blacks into the mainstream of news, not just in crime stories. A hint of newfound respect came when the *Times* published the photo of famed black scientist George Washington Carver in 1942 shortly before his death. Perhaps the first local black to be pictured in the full run of the *Times* was a woman recruited as a railroad laborer in World War II.

When blacks scored victories in entering society, the *Times* was eager to chronicle them. It reported in 1944 that, for the second time in the county's history, a black man had been named to a grand jury. The judge lectured the court on treating the juror with respect.[10] The paper also noted in 1947 when the city began hiring black policemen.

Taking the Ramparts

As the tide of new people and new ideas surged into Pinellas County after World War II, old barriers fell. Not only was new space needed, but new ways of life. But which space, and which ways?

Nelson Poynter wanted to help supply the answers. Confident as he was in his ideas, he had lost much of his cockiness of earlier decades. His natural shyness deterred him from becoming a power broker with the visibility of Colonel Robert R. McCormick at the *Chicago Tribune,* and Poynter deeply believed that duly selected officials were the best

Nelson Poynter, shown here in 1952, was harassed by charges of Communist sympathy during the McCarthy era. *St. Petersburg Times.*

ones to lead the people—so long as the *Times* had a hand in choosing and guiding them. The best way to do this, he felt, was by facts and logic, not bullying, so he needed an editorial writer he could rely on. Again, he drew on old friendships in Indiana.

Warren H. Pierce, like Poynter, had grown up in a small city in west-central Indiana where his parents had a daily newspaper. He browsed at various colleges, including Columbia and the University of Chicago, without earning a degree. He spent 1926–27 at the *St. Petersburg Times,* just as Poynter did.

After working with NBC and CBS radio networks in their founding years, Pierce returned to his hometown to take over the family paper. It was sold in 1935, and he became Poynter's chief editorial writer on the *Columbus Citizen.* Soon after Poynter left there, Pierce took a similar position at the *Chicago Sun-Times.* Once more the two friends were reunited when Pierce became Poynter's assistant at the Office of War Information branch in Hollywood. After the war Pierce returned to the *Sun-Times* and developed a professorial bent, teaching part-time at Northwestern University. Then his trail rejoined Poynter's, and he became the *Times*'s editorial chief.

Poynter and Pierce thought alike on public issues and would talk together at length, and because Poynter never was an adequate writer he relied on Pierce to put his ideas on paper. Bow-tied like Poynter, the balding, paunchy Hoosier became a fixture around the *Times,* known both for his Rooseveltian cigarette holder and his writing facility. He also was a primary liaison with the outside world, serving on a spate of civic boards and heading the county park board and the Friends of the Library.

The decade after Pierce's appointment was an explosion of editorial leadership unrivaled since Bill Straub's heyday at the beginning of the century. Much of its import grew out of a wide range of community-building drives. Some advocacies seemed trivial—getting catwalks for fishermen on bridges or a downtown Halloween party to reduce vandalism. Others were unglamorous but highly influential, such as a series on Florida's taxing and fiscal policies. Others nagged the readers, as in the case of traffic safety drives. There were carrots instead of sticks, notably the *Times*'s own awards for the most valuable state legislators, which became coveted and made excellence more esteemed.

The *Times*'s reformism developed a full head of steam in January

1951 with a series of eight articles about the high cost of running for office. The 1948 primary race for governor had appalled Poynter and Pierce. It had been a money-making carnival for advertising media, including the *Times.* The whirlwind of campaign dollars increased in the 1950 U.S. Senate contest between Claude Pepper and George Smathers. Morty Freedman, Tallahassee bureau chief, was assigned to probe the matter. After weeks of research in many parts of the state, he produced the stories. Written in lean, rapid prose and accompanied by cartoons, they laid out shocking excesses although no direct evidence of wrongdoing.

Typically for the *Times,* the articles attacked the system rather than people. Often they drew raw data into perspective. A senator who had spent a million dollars would have to work sixty-seven years to earn that much in legitimate pay, it was noted. Pepper had spent an average of forty cents per registered voter in Pinellas County.

Freedman did not mince words in saying the biggest reason for cost escalation was newspaper and radio advertising, giving figures on statewide costs. Freedman also dared to indict the media for their greed. They almost universally charged a higher than normal rate for political advertising, with the *St. Petersburg Times* and the two Tampa papers the only exceptions. Poynter always had preached that people who cared enough to run for office should not be penalized.

The series ended with an analysis of what was wrong with Florida's election laws and how some states had tried to solve the problem. Freedman put together a composite of solutions he felt were needed. As soon as the series ended, Pierce started hammering home the points with editorials that summarized the main ideas and showed their significance. Washington columnist Tom Stokes called the series "the most comprehensive job of this sort I have ever seen."

As Straub had done in his campaign to win independence for Pinellas County, Poynter made sure legislators read the material. As each article was printed, copies were mailed to all lawmakers. After all were published, a booklet containing them was sent the same way. And after more follow-up editorials, still another version was mailed.

It was a lonely fight for the *Times.* Whether through jealousy, shame, or anger, other newspapers made no special effort to support the reform, although some were friendly to it. But the election-law series became such a hot issue that legislators could not ignore it, and a reform was introduced. Then came a cliff-hanging melodrama in which members tried to maintain a public pose of favoring cleanup while covertly axing the bill. After one such ploy, Freedman alerted Pierce, who rushed out an editorial. Proofs were expressed to each member, and the bill was passed.

When the reform moved to the governor's office, many senators pressured him to veto it. He resisted and signed it with a ringing endorsement. It had come to be called the "Who Gave It—Who Got It?" law, after a headline in the *Times*.

After the law won approval, newspapers and radio stations challenged its constitutionality, but it survived two such tests. The press had reason to wince, as political advertising plummeted. The Associated Press reported that on one Sunday during that year's race for governor, not a single political ad appeared in the *Miami Herald*. On the same Sunday four years before, more than $1,000 worth of such ads had appeared.

The series received top honors in 1952 from both the Florida Daily Newspaper Association and the state's Associated Press Managing Editors Association. Then the National Headliners Club, a prestigious journalists' group, awarded its medal for public service to the newspaper and Freedman. The series did not win the Pulitzer Prize, although, ironically, Poynter was on that year's Pulitzer selection jury.

The editorial effort that won the most lasting respect for the *Times* was actually one of its most low-keyed—the slow, grinding haul toward racial justice. Poynter had shown his sympathies before World War II with the successful campaign to get public housing for blacks.

Nelson Poynter and Governor LeRoy Collins (*right*), shown here in 1959, supported each other in their lonely advocacy of racial justice. *Poynter Library, University of South Florida, St. Petersburg, Florida.*

Although the news page for blacks developed steadily during the war, editorial attention largely was directed elsewhere. The paper took a backhanded swipe at lynching, with praise for the swift conviction of three black rapists, which prevented mob action.[11] More forthrightly, it thumped for a movement to let blacks vote in the Florida Democratic primary, the winning of which was then tantamount to election.[12] This idea prevailed five months later when the state supreme court ruled favorably.

After the war the *Times*'s anger against lynching grew stronger. It condemned the 1945 gang murder of a black awaiting trial in North Florida, basing its appeal more on the reputation of the state than on justice for blacks. But after mulling over that case for three weeks, the paper called for a federal antilynching law. Referring to the recent case, it said, "If the local community can not enforce law and order, then outside agencies are bound to step in."[13]

The *Times* began laying the groundwork for basic attitude changes by whites toward blacks. It would occasionally run editorials espousing a general philosophy of justice and toleration. One such plea near the end of 1946 read: "The south can solve its distinctive problems in its own way, but in order to do so all good citizens must support those leaders who insist that justice displace violence, that tolerance really be practiced and that fair play prevail. We need to start action anew against those who would deny these democratic privileges and principles."[14]

Though insipid by modern standards, such rhetoric was daring for its time. The South, particularly more tolerant areas such as Pinellas, certainly was past the point where public expression of racial prejudice was acceptable. But it was equally taboo to mention the problem at all in a mass medium, which was considered "stirring up trouble."

The *Times* began advocating changes in the school system as early as 1949, when it advocated integration of colleges after blacks applied for graduate work at the University of Florida:

> Southern tradition and custom presumably will keep segregation alive in the south for a long time to come. But of all places where it is hard to defend this custom, it is in the institutions of higher learning. When colored college students—particularly those working for advanced degrees—can and do compete on equal terms with white students, the argument of inferiority breaks down badly. . . . If we want

Warren Pierce, as the *Times*'s chief editorial writer in 1948–54 and 1957–66, developed Nelson Poynter's ideas into powerful writing. *St. Petersburg Times.*

segregation we're going to have to pay for it by duplicate facilities for Negroes. . . . If our own consciences don't bring us to that conclusion, sooner or later the federal courts will.[15]

Although the paper still was not ready to advocate nonracial public schools, it pushed for efforts to improve the existing system for blacks.[16] In 1953 such caution began falling away. An editorial said St. Petersburg could not be satisfied until all of the city's racial and religious bigotry ended—"until we all judge each other upon our individual merits and not as a group of any race, color or creed."[17] The paper also called segregation unjust and un-American while recognizing the problems that would arise from "any drastic forcible assault upon the prejudices, traditions and mores of the southern states." So it endorsed a cautious and deliberate approach.[18] Even so, it apparently was the first major newspaper in the South to take such a stand.

Mixed in with the long-range editorials were those that pushed for justice on specific issues. The paper ran a series on dwellings showing that half the city's blacks had poor housing. It also backed establishment of a park for blacks and proudly cited the candidacy of a black running for the school board. The Council on Human Relations, considered dangerous by many, could count on support from *Times* editorials. This came naturally, as Warren Pierce was a council director.

Because Pierce was not the only person writing editorials, the paper drew up a code of editorial policies, one of which read: "We oppose any theory that says some citizens are second class because of race, creed or color. We believe in equal rights."

Thus the *Times* had laid a base of calm opposition to segregation when the watershed *Brown v. Board of Education* decision came down from the Supreme Court on May 17, 1954. The paper's editorial the next day called the decision "a major blow for man's freedom" because segregation "does violence to the spirit—to the dignity—of those who are segregated—and . . . deprives the citizens of something just as real and valuable to them as property itself." The *Times* soon advised the "all deliberate speed" approach that the Supreme Court later prescribed in law and praised the appointment of a biracial committee to plan Florida's desegregation.

Following this line—that the process must pursue a plan and a timetable—the *Times* did not object when St. Petersburg Junior College, under advice of the state attorney general, denied admission to two black students. It regretted that the question had to come up when policy was up in the air: "While it is inevitable that Negro students will be admitted to higher educational institutions at an early date we do not see how local school officials dependent upon the state for operating funds can do otherwise than follow the state rulings and orders at this time." When a timetable developed, it predicted, Pinellas would be one of the first counties to accept it.[19] Meanwhile, it publicized a drive to raise money to send the rejected applicants to a college outside Florida.

By the end of 1954 the *Times* had stopped applauding the official posture and had reclaimed its familiar ground as critic. It had become dissatisfied with what it considered foot-dragging: "Pinellas should be drawing up its plans now for an end to school segregation. It's not an impossible task. For the most part there will be little intermingling of the races in the schools because there still is residential segregation. . . . When the timing . . . is finally resolved, Pinellas then will be able to make the transition quickly and painlessly."[20]

The editorial page also lashed out at Willis McCall, a Central Florida sheriff who got national publicity for his defense of segregation. McCall had barred children in an American Indian family from attending white schools because he decided they were really blacks.

As Christmas of 1954 approached, the *Times* could have looked back on a difficult year and wondered whether it had taken the right path. The county supervisor of black schools gave his answer. The paper had taken the high ground, he said, and had been fearless in pointing the way toward a sensible and fair solution.[21]

The *Times* kept up the fight, which became steadily more difficult as a public backlash set in and politicians schemed about how to defuse the decision. The paper hailed the desegregation of the armed services' academies, but it continued to criticize the Supreme Court for not setting a timetable for local schools. Thus when another black's application was denied by St. Petersburg Junior College, it bemoaned the court's failure at guidance but urged community leaders to work "patiently, calmly and sensibly" on the problem. Referring to the latest admission case, it expressed hope that "this is the last time we must look on shame-faced as an intelligent young American is blocked in her efforts to get an education."[22]

Perhaps the most eloquent statement of the newspaper's outlook on how to end racial injustice came after the Supreme Court outlawed segregation in public facilities: "Bigots of both races will want to rush in with short cuts and over simplified answers to various, stubborn problems. . . . We have no misgivings about Americans' ability to meet these three challenges: the rise of the common man, the rise of the colored man, the rise of the Christian man. Our faith in democratic principles is founded on the common sense of the common man of every color—and the grace of the Christian man of every race."[23]

One of the sensational news stories of the era was the 1956 attempt to integrate Central High School in Little Rock, Arkansas, followed by Governor Orval Faubus's opposition and President Dwight D. Eisenhower's sending of federal troops to enforce the law. The *Times* suggested the action even before Eisenhower took it and called the issue "simply whether we are to have a constitution."[24]

Another cause that gripped Poynter's attention in the 1950s was a final victory over Pinellas's physical isolation. No less than Bill Straub and Paul Poynter, Nelson pursued the vision of a St. Petersburg solidly linked with the outside world. Although it had less reason to interact with the rest of Florida than most of the state's cities, St. Petersburg depended greatly on the northern states, and most travelers from there came by land.

So much had been done. The rutted tracks around the north end of Tampa Bay had yielded to hard roads and bridges over creeks. In 1924 the Gandy Bridge had spanned the bay itself to Tampa, and twenty years later the toll was removed. But as one stood on Point Pinellas looking southward toward the booming southwest Florida coast and a major route to Miami, only the sparkle of the bay could be seen. To get to the other side you still had to backtrack through Tampa or wait for the quaint old Bee Line Ferry.

A plan evolved to build a tunnel under Tampa Bay with private funds, raising ghosts of Bill Straub's feud with Tampa and Hillsborough County early in the century. Hillsborough was able to kill the plan out of jealousy because it owned the main channel running into the gulf.

After the war, Nelson Poynter conceived the solution—the state of Florida must back the bonds to build a bridge. As Straub had done to win independence for Pinellas, Poynter launched a two-pronged attack involving an editorial crusade and pressure politics. He won the support of Governor Fuller Warren, and construction on more than eleven miles of suspension bridge started. So high was its roadbed—up to 150 feet above the water—that it was called the Sunshine Skyway. Its main span was the longest open-water crossing in the country, and it was to St. Petersburg what the Golden Gate Bridge had been to San Francisco. When it was dedicated on Labor Day in 1954, former Governor Warren, the hour's hero, told the audience that no man had put more work into the project than Nelson Poynter.

In the same decade, Poynter came to national attention as a liberal maverick opposing the Republican majority in his county. Ironically, it proved a bed of nails he had built for himself.

The *Times* was born the year that Grover Cleveland won the presidency for the Democratic party for the first time since the Civil War. It retained its Democratic identity without lapse, even when that involved Bill Straub's changing allegiance after coming south. It was not a difficult path for the paper to follow, because the great majority of St. Petersburg residents were Democrats.

Although many immigrants from the North had been Republicans, most of them emulated Straub in changing registrations to keep some voice in politics. This was because all important electoral contests were settled in the Democratic primary, as few Republicans were registered in Florida. Other northerners were "winter residents" who customarily flocked south after Christmas, voting in their hometowns before they traveled. Poynter, as an ardent supporter of Democratic principles, believed the one-sidedness had to change. He had spent his youth in areas where two strong parties coexisted and provided a forum for debate. This, he felt, should be the case in Pinellas.

But elections are won by candidates, and the Republicans had none of any stature in the county. This began to change quietly after the arrival of a young lawyer from Ohio, Merle P. Rudy. He became county Republican chairman in 1936 and with infinite patience set about building the party. Rudy sensed a soulmate in Poynter, and they hit it off from the first. Poynter flatly told Rudy he would not support Republicans simply for the sake of bipartisanship, but if Rudy could find superior people to run for office, the *Times* would help.[25]

The big test came in 1948. Poynter endorsed Harry Truman with little enthusiasm, but at the local level, he threw aside his ties to the Democratic party. Late in October a *Times* editorial stated: "Casting our vote in the November general election in years past has generally been easy. . . . The situation is different this year. The Republicans are making a strong bid for office. They have 17 candidates for county office. They have worked hard to get up a good ticket."[26]

At that point, the bombshell fell. The *Times* endorsed Republicans for one of three county commission seats and for two of the highest elective offices. On election day, it was a Republican rout, with Republican presidential candidate Thomas Dewey getting his largest majority of any county in the nation. All the Republicans that the *Times* had backed won office, plus two others.

Once it was clear that Republicans could win elections, they began to dominate Pinellas politics. They came out of the closet in droves, changing their registrations back to their true conservative preference and flocking to the polls. Congressional and legislative delegations soon became heavily Republican.

Poynter's critics felt that he, still staunchly Democratic in his editorial policy, was betraying a duty to speak for the majority in his community. To his supporters, it seemed a lonely battle for political diversity.

Chapter 6

The Golden Egg

Once when Nelson Poynter was a young man he had lunch with his mother, Alice, at a restaurant. Afterward they quarreled because both wanted to pay the check. Nelson solved the impasse by throwing money down on the table and stalking off. This story, often told among the four Poynters, hinted at the discord and jealousy that would sour family relationships for more than half a century despite their intense love and frequent loyalty. Lawsuits, charges of extramarital romance, yearnings for approval, and struggles over control of a growing empire all made up part of the drama.

The scrapping endangered Nelson's dreams of building a great newspaper. Even after he succeeded and all the combatants were dead, the old menace to Nelson's creation burst out again, graver than ever.

Alice was the central figure. Although she was the only family member who did not aspire to run the *Times,* she never rested from trying to put the others' lives, jobs, and estates in order, but none submitted to her efforts.

On one occasion, referring to a wrap owned by her granddaughter Mary Alice, the matriarch wrote to Nelson's second wife, Henrietta, "Say nothing about ME suggesting it, but the short fur coat needs changes." Mary Alice, daughter of Eleanor Jamison, Nelson's sister, was staying with Nelson and Henrietta in Washington while working at *Congressional Quarterly.* After going on for two pages detailing what should be done to the coat, Alice reached a moral and political conclusion, as she often did: "It is a 'crime' to have it hang in the closet for three years without it being used—an economic crime of which no intelligent DEMOCRAT should be guilty!"[1]

When her son was thirty-nine and twice married, Alice was still trying to tell him what to wear. She sent him a check for a new suit and scolded his taste: "Three years ago that blue-green suit spoiled my summer—every negro in St. P. has its duplicate!" She enclosed a sample of the cloth she wanted him to use.[2]

A staunch Christian Scientist and traditionalist, she never hesitated to proclaim a norm. There was, she said, "a reason for every convention—for they 'go' toward making our own lives more normal—with real meaning, and we are not here to 'live our own lives,' follow every caprice regardless of the rights of others."[3]

If she had kept to family matters, even to marriages and divorces, she would have had little effect on the *Times*. But her enormous energy, curiosity, and range of interests made this limit impossible. Staffers were accustomed to seeing her chauffeured Cadillac park across the street from the building. Nelson, sometimes trailing a secretary, would hurry down from his office and join his mother for a conference on the back seat. She freely dispensed advice on how to run the paper and often made requests of employees. She tried to get them fired and in turn was cultivated by them.

Nelson's fraternity brother, Max Ulrich, who had been brought in as *Times* business manager, fell out with the matriarch. Nelson reported to his mother that Ulrich was "brokenhearted" and begged her to make up with him as a Christmas present: "Us Phi Gams have to stick together."[4] After Nelson fired one of his executives, the man turned to Alice for help. Nelson wrote her sternly that if the man could win concessions from her, "we might as well abandon all discipline."[5]

Nelson usually dealt with his mother in flattering banter, but he could lose his temper. After one bout, he wrote Alice and reminded her how much his management had added to her income and Eleanor's: "Last Saturday morning you upset the entire office and me over a matter of $30. . . . I think it is unsporting of you to upset so many people when I have bent every effort for years to place you and Eleanor in this position. . . . It is difficult enough to run a newspaper and a radio station in wartime without complicating our personnel problem further with unnecessary distractions."[6]

The main issue always remained that of who was to own and thus control the *Times*. Alice's efforts to mediate this fairly and lovingly may have helped Nelson stake his claim, but she could not prevent her two children from going to their graves with the quarrel still separating them.

Until Nelson reached middle age the matter seemed to him one of whether he would devote his career to the family business. He saw reasons not to do so: He believed he could not run the paper with meddling from his family, particularly Alice, and he was drawn by challenges on the national scene.

As a young man, Nelson continually drew up plans to acquire a majority of shares in the *Times* company. The first of these, which was agreed to by his father, Paul, surfaced at the dinner in 1927 when he introduced his first wife, Catherine, to his family. This scheme was vaporized by criticism from Alice and Eleanor that it did not give the latter a role. Another pact was signed by both parents in 1932, while Nelson was working in Washington but was trying to help his father with the tangled affairs of the *Times*. It gave Nelson the right to buy up to 49 percent of the stock. Stock owned by Paul, Alice, Eleanor, and her husband and daughters was "bound" by the agreement, although only Paul and Alice signed it.[7]

During the 1935 struggle to prevent the Smith brothers from ousting Paul as chief of the *Times*, Nelson borrowed money to buy stock.[8] But because the 1932 document did not give Nelson the control he insisted on, he was determined not to repeat the debacle of his first attempt to become an executive after graduating from college.

Paul's exhaustion and ill health—plus uneasiness by creditors—loosened his grip on the *Times* even after the Smith move was defeated. This situation pulled Nelson into management chores while he was still working at northern newspapers, so in 1937 he extracted an agreement signed by all members of the family. It was a brief letter that spoke of Nelson and Catherine as one party and the others as the second. On its face, the letter gave either party the option of preventing sale of the paper's shares to outsiders by buying at the price offered. But Nelson felt that he had shown he would not brook interference from his mother or sister and that he expected to succeed Paul as chief officer.[9] He apparently hoped to achieve this end through his power to sell his shares. Paul, desperately in debt, could not have raised the money to meet the challenge and thus would have had to sell out to Nelson.

When Nelson returned to manage the *Times* in 1938, he was in a position to invoke the agreement. But, he later recalled, "This would have been too cruel to father's dignity, which I wanted to maintain." Paul, he noted, deserved credit for being one of the few Florida publishers to weather the depression.[10]

Aside from putting new wind in the newspaper's sails, Nelson spent hundreds of hours unsnarling his father's personal finances. Federal agents demanded that Paul pay back taxes on sums he had borrowed from the *Times,* a problem solved by trading in some stock to the company. Nelson discovered that Paul had acquired shares in the local dog racing track and considered it an embarrassment to the paper. When the son insisted that Paul sell the property, the father instead gave it to Eleanor. It produced much income for her and continued to rankle Nelson.[11]

Nelson started spending most of his time helping Ralph Ingersoll found *PM* in mid-1939, but Alice beseeched him not to give up management of the *Times.* Florida was an adequate field for his talents, she wrote him, and he could pursue his vision of a statewide newspaper.[12] "Your father simply CANNOT carry on," she added. "He will never manage the Times again."

Nelson began his three-year stint at federal jobs in 1940 but continued to press his family for control of the paper. He always made it clear he wanted to buy the stock and did not care what his parents did with their personal wealth. To keep his distance from the family finances, he refused to be his father's executor.

Throughout the war years, Nelson and his mother exchanged long letters alternating between tender expressions and bitter invective. "After all," he wrote Alice in 1940, "I do expect implicit trust from you, and I am always hurt and enraged when you make your insulting implications. That's what brought the original rupture twelve years ago, and why I am determined that the best way for you and me to get along is to have no business relationships. . . . I am tired of being placed in the position that I am attempting to take something from you and Eleanor."[13]

Alice's rebukes of Nelson increasingly involved his wife, Catherine, in the last two years of their marriage. "It is most unbecoming to both of us for you to treat me as you do in the presence of other people," Alice told her son. "I have always been fair to you and cannot understand whatever Catherine's position is toward me."[14] Once she claimed that she had been "ordered out" of the couple's home, apparently by Catherine, and that they had refused ten straight dinner invitations from the parents.[15]

Alice also dwelled on all the care she gave to Paul in his declining health. She was always trying to get him to take more baths. Her own fading ability to hear plagued both her and those around her. It brought a crisis in her Christian Science faith as she began to question its effectiveness. "I know this may seem strange . . . but I have felt that unless I could be healed in CS . . . all I had thought and believed in since I was 28 years old was just shattered. . . . The doubt that assailed me has been worse to bear than any physical discomfort I have suffered."[16]

Paul's real estate remained a constant sore spot among the family in the 1940s. Alice continually criticized what both men did with it, then complained to Nelson that he did not do more to help.

As World War II approached, the tumult in the Poynter family rose to a crescendo. The first crisis came when Alice concluded that Paul had been "carrying on an affair with a woman for 12 years. . . an office girl—simple—necessarily clandestine—meeting in cars and elsewhere."[17] The sixty-two-year-old Alice, with her larger-than-life personality, was devastated. "This blow almost killed me, my pride in him, my self respect—and the way it has affected you children," she told Nelson. "You have concealed it, but Eleanor has been unable to conceal the 'hurt' of it."[18] To "stick it out" in St. Petersburg was unthinkable to her, Alice said. "Too many people know it. I am more miserable here than anywhere and believe he is too. I want to spend less time here and believe he too will enjoy having a home at Sullivan again," she wrote, adding that she intended to acquire a house next to Eleanor's in Indiana.[19] The couple continued to spend winters in St. Petersburg, however.

Alice talked of divorce, and she complained bitterly of Paul's dealings with her: "It is not pleasant to have passersby walk in and remonstrate at your language addressed to me," she wrote to her husband. But as his health worsened, her fierce protectiveness reasserted itself. "Surely you know that only my affection for you and the fact that I think you are ill causes me to endure it. . . . Paul, we can live many years quietly and happily. We can travel as soon as the war is over. With whom could I go that I would enjoy being with to the extent I would enjoy you?"[20] She declared the matter out of her hands, leaving it to Paul to decide on a dissolution of their marriage. She noted that their letters would be placed in the family archives.[21]

The couple apparently agreed that half of Paul's estate would be put formally in Alice's name. Nelson mediated the arrangement, which contained the key to Nelson's dream: Paul was to transfer his controlling stock to Nelson upon his retirement. All assets were to be appraised and parceled between the parents. Paul would get 51 percent of *Times* common stock, and Alice's share would be issued as participating preferred stock. Nelson pointed out that they had agreed that Paul and Alice would keep their business interests independent "and that neither of you is to interfere with the other."[22]

The implication that Alice was meddling with Paul's business interests infuriated her, as did a request that she relinquish claim to his estate. She took out her fury on Nelson at various times over the next year, with indications that she believed her son was sympathizing with his father in regard to the "other woman." Three days before Christmas 1941, she wrote her son: "Nelson, get this. I am going to live with your father until one of us dies. I shall look after his clothing, his real estate and anything I think necessary to be looked after. Your interference ALONE will cause trouble. . . . Just keep out— forget us."[23]

The next fall she accused Nelson of writing "terrible letters" to her for the past three years. (Although Alice did not mention it, Nelson, at age thirty-nine, had begun calling her Mother rather than the pet name Minno.) After he wrote that she had made herself look ridiculous "sleuthing around the Yacht Club" looking for Catherine and her new husband, she denied the charge vehemently. She countered that his thinking was "perverted" and "illogical" and that her reputation was better than his.[24]

It is unclear whether the agreement to divide the estate was ever completely executed. But Nelson, by then serving the government in Hollywood, decided to cut his ties with the *Times,* going off the payroll and turning in all his stock. "I honestly feel that it is the only way that any degree of family harmony can be established," he wrote his parents and sister. "The four members of the family have certain incompatible objectives. My withdrawal will make it easier to reconcile those of three people as compared with four."[25]

In the letter Nelson detailed his financial dealings over the four years he had managed the *Times,* apparently seeking to defend himself to his family. Although he cited the company's good health brought by his aggressiveness, he left the enterprise with his pockets nearly empty.

This resulted partly from the fact that he offered to assume the losses on radio station WTSP, which the other Poynters had always considered a folly that he had imposed on them. He predicted that after WTSP was sold at a distress price, he would have no assets or liabilities other than a fund to pay his debts to Catherine. Alice later noted in a marginal comment, "Tragic after all he has done for all of us."[26] She acknowledged that he was leaving because "we were all riding him and [Paul] was at his worst." No ordinary manager could have achieved Nelson's feats with the paper, she said.[27]

Family quarrels aside, Nelson had a more practical reason to turn his back on the *Times*. He estimated that under its existing structure he would have to work forty years or more to become its owner.[28] Still another reason was his courtship with Henrietta, which he kept secret from the family until just before their elopement in August 1942.

A Rush of Joy

When Nelson and Henrietta finished overseeing Hollywood's war effort, they obviously relished the prospect of new challenges. Both were too restless and strong-minded to remain either sybarites or bureaucrats. They had to create something of their own—together.

"You will never find two happier people in the world than Henrietta and I," Nelson wrote Alice.[29]

Even though he had severed relations with the *Times* in 1942, Nelson soon was drawn back into a part-time management role. All of the family frictions continued, somewhat less intensely. Alice arranged a beach cottage for the couple, and Nelson said that he and Henrietta were "perfectly willing to live there indefinitely when we are in St. Petersburg," although they would like to build a "bug-proof" home eventually.

The newlyweds clearly were more excited about getting back to their old haunts in Washington. A friend, Betty Garnett, found them a small downtown apartment, which they furnished with things Henrietta had stored in New York. They searched for two years before finding a house in Georgetown that met Henrietta's demanding taste. There they could entertain friends—mostly middle-level bureaucrats but also lawmakers such as Florida Senators Spessard Holland and Claude Pepper and the maverick Republican senator from Illinois, Paul Douglas. From the house, Nelson could take much-loved walks in a nearby park or hikes along the Chesapeake and Ohio Canal. The couple talked of teaming up as writers, but that was not Henrietta's strength, much less Nelson's. Both were attuned to creative management.

William Allen White, who long had been the soul of small-town America through his crusading paper in Emporia, Kansas, had complained to Poynter about the difficulty of getting information about Congress that went beyond headline political news. Even such simple data as a congressman's voting record was rarely available. Congress's official gazette, the *Congressional Record,* was too "full of wind and rain" to be of much use, White said. "Just give me the facts," White challenged Poynter, "and I will give them vitality!"[30] At the same time strategists for the 1944 Democratic presidential campaign sought similar data to make a case against Republicans.

These were causes close to Poynter's heart. The campaign was the more pressing of the two, and he organized a reference service to feed the political cannons. "Our stuff will be the basis for the most important publicity and radio outside the president's speeches," he boasted. It also gave him material for his assignment to set up the Democratic side of a "battle page" debate in the *New York Daily News.*

After Franklin Roosevelt won his fourth term, Nelson and Henrietta turned their full efforts to White's challenge. Busy newspaper people like White needed someone to digest *Congressional Record,* point up trends, and highlight notable events. Hezekiah Niles, a Baltimore journalist, had done that early in the nineteenth century with *Niles' Weekly Register.* It was bipartisan and thorough, so valuable to politicians and editors it was collected each year in bound volumes. The Poynters—particularly Henrietta—had the energy to create a modern-day version of the Niles service. They decided to make the reference service something that could be sold to dues-paying newspapers of all persuasions. They called it *Press Research.*

Henrietta was unaccustomed to the idleness she had known in Hollywood, and she found it difficult at first to fit into St. Petersburg society. Some people there resented the fact that she had taken Catherine's place, and many were put off by her brilliance, push, and New York ways. Nelson was careful to keep Alice from smothering the marriage. "Bless you," he wrote his mother, "I know that you would be perfectly willing to give Henrietta and I everything you have, and come over and wash our dishes, but you surely can understand that we want to stand on our own feet. We have a rare freedom and independence, and a partnership that we are jealous of."[31]

Henrietta was one of the few persons who read the *Congressional Record* every day—and enjoyed it. She was fascinated with the intricacies of Congress and knew people of all ranks who made it work. Nelson brought to the partnership an equally wide circle of influential friends and a sure sense of what editors wanted but were not getting in congressional reporting. He knew that they needed depth reports on their own representatives' performance, the background of legislation, and research data that deadline reporters could not provide.

To make the new service viable, Poynter had to put himself in the unaccustomed role of catering to fellow press barons. He felt more at home with editors than with owners, although he was both. Newspapers were massively conservative at the time, particularly in politics but also in all the other fields where Poynter wanted to innovate—news, production, circulation, and advertising. His innate courtesy and geniality enabled him to mix with people for whom he had no liking. Even so, he slowly withdrew from such involvements over the years as his patience wore thin.

While building *Press Research,* Poynter forged personal links with newspaper executives through an effort that came naturally to him—a crusade. When his colleagues gathered for their annual meeting of press organizations in 1944, he urged the American Society of Newspaper Editors to support his campaign to make the worldwide press free after the war. The society should petition Congress to declare a national policy refusing to "recognize the right of any government organization or person to infringe upon freedom of information or expression," he argued. He also proposed that the United States make treaties with other countries guaranteeing this right.

One of Poynter's few professional soulmates was the society's new president, John S. Knight, head of a chain which included the *Miami Herald.* Like Poynter, Knight was a writing editor with a liberal bent. He backed the press freedom project, and it got the organization's endorsement. Poynter set about garnering support from other powerful groups, including the American Newspaper Publishers Association. The plan struck welcome chords of idealism and won attention on front pages of major newspapers.

In late 1945, *Press Research* went through a metamorphosis. It became *Congressional Quarterly,* adopting the name of a respected earlier publication but remaining a weekly service. The Poynters continued to pour their energies into it, and they spent much of their time in Washington and New York, while a crisis was on the verge of erupting at the *Times*.

Conflict on First Avenue

To Sanford H. ("Sandy") Stiles, St. Petersburg was a great place to grow up. It was a sports paradise, offering him the chance to interview athletes in winter training, like Babe Ruth, for the high school paper. When he became a *Times* proofreader at seventeen, he found a new source of excitement that would never leave him. He didn't know it at the time, but he was the kind of person Nelson Poynter intended to build the *Times* with—young, talented, innovative, and energetic.

Stiles had been part of the 1920s land boom immigration. His parents brought him, at age four, from Connecticut. They pulled a trailer loaded with all their possessions and pitched a tent on a lot his father bought. Newspaper reading was a ritual in his home, so when he got a chance to earn $18 a week reading proof at the *Times,* he jumped at it. By the time he was twenty-two he had gone through the newsroom ranks and had become sports editor. During World War II, Stiles became editor of an airbase newspaper in Tampa. It was printed in the *Times* plant and won an award as the best service newspaper in the world.

After the war, Stiles started new *Times* projects such as a Sunday magazine and news features departments. He organized the team that introduced full process color to the paper. Years later a *Times* executive would describe Stiles as "the guy who catches the worst possible assignments and does them so very, very well."[32]

Stiles played a crucial role in the *Times*'s biggest crisis since the corporate ownership war in 1935, this time a conflict between management and labor. It was a collision no one would have predicted for Poynter, considered by some a knee-jerk liberal who would hand the country over to the unions.

In bursts of wartime patriotism, unions had taken no-strike pledges. War production contracts and spinoff prosperity filled workers' pockets with money. But with victory in sight, unions reached out for a larger share. Scattered strikes broke out, and after V-J Day they became a torrent.

The International Typographical Union (ITU) was the largest of several unions usually found in newspaper printing plants. It was one of the nation's oldest, steeped in traditions going back to medieval Europe. Its local branches were called chapels, recalling former quasi-religious rites. Newspaper technology had changed little since the late nineteenth century, which put a premium on mature, resourceful humans rather than on technology. Unions were confident that they could break a publisher who defied them.

For a half-century printers and publishers had gotten along well. Both sides accepted a role of public service; most conflicts were negotiated and strikes were rare. But an aggressive new ITU leadership saw innovation coming—machines that could improve efficiency and eliminate jobs—and they wanted protections.

Poynter always had championed labor when it was the underdog. He placed his editorship on the line in Columbus, Ohio, to defend strikers. Even when upholding management interests against unions as a Scripps-Howard executive he had won his opponents' respect. Soon after moving to St. Petersburg in 1938 he negotiated a contract with the ITU that had stood up all through the war.

Most publishers, despising unions, largely ignored organized workers in their news columns. But the *Times* ran a labor column every Monday, boasting that it was the first newspaper in the nation to give unions space to present their viewpoints. The *Times* also was the only major Florida newspaper to oppose Florida's "right-to-work" law, approved in a 1944 referendum. This measure prohibited any contract by which a business agreed to a closed shop—a ban on nonunion employees. That law, against which Poynter and the unions fought side by side, was to play a key role when they turned against each other.

ITU contracts with both the *Times* and the *Independent* expired June 30, 1945, shortly before the war ended. The union opened bargaining jointly with Poynter and the *Independent*'s owner, Lew Brown. Summer heat was at its worst. There was no air conditioning, but the tense sessions made progress.

The union presented twelve demands. The publishers agreed to four, arguing that some were illegal under the right-to-work law. Wages remained the sticking point. After raising its offer several times, management stood firm at $57.38 a week, or $3.37 below the union demand but nearly half again as much as the prewar rate. Besides,

Poynter had been told that this rate was more than the scale in Tampa, Nashville, Richmond, and other southern cities. Being larger, the other papers had higher advertising rates and a chance for more profits.

Under normal conditions, such a small difference between two sides would have resulted in arbitration. But the ITU required that its national rules be followed in any new contract, and that included a refusal to arbitrate. Negotiations dragged on toward the end of the year, when newspapers usually made much of the year's profit on holiday advertising. The union considered the papers specially vulnerable at that season. Although the union delayed taking a vote, Poynter realized a strike was in the offing. Max Ulrich was sure the union leaders were hell-bent on a walkout. He placed bets with colleagues who believed it would never happen.

Poynter had long felt that the printing process of ink on raised type, invented by Gutenberg five centuries earlier, was obsolete. Even before the war a few newspapers had experimented with the offset process, a combination of inking and photographic images. Ralph Ingersoll had wanted to use it for *PM,* but Poynter had helped persuade him it was feasible only for small papers at that time.

One of offset printing's strengths was that it could take advantage of "cold type." In the older process, lines of type (called hot type) would be cast from molten lead, only to be melted down after each use—the so-called hot type. The cold-type process could transfer any image, whether freehand drawing or typewriter copy, to newsprint. Its main merit for publishers was that it could ease backshop headaches. It reduced the necessity for the printing craft, and unskilled typists would replace the expensive—and unionized—printers.

Poynter had bought a small offset press so his executives could dabble with it and learn the concept. But it obviously was too slow to print the *Times,* which had large pages and a circulation of 26,000. Then he saw a way to gain the benefits of cold type without the limitations of offset. He would use cold type to prepare curved, engraved plates that could be adapted to the *Times*'s conventional letterpress. He had Ulrich start planning ways to do something the ITU thought was impossible—printing the two dailies jointly without printers. Ulrich ordered two machines called Vari-Typers, which arrived October 23, 1945. One was then sold to the *Independent.*

Ulrich installed the other Vari-Typer in the office next to his. Four young women, secretarial-level employees of the paper, were trained to operate it. The Vari-Typer looked like a typewriter, but it surpassed the conventional typewriter in two ways: It could produce various faces and sizes of type, and it could justify the right margin as readers had come to expect, although each line had to be typed twice.

Times employees came to work the morning of November 20, 1945, to find printers—many of them old friends—hanging around the building entrance. Although management had not been notified, word was out: The ITU local had voted fifty-seven to seven to strike both dailies.

The mood was lighthearted. ITU members were certain the action would stop operations, and they kidded their nonunion colleagues about wasting their time at the office. Many strikers went fishing. The idea of drawing strike benefits, something new to St. Petersburg, elated them. They had contributed to the fund for years.

The *Independent* felt the blow first, with its afternoon publication time. Its nonstrikers rushed to put together a four-page issue, a strange hybrid of cold type produced on an ordinary typewriter, type picked up from the previous day, photographs, and comic strips.

Sandy Stiles, who had just completed his military service, was recruited by Poynter and Harris to organize a production team for the *Times*. He had never been a printer, although as proofreader he had worked in the composing room—the typographers' area—and had picked up many skills by watching. Harris had done the same thing two decades earlier.

Other *Times* executives also got calls over breakfast and rushed to the office, warning their families they had no idea when they would be home. At 9:30 they gathered in Poynter's office and quickly decided to publish sixteen-page papers without interruption. And they welcomed the chance to try out all the labor-saving gadgets they had been hearing about.

Newsroom and advertising people had the idea that a strike could be fun. Everybody wanted to do something special to help. Copy boys dashed about, bringing coffee, paper, and typewriter ribbons and plunging out the door to fetch things from a stationery store. The one precious Vari-Typer was carried from Ulrich's office to the newsroom. It took the place of fourteen Intertype units normally used to produce hot type. The women who had been trained on the new machine alternated working on it. The first copy began coming in at 11 A.M., and a steady stream flowed in after that.

Because Stiles and others needed extra time to grope their way through things they had never done before, Tom Harris adjusted deadlines. Editorial and society pages were moved back seven to nine hours, and the hard news pages gave up two hours. Staff artists—people who usually did fancy lettering and illustrations for advertisements—found themselves working in the newsroom maelstrom. They drafted help from anyone with a steady hand to stick headlines together letter by letter, or paste up strips of typed copy on a page layout.

As the hours ticked away, pieces fell together. When press time of 2:30 A.M. on November 21 arrived, the motors groaned to life and a sixteen-page edition—only six pages smaller than the day before—slid out of the cast-iron womb. Ironically, the lead story was about a strike, but not the one at the *Times*. The United Auto Workers had paralyzed General Motors throughout the country, and the story carried an eight-column banner.

In the middle of the front page was a story headed "STATEMENT TO OUR READERS." It opened with "Don't shoot, we're doing the best we can" and apologized for the "fuzzy and inconvenient appearance" of the paper. It briskly explained the labor conflict and clearly laid the blame on the union. Uninterrupted publication was promised, as was an improved product.

Poynter realized his action seemed like an about-face. He conceded that the paper was getting "a hell of a ribbing" because it had been such a good friend of unions. "Despite this we still believe in collective bargaining as an American principle. It's better than government edict, but stubborn employers and stubborn unions which refuse to arbitrate invite labor relations by edict."[33] Next to the publisher's statement stood a gaping white hole headed "THIS SPACE RESERVED FOR UNION VIEW." A note said that the union had declined "with thanks" the paper's offer to present its view in equal space.

Despite its normal size, the front page had the amateurish look of a high school paper. The few headlines were lost in a sea of gray, largely because the Vari-Typer characters were half again as large as machine-set type, so they took up far more space.

The staff's titanic effort had produced nine of the sixteen pages in the new system of pasting typewritten copy on paper and photoengraving it. Four pages of continuing classified ads were picked up from the previous day in their original machine type. Three came from a junky array of syndicated material in the form of stereotype casts.

Nelson Poynter was ecstatic. He had no illusions about the quality, but he thought the *Times* had opened a new chapter in newspaper economics—the age of cold type. Leading figures in the drama held a postmortem as the press rolled to decide how to get out the kinks. This meeting became a nightly ritual.

Despite the paper's crude appearance, praise came from readers about some aspects. The larger body type pleased those who wore glasses—a sizable part of St. Petersburg's retirement-oriented community. A double-column line width adopted by necessity also proved popular, and many liked the decision not to continue stories from the front page. Emotional reactions poured in about the decision to keep publishing. "Don't give in to them bastards," some supporters phoned to say. Opponents canceled their subscriptions with outbursts like "So you're going to hire a lot of scabs, you sonsabitches!"[34]

Poynter wanted to buy the most avant-garde machinery to help him publish with relatively untrained help. Much of this technology was becoming available, although primarily adapted for small-scale printing in offices and commercial plants. But when Ulrich tried to buy some of these innovations, he ran into a curious lack of interest among equipment salesmen. It soon became clear that they wanted to sell the new items only to small commercial plants. They feared sales to larger operations would reduce demand for expensive conventional machines.[35] The difficulty in buying the equipment continued to hamper management's effort.

The conflict moved toward a climax in January 1946. Printers mounted picket lines January 10, and the *Independent*'s pressmen and engravers refused to cross them, although their national union's officers sent them back to work after one day. Then the ITU publicly accused the publishers of refusing to negotiate with the union. This quickly raised hackles in the newspapers' offices, as they were in effect being accused of violating federal law. Poynter, as president of the new joint printing company, fired back a telegram denying the charge. He said the papers planned to go back to normal printing soon and would be hiring nonunion printers unless the strike were settled.

The local ITU president responded by inviting Poynter to address an assembly of members on January 12. It was a Saturday morning, and the printers were weary and footsore from three-hour shifts of picketing around the clock. It was a tense moment. Men who had worked easily with Poynter for years now faced him as an adversary. Even Peck

Walters, a colorful Hoosier whom Paul Poynter had brought down in the early days as *Times* shop foreman, was there. He had long since left the paper to set up his own commercial printing plant but had kept up his union membership.

Poynter read a prepared statement. It was long and detailed, but it hit home to the members on two key points—jobs and wages. Poynter obviously had the upper hand. He confidently reviewed the employers' offer and argued how well it compared with the past and with other areas. Then he hit the most tender nerve. If the union rejected the offer, he said, the company would train a large number of apprentices "from returning war veterans and others with mechanical talent."

The message was clear: You are expendable. Most printers were middle-aged men who had been too old for the wartime draft. Now jobless young men fresh from military service were flooding the market. They were eager to get started on careers, and many held a grudge against men who had remained civilians, profiting from the war and living in ease. Poynter said the company would prefer to rehire ITU members and avoid the training program. He even said he would welcome a unionization movement among any nonunion printers he would hire as long as there was an arbitration clause in the contract.

After he finished, Poynter faced an hour of polite but barbed questioning. The toughest question—one that would bedevil Poynter for more than a year and cost the company tens of thousands of dollars—came from F. T. Carter, who had been sent down by the national union to watch over the strike. He asked Poynter whether News Printing Inc.—the temporary company created to print the *Times* and *Independent* jointly—would negotiate with the union local. Poynter at first would not answer, but then he gave a longer response which amounted to a refusal. The company would deal only with representatives of the majority of its workers, he said. He pledged to stick by this even if the union called it a lockout and the nonunionists he hired were branded as rats, scabs, or strikebreakers. Peck Walters immediately saw the legal trap Poynter had stepped into. He pointed out that federal law required that strikers be regarded as employees until the strike was settled, and refusing to deal with them violated the Wagner Labor Relations Act.

Poynter instantly regained the offensive. He asked Carter if Walters's comment meant the ITU was invoking the Wagner Act. If so, he said, he would immediately spread the news over the country by the wire services. Carter was on guard. He knew invoking the Wagner Act meant the case could go to arbitration, and the ITU firmly opposed that. Walters was ruled out of order. Poynter gave the union nine days to reply before he began training a new labor force. The only action that resulted was a few unionists' coming around to ask for their old jobs.

Finally, on January 26, 1946, the flirtation with cold type was over, to be rekindled two decades later. Linotype-set type began to reappear, and reconversion to hot type was almost complete within a month. The strike continued despite the gradual return to normal publication. The paper had not missed an issue, and no issue contained fewer than sixteen pages and one went up to forty-eight. The average was twenty-two. Instead of losing advertising, the *Times* had increased it by nearly a third over the year before.

Once the decision had been made to return to hot type, Linotype operators had to be found to replace strikers. Ads were placed in papers up north, but response was minimal. The solution was the Type-O-Writer, a device that converted the strange and sprawling keys of a Linotype or Intertype into a conventional typewriter keyboard. In theory this innovation allowed anyone who could type to operate the clattering, temperamental typesetting machine, but training proved to be long and tedious.

Soon after the January 12 meeting between Poynter and the printers, an agent of the National Labor Relations Board (NLRB) appeared ominously on the scene. Franklin Roosevelt had founded the NLRB as a special court system unburdened by the mossback conservatism he saw in the normal judicial process. The board's decisions were subject only to regular federal judges. Then Poynter was skewered by the very New Deal he had long applauded. The NLRB agent charged News Printing with four unfair labor practices, primarily hinging on a prolabor interpretation of Poynter's comments at the January 12 meeting. The NLRB agent claimed that Poynter had interfered with the formation of a union, discharged union members, refused to bargain collectively, and coerced employees.

The company hired some of the best legal talent available. It included Thurman Arnold, a former federal judge and chief trustbuster for Franklin Roosevelt, and Cody Fowler of Tampa, a former president of the American Bar Association.

The NLRB hearing—in effect a trial—opened June 25, 1946, in the St. Petersburg City Hall. Perspiration poured from 250 persons in the assembly room as two small fans barely stirred the air. The case obviously was a test, particularly because it might settle whether the ITU could impose its own rules on publishers without negotiation. Reporters from the wire services, several major newspapers, and syndicates covered the proceeding. Lawyers for both sides looked on it as a knotty matter.

Union lawyers presented a transcript of the meeting made for the ITU, quoting Poynter's response to a question inquiring whether Poynter felt he could negotiate: "News Printing Inc. has no employees, but we will be glad to negotiate with our employees when we have them. I want to make this clear, because I am not going to be placed in a position where you can say we will not negotiate. As far as we are concerned, we are always open for arbitration. We believe in it, but will not negotiate at the point of a gun, and as far as we are concerned, the strike is a gun being pointed at us."[36]

Trying to discredit the union's transcript, Arnold pointed out that it contained only about 2,400 words but that Poynter customarily spoke at 150 words a minute when calm and faster when excited. Because he talked for more than an hour at the meeting, the transcript obviously was incomplete and thus unacceptable, Arnold said. The NLRB examiner hearing the case overruled Arnold.

Arnold hammered away at the union's claim that Poynter refused to negotiate, citing conferences held by the two sides. The lawyer also presented evidence that NLRB agents had tried to pressure Poynter to settle the strike. Whenever he got a chance while testifying, Poynter expounded at length about the principles he was defending—protection of the rights of people who had been hired since the strike, the merits of arbitration, and the need to abide by Florida's right-to-work law. Once the examiner warned him to answer briefly.

Poynter brought in Lowell Mellett, his mentor from his Scripps-Howard days and former aide to President Roosevelt. Mellett testified that small, independent publishers like Poynter were dying out because of rising costs. It was ironic, he said, that most publishers considered Poynter unduly prolabor. Mellett also mentioned the case in his national column. Arguments went on an entire week. At the end, the *Times* ran long articles by each of the two top lawyers on Poynter's side and on the union's.

For four months the case gestated in NLRB secrecy. The *Times* and *Independent* went back to their separate printing operations much as before. The local ITU president flayed Poynter in a speech to the union's state meeting in St. Petersburg: "Nelson Poynter is an egotistical, somewhat hysterical radical who wants to be a hero in the industry. He it was who . . . told the world that he was through with printers . . . that he was going to revolutionize the industry."[37]

Tom Harris telephoned Poynter, who was in Washington, to tell him of the attack. Poynter ordered it reported. It seemed like a good way to show that unionists could not agitate for an opposition paper on the grounds that they could not get their news printed. Besides, he told his mother, "It's always a good idea to prove that we also can take it as well as dish it out."[38]

But the conflict weighed heavily on Poynter. He and Henrietta were desperately trying to get the new *Congressional Quarterly* reference service on its feet in Washington, and it seemed to him that the distraction would kill the newborn. "I could give it so little of real constructive thinking," he reflected.[39]

On October 31 the verdict came in—a victory for the union. The examiner had recommended to the NLRB that the St. Petersburg dailies be required to bargain with the ITU and give jobs to all fifty-five strikers. The finding had no teeth until the full board acted. The newspapers' lawyers launched an appeal.

After another three-month wait, the nightmare ended. The NLRB swept aside the examiner's findings and freed the papers from any obligation. The board's decision rested on the legal concept of good faith in negotiation, holding that the union did not show good faith when it refused to bargain over whether to impose its own rules on the employer. The finding also made it easier for employers to hire strike-breakers. The board vote was unanimous, and the decision was one of the most favorable management had ever received. As for Poynter's confusing remark at the January 12 meeting, the board called it "inept and misguided" but not a violation of law.

Poynter wrote a signed editorial headed "We're Not Gloating—It's a Hell of a Way to Cook a Pig" that bemoaned the fact that more than fifty old-line printers had to give up their homes and leave St. Petersburg. It also expressed regret that readers had been deprived of "super-quality" newspapers "while we fought a technological war and had litigation with our government." But the *Times* had prospered, he wrote, printing more copies than ever before.[40]

In the aftermath of the strike the *Times* published a manual on how other newspapers could survive a strike. Many publishers had visited St. Petersburg to find out how the strike was handled. Thus Poynter became known as the boss who broke the strike in St. Petersburg. It gained him admiration from fellow press lords, a group for which he had little affinity, and marred his emerging renown among liberals.

Never again would Poynter have to face a serious effort to unionize the composing room. But only two years after the NLRB decision, trouble arose in the press department. After the paper was printed each night, pressmen were accustomed to going home. One night three of them left before getting permission and were fired. Another was let go for incompetence. Pressmen walked off the job the next night, August 17, 1949, at 11 P.M., as presses were ready to roll for the Thursday paper. A substitute crew was hastily put together, and the thirty-six-page issue came out as usual.

Since the absent workers' jobs were filled, the union called the action a lockout. The newspaper charged that the union had conducted an illegal walkout. Negotiations went on for three days but reached an impasse: The union demanded that replacements for the protesters be fired. The company refused, and the foreman and assistant foreman, who had stayed on, also left. No agreement ever ensued, and the walkout was beaten.[41]

By 1952, the pressmen's union had again emerged, and negotiations with it broke down. Poynter saw the dispute once more as a question of who was going to run the paper—he or the union, with the critical issue relating to operations, not wages. He also objected to the union's insistence on cutting the apprenticeship period in half, giving workers full pay after two and a half years instead of after five. The union also wanted to say how many apprentices were hired and how many persons must run the press.[42]

A strike started on November 14, and the pressmen set up a picket line. As in the beginning of the printers' strike, the *Times* reserved space for the union to tell its side. The foreman, Charlie Watson, stayed on the job and saved the day for the paper, training stopgap help from *Times* management.

The paper continued with reduced color and tabloid sections, but it soon returned to normal with replacement pressmen. Reflecting on the strike, Poynter blamed himself and his managers for neglect and insensitivity—failures in communication. But once more a strike was broken. It would be the last such conflict until the 1970s.

A New Horizon

Nelson emerged from his victory over the printers' union still without owning the *St. Petersburg Times*. His parents in 1945 had signed an option allowing him to buy all their shares at $100 each, the market price. But the family bickering ground on, and he was sick of it. His sister, Eleanor, objected to the arrangement, and he saw as the reason her fear that Henrietta would take over the paper if Nelson died. He wrote his mother: "I frankly despise Eleanor's ghoulish pre-occupation with my death and estate. I am no longer upset by it. . . . You seem to all consider that it was perfectly all right to go on from month to month, year to year, with my not knowing what my plans could be so far as stock ownership. . . . I am now 42 years old, I have seen several friends . . . buy and pay for newspapers in the last eight years, while I was waiting the pleasure and whimsy of my family."[43]

Thanks to Henrietta's persistent graciousness, Alice had come over to her side. "I have only felt a sense of gratitude for Henrietta, and have grown fond of her—respect her highly," Alice told Nelson.[44] Later she would marvel that they had "such a complete understanding of one another, and such mutual love and trust."[45]

The family had transferred one-third ownership of the *Sullivan Times* to Eleanor, and she was publishing it with difficulty. Nelson continued to offer frequent suggestions about how the Indiana paper should be run, but he funneled them through his mother. Paul was out of the management picture, although Nelson insisted that he retain the title of company president. Alice had to hire servants to tend his needs and keep him amused. There was no doubt that, at seventy-two, he was approaching death.

Finally, in August 1947, the family reached an agreement for Nelson to buy all 500 shares of common (voting) stock. Other members received large holdings of preferred shares. Nelson borrowed $50,000 to pay Paul with cash that he could apply to his real estate obligations, freeing the older man from debt for the first time since he left college. Nelson also managed to fend off challenges by the Internal Revenue Service to Paul's $20,000 annual salary.[46]

For the first time Nelson spoke of the *Times* with the expansive zeal that became his hallmark. In a letter to his father, he said:

> As you know, I am terribly ambitious for the paper—to see it keep ahead of the parade as you kept it ahead. . . . This aggressiveness which is traditional is one of the reasons why we now have twice the circulation of The Independent, and The Tampa Tribune has dwindled in this territory. This is one of the reasons why a modern newspaper must embrace electronics. . . . Yet newspapering is not just equipment. Today we must fight to preserve the very idea of self-government . . . that the majority of men are good, and decent and intelligent, and that the majority of A MAN is the same—and therefore capable of self-government despite the doubts elsewhere in the world.[47]

Eleanor then had holdings exceeding $200,000 in value, more than Alice or Nelson held. Although Nelson's parents did not ask him to share his new control of the newspaper with his sister, he said it would "add to Minno's joy" if he did. So two months after the settlement he sold 200 of the 500 voting shares to Eleanor for $20,000.[48] This move would plague Nelson the rest of his life and his heirs afterward.

Nelson Poynter realized that he probably had kept the *Times* out of the hands of a less-qualified owner. But what if he and Henrietta should die? He knew what kind of paper he wanted to make of the *Times,* but did his heirs? During the month when he closed the stock deal, he sat down to write his ideas about the duties of a newspaper owner. This was not difficult; he simply wrote what had been forming in his mind for decades. It was done in about an hour.[49]

He had little precedent to go by. The newspaper industry had been notably reluctant to embrace professional standards. The American Society of Newspaper Editors had adopted a code of ethics in 1923, but it was intentionally vague, and it implied that the most relevant ethical questions were those for editors and reporters, not owners.

Poynter felt otherwise. He insisted that one person should have complete control over a newspaper and that person's ideas should be paramount. Only the owner could devise conditions necessary to put out the best newspaper the staff was capable of creating, he believed. He knew that if he and Henrietta died in the near future the paper would have to be sold to pay off the heavy debt he had incurred to buy it, so he wanted to provide some guideposts—even if not legally binding—for his executors when they chose a buyer.

Poynter wrote fifteen numbered paragraphs totaling 486 words, and he called them the Standards of Ownership (see the appendix). They came to be much more than guideposts for an executor, because Poynter lived three decades after they were written, and they served as both a declaration of independence and a constitution for the *Times*. They were much like the manifestos he and Ralph Ingersoll produced when they founded *PM*.

A widespread debate about newspapers was nearing a climax when Poynter wrote his standards. This concerned charges that American newspaper owners, because of rapidly disappearing competition resulting from closures, were becoming the country's greatest danger to freedom of expression. What good was the right to publish if only rich people could exercise it?

Harold L. Ickes, President Roosevelt's freewheeling secretary of the interior, had long hammered at press barons, calling them "America's House of Lords." Another controversial figure, *Time-Life* owner Henry R. Luce, entered the fray by commissioning a study led by the University of Chicago's president, Robert M. Hutchins. Hutchins put together a panel of thirteen distinguished intellectuals, most of them respected liberals. The study went on for five years, with a brilliant staff churning out 176 documents, some published later.

In the spring of 1947, a few months before Poynter wrote his standards, the Hutchins Commission published its main findings amid much furor. Its recommendations rested on some radical new assumptions, including the one that even owners of newspapers should not limit press freedom by impeding their employees from doing their jobs. The First Amendment guarantees were intended not to fatten publishers but rather to meet community needs, it indicated, and editors must give space for all viewpoints.

Poynter's first four standards invite close comparison with the Hutchins Commission credo. Owning a mass medium is "a sacred trust and a great privilege," he said, and each such property had "unusual obligations" to its community. This ran head-on into the common view among publishers that the newspaper had no constitutional obligation to the reader. Poynter's idea of "unusual obligations" to the community tied in with his fourth point, which stressed taking the initiative in serving the public rather than waiting "to be prodded into rendering that service." Similarly, the Hutchins report stressed that the press had a duty to set society's goals.

Many people—including some publishers—thought that one privilege of a newspaper owner was to keep out of the paper news that the owner did not like. Poynter apparently was thinking of this when, in his third standard, he drew the line against any "compromise with the integrity of the news." Years later, Poynter also justified such a stand on a basis of prudence: "Some people are going to know that we didn't print that story, and we're going to lose the confidence of those people. And then if a news story comes up that affects them, the people who knew we suppressed this story will say, 'You didn't print so-and-so. Why should you print the fact that I was arrested for driving while drunk?' "[50]

Most radical and original of the fifteen standards was the last one, providing the pivot for all the others. It said that one person must have "complete control" of the newspaper. Poynter had before him the memory of his father's pathetic battle to regain control of the *Times* in 1935 after stock slipped into unfriendly hands. Poynter also saw how once-great newspapers like the late Joseph Pulitzer's *New York World* and *St. Louis Post-Dispatch* had weakened steadily after control dissipated as stock spread among the heirs. Even though he had bought a majority of the stock and complete control with it, Poynter worried about even the minority's becoming scattered. His parents and his sister still had part of the shares, and they could sell or will it to others. Besides, Poynter felt, a minority stockholder could create havoc in an organization and keep its executives from doing a good job.[51]

The only way to build up a newspaper, aside from making more money, was to reinvest the profits. Several of Poynter's standards stressed this outlook. They called for reserves to be built up, debts paid off, and top-quality equipment bought, and these were to take priority over profits. A cap of 6 percent on dividends was set until all other needs were met.

Poynter also was chagrined to look about him at family-owned newspapers and see the staffs loaded with relatives drawing salaries for jobs they were not qualified to do.[52] Closer at hand, Eleanor had at various times asked that she or her husband be put on the *Times* payroll. Nelson felt that, besides wasting money, nepotism could kill the incentive of staffers who were not family members. He developed a rigid dislike for the practice, so he inserted a standard that banned owners from getting unearned salaries.

Keen businessman that he was, Poynter overtly tied his own hands at money-making in two respects—he condemned both chain owner-ship and the ownership of properties outside journalism. At the time Poynter wrote his standards, press critics were appalled at the cynical abuse of power by some chain owners, particularly William Randolph Hearst. They could pull strings stretching into editorial offices across the nation, forcing local editors to endorse a candidate or support a cause en masse. Because chains lent themselves to public ownership—sale of stock on the open market—they posed a particular danger to Poynter's ideal of concentrated power in one individual. He shuddered at the nightmare of annual stockholder meetings' becoming the arena for attacks on editorial decisions. Forswearing chain ownership also underscored the fact that Poynter had made his final decision to stay in St. Petersburg. Although he maintained a home in Washington and operated *Congressional Quarterly* there, he apparently did not con-sider it part of a chain.

Paul Poynter had owned a chain of small newspapers, and he also had financial interests outside the papers, notably in land. But Nelson Poynter had set about selling off the *Times*'s speculative property as soon as he arrived in the city. Because of pressures to make Florida land easier to sell, proposed zoning changes stirred continual squab-bles. Poynter knew that such changes were bound to affect the value of the newspaper's land. That would inevitably make readers suspicious of how news stories and editorials treated the matter.

Much space in the standards went to staff matters, where a curious ambivalence emerged. Poynter insisted on having the last word on every question about the *Times,* and he doted on its staff like an indulgent father. But he winced at anything that seemed patronizing, and he avoided the term "benefits." To him they were "earned divi-dends." Whenever a staff member would thank him for some advan-tages in working there, he would reply, "Don't thank me . . . ; you've earned them or you shouldn't be here." Apparently in sincerity, he would say how grateful he was to have anyone willing to work on the same staff as he.[53]

In the standards, Poynter declared that he expected every member of the staff to be above average. To merit that, he added, the paper must pay above average, even to the point of putting personnel outlays above equipment. But he did not stop there. In an era when most newspaper owners still grumbled about Social Security, Poynter talked of doing more. He preached that capitalists must provide pensions that promise "honest and dignified" retirement, and he started a pension plan in 1947. Nine years later he set up a profit-sharing system.

The standards were intended as a message to the staff, but Poynter also sent them to Eleanor, who had disapproved of some of his ideas. Years went by before they were published. Looking back later, Poynter would call the standards "rather corny" and "self-evident in the printing business."[54] He was right in that they were awkward, didactic, and repetitious in places. He was wrong to indicate that most newspaper owners endorsed them.

It took a while for the *Times*'s readers to accept that Nelson Poynter was fully in charge even though his family held only a minority share. Soon after writing the Standards of Ownership he had to set the public straight. Alice Poynter, perhaps more liberal than her son, had donated $1,000 to the doomed third-party quest for the presidency by Henry A. Wallace, whom mainline Democrats by then considered a dangerous radical. The *Times* had reported Mrs. Poynter's contribution. The paper came under fire for allegedly being two-faced because it had editorially condemned the Wallace candidacy. Nelson answered critics in a signed editorial. The graciously written article defended Mrs. Poynter's support of unpopular causes. If she as a stockholder could not exercise freedom of expression, the paper's employees might fear to do likewise, it argued. But it made clear that Nelson had control of the paper by virtue of his majority ownership.

As Paul Poynter year by year grew weaker and more dependent on his wife, Nelson chafed at how Alice's normally robust way of life was being cramped. He constantly coaxed her to take the trips abroad that she so enjoyed. When Alice passed up a trip to Europe to stay near Paul, Nelson frankly told her that her decision made him jealous: "You read, and improved yourself and deserved the best, and I regret that your marriage was such that you and Dad could not have had tastes that were more compatible. I have always thought you should have been the wife of an ambassador. I know you will understand, and that I am not critical of Dad—and realize how sweet and generous he has always been to all of us—but you had a drive that would have netted a lot of fun for you if you had a trip almost every year."[55]

When Paul greeted his son for the last time, he said, "Hello, Mr.

Editor!" Finally, on November 21, 1950, his life ended in the home on Coffee Pot Bayou. The honorary pallbearer list was a who's who of St. Petersburg and the *Times* staff, as few persons who had lived even a fraction of his seventy-five years had made so few enemies. Alice had once referred to him as father confessor to half the newspaper's employees. He was buried in Sullivan.

The next year Nelson changed gears at the *Times,* and Alice took an extended tour of Europe.

The Money-Makers

As the 1950s began, Nelson Poynter was content with Tom Harris and a news staff that was home-grown or had drifted down from the North. They were nimble and aggressive people, perhaps not polished in New York ways but able to push the *Times* ahead.

The business side was another matter. C. C. Carr, a professional who held the paper together in the 1920s and 1930s, had left St. Petersburg to sell Alcoa's image from a plush Pittsburgh office. The paper missed his firm hand.

Poynter had heard about exciting trends in management—techniques such as goal-setting, incentives, and the use of psychology in hiring. He prided himself on his own feats as a manager at the *Washington Daily News,* but he knew he had to find people even more skilled than he.

Advertising held first priority. World War II prosperity was promising a golden harvest, but there had to be someone qualified to take advantage of it. As it was, ad selling was divided up into little fiefdoms at the *Times,* none as productive as it should be. For years the paper's best friend in New York had been the S. C. Theis "publishers' representative" firm, a channel for getting national advertising. The main contact there was an urbane executive named Irwin Simpson whose white hair and cool manner would later get him called the Silver Fox.

Simpson had dealt with Paul Poynter but quickly recognized superior business instincts in Nelson upon the son's arrival in 1938.[56] When Nelson offered Simpson the new title of advertising director six years later—combining all the scattered functions—he took it. During the nearly twenty years until his retirement, the ad department turned into a finely tooled harvesting machine.

Simpson also was the joiner that Carr had been and Nelson Poynter wasn't. He forged links with the power structure through groups like the Chamber of Commerce board of directors and the Rotary Club. He collected shelves of civic and professional awards.

Before Simpson, ad salesmen had been accustomed to picayune office practices. To get a new pencil, one had to turn in a stub. Simpson held out a sky-is-the-limit prospect for making money through bonuses, but salesmen had to go through constant training. Once a week they reported at the office at eight o'clock to take sales classes. Advertising artists were brought in to draw high-fashion clothes from the originals. Simpson wanted *Times* advertising to project youthfulness to beat down St. Petersburg's unprofitable image as an old folks' home.

The *Times* had been letting its ad space go at bargain rates, and Simpson set out to raise them to the norm. Advertisers howled when rates went up. Merchants were used to getting free publicity when they promoted an employee or stocked a new line. Simpson set up a column for such trivia and removed it from the news mainstream.

Advertisers also learned that Poynter was serious about ethics. One supermarket manager with a large lineage account got in trouble for public drunkenness. He asked Simpson to see that it stayed out of the paper, but the ad manager said the best way to make sure it got printed was for him to ask Poynter otherwise.

Poynter chafed at the intrusion of ads into editorial space. Simpson suggested that some ads should appear on the editorial page, and the boss snapped back: "You listen to me. You've got ads on the front page, ads practically every place except the editorial page. Out of 48 pages I've got one lousy page for my stuff, and the hell with you."[57] Editors even were allowed to throw ads out of the paper when a big news story demanded space. Simpson had to persuade advertisers to reschedule the insertions.

Simpson drew up the paper's first "standards of acceptability," a manual detailing which ads were considered too offensive or dishonest, a particular problem in a city with as many seasonal residents as St. Petersburg. Often fly-by-night shysters would look on transients as easy pickings through trick ads.

One standard was loosened after Simpson arrived. The tradition of Straub and Paul Poynter that banned alcohol from *Times* ads still stood long after Nelson, a social drinker, took over. Simpson aimed first at beer.

"Why should we advertise all other kinds of nutritious food when we leave out beer, Nelson?" Simpson cajoled him. "Beer is a food too!"

"It is?"

After thinking it over, Poynter allowed beer advertising, but hard liquor remained forbidden. This policy continued for nearly a decade. A delegation of clergymen visited the paper in 1955 to protest what they thought was unlimited alcoholic-beverage advertising. Poynter decided that if they paid so little attention that they were unaware that hard liquor ads were not running, why not go ahead and run them? So he did.

Before suburban shopping centers opened their cornucopia of advertising in the 1950s, downtown department stores were the mainstay of daily newspapers. St. Petersburg lacked such a retailer until 1948, when the Tampa-based Maas Brothers chain opened a branch in St. Petersburg's downtown. It was a huge success, and it advertised heavily. Webb's City remained the best all-weather source of ad money. Doc Webb thought *Times* advertising was his salvation, but he knew the dependence was mutual. For public consumption, Webb appeared to despise Poynter. But the two viewed each other with grudging admiration. While they were poles apart politically and socially, their instincts were the same: Both wanted to help the little man. Doc wanted to give him the necessities of life as cheaply as possible, and Poynter wanted to give him the ultimate in food for thought.

In the dawn of the civil rights movement, St. Petersburg's blacks set out to get official approval of an integrated beach. Doc Webb told Simpson he and others wanted to take out a full-page ad opposing the plan. Simpson checked it with Poynter, who refused unless the protesters put their names in the ad. Blacks by then made up a sizable part of retail trade, and this would have alienated them. Webb pointed out that Poynter did not sign his editorials. "Nobody has any doubt about who is running this paper," Poynter replied, "but the public has never heard of the group behind this ad." The ad never ran.

Despite Simpson's success with bold new ways, most *Times* executives continued to move at their leisurely pace. Some department heads dated back to Paul Poynter's time, and they liked his easygoing tolerance. Certainly they could not be expected to take it seriously when the young boss let fly with high-sounding pieties about the mission of a newspaper. That was for public consumption, they figured. Poynter was too busy getting *Congressional Quarterly* started in the late 1940s to take radical action at the *Times*. But after his father's death he made his next big move in management-building, and changes came rapidly after that.

Poynter had long admired Claud F. ("Doc") Weimer, who had been his managing editor when he was editor of the *Columbus Citizen* in Ohio. They shared the scar of having been fired by Scripps-Howard for policy decisions, although at different times. Poynter knew that Weimer was tough enough not to be a yes man, someone who would speak up if he thought one of the boss's ideas was impracticable, so he hired Weimer down with the title of associate editor. In reality he served as a troubleshooter, particularly on the business side.

One of Weimer's first jobs was to bring more order into the paper's budgeting. He was shocked to find that Max Ulrich's way of avoiding shortfalls was to tuck miscellaneous reserve funds around various places in the budget. It also fell to Weimer to handle the 1952 pressmen's strike. He refused to give in, and his solution was to hire people with engineering ability to be replacements. Heart trouble cut short Weimer's rise, however, and he died in an early experiment with open-heart surgery in 1955.

Poynter passionately believed the staff made up the heart of the newspaper. It was up to him, he felt, to put together the best possible people, give them the best possible benefits—and make them work to their limits. He also had a theory that many people could fill all sorts of jobs if only management could discover their hidden talents. So Poynter plunged into the heart of scientific personnel management in 1951. A young industrial psychologist named Byron Harless got a call from the St. Petersburg editor, who said he had read about Harless's work and was interested in talking with him.[58]

Harless, a Virginian, had earned a master's degree at the University of Florida and later taught there. During World War II he served as an aviation psychologist. He started a partnership in Tampa that soon built a national reputation for showing executives how to choose management personnel. He had utility companies, banks, hospitals, and department stores as clients, but no newspapers.

When they first met, Poynter questioned Harless closely. The *Times* had a previous linkage with a personnel consultant, and it had not worked out. The two warmed to each other, and Poynter poured out his dreams to Harless. He wanted to make the *Times* one of the top papers in the country, although he had too much turnover and wanted to improve his hiring in all ranks from unskilled personnel to executives. Above all, Poynter told the psychologist, he did not want a consultant who would play God, someone who would treat employees like pawns.

Poynter checked Harless out thoroughly, summoned him back in two weeks, and asked him to set up an experimental program. For a social scientist it was a dream come true to have so much latitude. Harless first had to learn the newspaper business. He could live on little sleep, so he spent three or four weekdays each week plus Saturday and Sunday doing all sorts of jobs at the paper while keeping up his Tampa practice.

With Poynter's encouragement, Harless put together a personnel program that both protected the company from mistakes in hiring and opened up transfers for existing staffers who had hidden abilities. All newcomers had to take a battery of tests that touched intimate parts of one's psyche, such as asking hard-bitten war veterans about their dating habits. Even existing personnel had to submit, amid much grumbling. But Harless maintained that no employee was hurt by the results, only allowed to move up.

Job applicants faced much more than tests. Patterned interviews probed dim corners not usually reached. Investigators checked behind job records into realities of past performance. College transcripts were analyzed line by line.

Poynter, Harless realized, was looking for people like himself. He wanted staffers who doted on their jobs twenty-four hours a day and were never satisfied with what they did. This meant frayed nerves for some who could not take it.

On one occasion the psychologist was watching as pictures from a major story were spread on the desks and floor in the managing editor's office. The *Times* had flown a full crew 1,000 miles to Corpus Christi, Texas, to report on a disastrous chemical explosion. Glowing with pride, the newsmen narrowed choices to a half-dozen photos to print. Then they heard Poynter's feet tapping downward on the private staircase that connected his office with the managing editor's.

"What do you have here?" he asked cheerily. He looked over the pictures and said, "They're not any good. You can't use those."

"Well, they're all we've got," he was told.

"Then get your ass back on the plane and get some more."

Harless counseled Poynter that he should soften employees' disappointment when they made mistakes, but Poynter refused. He would stack tremendous demands on them and expect the best possible results.

One day Harless got a call from a young staffer who had made a smashing success on the *Times*. The youth said the experience had been a great opportunity but he had to quit because he could take the torment no longer. So Harless told Poynter he was burning people out with his demands (long before burnout had been widely recognized). The editor was deeply touched, and tears came to his eyes. "I don't want to hurt people—I don't want to cause them these kinds of personal problems. You've got to help me not do that." Harless saw that Poynter was sincere. But he was nearly fifty, and his ways were deeply rooted.

The two men began putting together a wide-ranging personnel program—pensions, health and life insurance, long-term incentives—that far exceeded the norm for newspapers. Most journalists had nothing more than Social Security to look forward to. The keystone of the project was to be a profit-sharing trust. Harless found a consultant who designed a plan. Poynter started grilling him about how it would help the average staff member.

"Sir," he said, meaning he was on the offensive, "tell me again what the benefits are."

The consultant told him the beauty of the plan was that the company, not the employee, would keep control of the money. What's more, the worker would have to stay in service a long time before he could carry off his profits. Poynter grew furious. "I don't want to handcuff somebody! I want that to be called a 'Go to hell, Nelson Poynter' fund. If they don't want to stay here, they can say, 'Nelson, I'm taking my money and going.' " Poynter wanted short-term vesting of employee benefits, unheard of at that time and rare three decades later.

Another of Poynter's uncommon habits was his openness to women and black employees. He had no affirmative action program—the concept did not exist then—but rather was blind to the supposed debilities of such workers. He encouraged inclusion of girls in a high school training program.

Harless, like several other young executives, became like a son to Poynter. As a trained observer of minds, Harless was fascinated with how his boss's intellect worked. He was entirely uninhibited, Harless decided, "a tremendous lateral and upside-down thinker." But the psychologist doubted that Poynter would have flourished nearly as well if he were not in charge of in the operation.

Poynter loved to tinker with others' lives, somewhat as his mother always had, although he was less overbearing than she was. He would urge staff members to take better jobs elsewhere if he thought it benefited them. A favorite ploy was planning people's vacations for them unasked. Once Harless, coming up for a vacation, discovered that Poynter had mapped out the whole itinerary—dates, routes, hotels, and more. Poynter realized that his zeal was excessive. "No one ever takes my travel suggestions," he complained to his mother. "I would go broke as a travel agent though I think it is a fine career."[59] The editor also found delight in children. When he encountered an employee's family, he would drop everything to get to know the kids.

Only once did Poynter flatly turn down Harless's ideas. He invited his consultant to lunch at the Yacht Club and asked him to be completely candid about his views. Harless responded, "You know, one of the things I'm having trouble understanding is this dual management situation where you have a general manager who operates the business side, and over here you've got an executive editor. I think that's inefficient."

Poynter listened quietly as Harless continued. "Another thing I find is that you have a tremendous impact on the people in this organization. I can walk in that door on a Monday morning and tell whether you're in the building. If an executive is not sure of himself, you can have a negative effect on him. You've cut off communication, and you may cut off contributions he can make. You might consider moving your office from the fourth floor up to the top floor."

Without criticizing, Poynter gave Harless a lecture on the need for balance between editorial and business and convinced him of its wisdom. Poynter conceded his impact on people, but he refused to move his office. Harless later realized Poynter needed to be in the center, involved with everything about the paper and its people.

Poynter was so delighted with what was emerging from the personnel venture that he put Harless before national organizations to boast about the vision. It did attract attention, and many publishers drew on it.

Pin-Striped Camelot

Tom Harris was a frustrated newspaper designer, but the paper's stodgy, muddy, and sober appearance did not show it. Little could be done as long as the paper did not have a production operation that came up to the current standard of technology or went beyond it. Poynter had put the union problem behind him, but he still needed a professional hand controlling the printing.

In 1951, a man who took a Florida winter vacation every year with his wife decided he ought to move there. He was a forty-year-old native of Montreal named Donnell Shortell who was composing room foreman of the small daily newspaper in Asbury Park, New Jersey. A compact, balding man with an air of friendly vitality, Shortell applied to the *St. Petersburg Times* for work.

Nelson and Henrietta Poynter talked with Shortell and had his background checked out. The Asbury Park printing plant was a place where perfection came first. Shortell had gone to a General Electric engineering school for a while and had run the nonunion newspaper shop for more than a decade.

Poynter decided that Shortell could grow with the paper and pick up ideas quickly, and hired him as mechanical superintendent. Shortell soon learned that innovating was the only way to keep Poynter off his back, which meant always making the product better than the year before. Improvement was a fetish with Poynter. He continually nagged manufacturers of printing equipment to develop new approaches. He had never been a printer, but this did not deter him from demanding better work.

In 1950 the *Times* bought and tore down an old two-story building next to the eight-story downtown tower it had occupied since 1926. On the site the paper spent $400,000 to put up a four-story structure linked to its 1920 building. The new building housed eight new units of press. Added to its previous units, this allowed printing of 128 pages, twice the previous capacity. The new presses occupied the first two floors, running sleekly behind plate-glass windows and offering a show for passersby. Within two years, though, it was plain that these machines would be overloaded by the end of the decade.

Ironically, many publishers felt letterpress printing was doomed because it produced unattractive newspapers in all but a few cases, such as the *New York Herald Tribune*. And everyone knew that offset was the technique of the future. The snag was the lack of presses fast and large enough for a major daily. Papers that needed offset most were those that emphasized photography, as it made pictures look immeasurably better than the blurry images in letterpress. The *Times* was developing one of the best photo departments in the country; only offset could do it justice.

Poynter's solution was to keep improving letterpress printing while phasing in offset for parts of the paper that could be printed in advance. A Sunday magazine section, *The Floridian,* was the guinea pig for offset. Poynter bought a Goss offset with every gadget available, and press crews slaved to make it turn out a masterpiece, whetting Poynter's appetite for offset. From then on, letterpress seemed a compromise with the future.

Meanwhile, Poynter was caught up again in his dream of cold type, which had gone on the shelf after recovery from the 1945 printers' strike. Poynter had joked, "I never have a bad idea—only a premature one." In 1954 he was able to bear this out. The *Times* became the first newspaper in the country to use photocomposition with typesetting machines designed for that purpose. They were used for advertising, where the need for flexibility was greatest. Life became easier for printers making up Doc Webb's splashy display ads.

The same year Poynter made a breakthrough with another dream— color photography. This always had been impractical in newspapers because of the speed and volume of press runs and the slow process of preparing color photos for printing. Now the *Times* collaborated with the Rochester Institute of Technology in experiments using the Spectacolor technique, which opened up a new world of visual journalism. In 1956 the *Times* was one of the first customers for the newly developed Curtis color analyzer. It sharply reduced the time needed to prepare true-to-life news and feature photos for newspaper printing. Soon the paper would become known as one of the most colorful in the nation.

In 1953 there appeared in a national trade bulletin a help-wanted ad for a "creative financial officer." This did not seem to be an oxymoron to a thirty-two-year-old newspaper bookkeeper in Little Rock, Arkansas, named John B. ("Jack") Olson. The ad gave no indication where the job was, but he believed the idea that someone cared about what a money man thought was novel.

Olson sent in a reply, and he found out that the curious ad had come from the *St. Petersburg Times,* which was gaining a reputation outside

Florida. The 1945 strike and NLRB fight had attracted some attention, as had the personnel program. Poynter had bragged about the paper in trade journal ads, and other publishers liked to visit to see the experiments in production.

Soon Olson was in Byron Harless's office undergoing three days of testing. This struck Olson as an invasion of his privacy, and he discovered that Poynter sympathized. But the editor felt that the matter was too important to pass up a complete scrutiny of the candidate. Olson passed the ordeal—only, Poynter joked, because he had married a girl from Indiana.

Olson's title was comptroller-treasurer. His first job was straightening out the paper's tangled money matters. Soon after arriving he found that a load of newsprint was routinely awaiting delivery to the *Times,* but there wasn't enough cash in the bank to pay for it. He spent a whole day scurrying around to scrape up the payment.

The new man won Poynter's confidence quickly. This was a mixed blessing, because when it happened the editor's normal shyness slipped away and he could talk a person to death. There were phone calls at midnight when ideas struck Poynter, an insomniac. And Sunday afternoons there were long, pleasant walks on the beach. Olson enjoyed seeing Poynter's mind work. He thought his boss was something of a frustrated educator, because he wanted to teach the world the right way to publish a newspaper. But he was determined to do it by example, not lecture.

Liberal as he was, Poynter told Olson about his admiration for Colonel Robert R. McCormick, arch-conservative owner of the *Chicago Tribune.* The colonel's independence, assertive in-charge style, and success appealed to Poynter. He also held much affection for Roy Howard, who had fired him from Scripps-Howard.

As Poynter let down his guard somewhat, Olson was able to see that his usually cheerful facade was not his only mood. There were times of depression. The fact that the rest of the world lagged behind his pace disappointed him. Manufacturers of printing equipment were a particular bane, as they seemed to shrug off Poynter's pleas to move faster. The impurities of politics also weighed heavily.

Poynter's total immersion in his newspaper also struck the younger man. Poynter hardly knew his neighbors, but Olson was impressed as much as Harless with their employer's kindness to *Times* people. With tact and good taste, the Poynters would press upon their aides presents

Alvah H. Chapman (*right*) put the *Times* on a highly profitable path in the 1950s as general manager. John B. Olson (*left*) continued the growth as his successor. *St. Petersburg Times.*

from their trips abroad. Once when Olson visited them in Washington, Nelson brought out some tweed they had bought in Wales and insisted that Olson have a suit made of it as a gift.

Although Poynter and Harless found good talent for the management team, the editor longed for someone who could be the capstone— a general manager. Poynter wrote his mother that it was difficult to find people "that would suit me."

Poynter found his man in June 1953. He was Alvah H. Chapman, Jr., a tall, handsome thirty-two-year-old who was the third generation in a publishing family. Chapman's father owned a small daily in Bradenton, Florida, across the bay from St. Petersburg. Young Alvah graduated in business from a military college, the Citadel, where he was cadet commander. He flew thirty-seven combat missions as a B-17 pilot in World War II, coming home with a chestful of medals, including the Distinguished Flying Cross. Before he moved to St. Petersburg, he was business manager of the *Ledger-Enquirer* in Columbus, Georgia, a paper that Poynter admired.

Poynter was delighted with his new man. He bragged to his mother that Chapman, a Methodist and Republican, was fitting into St. Petersburg quickly. "He is thoroughly sold on the fact we can make this the best newspaper in the country—and what a relief he will be. He will be better than any we have ever had in the past—and by October I'll be able to take a real vacation."[60] The appointment allowed Poynter and Harris to spend more time on the editorial product. When Chapman started work in September the editor told his mother that he felt as if he had just inherited a million dollars.[61]

The first thing Chapman decided was that profits were too low and could be improved with good management. The *Times* seemed to him a laid-back operation, with too many executives not up to their duties. Budgeting was slipshod, planning was short-term, coordination of departments was lacking, and costs were out of control.

Despite his background, Chapman realized that newspapers were evolving from intimate family operations into professional institutions. He was determined to put the *Times* on the cutting edge of that trend. And he would do it with what Poynter esteemed most—management by goal-setting. One thing was clear: Chapman expected and got delegation of authority from Poynter. The editor restrained himself from meddling in day-to-day details and did not go around Chapman to his subordinates. Poynter's avalanche of ideas continued, but Chapman saw himself as a counterweight who could say no to the boss. He did not like to chat over the phone at midnight, and Poynter desisted from calling him.

The process was messy at first. Several department heads were fired, and men who would play key roles in later development came in as part of the Chapman team. Among them were Joe Yauch, former circulation director for Long Island's *Newsday,* a rotund giant whose affable exterior masked a driving genius for expanding the paper's sales. Clifton Camp came in from an accounting firm to be Jack Olson's assistant, learned the Chapman methods, and carried them into later decades while rising toward the top. Poynter not only supported

Chapman as he put together his new team but left town to give him a free hand. He was delighted to be able to take long foreign trips with Henrietta.

To get his ideas over, particularly to young men like Olson and Camp, Chapman set up a training program. Only half in jest they called it the *"Times* College of Newspaper Knowledge." It was an honor for staffers to be chosen for the twenty-six-week course, because its purpose was not only to learn their own jobs but those of others. Chapman and Poynter felt that any executive must understand the problems of his colleagues. That way, when a department head asked something of a person, he could be realistic.

A cadre of young comers signed up for the program. Junior-level editors were invited, but the newsroom generally scorned the idea. Trainees also had to stumble through the paces of other jobs. Cliff Camp found himself seated at a typewriter in the sports department. He considered the sports editor, Bill Beck, something of a sadist. Beck handed him a picture and told him to write a cutline. Camp had to look in the dictionary to find out what a cutline was. The ordeal developed toughness—as well as personal links. Graduates felt a kinship for people they had studied and breakfasted with, and this feeling lasted for decades as they rose in the ranks.

Chapman did not consider the *Times* to be in precarious condition when he arrived. Although Nelson Poynter privately criticized his father for "almost putting under" the paper with his real estate deals, Nelson's financial goals were modest—lower than Chapman's, in fact.

Self-confidence was Chapman's strong point, and he knew he could raise profits. He cut expenses by putting them in the hands of people who could control them. Too many slips, and the executive who missed the mark would find his bonus cut. There were staff reductions, particularly in production. Ad revenues were good when Chapman came, thanks to Simpson's direction, but together they pushed to broaden the sources.

Newspapers traditionally tried only to make more money than they spent. If there were profits, owners would decide how to use them. Chapman was determined to do something new—set up a budget that would project how much each department needed, how money would be raised, how much profit could be expected, even what would be done with the profit.

The first results were ragged. Department heads would either underestimate their needs to appear frugal or would set them too high so as to look good when they spent less. It took years for executives to become comfortable with Chapman's plan, but eventually it worked. Projections of even five or ten years could be made.

Congressional Quarterly represented a drain on the *Times*'s finances when Chapman arrived. Most people at the paper seemed willing to shoulder this burden, and Poynter was able to devote more time to the Washington operation because of Chapman's help. Within four years, *CQ* was in the black.

Poynter liked to show off his blueprint for management, and he encouraged Chapman to make speeches. The American Press Institute, an in-service training operation, invited him to lecture, and many of the *Times*'s ideas spun off into other papers. Poynter treated Chapman not so much as a son but as a social equal. He steadily decreased his own salary while raising Chapman's until the manager made more money. When Chapman reproached him about this, Poynter seemed surprised: "You're taking over work I used to have to do, so why shouldn't you get more?"

Profits trebled at the *Times* after four years, while the economy was going up at a modest pace. Chapman, clearly a young man on the rise, left in 1957 to become part owner and president of the dailies in Savannah, Georgia. He went on to manage the *Miami Herald* and later became chairman of its parent chain, Knight-Ridder. Systems he set up at the *Times* proved so workable that some were in use decades later. And his stint spawned a generation of newly trained business executives who would continue working into the 1980s, making ever-bigger profits.

The Trouble with Television

For someone as shy of the public glare as Nelson Poynter, he had a way of getting drawn into it. Every few years something would thrust him against his will into headlines. In the 1950s it was television.

Americans were in a frenzy after World War II to make up for lost fun time. Unmarried young people cozied up to drive-in movies and their opportunity for forbidden groping. Those who had married and settled into suburban living wanted television, the magic lantern that had been dimmed by the war.

Under this pressure, the Federal Communications Commission

(FCC) plunged into assigning channels. Entrepreneurs hired expensive Washington lawyers to help them get what were generally considered licenses to make money. Poynter, like many newspaper owners, already had a radio station, and like many he decided to bid for a television operation.

The FCC had passed out 108 of a projected 2,000-plus licenses when it decided in 1948 to put a freeze on the process. It saw the enormous competition ahead and wanted to plan carefully the jigsaw puzzle of signal locations and strengths to minimize channel interference.

Before the freeze, Florida had gotten only two channels, in Jacksonville and Miami. The entire west coast was left out, and in that area only a determined few with large antennas could pick up a weak image from Jacksonville. Meanwhile, Suncoast residents had to content themselves with radio, then in its last days of glory before the television deluge. Paradoxically, it was becoming clear that a station that tried harder to provide local public service was only taking away time from what the public wanted most, the high-powered entertainment of national network programming.

Tampa radio stations were the only ones in the bay area with the two major networks. WFLA, owned by the *Tampa Tribune,* had NBC, and WDAE, the afternoon *Tampa Times*'s property, had CBS. The two lesser networks were heard from St. Petersburg. City-owned WSUN had ABC, and Poynter's WTSP could get only news and sports from its affiliation with Mutual. Radio also was proving that, while each city might support its own newspapers, the Tampa Bay area was one big market for broadcasters. This point was not lost on those who sought a television license.

In radio Poynter proved his true colors as a broadcaster. To him, WTSP offered an opportunity for public service. Entertainment and advertising profits always came second to political talk shows, bake sales, educational programs, club notes, and the like. Poynter took delight in doing what the government unsuccessfully twisted the arms of other station owners to do.

Poynter also marched to a different beat by insisting in editorials that the government reserve valuable VHF channels for educational stations (ETV), which later would become public television. VHF— very high frequency—included channels two through thirteen, those with longer reach and thus more possibility for selling commercials.

With so few VHF channels available for so many bidders, other newspapers grumbled that educational VHF allocations would be wasteful.

To Poynter, ETV held out the prospects of surgeons' being trained by watching delicate operations on a screen. He predicted a vast improvement in all kinds of education, where films already had proven invaluable. "Television offers everything that the talking pictures do, plus instantaneous transmission of current events and, after the initial investment, much lower costs," the *Times* editorialized.[62]

The paper started calling for ETV allocation while the FCC's freeze was on, arguing that then was the best time because commercial pressures were lower than they would be in the future. The FCC did not act then but later reserved 242 VHF licenses for education.

On Easter Sunday 1952, the FCC opened its treasure chest. It trumpeted the good news that it had figured out how to assign 2,052 licenses to 1,291 communities by opening up seventy more channels above VHF channel thirteen. These stations were in the UHF (ultra-high frequency) range, which had a much smaller reach; thus they were less likely to interfere with stations in other cities. This was little comfort to private license-seekers. UHF stations were considered commercial poison, with little effectiveness in satisfying advertisers. Besides, a normal television set would not pick up UHF signals. A new set or an expensive converter would be needed.

The outlook was grim for the Tampa Bay area. St. Petersburg and Tampa would have to share four channels, fewer than expected. One of these was channel three for educational television, and one was channel thirty-eight, in the UHF range. The smaller cities in the area, Clearwater, Bradenton, and Sarasota, got only one UHF slot each. This left only two commercial VHF channels, eight and thirteen, for the entire region. Before the freeze there had been five commercial applicants.

The villain was Florida's population boom. Eleven metropolitan areas received VHF allocations, presenting a tricky interference problem. Most of these fast-growing cities were on the state's narrow peninsula and could not use the same channels.

Joe Kelley, WTSP's manager, was waiting in Washington, armed with engineering evidence, when the Easter announcement came. He and a *Times* attorney worked around the clock to revise the prefreeze application. Three stenographers hurried to finish the sixty-page form.

Tuesday morning, when the FCC opened, Kelley was at the door, ready to become the nation's first applicant under the new allocations.

Poynter requested channel eight, for which another strong contender was the *Tampa Tribune*'s WFLA. A group of Tampa and St. Petersburg businessman not connected with a mass medium also applied. All three petitioners for channel thirteen were from Tampa. Thus, Poynter's was the only pure-Pinellas bid.

The City of St. Petersburg's WSUN applied for UHF channel thirty-eight, along with a little-known applicant who soon withdrew. This would saddle WSUN with the technical problems of UHF, but it also would mean it could get on the air first amid what was shaping up as a lengthy battle over the VHF channels. Television fever struck St. Petersburg as stores began selling sets and WSUN tooled up at its studios at the tip of the Million-Dollar Pier.

The channel eight case ground on for a year in Washington. Poynter told the FCC that he had already installed $50,000 worth of television equipment and had bought forty acres east of Tampa for an antenna. He had long before turned the WTSP studio into a mock television operation, organizing events like the winners-losers postelection party as a closed-circuit broadcast. There was an auditorium seating 250 to watch the action.

One of the first arguments Poynter offered in his application for a channel was his Standards of Ownership, making them public for the first time. As for programming, Poynter flashed before the commission his dream of a station anchored in local needs. Programs would include a fishing show starring Rube Allyn and one called "Can You Draw It?" that featured famous cartoonists living in the area. Also on the list were "Know Your Policeman," "World Affairs," and a cooking school.

Although WTSP had $300,000 cash, it proposed to borrow most of the start-up costs from the *Times* and from Jefferson Standard Life Insurance Company. Poynter predicted that he would lose less than $5,000 the first year.

The battle centered on two bidders, the *Times* and the *Tribune,* and it was uphill for Poynter. Tampa was the larger city, and WFLA was a big-league radio station with a major network. Its most vulnerable point was the fact that it had absentee owners. Daily newspapers in Richmond, Virginia, owned the *Tribune* and its broadcast facilities.

Even so, Poynter did not hesitate to come to the *Tribune*'s defense when he thought his rival had suffered unduly. In doing so, he took on the governor of Florida. Governor Fuller Warren, with whom the *Times* had a love-hate relationship, sent the FCC a letter asking it to deny channel eight to WFLA. The *Tribune* had consistently criticized the controversial governor. Rather than relishing his advantage, Poynter criticized Warren in an editorial for an "unwarranted and unwelcome intrusion" in the FCC case.

Warren snapped back with another letter to the FCC. It accused Poynter of "an inordinate craving for political power." Although he often supported worthy causes, Warren wrote, the editor was widely regarded as emotionally unstable and "a man of radical and erratic tendencies."[63] The wire services shied away from carrying the letter because they considered it libelous. The *Times* printed it and gave permission to any other paper to do the same.

Unlike the other two bidders, who presented a parade of community figures as witnesses praising their abilities, the *Tribune* put only its officials and technicians on the stand. Testimonials from civic leaders came as letters.

In mid-1953 the examiner who had heard the case submitted his recommendation to the full commission: Give channel eight to the *Tribune*. The examiner found the three bidders equally qualified in most ways, but he gave the edge to WFLA's larger, better, and more accessible studios.

It had been the longest and costliest TV hearing in the FCC's history. Both losers filed protests to the findings, but these actions were on relatively minor grounds compared with a conspiracy against Poynter that was occurring behind scenes as the FCC moved toward action on its examiner's recommendation. Poynter apparently did not know about it until nearly two decades later.

One of the FCC members, Robert E. Lee, was a former FBI agent, and he contacted his old employer about the case. He said he had found in the application files some allegations that Poynter had Communist affiliations. He also passed on a letter Poynter had sent to the FCC dealing with the allegations.

Two points in the letter raised hackles at FBI headquarters. For one thing, Poynter apparently had mistakenly recalled the date of the 1952 letter FBI Director J. Edgar Hoover had sent him about a minor incident and had reported a date of April 19, 1953. (See chapter 7.) Second, he had said that David Loth, an editor he hired for *Congressional Quarterly* who testified before a congressional committee about

Communist activities, had been cleared by the FBI. On an internal memo, Hoover had written, "We clear no one!" This was a touchy point inside the bureau. Its often-voiced position was that it did not clear or condemn anyone but rather provided information.[64]

Hoover approved of Lee's being "confidentially advised" of what was in the FBI files about Poynter. Lee was to be told that Hoover's 1952 letter "was obviously being misused by Poynter and was a pure fabrication."[65] Once the FBI agent had told this to Lee, the commissioner devised an elaborate scenario to make sure that Poynter did not receive the license. It involved arranging for a formal letter from the FCC chairman, Rosel Hyde, asking Hoover about the accuracy of the Georgetown letter's date and requesting "any other pertinent information you can make available." After receipt of a response from Hoover, Lee said, another FCC hearing was to be held and he would be in a position to vote formally against granting the station to Poynter. Lee predicted that "a couple of other Commissioners will follow . . . and that probably will be an end to the issue. It will not be necessary to have hearings on any subversive, derogatory information on Poynter."[66]

The plan worked. More than a year after the examiner's judgment, the full commission made its award—to the *Tribune*'s WFLA. Four commissioners—a bare majority—had voted for WFLA. There were two votes for the *Times*'s WTSP and one for the third applicant. Again, the losers appealed the decision, asking the FCC to reconsider. Poynter's main argument concerned the *Tribune*'s absentee ownership.

Poynter's appeal meant Tampa Bay area people would have to wait still longer for television during a squabble they cared nothing for. Poynter, apparently sensitive to this, suggested to the other two bidders that all three jointly operate the channel, getting it on the air immediately. Poynter publicized this suggestion while WFLA mulled it over but then rejected it. The idea was contrary to sound business practice, WFLA management said, and still would have to be approved by the FCC. That would mean even more delay.

Finally, in December 1954, the FCC denied the appeal and concluded that WFLA must have channel thirty-eight. It went on the air two months later with festive coverage of Tampa's Gasparilla festival. Poynter filed suit in federal court to block the award, but the suit failed.

Washington columnist Drew Pearson, whom Poynter had long admired, went to the *Times*'s aid with a report that the *Tribune* had received the license because of political influence. He asserted that an assistant to President Eisenhower had decided that the Richmond newspapers must be rewarded for their editorial support in the presidential election. The commission was leaning toward the *Times* when the White House aide influenced Republican commissioners to swing over for the *Tribune*, Pearson alleged.[67] Nothing came of the charges.

Poynter's radio station hung heavily on his hands, weighted by the fruitless nine-year struggle for a TV channel. Besides, he didn't like the new rock-and-roll music that was gaining airtime on disk jockey shows. In 1956 he announced the sale of WTSP to brothers Farris, Joe, and Sam Rahall. At first glance it appeared that Poynter was washing his hands of broadcasting. But in his sale announcement he noted that the *Times* still held forty acres on which to put an antenna. "We . . . are retaining the site for possible Suncoast TV needs in the future," he said.[68]

The next year the FCC announced it was allotting another VHF channel, channel ten, to the Bay Area. The frequency would be shared with Miami, and to minimize interference the transmitter had to be near New Port Richey, thirty miles north of St. Petersburg. Poynter again entered the fray, as did the third-ranking applicant for channel eight and the Rahalls. That conflict would drag on for years, and Poynter also would emerge a loser from it.

Sibling Rivalry

Alice Poynter, who had the temerity of a battleship, saw her daughter as a person beset by fears. When Eleanor was a small girl she was afraid that every pair of new shoes was either too small or large. Her little brother, Nelson, would trot off to the store and exchange them, and she would reward him by reading books aloud.

When they grew up, Eleanor feared that Nelson's children would have a larger inheritance than hers and that his plans for expanding the *Times* facilities and founding *Congressional Quarterly* and a television station would reduce her dividends.[69]

Alice often expressed concern for Eleanor's health, and she told Nelson of the despair that came out in the daughter's letters. Of her work with the Sullivan paper, Eleanor said, "I cannot go on longer, Mother, I am so very, very tired—will have to give it up this year, am certain. . . . I just cannot go into that office—look at that desk again—and go on with it." Of her deeper feelings, she wrote, "I do not

Alice Poynter (*left*) felt free to make a number of foreign trips after her husband's death in 1950. Often she was accompanied by Eleanor, her daughter. *Poynter Library, University of South Florida, St. Petersburg, Florida.*

know why I am so fearful—of everything—of you—of Nelson—of everyone."[70] Nelson had hoped he would placate Eleanor by selling her two-fifths of the voting stock in 1947, but tension continued to build.

Three years later, a team of Indiana lawyers and auditors representing Eleanor showed up in St. Petersburg without prior notice. They demanded of Nelson's lawyer that they see the *Times*'s records. Although he was obligated only to show the audit, Nelson threw open his books.[71] Nelson was appalled as rumors about the visit spread through the city, seeing the request as a public slur on his integrity and management ability. Alice drove down to the office late one night to pledge Nelson all her resources to keep him from going to prison. He assured her that the investigators would find nothing amiss, as was the case.

Nelson decided he must acquire the preferred stock remaining in his family's hands after Paul Poynter's death in 1950. The 1945 agreement had given him the option to do this. He purchased his mother's stock at its price when issued, according to terms of the original deed. Eleanor objected to Alice's doing this, but she went ahead and sold it to him for $263,000, less $85,000 as a gift. Alice gave Eleanor the remaining two-thirds of the paper in Sullivan, the family home there, and the newspaper's cash account. In December 1955 Nelson exercised his option and offered Eleanor $100,000 to buy her 200 shares of voting stock. He believed she had shown herself incompatible with his Standards of Ownership.[72]

Alice was eager for Nelson to pursue the plan, even urging him to sue if necessary and offering to testify in his behalf. Of Eleanor, she wrote, "I am torn, between believing she is absolutely irresponsible and believing that she is just MEAN, Nelson." She indicated that in the unlikely event a court gave Eleanor more than $100,000, in her will she would penalize her daughter to the extent of the excess.[73]

Within two weeks Nelson had raised his offer to $200,000. Alice called this generous but not too much, as she hoped for a truce in family affairs and an end to name-calling. She thought Eleanor was suffering complete nervous exhaustion.[74] But few days had passed before Alice urged Nelson to raise the offer to $300,000. He sent back an angry letter saying Alice had "abused unmercifully" his love for his parents even though he had enabled them to have their highest standard of living ever.[75]

Eleanor refused the $200,000 offer, and the matter went into arbitration as provided in the 1947 agreement. She arrived in St. Petersburg in February 1956 with her attorney and a newspaper broker who was to serve as her member of an arbitration board. They met Nelson in the office of his lawyer along with his arbiter, a law school dean.

The Indiana group failed to reappear after the lunch break. Five days later Nelson received a letter from the Miami law office of U.S. Senator George Smathers, a political enemy of the *Times*. The letter said Eleanor had directed that the 1947 option agreement be repudiated.[76]

Nelson filed a federal suit in Indianapolis to force Eleanor to abide by the agreement, but he dropped it when Alice became upset that her children were litigating in public.[77] Eleanor brought a countersuit over Nelson's dealings with *Congressional Quarterly*. The *Times* company had voted Nelson a $30,000 bonus when he deeded the Washington publication to the *Times* in 1948. It had lost money afterward, beginning to break even the year Eleanor sued. She withdrew her action after her attorneys found insufficient basis.[78]

Nelson, resilient as ever, was glad the encounter had ended. He told his mother that he almost wept when she told him, "Sometimes I go a whole day without thinking of this." His desire for the stock did not justify such suffering, he said. On the last day of 1956, he looked forward to a happier new year. His lawyers felt he had not harmed the long-term stability of the company by dropping the suit.[79]

Now, he felt relief that he no longer was obliged to buy Eleanor's stock at a price higher than he could afford. But his expectation of an end to discord might have seemed ironic three decades later to those who succeeded him.

Chapter 7

Getting on the Map

In fall 1957, journalists' pulses ran fast, particularly in a world news capital like Tokyo, where Don Baldwin was serving as Far Eastern news editor for the Associated Press. The two Chinas were exchanging artillery volleys between islands near the coast, raising jitters about a new Asian war. Anti-Yankee feeling erupted when an American soldier shot a Japanese woman scavenging shells on a firing range. The Third World concept was being invented at a meeting in Bandung, Indonesia.

Baldwin covered all these events, often on the spot. At forty he was looking toward a breakthrough in his career. He had received word that he soon would head the AP's whole Far Eastern operation. Tokyo intrigued him and his family. They lived much like the Japanese in a turn-of-the century house.

Baldwin's superior, the bureau chief, had the chore of playing host to a steady stream of junketing American newspaper owners, usually seeking a good time. When an AP member editor and his wife from St. Petersburg, Florida, arrived, however, the chief assigned Baldwin to entertain them. Baldwin gave them the full treatment—the best room at the Imperial Hotel, with flowers, candy, their favorite liquor, magazines, and books—and, if they needed them, a private car with a bilingual driver, a shopping secretary, and other perks.

But Baldwin soon discovered that Nelson and Henrietta Poynter were not stuffed shirts eager to be charmed by the natives. They were keenly informed and interested in big issues, and they were prowling

Donald K. Baldwin brought in a surge of innovation when he became *Times* managing editor in 1958. *St. Petersburg Times*.

for column material. Nelson knew the Far East from his youthful stint as a journalist there, and Henrietta had visited before their marriage.

Baldwin treated the Poynters with his usual quick geniality, and he developed a friendship with Nelson. Henrietta and Madelyn, Baldwin's wife, had much in common. The couples traded social dinners, the Baldwins arranging a traditional evening at a former princely palace. There was no inkling that any business involving Don's future was afoot. After two weeks in Japan while Nelson showed Henrietta all his old haunts, the Poynters moved on with their Asian tour. There the matter ended, Baldwin thought. Two months later he got a letter from Poynter, back in St. Petersburg, asking if there were any conditions under which Baldwin would leave the AP. The response was yes—more money and time enough to put his affairs in order and to take a leisurely vacation coming home.

Poynter met the terms and invited Baldwin to become his managing editor. Most of Baldwin's career had been with a wire service, which has a simple staff structure little like that of a newspaper, so Baldwin did not really understand what a managing editor does. He went to the foreign correspondents' club, borrowed a book, and found out. Then he accepted. With a $1,500 gift from Poynter, Baldwin and his family took their long vacation.

It was a strange turn in a career that mostly had looked westward. Donald K. Baldwin's parents were from the farm country of southeastern Kansas. They moved to South Dakota, where he was born, and settled in Pocatello, Idaho, where the father taught chemistry at Idaho State University. It was a traditional family, with Baldwin's mother and two sisters remaining housewives. After finishing at the university, Baldwin worked on two small dailies in Idaho, rising to be city editor in Idaho Falls. He married and had a child.

Then one Sunday in December 1941 Baldwin and his family were on a picnic when they heard on the car radio that the Japanese had attacked Pearl Harbor. Baldwin rushed back to the office to put out an extra. Many of Baldwin's friends volunteered for service, and he planned to do the same at first. The draft board turned him down because of his work, and he stuck with newspapering.

Idaho Falls was a dull place in wartime—its only defense industry was growing potatoes for making alcohol. So Baldwin jumped at a chance to join a paper in Santa Barbara, California, where he knew he was getting close to the war when a Japanese submarine shelled a petroleum tank farm outside town.

After three months, Baldwin's chance at the big time came when the San Francisco bureau of the AP hired him. During his thirteen-year AP career he learned the precise, fast, punchy way a wire service person writes and processes news. Because San Francisco was the funnel for all AP news from East Asia, Baldwin gained an intimate if distant insight into the area.

Baldwin was troubled by his feelings about the war. He felt guilt at being out of uniform, although no one was ever hostile about it. He often gave blood and served in the Coast Guard Auxiliary, doing necessary but routine work in San Francisco Bay. Evacuation of the Nisei—American citizens of Japanese descent—disturbed him deeply. He had gone to school with some of them in Idaho, and he liked them. In his talks with Nisei in Santa Barbara, the feeling surfaced that rich white landowners were grasping for their lands.

At any rate, Baldwin's work absorbed him. Later he moved to the AP world headquarters in New York. He made it clear that he wanted to go abroad, so he was sent to Japan in 1955. He had followed the setting sun as far as he intended—until Nelson Poynter arrived.

The Kiddy Corps

Tom Harris at fifty was as hard-driving as ever. The slash of dark hair that remained on his balding head rose like an exclamation mark above penetrating eyes and bushy brows. He liked to laugh about the times he had been mistaken for Communist-hunter Joseph McCarthy. But Harris was only five years younger than Nelson Poynter, who wanted to pass his mantle on to someone who could lead the *Times* into the late twentieth century. Besides, Harris had learned newspapering in the 1920s, and Poynter wanted fresh ideas. He had rejuvenated the business department of the paper, and now he wanted to do the same on the editorial side.

Although Baldwin did not know it at the time, Poynter had been searching for a managing editor as part of his trip through Asia. Besides Baldwin, he hired Robert W. Brown, who had won a Pulitzer

Tom Harris, caricatured at right, enjoyed jokes about his resemblance to Senator Joseph McCarthy, no hero of his. *Jim Ivey.*

Prize in Columbus, Georgia, before working for the U.S. Information Agency in India. With Baldwin handling news, Brown was engaged to fill the void in writing editorials left by departure of Warren Pierce. It had been a fruitful shopping trip.

The vast respect and affection Harris inspired in his staff could have snarled the transition. But during the first three months after Baldwin arrived, Harris handed over authority at the pace Baldwin wanted, never undercutting him. The main problem was that staff members accustomed to taking their problems to Harris continued to do so, some defiantly.

Poynter orchestrated the changeover deftly. He assigned department heads to travel with Baldwin for a day or so, visiting news sources and getting to know Florida. To remove the problem of divided loyalties, Poynter acted boldly. He sent Harris off on a three-month tour through Latin America. Harris relished the experience, sending back detailed political features.

It was a wrenching change for Baldwin, who knew little about how a sizable daily newspaper was put out. But he met the challenge head-on, working eighteen-hour days at first and haunting various departments with constant questions.

Soon after he arrived Harris remarked: "They shot the weather map half-tone and it should have been line." It mystified Baldwin, so he went to the engraving department and asked for a lesson on the subject. Step by step, he reduced his ignorance.

To the staff, Baldwin was an exotic import. He let people call him what they wanted to, and younger ones down to copy boys called him Don. Older ones kept their distance by using "Mr. B" or Mr. Baldwin.

One always knew when Baldwin was around. He was six feet three, loose-jointed and slim in a way that made him seem taller. He had a loud but modulated voice that would have been stagy except for his obvious sincerity. His moods were mercurial—usually upbeat and joking, turning hard-eyed and angry in an instant. His years with the wire service had trained him to work at lightning speed, and it took him two years to slow down even to the fast pace of a newspaper.

Above all, staffers recognized a throbbing new force that would demand the best they had to offer and then some. They might be struggling to come up with the right lead paragraph, and Baldwin would plop down alongside them at a typewriter, bat out a snappy version and say, "Why don't we try it like this?" Some reporters found it stimulating, others humiliating.

An incident that became legend at the *Times* occurred soon after Baldwin arrived. He and his wife were attending a play one night when he was called to the phone and told that Webb's City—still the city's largest shopping center—was on fire. He rushed back to the office. It was near deadline, and he sent all available reporters and photographers to the fire. They started pouring back their reports by phone, and Baldwin took them all. He alone wrote the story, spinning out a coherent account from the fragments as he got them. It was standard AP practice but a strange sight in the *Times* newsroom.

Baldwin clearly expected the same speed of all who worked for him. "Goddammit, let's get it *now*!" became the byword. He was particularly rankled by the leisurely pace of enterprise writers like Lowell Brandle and John Gardner, who would spend the morning filling up their notebooks, knock off for a long lunch, and amble back to the office trusting that their golden words would find their way onto paper. Baldwin could not accept their not writing their stories *before* lunch.

Just as Alvah Chapman had overhauled the business operation by bringing in a young team, so Baldwin fashioned his revolution by nailing together a corps of second-level editors who would approach each day's work as if it were a commando raid. All were under thirty, and most had replaced people twenty years older.

To the Young Turks it was an exciting opportunity. They knew Baldwin would not require them to stand in line to get promoted, waiting for senior people to die off. They responded by toiling madly, heedless as the workday ran up to fourteen hours. It was bad for their health and, if married, for their families. After the paper was put to bed every night, all would head for the same bar and let off steam. The more seasoned staff of the *Tampa Tribune* called them Baldwin's Kiddy Corps.

To older workers—anyone past forty—and those who could not adapt to Baldwin's ways, the newsroom seemed a jungle of backstabbers. This probably resulted from Baldwin's practice—heartily endorsed by Poynter—of giving young people even more responsibility than they could be expected to handle and see what happened. The result was fiendish energy and often brilliant work.

Some not hired by Baldwin found themselves squeezed out or left.

At a meeting of his editors after most of the changes had been made, Baldwin was whipping them up to undertake some new challenge. "You're all my guys," he exhorted them. "You're in your job because I put you there." Gloria Biggs, family editor and a holdover from the Harris days, quietly objected: "Not including me, Don." Baldwin just as casually replied, "Yes, that's right, Gloria." Within a few months she was gone.

Although few radicals worked on the *Times* staff in the early 1960s, most young journalists were caught up by social changes. They worshiped Poynter from a distance, but Baldwin seemed even more a practicing liberal on such new issues as race, gender equity, and ecology. Unlike most top editors he had no interest in writing columns and editorials. His grass-roots progressivism emerged if bad old ways impinged on operation of the paper.

Baldwin came to the *Times* when it was still defining the social status of brides by the size of their engagement pictures, ranging from quarter-page to one-column width. One day a caller, a woman obviously of modest means, was shown into his office. She was crying. She had just come from the women's department, where she had taken an announcement of her daughter's engagement and had asked that a large picture be run.

"They tell me I can't have one. And when I asked why, they get all sort of red-faced and can't explain. They say something about prominence. What does prominence have to do with it? Do you want me to tell you how much my husband and I love our daughter, how smart she is, what a wonderful man she's marrying?"

Baldwin couldn't tell whether she was naive or was goading him. Either way, she deserved an explanation, and he realized he could not pretend there was anything fair about the system. So he decreed that from then on all brides would get the same modest size of pictures. One of the first casualties was the debutante daughter of John B. Lake, publisher of the *Times* who moved in stylish circles.

Perhaps Baldwin's biggest challenge was getting along with Nelson Poynter. The top man had no less of an obsession for improvement than Baldwin but had his own ideas on how to achieve it. They never argued except behind closed doors, and staffers appreciated the degree to which the managing editor acted as a buffer between them and Poynter.

But when Poynter was excited about some news story, which was almost constantly, he would go straight to the journalist involved. In his incursions into the newsroom he was always courtly and gentle, phrasing his ideas as suggestions rather than commands. He had a maddening way of not finishing a sentence, or of using a pregnant pause when the staffer did not respond as Poynter wished. When he would telephone in his suggestions or when the victim was someone new to the paper, the treatment could shred a person's nerves. Those who were around for a while would pride themselves on learning "how to speak NP," as they called the boss's language.

Poynter was a prolific memo writer. Praise, which often came, usually was put down with green ink in a barely legible hand. He tended to type suggestions or criticisms.

Every editor who survived had to develop a strategy for dealing with Poynter's ideas, which could throw a wrench into the best-laid plans. The most apt learners knew not to argue but, if the idea was not feasible, to be ready with a good reason if they did not comply. The defense had to be good because Poynter knew newspapering inside and out.

One deskman who caught on fast was Robert J. Haiman. This alertness would propel him to the highest levels. Bob Haiman was wire editor, a position later dignified as national editor. It was a particularly hot spot, as Poynter was most primed on news out of Washington and from abroad, rather than local. It seemed that whenever Haiman was most rushed, there Poynter would be with a recommendation that he dig some forgotten nugget from the files and put it in the paper to give the reader the proper perspective.

Haiman lived with a gang of *Times* bachelors in a beach cottage. They played as hard as they worked, devoting spare time to drinking beer, playing softball, chasing women, and sitting around reading their own poetry while candles dripped on Chianti bottles.

On weekends they would party with young politicians and policemen or zoom around the state looking for a sports car rally so they could enter their MG. Once, during the early exciting days of space shots, they put out an edition telling of preparations for a dawn launch, then dashed 150 miles across the peninsula to Cape Canaveral and watched the event. They returned to work as the story was coming out. After a few years of this, Haiman, like most of the others, married and settled down. "Living together" was rare at the time.

Haiman was a transplant from Norwich, Connecticut. He attended

Robert J. Haiman was Don Baldwin's chief adjutant in the 1960s and became executive editor in 1976, but he lost out in the succession to control the newspaper and became president of the Poynter Institute. *St. Petersburg Times.*

prep school and went to the University of Connecticut to become a doctor or dentist like several relatives. But writing always was his hobby, and as a sophomore he decided to write the great American novel.

Haiman's parents planned to retire to Florida, so he transferred to the University of Florida, majored in journalism, and entered a select creative writing program. But because of two magnetic journalism professors, H. G. Davis, Jr., and Hugh Cunningham, he switched to a journalistic career as a senior.

Although he had a chance to start as an apprentice at *Time* magazine, Haiman liked Florida. Newspapers there were making money,
and job openings were plentiful. Haiman put an ad in an editors'
bulletin and received five offers, including one from the *Times*. He
wasn't sure where St. Petersburg was, but he went down and interviewed. Harris hired him at $75 a week, saying it was the most he had
ever paid such a recruit. Haiman came to work the same month that
Don Baldwin arrived. Baldwin spotted the young man as a comer and
wanted to test him on the copy desk, which seemed to Haiman to be
dull stuff compared with reporting. Haiman threatened to quit rather
than do it, but Baldwin asked him to try it for ninety days with the
assurance he could resume writing if he wished. Haiman fell in love
with the challenge of creating a newspaper and moved up rapidly.
When Baldwin became executive editor in 1966, he chose Haiman to
succeed him as managing editor.

Nelson Poynter liked to say staffers must make every effort to
produce Florida's best newspaper. Norms of journalistic hype held that
the only requirement for a newspaper to call itself the best of anything
was for it to decide that it was, and some editors of the *Times* thought
they could honestly award themselves the state crown. Year after year
Poynter countered that the honor had to be earned. From the time
Baldwin arrived, public recognition of the paper began building from
an occasional tap into a drumroll. Many staffers whose work caught
attention had been hired and trained by Tom Harris, but things were
coming together with Baldwin in charge.

Time magazine led its press section one week in 1959 with a story
that placed the *St. Petersburg Times* "among the South's most solid
newspapers."[1] The compliment was somewhat backhanded, as the
story focused on the large number of old people who subscribed. But it
gave the *Times* high marks for painstaking accuracy, a necessity with
so many cranky readers. One staffer was quoted as saying, "They
make you think twice before generalizing. They really read the newspaper. They not only have the time, they have the informed interest."

Newsweek also waxed lyrical about the paper's merits, particularly
Poynter's leadership.[2] The article referred to Poynter as "the Idea
Factory" with a "whiz-bang personality" who "nurses a passion for
his profession usually evident only in the greenest cub reporter."
Henrietta Poynter's vital role also was cited. Among the paper's strong
points, *Newsweek* said, were its aggressive news coverage (it had just

dispatched a team to cover the Berlin Wall crisis), the authority of editors to throw out ads to make room for news, and the practice of printing important speeches verbatim. As for integrity, it noted that Poynter had sold off the *Times*'s real estate holdings to avoid conflict of interest.

Awards soon began arriving in rapid succession. Photographers broke through to national prominence in 1963 when Bob Moreland was honored by the National Press Photographers Association for the best color photo of the year in 1963.

Reporters also began to hit their stride in national standing. Repeated exposés were coming from Frank Trippett in the Tallahassee bureau. Lowell Brandle trekked northward along the routes that winter visitors to St. Petersburg followed, uncovering gross abuses in speed traps. The University of Missouri gold medal for a distinguished newspaper represented one of the peaks of journalistic glory, close to the Pulitzer Prize in status, and in 1961 the *Times* won the award.

In 1961, Nelson Poynter shared national attention with James B. Reston (*left*), *New York Times* political writer, and Herbert Block, *Washington Post* cartoonist, when they won the University of Missouri Journalism School's Distinguished Service Award. *St. Petersburg Times.*

Winning most attention for *Times* reporting efforts were chiefs of the state capital bureau in Tallahassee. A series of men whose names became bywords in journalism before they moved on to national publications included Frank Trippett, Robert Sherrill, and Martin Waldron.

Trippett set the pace. He coined phrases that became part of history—porkchoppers for backwoods power brokers, the old he-coon for a populist congressman. He liked to say that a newspaperman in Tallahassee ought to have such prestige that the attorney general would tip his hat to the reporter. He was tall and courtly but could be blunt. When Byron Harless ran into resistance from Trippett to his psychological tests, he remarked, "Frank, you don't think these tests are worth a shit, do you?" Trippett replied, "Yeah, I think they're worth a shit." Trippett wrote a book on state legislatures that became known around the country. He later worked for *Time* magazine.

One of Trippett's successors, Martin ("Mo") Waldron became the most celebrated reporter in the *Times*'s history not only for his work but also for his personality. At thirty-seven he looked like a pro football lineman with a beer belly, a gruff voice, and bushy eyebrows that rivaled those of John L. Lewis. He could easily intimidate most politicians just by staring at them. A cigarette butt usually hung from his lips, and if he wanted to unnerve someone he would flip the butt with his lip so that the whole thing was held backward in his mouth, fully lit. Legend had it that he could down two steak dinners and eight martinis at a sitting.

Waldron often was unshaven and appeared to have slept in his clothes. Governor LeRoy Collins observed that, to Waldron, semi-formal dress was tucking in his shirttail. He liked to call himself "just a dumb kid from a turpentine camp in south Georgia." His car was a battered Ford convertible with the top gone, the back seat strewn with newspapers, potato chip bags, and stubs of pencils. When he found it full of rain water, he would just open the door, let it drain, and drive off.

Baldwin hired Waldron after he had made his mark with the Associated Press and the *Tampa Tribune*. Even though the Kiddy Corps editors dispirited some past-thirty reporters, Waldron soon made it clear he would not be regimented. Although reporters were expected to give their editors a budget at the start of every workday so they could lay out the stories into pages, Waldron blithely filed major

Martin ("Mo") Waldron, widely known for his colorful personality, led a team which won the *Times*'s first Pulitzer Prize in 1964. *St. Petersburg Times*.

unannounced stories long after the pages were planned. This offense might have gotten one fired, but Waldron could get away with it.

In fact, Waldron had little use for editors at all. When Haiman became managing editor at age thirty, he was apprehensive about many of the challenges before him—especially that of dealing with Waldron.

Haiman's phone rang. It was Waldron. "This my boss? Congratulations."

"Thank you, Martin. I appreciate that. I'll be coming up to Tallahassee real soon so we can have a chat."

"We don't need a chat. You gonna fuck with me?"

Haiman was shocked: "Well, of course not, Martin."

"Good. You don't fuck with me, I won't fuck with you. Call me anytime you're in town and we'll have lunch."

Waldron's integrity and zeal made him popular with whistle-blowers. One call concerned the Florida Turnpike Authority, an agency set up to build a toll expressway down the peninsula before the days of interstates. The authority was nearly autonomous, and its finances had not been audited for several years. The caller, former pilot of a rented plane used by the authority's chairman, claimed to have the goods on his former bosses, and Waldron talked him into handing over boxfuls of records.

Exuberant as always, Waldron alerted Baldwin: "I think we've really got a hot one here." He hopped in the convertible and headed for Fort Lauderdale, where the authority had its headquarters away from the powers in Tallahassee. He asked to see the authority's files, but Florida did not have laws allowing easy access to public records then, and the request was refused. He went back to St. Petersburg, and the editors decided to file suit. Rather than go to trial, the authority conceded and opened its records.

Waldron and other reporters spent weeks poring over data. Although incriminating facts were buried deep in financial archives, the team put together a series that revealed a sordid history of high living by authority personnel and misuse of public money. It resulted in the resignation of the authority's chairman, the jailing of a judge, and the overhauling of the state's bonding and auditing policies.

Waldron's sense of the absurd emerged when he and fellow reporter Don Meiklejohn came across an expense account item for a $30 dinner for two, an astronomical amount in 1963. As an experiment—at the *Times*'s expense—Waldron and Meiklejohn went to dinner at the same elegant Miami restaurant where the tab had been run up.

After two drinks each they scanned the menu for the most expensive items—steaks, salads, cherries jubilee, coffee, and several rounds of brandy—and finally topped $30. They proved that it *was* possible to be so gluttonous with public money, and *Times* readers loved it.

Poynter and his editors knew that they had pulled off a major coup with the series. Public service and promotion manager Sandy Stiles entered it in various contests, including the Pulitzer.

More than a year had passed after the series ended when a tip reached *Times* editors, advising them to watch the Pulitzer announcements. On a Monday morning early in May, bells sounded on the Associated Press machine and the Pulitzer results started tapping out.

Haiman and others rushed over. There it was: The *Times* had won the prize for public service. Haiman looked up in ecstasy to see Poynter, normally a man of great reserve, perched on a desk with his legs crossed like a small child. Then he tossed a phone book toward the ceiling and let out a howl of delight.

For years to come, those present would relive that moment together. The staff had long known they had built a quality newspaper, but its reputation had been overshadowed by St. Petersburg's image as a retirement haven. Now the newspaper's excellence bore the stamp of national recognition.

Many Pulitzer-winning newspapers have sunk back into obscurity as quickly as they emerged, but Poynter would allow no faded laurels around the office. When reminded of victories like the Pulitzer, he would say, "That was yesterday. What have you done for me today?" He was immensely proud that the *Times* staff had grasped the brass

Celebrating the *Times*'s first Pulitzer Prize are Don Baldwin, executive editor; Tom C. Harris, general manager; Nelson Poynter; and Cortland Anderson, managing editor. *Poynter Library, University of South Florida, St. Petersburg, Florida.*

ring. Copies of the Pulitzer medallion were cast for all staffers, and on the next January 1 a motto quietly appeared under the paper's front-page nameplate: Florida's Best Newspaper.

Awards continued to roll in. Anne Rowe twice won the coveted J.C. Penney award for family sections given by the University of Missouri. The National Press Photographers Association declared George Sweers the photo editor of the year. Bette Orsini won first place in national judging of education writers and a year later she won a National Headliners prize. The new editor of the editorial page, Robert Pittman, was named the nation's best in his field in 1965.

Statewide awards became almost routine, but they bore a special edge because of the relatively high level of journalistic quality of Florida's newspapers. Some outsiders credited the state with the highest concentration of good newspapering in the country. After the *Times* swept top awards among one year's state entries, one judge from another region complained, "Your Florida journalism is too damn good."

Somewhat Less Independent

The *Times* had its share of hard-drinking editors, madcap reporters, and loony photographers, but compared with the hell-for-leather neighbors next door the crew on the morning paper was a well-scrubbed Sunday school class. The *St. Petersburg Evening Independent* crouched in a gracious if grubby old building in the shadow of the eight-story *Times* tower. The *Independent*'s two floors, somewhat in the Spanish style, stretched back from a periscope-like cupola. An arched colonnade invited one to come across the railroad tracks that divided First Avenue and enter the dark offices.

In its early days the *Independent* had been a grander affair than the *Times,* having become a daily nearly five years before Straub converted his paper. Its political stands were far closer to mainstream public opinion, and its owners were, for much of its life, more popular and flamboyant public figures in the city than those of the *Times*.

But as the years added strength and depth to the *Times,* they eroded them from the *Independent*. Its staff kept spirits up like defenders of an encircled fort. A survivor, former sports writer Jimmy Mann, recalled that the closing of each edition "was celebrated and/or mourned by editors and staffers openly drinking whiskey from flasks, thermos jugs

The *Evening Independent,* daily rival of the *Times,* had offices abutting the morning paper's on 2nd Avenue South, next to the downtown railroad tracks. *St. Petersburg Times.*

or bottles hidden in desk drawers." Working conditions were deplorable, with weeks sometimes running six days and workdays seventeen hours.[3]

Daily journalism came to St. Petersburg near the high tide of newspapers in the United States. The 1910 census counted more dailies than at any other time. Publishers like Hearst and Scripps were making fortunes, although most plungers who started papers soon went out of business. Founding a daily was a relatively low-budget venture in the first decade of this century. Large investments in equipment were not necessary, and salaries of $10 a week were generous. Publishers still could make money on per-copy sales, and fat advertising contracts were not vital. Competition was taken for granted. In 1910, of all the cities that had dailies, 57 percent had more than one that was separately owned. This intracity competition would almost disappear toward the end of the twentieth century.

Most expansion took place in small, new cities like St. Petersburg. The country had just finished dominating its terrain, overrunning the Indians and extending railroads to the farthest corners. Victory in the Spanish-American War had lent the confidence of a world power, and the boomer spirit was rampant.

Bill Straub had wanted to go daily from the moment he bought the *Times,* but he lacked the audacity of a good entrepreneur. One of his weekly competitors was the *Independent,* founded in 1906. Its owner, Willis B. Powell, took the plunge the next year. He bought a lot across the street from Straub's wood-frame shop, put up a one-story building, and offered the paper every evening for three cents. By establishing his daily first, he took a firm hold on the afternoon field, more profitable than morning publication at that time. Powell held his daily only a year before selling it to Lew B. Brown, a Kentucky lawyer with extensive newspaper experience. Brown's entry into St. Petersburg journalism, like that of Straub and Paul Poynter, was love at first sight. He was vacationing in Pinellas, and within a few days he bought the *Independent* for $10,000.

The dependability of St. Petersburg's sunshine intrigued Brown. In 1910 he announced in a full-page ad that he would give away all copies on any day when the sun did not shine before the newspaper came off the press. Soon afterward he had to make good on his offer for two straight days during a hurricane, but over the three-quarters of a century before the policy was abandoned it was activated an average of only four times a year. The Sunshine Offer became known all over the country as St. Petersburg's most notable feature.

Using wartime problems as a reason, the *Independent* dropped its Sunshine Offer in 1942. The *Times* jumped into the breach and adopted the policy. There was enough fight left in the *Independent* to reject this humiliation. Before the week was over it announced it would resume the offer, and the *Times* gallantly bowed out.

Circulation of the two dailies had been virtually equal until a local politician, Frank Pulver, entered the fray with a third daily in 1925. It lasted only a year, but the *Times* took on the challenge with an outburst of enterprise whereas the *Independent* ignored it. From then on the *Times* slowly pulled ahead of the evening paper in sales.[4]

Like Paul Poynter, the *Independent's* owner groomed his son as successor. L. Chauncey Brown became president and publisher in

1927, although Lew Brown remained influential on the paper until his death in 1944.

After that, nothing seemed to go right for the *Independent*. It survived the ordeal of the 1945 printers' strike alongside the *Times* but did not snap back as well. The movement to the suburbs favored morning newspapers. About the only thing helping the *Independent* was its rock-ribbed conservative politics, for which the booming Republican electorate in Pinellas was grateful. This admiration did not translate into enough sales, and circulation continued to sag.

The year Paul Poynter died, 1950, the Brown era ended. Chauncey Brown sold the paper to Ralph Nicholson, co-owner of the *Tampa Times,* also an evening paper. The *Independent* got a firm hand at its helm in 1951 when Loyal Phillips took over as general manager (later publisher).

Bad blood developed between Phillips and Nelson Poynter. The *Independent* had accused the *Times* of self-serving hypocrisy in connection with proposed electricity rates. Poynter sued for libel but soon dropped the suit, saying he did not want to make a martyr of the rival paper.

In 1952, Nicholson sold the *Independent* to Roy Thomson, a Canadian radio salesman who had risen to be owner of the world's largest newspaper empire. The chain was mostly a ragtag collection of minor papers that Thomson had picked up cheaply. He paid $750,000 for the *Independent,* reportedly so he could have a local office when his yacht docked in St. Petersburg. At any rate, he planned to make his winter home there.

Roy Thomson's primary goal in journalism was to make money, so the mounting losses at the *Independent* galled him. Besides, he had given up his idea of spending winters in St. Petersburg, having centered his operations in London. Thomson tried to sell the *Independent* for years, but prospective buyers would take one look at the *Times* and decide they did not want to compete with it.

By 1962 the losses rose to $300,000 a year. On Saturday, June 19, Poynter got a call from Thomson, then in Toronto, asking him to come to a meeting in New York City. Thomson and his aides came to Poynter's room at the Waldorf and told him they would close the *Independent* unless he bought it. Poynter realized the physical assets of the opposition were of little value, as the equipment had not been maintained properly for decades, and the Browns had retained ownership of the building. In such a case, the most valuable assets were the name, circulation list and good will (buyer loyalty) of the paper. After brief negotiations, Thomson concluded, "It will cost $300,000 to get us out of town." Poynter agreed, they shook hands, and both were back home that night.[5]

Poynter had the option of just letting the paper die, which would relieve him of a long and costly challenge to make it solvent. But he was quite aware that a competitor might start a successor, and he felt St. Petersburg deserved the strong afternoon paper he was confident he could provide.[6]

Strict secrecy cloaked the deal until July 1, when the *Times* started publishing the *Independent*. This left little time for planning. Most new *Independent* staffers came from the *Times,* as only a few were hired from the old rival. They generally were seasoned people like Stan Witwer, who became managing editor.

Shortly afterward Poynter made a separate deal with the Brown family to acquire the *Independent* building and land. Within a few months after the paper was sold, a wrecking ball was swinging into the old stucco structure. A parking lot for staffers emerged.

The *Independent* set up offices, almost equal to those of the morning paper, on the third floor of the *Times* building. Its news and opinion staff was separate from that of its sister, but photographic, mechanical, advertising, circulation, and business operations were combined. The news staff refused to concede an inch to the *Times* in brightness and freshness of local news, if not in comprehensiveness. They took glee in beating the opposition with important stories, particularly from the county courthouse.

Full-page photo essays, artistically laid out, were nearly a daily feature. Some photographers preferred to take assignments from the *Independent* because it displayed their work better. A zippy family department under Anne Rowe came up with far more original ideas than its opposite number on the *Times*. The company spurred competition with a joint contest for staff work each week for newswriting, headlines, and photos, and the *Independent* often humbled the *Times*.

A wild succession of ideas was tried with the paper's physical appearance. An edict required that Page 1 must have a banner headline every day—in color. One morning a tentative report came in that a nearby bank had been held up by robbers with purple hair. Alex

Radford, news editor, ordered printers to prepare a brilliant purple ink for the headline. Just before deadline the story fizzled. Radford was stuck with the purple ink, and he had to use it on a more sober story.

Apparently Poynter was tempted to try out some ideas he had pushed for the experimental newspaper *PM* in 1940. He wanted to turn the *Independent* into a tabloid, but the advertising department talked him out of it. He also toyed with starting classified display advertising, which Ralph Ingersoll had rejected at *PM*.

Editorials were another matter, not open to tinkering. Poynter's ethics ruled out speaking with two voices. As civil rights and Vietnam War issues were coming to a head, ideological position was even more crucial than earlier. "We must not be hypocritical and have two editorial policies," Poynter decreed. He put Pulitzer winner Robert Brown in charge of writing *Independent* editorials, but Brown coordinated them with the *Times* editorial board.

Times executives had believed the *Independent*'s circulation was nearly 34,000. After the purchase they audited the accounts and found there were 19,561 subscribers.[7] Considering how weak the *Independent* had been in the decade before its purchase, Poynter was confident that making it a good, complete afternoon newspaper would buck it up to 50,000 circulation in five years.

The magic touch did not work. Sales actually went down about 3,000 in the first two years. Experts had various explanations, but they generally agreed the problem was mainly in the public's perception rather than in the reality of the paper itself. No matter how good the paper was, the public saw no reason to buy two Poynter newspapers. Two national trends stimulated by the rise of television also were at work in St. Petersburg: Households were tending to be content with one newspaper, if any, and evening papers were losing favor.

Ironically, just as he was hurting most from his purchase of the *Independent*, Poynter had to defend himself on the national scene from charges of a monopolistic grab. A congressional committee was trying vainly to find a way to stem the tide of newspaper mergers, and it called Poynter and Phillips to Washington to testify.

Poynter presented a two-page statement plus six exhibits aimed at showing what every journalist in his area knew: Competition was fierce in the Tampa Bay area, even without a separate *Independent*. Tampa and Clearwater dailies fought the St. Petersburg papers for

Pinellas coverage, and so did a profusion of broadcast stations. Poynter also gave the committee statements that only an idealist like him would have the nerve to bring up—his Standards of Ownership and his editorial philosophy. Nothing more came of the federal challenge to the St. Petersburg merger.

Poynter and Baldwin agreed in 1964 the evening paper must change drastically to survive. As George Sweers, photo chief, observed, "The *Times,* having murdered its opposition, then had to find a way of breathing new life into it."[8] Baldwin chose five of his most innovative news staffers and told them they were to disappear together. "Don't come back without a new format," he ordered. His only other instruction was to find a way to complement but not compete with the *Times.* The Filthy Five, as they called themselves, decamped to a beach motel one Monday in May, a blessed month between winter and summer tourist seasons. Only Baldwin and their spouses knew where the conspirators were.

By Thursday afternoon they were ready. Keynotes of their prescription: Localism, good looks, and informality. "The *Independent* will be St. Petersburg's LOCAL newspaper," the committee report read. "It will take an intensely personal approach to the news. It will center on the needs and desires of the people of St. Petersburg. It will be wedded to the reader as no newspaper has ever been."

The concept resembled manifestos of countless entrepreneurs who made newspaper fortunes undercutting established papers through chumminess with the reader, including James Gordon Bennett, Joseph Pulitzer, William Randolph Hearst, and E. W. Scripps. The committee did not give credit to them or concede that times had changed since they performed their miracles.

The evening paper was to look "light, airy, and coherent as possible—with the emphasis on display and packaging." Horizontal layout, an innovation at the time, was to be the *Independent*'s mode.

The paper slowly began to turn the corner, and it made a modest profit by the end of the decade because of better advertiser response. Circulation rose 65 percent by the end of the Baldwin era, but at 28,000 it still was inconsequential. With Robert Stiff as editor, the staff came to be a proud band of highly competent innovators. They adopted an affectionate nickname for their paper, the *Indy,* but their work remained something of a secret in the trade, as the paper never circulated outside Pinellas County.

The Package

Good looks, like good writing, always had been considered the special province of magazines. Newspapers generally were content to be little more than startling, and to be graphically pleasing was put down as somewhat effete.

But because newspaper people secretly admired elegance as much as anyone, they designed their own Sunday magazine supplements with a dash of style. Thus the Eden of hard-nosed journalism could keep its forbidden fruit segregated from the starkness of the news pages. The *St. Petersburg Times* had its own much-admired Sunday magazine, but Nelson Poynter was not content to let the matter stop there. He looked on creative newspaper graphics not as entertainment but as a tool to convey information seven days a week, on all pages.

As in so many instances, he took as his model the newsmagazines. Henry Luce had excited Poynter's generation in its youth with his graphic triumphs in *Life, Time,* and *Fortune,* and these publications had continued to leave newspapers far behind in this respect. Most daily newspaper proprietors excused their staffs for not matching magazines' brilliance on the grounds that they had only one-seventh the time that weekly publications had to create their miracles. Poynter turned this logic on its head by saying his editors had seven times as many chances as the magazines to get it right, and he maintained his habit of demanding a level of quality that seemed impossible.

In the late 1950s, when Poynter stepped up the pressure for graphic excellence, this was no easy matter. Although newspaper business management was developing as a well-rounded craft, journalism schools were still teaching traditional ways of writing and designing newspapers. In fact, the term *newspaper design* remained rare. The byword was *makeup,* which grew out of the backshop mechanical process of stacking type into a page form. Even *layout*—the use of pencil and paper to specify where type and pictures were to be positioned in the paper—was looked on as rather fancy and better confined to advertising.

Radically new ideas about newspaper appearance inched over the horizon, and a few daring newspapers tried them. But these visions were so occult that they existed only in the minds of a few consultants who, for a hefty fee, would visit a newspaper and create a special format for it. Such gurus pointedly avoided putting their concepts into books, where they could be shared by all.

Poynter took another tack, as he had in developing enterprise reporting. He and Baldwin encouraged young people on the staff to come up with new design ideas and try them out, even if they stumbled. In the end the paper developed what some say is the *Times*'s greatest merit—the marriage of word and image to produce maximum impact and clarity of a message.

This effort demonstrated the teamwork that had brought success. Three strands were woven into the visual package: the written material (copy), drawings (graphics), and photographs. Among those who won respect by melding their efforts were three young staffers, David Laventhol, a desk editor, George Sweers, head of the photo operation, and Frank Peters, a staff artist.

Laventhol was one of the first youths to benefit from an informal shuttle of staffers between the *Times* and newspapers in Washington, D.C. He had grown up in the capital, where his father was a journalist, and had been a copy boy on the *Star*. While earning an English degree from Yale, he worked as a summer intern at the *Times*. He was liked there, and Tom Harris gave him his first job out of college.

Laventhol watched the newsmagazines and picked up tricks of layout from innovative editors. He also pondered the way that television was invading the news field and giving many readers their first knowledge of news breaks. He saw this as a challenge to newspapers to present items that complemented rather than competed head-on with the tube.

When he became editor of Section A and dummied all its pages, Laventhol looked for ways to bring a sense of order to the news. He and his helpers did much rewriting to pull together related stories, a luxury of time few papers could afford. The *Times* desk did it mostly because its young editors were quick enough to work it in among other tasks.

The desk faced another challenge. Baldwin had ordered that the front page of each section carry color every day—either full-color photographs (process color) or tone blocks used in drawings, charts, and graphs (spot color).

Good process color was hard to come by. Wire services and syndicates did not supply it, so the *Times* photo staff was the only source. Because of time pressures, most of these had to be feature pictures, often beach scenes. Red stood out well, so one photographer carried a red beach ball around in his car and had someone—preferably a pretty girl—hold it whenever possible.

Laventhol reached out for spot color. He saw that it could abet his drive to make the news attractive and clear. He found support from an intense young redhead named Frank Peters, a staff artist who liked to hang around the news desk.

Peters had no particular direction in life when he finished a stint in the navy at age twenty, the year Baldwin arrived at the *Times*. He had played around with drawing while in high school, and when he applied for a job at the paper and took Byron Harless's aptitude tests, he displayed artistic and mechanical skills. He became a copy boy and eventually an artist. But Peters had learned to love news, and he jumped at any chance to do things for the editorial side. Other staff artists saw cartooning as their highest calling and disdained maps and charts; Peters delighted in them.

Dissatisfied with his editorial artists, Baldwin fired all three. He carved a new staff out of the ad art department, including Peters. *Times* editors wanted a drastic change from what editorial art had been before. They wanted to get away from the idea that editorial art was decoration. The low-level cartooning that had infested newspapers for decades particularly galled them.

They also ditched the concept that informational graphics were suitable only for time copy, features that could be prepared well in advance of publication. Why not use them to give depth to that day's news? Hard, breaking events needed explanation even more than older, more familiar situations. And, in a sharp departure from newspaper practice, they rejected the belief that fact-packed graphics such as charts, graphs, and tables had to be dull. They were determined to exploit their new luxury of color not just as visual accent but as a new dimension to indicate trends and comparisons. Showing one bar on a black-inked graph as longer than another was not nearly as effective as printing it in a contrasting color. Even photographs and sketches could be integrated.

This frame of mind made the move a success. Editors began thinking graphically and artists began thinking verbally, and both groups talked together. Sometimes the brainstorming produced startling results. In the early days of space travel, Peters and managing editor Cortland Anderson struggled with the problem of how to have enough room on the front page to explain graphically a multiple-orbit mission. Their solution was to run the graphic around the perimeter of the page, completely enclosing it in art.

Ever since Baldwin had arrived, he had looked for a way to integrate photography with the rest of the editorial product. The *Times* had some prize-winning photographers, but their work tended to be used either as routine illustration of the news or as page brighteners. The new ideas sweeping through the newsroom posed a new possibility: If word and hand-drawn image could enhance each other, why not photography also?

Baldwin knew that this innovation required a new way of thinking about photojournalism. Instead of having photographers who took assignments from the city desk, a photo editor who worked as an equal to word editors was needed. The new editor would be aware of news strategy and would even suggest ways to cover things.

To find such a person, Baldwin thought back to his AP years in Tokyo. He had left behind a thirty-year-old named George Sweers, who was photo editor of the bureau there. Having supervised Sweers in a number of tight situations, Baldwin knew that he not only could make excellent pictures but could also, without going onto a news scene, project in his mind how a story might be told through a lens. He wrote his former AP colleague: "I remember how shocked you were when I was offered a job at the *Times*. Now it's your turn." Sweers accepted.

Like Frank Peters, Sweers had come up through the ranks. After high school he had gotten a menial job with the AP, wangled work in the darkroom, and then moved into making photos. After army service, he returned to the AP as a technician and pestered his bosses to let him try out as a photographer. He talked his way into an assignment covering the Korean War and soon found himself working as photo editor in Tokyo. Like Baldwin, he covered all the big-news events breaking in Asia and observed the greatest photographers in the business—those working for *Life* magazine.

When Sweers arrived at the *Times*, Baldwin told him that he already had two photographers good enough to work for *Life*. In fact, the whole staff was excellent, but some members were prima donnas, one even refusing to trade technical data with colleagues. Sweers assured them that he usually would not compete with them as a photographer. His job was to get great pictures in the paper; theirs was to make them.

Even so, Sweers kept his hand in. Soon after arriving, he and magazine editor Don Sider decided to find out how safe air bases in Florida were from enemy attack. They rented a plane and casually buzzed base after base, never being challenged. Sider's story and Sweers's pictures left several generals red-faced.

Sweers's biggest challenge was the Baldwin edict to have color on each section page, every day. As in the case of Frank Peters' art, it had to be timely. Processing color film was cumbersome and slow, so the photo staff worked out tricks to take advantage of every minute between shooting the picture and printing it. The back seat was taken out of a photographer's car and a portable darkroom installed for use when returning from an assignment. When color photos of the legislature's opening day in Tallahassee were scheduled for that night's press run, the same thing was done on a plane. A milestone was reached in 1963 when the last train pulled out of the downtown station and a color picture was shot almost at sunset for publication that night.

Although the *Milwaukee Journal* and the *Miami News* had pioneered color photography, the *Times* soon overtook them and set the pace for the country. This was two decades before *USA Today* gained much publicity for "discovering" the idea that color photography could be just as routine as black and white.

Living for the Day

Henrietta Poynter's Bible, it was said, was Betty Friedan's book *The Feminine Mystique.* As the daughter of a strong career woman and herself well aware of her superior mind, Mrs. Poynter had a firm hand in changing the *Times* as to both female staffing and the kind of fare offered women readers, a process that also affected how the paper spoke to men. Thus the last decade of Henrietta's life, ending in 1968, marked a watershed in *Times* features—all material except the hard news of politics, crime, and business and the mostly male preserve of sports.

America's attitude that women's place was in the home was reflected and nurtured by newspapers. They segregated "women's" matters to their back parlor, the society pages. There, at the hand of female journalists who often had come from modest homes, women were instructed that life was a velvet jail that locked people into social and economic class. If they came from a "good" family, they found themselves fawned upon in gushy articles and smiling pictures. It was a world of neat hairdos, perfect lipstick, and straight seams. And women journalists were generally expected to take their own medicine, not asking for the sweatier jobs reserved for men. The society department could be found in a sedate room well away from the grinding gears of news production.

Over the decades, a scattering of women had gone against the tide. Some inherited papers and did well with them, like the imperious Eleanor Patterson of the *Washington Times-Herald*. Her cousin, Alicia Patterson, created Long Island's innovative daily, *Newsday*. Reporter Ida M. Tarbell, columnist Dorothy Thompson, and photographer Margaret Bourke-White typified hundreds who refused to be typecast.

The *St. Petersburg Times* had always been close to the norm but somewhat more liberal. When it was a weekly, it had a woman city editor named Alliene Mitchell. This meant little, as such a job on a weekly usually went to whoever would take the least pay. A few female journalists appeared over the following three decades—a general feature writer, a real estate columnist, and the like. During World War II a brigade of women replaced men who had gone into uniform, but they were fired after victory. Bette Orsini, later to share in a Pulitzer Prize, was one of the few who survived in general news.

News directed toward women was even more conventional. Nearly all cities had a grande dame journalist who guarded the gate to social paradise. St. Petersburg's was Diana Rowell, a white-haired dowager with rimless glasses and high-top shoes.[9] She ruled as *Times* society editor for seventeen years until 1948 and kept much influence as food editor until 1956.

Ruling a swarm of helpers who called her the Duchess among themselves, Rowell gave the ultimate word on social success. She originated the city's debutante ball in 1937 and helped select the honorees until her death in 1973. Deciding which weddings, teas and meetings deserved the cachet of big pictures and headlines remained solely her prerogative. From the paper's reporting, life seemed a whirl of dances, yachting, churchgoing, and homemaking.

The *Times* softened the elitism of its society section label in the early 1950s. Over the next decade the section heading edged toward modernity, being given names such as "and now . . . about WOMEN," "Women Today," and "Family Today." The bride pictures slowly

Diana Rowell, 1931–48
society editor of the
Times, set the sedate
tone for the paper's
feature material before
it became consumer-
oriented. Here she
poses in a 1956 fashion
picture. *St. Petersburg
Times.*

ebbed and the joys of decorating, cooking, and dressing gained ground. It was a decided shift toward middle-class values.

Henrietta Poynter's ideas, derived from her magazine jobs in New York, began to supplant Diana Rowell's. The old social order had cold-shouldered Henrietta as an outsider, and as she carved out her own position she celebrated the new generation that made it possible. She championed sophistication and intellect at the expense of tight girdles. One of her ideas was to bring in a Washington journalist, Nancy Osgood, to pump some flair into the section.

Several modernizing blows were struck in the mid-1950s. The paper's troubleshooter, Sandy Stiles, was editing the Sunday magazine, the *Floridian.* He was named news features editor—a new position— with authority over the women's department, the magazine, religion, real estate, and entertainment. All these desks moved into fourth-floor quarters vacated when Poynter sold his radio station. The new women's editor, Gloria Biggs, was a soulmate of Henrietta Poynter's.

Both Poynters would flood Biggs with ideas, and Henrietta would bring back notes from parties.

The wind was right for change upon Don Baldwin's arrival as managing editor in 1958. He had grown up in the classless western mountains, and he had seen enough of the world to know St. Petersburg's pretensions at high society were a puerile imitation of larger cities. But instead of killing the section, he wanted to expand it into something that caught the vitality of the 1960s.

The changes stirred the wrath of the establishment. No longer was social position a key to getting a big splash in the paper. Howls arose from aristocrats stung by the putdown and from club leaders whose trivial doings were ignored. Again, Stiles was sent in to handle the crisis. With the title of public service editor, he acted as an ombudsman who soothed the grumblers and explained to them the bright new future that was coming. Biggs took over the news features helm.

Biggs was older than Baldwin's Kiddy Corps, and coming up fast was a woman barely in her twenties, Anne Rowe (later Goldman). She had talked her way into a copygirl's job just out of high school and seized any chance she had to learn how to be a journalist. This won her a place in Biggs's department, where she caught Henrietta Poynter's sharp eye. Henrietta once sent her home from a public occasion because her dress was not right, and another time she told Rowe she had too much eye makeup. But Rowe became the older woman's protégé, and Henrietta later insisted on lending Rowe a mink jacket when she covered the New York fashion shows.

Rowe got her break when the *Times* bought the *Independent*. She became the paper's features editor, and she plunged into the challenge of making the section relevant. Every day she had a magazine-type spread on a cover page. It was sassy, up-to-date, and helpful, and it raced ahead of the *Times* in ideas. Even its name—Suncoast Living—signaled a new day. Bad blood came between Baldwin and Biggs, and she left for a successful career in the Gannett chain. Rowe followed her as news features boss of both papers.

Soft news had always been the disparaging label journalists put on features. They were the hors d'oeuvres of journalism, pleasant but expendable. Now Baldwin insisted that everything under the features umbrella—health, consumerism, entertainment, personal finances, and fashion—be covered as regular news. It even entered the realm of opinion. The weekend that President John Kennedy was shot, Rowe

Anne Rowe (later Goldman), here being kissed by Elvis Presley, led the modernization of the *Times*'s feature pages. *St. Petersburg Times.*

learned that the Yacht Club was going ahead with its Venetian Ball, ice sculptures and all. The family section printed an editorial criticizing the callousness, heading it "An Island of Gaiety in a Sea of Tragedy."

Still, family news had no home of its own; it was tacked on the back of the second section. The *Times* had pioneered departmentalizing of news, putting national and international news in the front section, local news in another and sports in a third, each with cover pages free of ads. Then Baldwin decided that family news had to have its own cover page. The advertising department resisted, pleading that this was too valuable a money-maker to give up. First Baldwin won half a cover page and later a full one. Part of his strategy was using the popular Ann Landers advice column as a stalking horse, moving it from the cover page to the third page, thus making another page solid gold for advertisers.

Pressure for change mounted in 1966 when Tom Harris retired, Baldwin became editor-president, and Haiman was promoted to managing editor. Both Baldwin and Haiman felt that the section did a disservice to both sexes—to men because it largely ignored them and to women because it condescended to them. The editors' zeal took on a messianic edge.

Even with the odor of high society hanging over from earlier days, surveys showed 20 percent of males who looked at the paper read the family section, as did 90 percent of women. The editors sought to equalize those figures. Sexism still reigned in staffing and content.

Baldwin and Haiman decided to completely overhaul the section, calling on talents of the best editors, writers, photographers, and artists. It aimed at what would later be called the "me generation"— young people who were alternately thrilled and bewildered by new doors opening for them in society.

Quality of life became a byword, and Haiman was intrigued by the ideas of Clay Felker, who had made his *New York* magazine a symbol of the new wave. Felker preached that the journalist must offer the reader a survival kit that tells him or her where to find a good plumber or the best bagel, how to engage a babysitter, which cheap restaurants are best. Although yuppies had not been discovered, the new audience was their precursor.

The *Times* planners discovered the same thing was happening at the *Washington Post*. Dave Laventhol, one of the Kiddy Corps stars, had ended up there along with several other former *Times* staffers. He was put in charge of a project that brought about a replacement for the society/women's section. Simply called "Style," it unleashed a revolution in journalists' attitudes. *Post* owner Katharine Graham, one of the capital's best-known socialites, was beset by protests from her friends.

Style stole the march from the *Times*, but within a few weeks the Florida paper completed its long planning. All the new ideas were in the proposal, plus a new one. Each weekday's edition of the section would have a different theme—consumer news, arts and leisure, food, home and garden, or the weekend's entertainment events. It was hedonism wrapped in a designer scarf.

Nothing flaunted trendiness more than the title. It was called the "Day" section, as the day of the week was the name of the edition, with the end in capitals—monDAY, tuesDAY, and so forth. Anne Rowe headed the project as news features editor, although she put a premium on hiring men. Total staffing for the department had risen to about thirty by 1972.

Although Nelson Poynter kept his hands off, he disliked the whole concept. To him it seemed frivolous and elitist. He much preferred self-sacrifice to self-indulgence.

On the Move

When Baldwin reported for work in June 1958, St. Petersburg had become the jewel of the subpeninsula, as Bill Straub had dreamed. It was a safe and healthful place to work, without traffic jams or notable price gouging. Schools were good, jobs were plentiful, and homes were easy to buy. There were no real slums, even for the one in seven area residents who was black. Compared with the rest of the nation, whites in St. Petersburg were more likely to be well endowed, educated, Republican, and churchgoing.

During the 1950s the city's population nearly doubled to 186,000, but in the next decade growth slackened to only 19 percent. It was the smallest percentage rise for any decade in the city's history to that point, although the number of people added nearly equaled the entire growth in the first four decades. Sun-seekers fleeing the North still accounted for a majority of the growth. The green benches on Central Avenue were thronged at the height of the winter season with old people knitting new friendships and mending old ones. Social Security checks clogged the post office at the beginning of each month.

Retirees came mainly from a few states. New York accounted for 15 percent, and the five states stretching from Pennsylvania through Illinois made up 38 percent. Unlike Florida's east coast, which tended to attract people from big cities, those going to St. Petersburg were predominantly from outside metropolitan areas.

The average household size captured the retiree syndrome more than any other. St. Petersburg's average of 2.6 represented one of the lowest rates in the country. Also, the population's age was skewed toward the upper end. More than a fourth of St. Petersburg residents were over sixty-five, compared with 11 percent in all of Florida. Their median age was forty-seven, while the state's was thirty-one.

These two indexes taken together mean that the typical household consisted of a middle-aged or elderly couple. More than likely they had sought out St. Petersburg for the good life rather than the nightclubs, expensive restaurants, and racetracks of the east coast. The retirees centered their activities on the historic downtown area where Demens had brought his train in 1888, with linkages to the gulf beaches. They fished, puttered about on the beach, played shuffleboard, watched winter baseball practice, and above all enjoyed the Million-Dollar Pier. A roadway jutted from the downtown waterfront 1,400 feet offshore, to a depth of twenty-eight feet. The three-story Spanish-style casino at its tip sheltered dances, card games, and other polite pleasures.

All this would change in the 1960s. Pressure for a shift had mounted since the postwar invasion of newly married veterans. They had poured into the subdivisions that popped up north, west, and south of the downtown area. A scattering of suburban shopping centers had come with them.

Just as the automobile made suburban commuting possible, so the air conditioner made it comfortable on a year-round basis. By the

The ornate "Million-Dollar Pier" on St. Petersburg's downtown bayfront attracted hordes of northern tourists. *Heritage Park, Largo, Florida.*

mid-1960s the subdivisions hummed with window units, followed later by the deeper drone of central units that cooled the whole house.

The pace of home construction had been so hectic in the 1950s that the city started the next decade vastly overbuilt. Wild speculation led to development far beyond what the market demanded and often to shoddy quality. The orgy went on even after the truth became evident. In 1959, when 3,500 homes remained unsold, developers churned out 3,539 new ones. Overbuilding threatened major problems for the home construction industry within St. Petersburg's limits. Employment dropped by more than half from 1959 through 1963. But growth continued for suburbs and exurbs, a freckling of new little towns between St. Petersburg and Clearwater. Retirees who could afford it moved from downtown to outlying areas.

Also bringing new home buyers was the wave of electronic industries that swept in just as the building boom collapsed. Manufacturing employment, which had been negligible in 1959, soared above 16,000 in 1965 and kept growing. City boomers dreamed of new residents like those working for the electronic giants. They were young, well-educated engineers just starting families, eager and able to buy upper-bracket houses plus all the fittings. Because they wanted to enjoy the newfound joys of water sports, they spread out all around the county's shoreline, not just in industrial enclaves.

Giving an edge to the city's pride was the new Florida Presbyterian College, later Eckerd College. From the first it put a premium not on size but on excellence. Faculty came from prestige institutions all over the country, and they were among the nation's best paid. The college's founders ignored many academic conventions and adopted an innovative curriculum. Soon the college moved from temporary quarters to a spacious, modernistic campus beside Boca Ciega Bay in the extreme southwest part of the city.

Just as St. Petersburg had the luck to escape from the housing debacle in the suburbs, so it averted an impending calamity in the makeup of downtown. As the retiree trade in the city's center steadily dried up, leaders desperately grabbed at stopgap remedies. Some blamed the green benches, a symbol of senility. The city first painted them a rainbow of colors, then removed most of them. The real salvation came as the city experienced a movement like that in such booming commercial cities as Houston and Atlanta. The downtown converted itself from a shopping area into a financial, governmental, and professional center. Leading the way was a $4.5 million arena, convention center, and theater called the Bayfront Center, which opened in 1965. Its modernistic lines loomed into the sky near the old downtown airport and cast a reflection on the South Yacht Basin. The same year, the city's first major art museum opened in a million-dollar building in Straub Park overlooking the North Yacht Basin. Nelson Poynter endowed one of the major rooms in honor of his parents.

Sore spot of the downtown panorama, in the eyes of the city's planners, was the forty-year-old Municipal Pier. The engineers' verdict was that needed repairs would be too expensive to be feasible, so the city council decided to tear the pier down in 1967 and replaced it with an inverted pyramid, each upper floor cantilevered wider than the one beneath it. Furious protests stemmed not only from a generation's nostalgia but also from widespread distaste for the new design.

Alongside the pier another change swept across the waterfront. Postwar prosperity had written an end to the era when only rich people could go to sea in their own boats. To accommodate the exploding numbers of private craft—both power and sailing vessels—the city built a 389-berth marina in the Central Yacht Basin. The ranks of masts and hulls sparkled in the sun.

Turning the Page

To Don Baldwin, who never had been south of Washington, St. Petersburg in 1958 was a strange place, albeit not nearly so alien as some counties that surrounded it. The time was not long past when the leading hotels would not admit Jewish guests and the Jaycees did not welcome Jewish businessmen. Golf, yacht, and country clubs often blackballed Jews and Catholics.

The situation was far worse for blacks. When found in the exclusive Snell Isle neighborhood after dark, blacks would be picked up by police for questioning if they had no excuse for being there. When Florida Presbyterian College arranged a concert by William Warfield, famed black baritone, the only lodging it could find for him was at a Howard Johnson's. A welcoming supper was stymied until one restaurant agreed to have it hidden away in a private dining room.

The week Baldwin began work at the *Times,* the paper covered two incidents that verged on the surreal. First, eight blacks showed up to swim at the Spa Beach, a haven of elderly visitors on the Tampa Bay waterfront. The city promptly closed the beach. Although a segregated beach nearby was open to them, blacks had been quietly protesting beach segregation off and on for three years. The *Times* waffled somewhat on its editorial page by calling for blacks-only beaches all over the county. It declared legally enforced segregation a dead issue, but it said that other areas that had provided ample beach access had seen the races segregate themselves voluntarily.

Toward the end of the summer, after the appearance of a lone black girl brought another closing at the Spa, an editorial accused the city government of bankrupt leadership on the issue. Racial prejudice was foreign to three-fourths of the residents, it declared. "Are we going to have Pinellas and St. Petersburg known not for their hospitality and wonderful recreational facilities but as 'someplace they're always having racial troubles'?"[10]

The other occurrence that greeted Baldwin was the announcement of plans to dedicate the new Gibbs Junior College, a public institution for blacks. The state attorney general had taken the position that St. Petersburg Junior College could not admit blacks until all state colleges were opened to them, and the *Times* concurred while demanding a statewide open-door policy. A politician told the Citizens Council, a segregationist group, that the only way to maintain segregation in Pinellas was to give blacks equal opportunities, which meant a separate junior college.

The *Times* fought the founding of Gibbs every step of the way. It declared that "the idea of investing one more penny in segregated school facilities—especially at advanced levels—is utterly unthinkable. It is incredibly naive, let alone being legally untenable."[11] The solution, the paper said in a shift of position, was to admit blacks to St. Petersburg Junior College immediately.

But for St. Petersburg blacks it was much more comfortable to remain in the ghetto. They found it impossible to buy a cup of coffee in the center of the city and almost as difficult to use a restroom. They did not see people of their race basking in the sunshine on green benches. Blacks visible in the downtown drove trucks, pushed brooms, and did similar menial jobs.

An oasis was the *Times* building. Since 1951, full-time black journalists had worked on the black news page at desks in the middle of the newsroom and used all facilities. Even this was too much for many rabid segregationists. In 1957 Poynter received an anonymous letter reading, "Keep all Nigger news out of your paper or you will meet with early death." Ku Klux Klan literature was found near the building. It stated, "The KKK has started a campaign against Poynter and his ilk." The paper's coverage continued as before.

The *Times*'s attention to black issues increased markedly in 1960 when it hired Samuel Adams, a black man with an outgoing personality and dogged stubbornness; he held two bachelor's degrees and a master's. Soon his name began appearing in bylines on the white news pages. The paper had decided to go after the integration story aggressively, and it sent Adams wherever attacks on segregation arose—the rally in Washington, bus integration in Birmingham, the march on Selma, and soda fountain encounters in St. Augustine. When the Freedom Rider buses came to Florida, two *Times* reporters went along.

The *Times* was not content to assign Adams to the obvious news events. After President Lyndon Johnson pushed through the Civil Rights Act of 1964, Baldwin decided to test the South's compliance. He refused to send a black man alone—he wanted a couple like any other tourists. Adams' wife, Elenora, felt it was a risky assignment, and this later proved true. But she and Sam set off in their car on a meandering route through Dixie, asking over and over at motels and restaurants until they found acceptance.

The results ranged from harrowing to heartening, and the series ran under the title "Highways to Hope." *Newsweek* magazine called Adams one of the best reporters on racial matters—the "most dangerous domestic assignment in U.S. journalism." After a series on conditions for blacks in migrant labor camps, Adams won top honors in a southeastern journalistic competition.[12]

But the most difficult issue—black community news—was boiling up inside the *Times* itself. In an age when barriers between races were eroding, some young blacks said the *Times* remained one of the worst offenders because it printed its pages of black news, although many other blacks disagreed. For several years the *Times* had given black brides the option of having their pictures printed in the general family section or on the blacks' page. Few asked for the general section.

Black militants began presenting a case for elimination of the black page, and Baldwin set up meetings. Officers of the National Association for the Advancement of Colored People, representing a relatively moderate bloc, argued against the change, as did some black staff members of the newspaper.

The paper went public with the debate, inviting readers to send in letters. One, from a former black contributor, said the page resulted in one of the best-informed black communities in the country. He saw an irony that the very organizations that had benefited most from the page "were stampeded into condemning the instrument which contributed greatly to their growth."[13]

But letters ran twenty to one for killing the page, and in 1967 Baldwin ordered it to cease. Black news was to be integrated with that of whites, which meant the small news about ordinary black people—church parties, club elections, lodge dinners—was swept away as metropolitan standards of news judgment were applied to them also.

Poynter was out of town. When he learned of the decision, he was unhappy. To Baldwin, he seemed more perplexed than angry. "You're robbing people of some coverage that does a wonderful thing for them," he told Baldwin. "It lets people who are potential leaders in the black community gain the recognition they need to become leaders." He recalled the press of America's pioneer days, which made it possible for political spokesmen to emerge.

Years later the paper would try to compensate for the lost benefits of the black page with a glitzy monthly supplement for blacks. But it never replaced the down-home familiarity of the black page.

A month before the black page died, the new scrutiny of black issues resulted in the discovery of financial misdeeds by several black officials at Gibbs Junior College, one of whom went to jail. The college closed and was merged with the white college. The *Times* hailed the decision: "The closing . . . finally will erase a costly error made in 1957. It was an error committed under the misguided concept that there was such a thing as separate but equal education for Negroes."[14]

The newspaper's role in the college's closing brought an even more bitter dispute among blacks than the end of the special page. Some blacks charged that Sam Adams had betrayed a black institution and had misused his former connection with the college to pry out secrets. His longtime assistant, Mamie Brown, resigned, in part because of the incident.

Peggy Peterman, who replaced Brown, also resented Adams's actions. The closing damaged the education of black students, she said, as they found it more difficult to be admitted to St. Petersburg Junior

College. A law school graduate, Peterman brought a new militancy to the staff. She chafed at insults blacks suffered in economic life as well as in political arenas. She had been refused diaper service when she had a baby, and even a portrait photographer declined to take her son's picture. Before she joined the staff, she wrote in a letter to the editor: "How do you explain to the most innocent human form on Earth that he is not wanted in certain businesses not because of his structure, his features or his background, but simply because he is of color? . . . I will tell him that it is his moral, Christian duty to fight this ugliness. . . . I will dedicate my life to the liberation of the Negro from second-class citizenship."[15]

The crowning tribute to the *Times*'s long struggle for racial justice and accord came in 1971, a few months before Baldwin left the paper. Public schools throughout Pinellas were to start the year integrated, and the paper posted a reporter in every school. They had little to report, as the milestone passed peacefully.

Angels and Ghosts

"I have a superstition that good weather follows me," Nelson Poynter wrote his mother, and returning to the theme later, "I also know we are the most lucky family in the world and have everything that any family could need."

As the *Times* and *Congressional Quarterly* moved toward maturity and stability, it did seem the angels were on Poynter's side. He was tough as ever, at least strong enough to handle the sorrows that would visit him in the next decade. With his management team shaping up, he and Henrietta allowed themselves more travel, their favorite luxury. They were intrigued by different cultures and used interviews rather than tourism to fill their editorial notebooks.

This was particularly true in Henrietta's case. She could be frugal enough to haul an ironing board around town for repair, and once while her mother-in-law was touring the world she sent her a letter in advance to Guam to save foreign postage. But she passionately shopped for just the right thing at the right price—clothing or jewelry for herself or, more often, a gift for a friend or employee. "Nelson bought out Hong Kong and I've bought out Bangkok," she wrote home, "a princess ring and earrings—stoles and scarfs and what have you."[16] When Nelson's mother and sister were to visit Paris, Henrietta sent them a long list of places where they could buy clothes or gifts. She even told Eleanor where to get a Chinese pedicure.

While the Poynters' status opened doors, they sought brains, wit, and involvement, not social cachet. Nowhere were they more exhilarated than in Washington. Nelson once greeted his mother to their capital apartment with a note: "This is the payoff—the things you dreamed of when you were a little girl in Sullivan—and the things that Nelson Wilkey [her father] dreamed of for you."[17]

Their trip through East Asia, when they hired Don Baldwin, produced a series of such dazzlements. Most encounters were arranged well in advance by friends. Before they left, the Taiwanese ambassador had invited them to lunch so he could personally sign their visas.

Stopping off in Hollywood just before setting out, they had dinner with the Ira Gershwins. In Taiwan, they had tea with Generalissimo and Madame Chiang Kai-Shek and were honored at parties by the U.S. Embassy and the Associated Press. In Singapore, novelist Han Suyin invited them to tea and the British commissioner general hosted them at lunch. They visited U Nu, famous liberal prime minister of Burma. In Sri Lanka, where the conference was held, they turned down the governor-general's invitation to stay at his mansion so they could have more freedom of movement.

When they went to London, Henrietta's old friendships with the cultural elite gave them entrée to the insiders' life. The Tate Gallery was opened two hours early for them to preview the biggest Picasso show ever. They had lunch with Lord Roy Thomson, who owned the *Evening Independent* in St. Petersburg. There also were evenings with literary lights such as G. B. Stern and Louis Golding.

Their favorite vacation was holing up in some rustic resort or taking a tramp steamer trip—anything for quietness and escape. They would take along an armful of books, mostly current titles on economics and politics. And they would enjoy each other's company.

In one rare case, tranquillity was combined with the good conversation they enjoyed. They used their London connections to get into an exclusive retreat in Wales, formerly part of a great estate. It was owned by the sister of John Strachey, author and Labourite cabinet minister. Nelson wrote his mother that "they still only take people they know, so that the intellectual level there is sure to be above most resorts . . . at least we're likely to find people who agree with us politically."[18]

Far more than for himself, Poynter pressed on his mother a life of ease. He was continually coaxing her to spend more on servants and indulge in the foreign travel she too loved. Although she made the circuit of St. Petersburg, Sullivan, and eastern resorts such as Asheville, North Carolina, Nelson tried to ensure she had all possible comforts at her residence on Snell Isle. To get her to go to resorts, he played a game that humored her frugality. He let her think she was using due bills—hotels' debts to the *Times* for advertising—but he was secretly paying the charges himself.

Alice Poynter constantly fretted about her will. She was worried about satisfying the desires of her daughter, Eleanor, and Eleanor's two daughters while still treating Nelson and his daughters fairly. Nelson declined his mother's request that he serve as her executor "because I do not want to be in the position of administering anything for Eleanor." He recommended a bank instead. He also said he did not want to pick out any favorite things from her home "because that would just be the thing that Eleanor had set her heart on, and you know that we don't care enough about material things to upset anyone."[19]

The quarrel came to a head in 1965. In an adoring letter to Alice, Nelson apparently gave up any claim to her home and household effects. He also returned a ring that Alice had given to Henrietta and his father's gold watch. His daughters would thus go without mementos from their grandmother, but he said he was sure they would understand. They would receive silver and jewelry from Catherine, his first wife, and from Henrietta. He wrote to her: "Erase your mind of these material things, and know that only one Will really counts—and that's the Will of God which you so richly understand if only you will refuse to be side-tracked by material things. Many years ago I discovered these values with your guidance. They are my great heritage, and I hope to pass them on to Nancy and Sally.[20]

Although Poynter left many questions unanswered about the nature of his religious faith, he never showed any disbelief to his mother. He repeatedly recited Christian Science dogma to her, particularly as a way to buck up her spirits. After her hearing had taken a turn for the worse, he intoned: "I think it is *fear*—and C.S. more than any one thing can help all of us to overcome fear—you are God's Child—and have no reason to have fear of *anything*. You know this—it was you who taught it to me—and I am thus merely reminding you of something that is yours—and you can regain it INSTANTLY."[21]

Politics was another matter. He poured out his opinions in letters to his mother with the tone not of a patronizing son but of an intellectual equal. It was a subject both were fervent and informed about. The greatest political heresy to Poynter, who thrived on ideas, was to be boring. Midway through the Eisenhower doldrums he pronounced the Republicans dull—"I have that against them more than anything." After John F. Kennedy's victory, he exulted that the Democrats were "more fun." But he swallowed hard and supported a Republican for Congress when the Democrats offered lesser men. "In a way this is a break for The Times because it gives us an opportunity to prove our non-partisanship."[22]

Although he remained true to his Wilsonian ideals all his life, Poynter was not fooled by labels. In a historic battle for the U.S. Senate between Claude Pepper, an orthodox New Dealer, and Spessard Holland, identified with Bourbon conservatism, he chose to support Holland. First, he said, the labels had grown out of press agentry and both men were rather moderate. But he believed that Holland had grown while Pepper had nothing to offer but "warmed over New Deals." He concluded: "Finally—Pepper would be a captive of Big Labor and labor is not a Liberal force in America. Most of it is quite reactionary—with featherbedding standing in the way of massive production—and therefore aiding inflation which is the biggest domestic issue today."[23]

Poynter was elated with John F. Kennedy's triumph and his early appointments. "I am amazed at the variety of new issues and public affairs that Kennedy brings to Washington," he wrote. But after the president cast a slur on Adlai Stevenson following the Bay of Pigs fiasco, Poynter termed the Kennedys "a ruthless tribe." In 1964 he told his mother that he would rather see Goldwater as president than Nixon if the Republicans should win. She agreed obliquely: "If Johnson does not accept R. Kennedy on ticket—may vote for Goldwater. I do not fear him. Jews are smart."[24]

As an editor who always had supported Democratic presidential candidates, even in the face of Republican majorities in Florida the last three elections, Poynter no doubt could have had almost his pick of offices in the Kennedy administration. But he declared that he would not have a government job "for all the tea in China." He had his fill of that during World War II and felt he could contribute more to his country as a newspaperman. A dedicated journalist should never leave the business, even temporarily, he said. "It's a big calling and commands all the time and mind."[25]

Certainly he was feeling good about his accomplishments with the *Times*. The internship program he started in the mid-1950s was bearing fruit, and he boasted that it set the pace for other newspapers. He was proud of hiring Baldwin and Brown, as it "required some management art on my part in bringing them in," he told his mother. He believed that the *Times* "has never been at a higher peak from a public relations standpoint."[26]

Early projects of the Poynter Fund also delighted him, and he thought his profit-minded father also would have been proud of how its grants were paying off in the education of political writers. "This is 'profit' that is just as exciting—much more exciting to me—than making a large real estate deal."

After he had been away on a three-month trip, he conceded that his absence had been good for the paper, as "the younger men on the staff have responded wonderfully to the challenge." He resolved to make a habit of it, although he never did.

Congressional Quarterly also was coming up to his standards: "I am delighted with CQ's prospects this year—the best since we founded the service which is now more than 12 years ago. Anyone less stubborn would have sunk it after the numerous disappointments—but that makes it all the more thrilling as it now matures and flowers."[27] Nelson continually gave his wife credit for success of CQ, which he said "would not have been possible without Henrietta who bore the professional brunt for months at a time." Besides her hard work, her brilliance never ceased to fascinate him: "Henrietta is marvelous in her grasp of the whole project. The men at the office stand in awe of her knowledge."[28]

Accused

In 1951, soon after Senator Joseph McCarthy began his campaign against a supposed Communist conspiracy in American public life, the *St. Petersburg Times* gave voice to a staunch anticommunism it had long espoused and would keep up for years to come. McCarthy himself could hardly have been more eloquent than the *Times* editorial:

There is no mystery about the ultimate aim of communism. The great Russian leader, Lenin, gave inspiration to the present drive by the Kremlin when he said "As long as capitalism and socialism exist, we cannot live in peace; in the end one or the other will triumph—a funeral dirge will be sung over the Soviet Republic or over world capitalism." But there is some mystery as to when, where and how Russia will strike. Because no one knows the plans or the whims of a handful of willful men in the Kremlin, it becomes necessary for the free world to prepare for its defense.[29]

But as the air became poisoned with the cold war, no amount of flag-waving could protect one from suspicion. Poynter infuriated thousands with his stands for desegregation. His opponents could not fault him for lack of public spirit, so they looked for something else to prove guilt by association. For years there had been whispers that Poynter was a Communist. Hate mail came regularly, and he passed on some to the FBI. Local extremist sheets delighted in printing charges that Poynter had been linked with subversive organizations. Employees of the *Times* were inured to being told by acquaintances that their boss was a red.

The ugly talk came to the surface in March 1960, when blacks were trying to integrate downtown lunch counters and a black woman had just announced for the school board. Members of the Women's Republican Club of St. Petersburg, a bastion of the elite, received their March bulletin and read a chilling letter to the members from their local president, Mrs. Lyle L. Chaffee. The letter said, in effect, that Poynter had been a member of Communist fronts. Although she made no specific allegations, the letter made clear that what had upset Chaffee was the news in the paper. Noting the power of the press, she wrote: "Repeat a thing in print enough times and even though it may be untrue or only slightly factual the insinuation has sown a seed in the public mind. The resemblance to the Nazi and Communist machines is strong and the citizens of St. Petersburg should ask themselves if the St. Petersburg Times is applying these tactics in reporting both local and national news." To cope with the problem of *Times* coverage, she suggested, club members "should ascertain if its editor and publisher, Mr. Poynter, was ever a member of any alleged Communist front organizations. The affirmative answers are contained in the Congressional Record."

Although it stung Poynter to have such things publicized among St. Petersburg's respectable folk, at least he finally could strike back at the rumors. In a much more polite tone than Chaffee had used, he mounted a fierce defense. He called Chaffee's attack "a libelous and untruthful smear" that did not square with the national policy of her group. He had ignored such slurs from groups like the Ku Klux Klan, he told her in a letter, but he had expected her club to be more responsible.[30]

Poynter flatly denied ever having been a member of a Fascist or Communist front. He also cited the *Times*'s long support for a two-party system in the South. Without a specific charge to disprove, Poynter could only speculate that Chaffee's reference to the *Congressional Record* concerned an instance in 1944 when he had tangled with the U.S. House Un-American Activities Committee (HUAC) over the impugned loyalty of a CQ editor.

Poynter asked Chaffee to pass on his letter to the club's members, but she refused to do so or to give him their names, so *Times* staffers scoured their files for likely members and sent registered letters to all. A three-quarter-page ad also ran, primarily stressing all the help the *Times* had given to the Republican party. The ad contained long quotes praising the newspaper from former and present county GOP chairmen and even Richard Nixon, then vice-president. A typical comment was that of Clare B. Williams, Chaffee's predecessor and then Republican national vice-chairwoman: "I don't know of any other newspaper which endeavors to bring so much impartial information to the electorate—information which they themselves submit. . . . The Times has made a frequent effort to bring before the public the advantages of competition in government—that is the two-party system—and we, as Republican leaders, appreciate the foresight of this editorial policy."[31] In fact, the state federation of Chaffee's group had just the year before named the *Times* as one of only two papers to be thanked for help.

The Chaffee affair blew over quickly, but apparently not even Poynter realized that it was related to an FBI effort to discredit him. It had dogged him for a decade and would continue almost until his death. FBI records of Poynter started ironically with a letter from Director J. Edgar Hoover in 1936 thanking him for an editorial he had written in the *Columbus Citizen* praising Hoover's leadership. As a courtesy, Hoover placed Poynter on the bureau's mailing list, although he was deleted when he left Columbus.[32]

Poynter's folder grew much fatter in 1941 when he applied for work with Nelson Rockefeller's office. Such an important appointment required a routine FBI study of his background, the only field investigation the bureau ever conducted on him. Although glowingly favorable, it did not prevent the FBI from collecting and spreading gossip and half-truths about him from then on.

To compile the report for Rockefeller, agents in six offices near Poynter's residences gathered information. Although the version later released to Poynter by the FBI was heavily censored, it reflected vigorous legwork by the agents. They apparently talked with knowledgeable sources and recorded the data in a relatively fair manner.

Poynter "was very liberal in his views towards labor movements, although he was not supposed to be a communist," the Cincinnati agent wrote, and added, "One hundred percent American, being thoroughly loyal and true to his country." The word from the St. Paul agent was: "Morally straight, makes an excellent appearance and possesses a magnetic personality." Most of the agents commented on Poynter's aggressive business habits and brilliance. The Miami agent, after probing in St. Petersburg, called him "smart as a whip, nobody's fool" and said that Poynter had "the keenest mind of any young man in town." Perhaps as a signal to Hoover to be on guard politically, most of the agents noted that Poynter was a close friend of Lowell Mellett, then executive assistant to President Franklin Roosevelt.

When Poynter switched to the Donovan propaganda operation the same year, he apparently did not have to go through another investigation. On the application, he answered no to the question: "Are you a member of any party or organization which advocates the overthrow of a constitutional form of government in the United States?"

It was in his propaganda work that Poynter got his first black marks from the FBI. He chaired an interagency meeting the day after Pearl Harbor to set up a way to censor commercial shortwave broadcast operations. He asked the FBI representative to run security checks on about 350 people working at the stations, and the agent agreed. But military representatives disagreed bitterly with civilians about who would be in charge of censorship, and Poynter tried to bring about some calm. Nevertheless, the FBI agent turned in a disparaging report that called the conference "chaotic to say the least."

Even sharper criticism entered the files when a Civil Service Commission investigator told Poynter that "Communist infiltration" had penetrated the highest levels of the Donovan office. The investigator told the FBI he had "a terrible time" with Poynter when he presented allegations against several employees and demanded that they be fired. Poynter defended them heatedly, the investigator said, and gave the impression that he was "deliberately shielding Communists."

While serving as federal liaison with Hollywood filmmakers, Poynter found himself caught between conservatives and liberals. The feud went back to the early New Deal days, when producers generally were Republicans and creative people—writers, directors, and actors—mostly were Roosevelt partisans. It also revealed the moguls' view that the function of movies was to make money. The other side wanted to send out a message—to remake the world into a better place. Producer Sam Goldwyn had shown his contempt for this idea with his aphorism "If you want to send a message, use Western Union."

Name-calling became more bitter during World War II. To the artists, producers were fascists; to producers, their critics were Communists. Poynter's specific assignment was to persuade Hollywood to help win the war with films, so to some critics it appeared he was siding against the producers. The bosses were as committed to the war effort as the workers, but they believed that entertainment could be profitable. In the end the industry both entertained and propagandized, syndicated columnist Peter Edson later reflected: "And if Hollywood's production for the war were run thru continuously from beginning to end, it would show that no segment of the population had a better patriotic record."[33]

But Poynter had his hands full of issues involving loyalty. His boss at the Donovan office, Mellett, had pointedly told him not to get anyone deferred from the draft. Studio owners pressured Poynter to keep Clark Gable out of the service, as he supposedly could do more for the war effort making movies. Poynter refused, although he did get a few weeks' delay in induction for Robert Taylor, who was starring in *Song of Russia,* a bit of fluff that made the Soviet allies look good. As a result, an entry from a "confidential informant" went into Poynter's FBI file. It exaggerated his power over the film industry and said all productions fell under his "direct control and supervision," and went on to say: "The informant added that Poynter practically always insisted that World War II started at the completion of World War I . . . and that if the picture did not have a definite Russian leaning, it could not get by at all. Referring to another film about the Soviet Union, the informant added that 'Mission to Moscow' . . . would not have received the approval of Poynter if it had not pictured the Russian situation in glowing colors."[34]

The report made much of the fact that Poynter spoke to a public meeting called by the Hollywood Writers Mobilization, which nearly a decade later was listed by the attorney general as a Communist front. It did not note that Poynter was there to explain Washington policy to the writers. Also cast in a subversive light was a notation that Poynter had spoken at a dinner given by the Joint Anti-Fascist Refugee Committee, later put on the list of fronts, and that music was provided by Paul Robeson, a baritone who later became a Communist leader. (See chapter 4.)

Poynter bitterly resented aspersions that HUAC, in a 1947 series of hearings, cast on the government's role in wartime Hollywood, although he apparently was not cited by name. He wrote a three-page letter trying to persuade the congressman from his district, a member of HUAC, to keep the hearings from running wild. He also ran a series of columns in the *Times* defending the filmland project.

Many liberal organizations went through internal struggles in the 1930s and 1940s between non-Communists—orthodox New Dealers and theoretical socialists—and card-carrying Communists. Senator Olin Johnston of South Carolina, a leading Communist hunter, noted that Communists had infiltrated groups "of probably once innocent nature or high purpose, and taken control and turned these organizations into tools of the Communist Party."[35]

The FBI did not claim that Nelson Poynter was ever a member of any group while it was on the U. S. attorney general's list of subversive organizations, although the bureau did claim that Henrietta Poynter belonged to the Washington Bookshop Association, which was listed. She quit paying dues to it in 1943, the file noted. But the FBI files detailed a host of other brushes Nelson Poynter had with political groups, all in the mid-1940s. The reason given for reporting his affiliations was that the groups had been cited late in the decade by HUAC, then headed by Rep. Martin Dies, and the California Committee on Un-American Activities. These were infamous for being far less accurate than the attorney general.

One such link was the Independent Citizens Committee of the Arts and Sciences, formed in 1944 to help reelect Franklin D. Roosevelt and including such luminaries such as comedian Eddie Cantor, playwright Russell Crouse, and literary editor Henry Seidel Canby. Poynter resigned after the election, three years before Henry Wallace's Progressives took it over and five years before it was listed by HUAC. Poynter also was a member of another Roosevelt campaign group, the National Citizens Political Action Committee, along with Mrs. Marshall Field, Mrs. J. Borden Harriman, and Gifford Pinchot, father of American forestry and former Republican governor of Pennsylvania. It was investigated by HUAC, but Senator Pat McCarran, a prominent Redhunter, pointed out later that it had never been cited as a Communist front by any agency.

In repeated security checks on Poynter over the decades, the whispers in the FBI files grew into a litany of suspicion. The reports also went on at length about extremely tenuous connections with groups that the FBI hinted were less than loyal. Some FBI gossip even confused Nelson with his father, who had served on a blue-ribbon commission appointed by Roosevelt and cast in a bad light.

Poynter had no inkling that he was caught up in the web of FBI innuendo during the 1940s except in one case. In 1944, David Loth served as managing editor of Poynter's *Press Research*. According to newspaper stories quoted in Poynter's FBI file, Loth had been called in 1944 to testify at a HUAC hearing on whether Communists, through the political arm of the Congress of Industrial Organizations, were trying to take over the Democratic party. Poynter had founded *Press Research* to provide campaign data for the Democrats, although it soon turned nonpartisan as *Congressional Quarterly*. At issue in the Loth case was a long report issued by *Press Research* on Thomas E. Dewey, Republican candidate for president.

When Loth testified, the HUAC chief investigator put into the record a 1936 election archive listing Loth as a Communist party member. Loth admitted that the name and address were his but denied that he had registered as a Communist. He did say that a Treasury Department investigator had exonerated him of communism when he joined the Rockefeller office in 1941 (the same year as Poynter). The HUAC investigator also accused Loth of contributing to *New Masses,* a Communist publication, but Loth said this was not significant.[36]

Poynter apparently heard about the Loth testimony the day it occurred. He sent a telegram to the hearing's press table: "Word indicates my name used in Un-American Activities Committee hearings in unfair and what I believe libelous manner. Will have statement available for press in few minutes for simultaneous release if you're using any reference to me."[37] The *New York Times* carried an inside-page story headed "Dies Group Uses Gestapo Ways, Says Poynter As It Opens Inquiry On Anti-Dewey Pamphlet."[38] Years later Poynter recalled that the accusations against Loth had brought protests from famous editors Josephus Daniels of Raleigh, North Carolina, and Barry Bingham of Louisville. Loth worked for Poynter less than a year, then was hired for a succession of jobs by Stuart Symington, later secretary of defense; by Nelson Rockefeller, in two government projects; and by Columbia University when Dwight Eisenhower was its president.

A tragicomic episode in 1952 demonstrated Poynter's unawareness that the FBI had been amassing a damaging dossier on him. Early in April he heard that FBI operatives had been asking questions about Henrietta and him in the neighborhood of their Georgetown home. The Poynters sent J. Edgar Hoover an angry letter questioning the investigation, as they were not candidates for any elective or appointive office. They referred Hoover to some of their friends—a list of Washington VIPs—and asked that the agent question the Poynters directly. Copies were sent to Senator Holland and to the attorney general.

It soon developed that the agent was making a routine hiring check on a man who was staying in the Poynter house temporarily while they were in Florida. Because the neighbors did not know the guest by name, the agent referred to him as the man who was living in the Poynters' house, causing much excitement on the block. The confusion was heightened by a normal credit check on the Poynters that was being done during the same week by a Dun and Bradstreet agent.

The episode apparently caused embarrassment at FBI headquarters, because Hoover made a note on the Poynters' letter asking an assistant, "Why would agt handle it this way?" Hoover immediately wrote Poynter by air mail, special delivery that the FBI had not investigated him since the "commencement of World War II"; a copy of the letter went to Holland.[39] Meanwhile, Hoover's aides put together an explanation that exculpated everyone concerned—the Poynters, the house guest, Dun and Bradstreet, and above all the FBI. Hoover politely communicated this to Poynter, again with a copy to the senator, but he made no mention of the rumors and innuendoes about Poynter that the FBI was passing on to any official who inquired.[40]

Just how hurtful the dossier could be came clear in 1954 when

Poynter lost out in bidding for the valuable channel eight television license after Hoover and an FCC commissioner had acted secretly to plant suspicions in the mind of other FCC members. The commission's examiner had ranked the three applicants closely, and the *Tampa Tribune,* Poynter's rival, won by a one-vote majority. (See chapter 6.)

The FBI files on Poynter grew over the remaining two decades of his life. The entries usually were scurrilous attacks by persons in St. Petersburg. The Miami FBI office passed along one of these to Washington, noting that "it is believed" that the *Times*'s endorsement of a candidate for mayor prompted the attack. On another occasion the Los Angeles bureau referred to Poynter as "editor of the St. Petersburg, Florida, Press" and noted that a Florida legislative committee had "apparently found Poynter to be against the philosophy of conservative Floridan [*sic*] and to have socialistic tendencies."[41]

Poynter's only substantial contact with the federal government after the channel 8 episode was his unsuccessful application for channel 10. In 1959, the FBI received a letter from St. Petersburg reviewing all the old charges against Poynter and saying that a station should not be awarded to "this controversial, tinged person." The bureau passed the letter on to the FCC with the sender's name blacked out.

Many enemies outside government asked the FBI for data on Poynter in later years, and they always were refused. Law restricted such reports to official requests, but there were plenty of these. Various officeholders asked for "name checks" on Poynter, although reasons were not recorded. The Central Intelligence Agency filed such a request, as did the U.S. Information Agency and the Johnson, Nixon, and Ford White House staffs. The FBI responses continued to cover the same ground, although more briefly in the 1970s.

Unheeded Prophecies

Hearst and Pulitzer created the image of the bombastic editor who becomes a national figure by directing aggressive journalism. They sent boatloads of reporters into the middle of Spanish-American War battles. They paid for stunts like Nelly Bly's attempt to go around the world in less than eighty days. Orson Welles savagely delineated the Hearst myth in his movie *Citizen Kane.* But by the time Welles made his film in 1939, newspaper editors had begun to slip into the shadows.

A journalist made a name by being a prominent reporter, a syndicated columnist, or a commentator.

Such a situation suited Nelson Poynter perfectly; he had a distaste for putting his personality above the mission of telling the day's news. On the editorial page, where he spoke with the authority of ownership, he could have been excused a bit of self-display. But aside from the Sunday column he coauthored with Henrietta, he did his best to make the editorial "we" truly mean the institutional voice of the newspaper, not a pluralized ego. This was a far cry from the personal pulpit in which Bill Straub had gloried.

After the Chaffee attack on his loyalty and the charges that he had grabbed the *Independent* to gain a monopoly, it became difficult for Poynter to keep a low profile. He was setting the paper on a course that would face it into the wind of majority opinion, requiring him to serve as a visible target for criticism. It also added to growing respect for his flinty "butt-headedness," as he called it.

Warren Pierce, who served as Poynter's editorial right hand, had returned from a brief fling with his own magazine and troubles with alcohol. Every morning Poynter would bring around his list of a dozen or so things he was concerned about. First, he would drop in on Baldwin and other news-side editors, and then he would engage in a stimulating chat with Pierce. They would meld their ideas, and he would leave Pierce to write the day's editorials, churning them out with flawless, informed prose.

But a year after buying the *Independent,* Poynter made a staff decision that would affect the paper for decades to come. He demoted Pierce and brought in a new editorial chief. Poynter said he wanted to free Pierce from administrative chores so that he could write more. The editorialist was not content, and in 1966 he bought two weeklies in Georgia. He left the staff cheerfully, saying the deal—a family matter—was too good to pass up. But he was fifty-eight and his health was too frail for the rigors of weekly publishing. He died soon afterward.

After Pierce's demotion, control of the page was soon taken over by a thirty-five-year-old North Carolinian named Robert Pittman. As in Pierce's case, his background as an academic reflected Poynter's life-long fascination for intellectuals.

Bob Pittman had been close to journalism since he edited his high school paper, the *Pea Picker.* He served as managing editor of the College of William and Mary paper and took his first full-time job with Virginia's leading newspaper, the *Richmond Times-Dispatch.* After a Korean War stint, he earned a master's in journalism at the University of North Carolina and then started on a doctorate in political science.

In his second year of doctoral work, Pittman had a chance to become part owner of a weekly in Montana. It was springtime, and life under the big sky was great fun. But after a horrible winter, he decided not only to head south again but to aim for Florida. He sent letters to every daily in the state, but only the *Florida Times-Union* in Jacksonville made an offer. He accepted it and spent several miserable years there as editorial writer. The *Times-Union,* owned by a railroad, did not have the standards he sought, so he applied to the *St. Petersburg Times.* Robert Brown had left the staff, and Pittman was hired to fill the vacancy. A few months later he stepped up as chief.

Pittman, whose soft-spoken courtliness resembled Poynter's, found it easy to slide into the necessary accord with the top man. He became Poynter's favorite partner for conversations about issues after Pierce left. Although Poynter had given up some degree of involvement with minutiae by the time of the new man's arrival, Pittman found out, as other *Times* executives had, that his biggest challenge was learning to play the game of ideas with the owner. Pittman had it somewhat easier than for managers and news editors, because with editorials the ideas were ends in themselves rather than merely means.

On issues, Poynter was inclined to plumb the minds of his editorialists. His favorite opener every morning was "What do you know that I should know?" When moving toward taking an opinion stand, he would engage in a Socratic cat-and-mouse dialogue. He would take a position just to bait the writer, then shift to another, leaving open the option of agreeing with the other person, reach a compromise, or win him over to his side. Politics was his passion, and he liked to toy with various candidacies as a campaign went on, whereas Pittman preferred to pick one early on and stick with it.

Poynter hammered into Pittman a stubborn respect for the reader. He wanted editorials that would persuade rather than preach, and he wanted facts to be the main tool of argument. He also was reluctant to bore or nag the reader and insisted that the editorial page move on to new subjects, although he broke his own rule in notable cases. Letters from readers delighted Poynter, particularly those that took issue with editorials. He banned the snippy replies some newspapers would tack below letters. "The editorial writer has had a clear shot, and the reader should have his," he declared.

Poynter clung to the hope that his readers were not as opposed to his ideas as generally supposed, despite the fact that the area continued to vote heavily Republican although he supported mostly Democratic candidates. He repeatedly took unpopular editorial stands in the 1960s; in some things he went with the national tide if not with local sentiment. He strongly backed the Kennedy and Johnson domestic programs, although personally he seemed to prefer Hubert Humphrey as a politician. Like Johnson, he most resented the Vietnam conflict because it interfered with progress at home.

Poynter's most spectacular defeat in Pinellas County concerned the sparkling waters of Tampa and Boca Ciega bays, which had mesmerized newcomers for generations. Poynter habitually took passionate stands in favor of free bridges and against land developments that would fill up the bays. Having seen the Gandy Bridge toll restrict traffic between Tampa and St. Petersburg for two decades, he was determined to unchain the new Sunshine Skyway from eternal charges. Some commercial boosters like Doc Webb believed that a golden stream of shoppers would cross the bridge northward from Bradenton and Sarasota if it were free. Poynter was more enthralled by the trip's scenic splendor. He believed it was one of the most beautiful drives in the country and visitors from all over the world should be able to enjoy it unimpeded. Also, the toll served as a nagging reminder of Pinellas's earlier isolation.

Although Poynter yearned for people to be able to marvel at the bay from the soaring arch of the Skyway, he was dead-set against allowing land developers to fill in the bay in the name of progress. Since the 1920s, developers had coveted the mud flats that ringed both bays. Often only a few inches below the water's surface at high tide, they emerged as an untidy runway for sandpipers at low tide. It was difficult for any kind of boat to cross them, so passages had to be dredged to allow fishermen to move from channels to moorings.

Business boomers argued: Why let such marine deserts go to waste? Why not dredge the channels deeper? The soil could be used to raise the mudbanks enough to build houses on them, leaving mini-channels to each owner's front door. This would attract more permanent customers from the North and fatten the tax base, supposedly solving all public finance problems. During the 1920s land boom, this concept had created Snell Isle on Tampa Bay, an opulent enclave of millionaires.

And look at those islands at the mouth of Tampa Bay going to waste, they said. Hermits had lived there for centuries, and an ancient fort pointed dead cannons at the sky. Now the islands were used by picnickers trekking over by boat, hearing only the wind and smelling only the sea. Shouldn't the hundreds of thousands who owned cars but not boats be able to do the same, via causeways that could poke straight across the bay, even bridging channels?

Poynter, like Straub before him, was concerned with a different kind of waste—careless discard of the county's gifts of nature. Soon after Poynter returned to the *Times* in 1938, it editorialized:

> Pinellas waters and woods naturally abound with wild life as our beaches abound with sunshine. But wasteful commercial fishing, wasteful grass fires, careless husbandry of these assets, have resulted in their partial depletion. How long shall this continue?
>
> Waste destroyed the buffalo and the carrier pigeon. Waste destroyed valuable farm lands in the old south and in the wheat belt through erosion. Let us learn from the tragic experience of other areas.[42]

After World War II, scientists began to prove some things that old fishermen had long known. Mud flats were not useless; they were indispensable to marine life. Also, the water had a will of its own, and channels did not always stay where engineers tried to put them.

Rachel Carson, whose book *Silent Spring* awakened the country to environmental dangers, took on Tampa Bay as a prime laboratory to study marine ecology. She and the Poynters became friends, and her concepts made a deep impact on Nelson.

Poynter had fought hard through the paper to save Mullet Key, one of the bay-mouth islands, from exploitation by getting it into the county's hands. It became a quiet, unspoiled park accessible by boat. He also had taken an early stand against bay-bottom filling. Anyone wanting to do this had to buy submerged lands from the Internal Improvement Fund, made up of elected state cabinet officers. Well-placed campaign contributions worked wonders, but in 1954 the *Times* raised such an outcry that the fund put a two-year freeze on such sales, which only slowed the dredging.

The two issues—Skyway tolls and bay filling—became intertwined over the years. The boomers, backed by much of the population, lusted after anticipated riches. The *Times* and the weak, newborn ecology movement stood against them.

Every governor involved with the Skyway had itched to see it produce revenues to construct roads elsewhere. It was built with a promise that the $1.75 toll would be eliminated when the $21 million original bond issue was paid off from revenues. The bridge proved a golden goose, with about $2 million a year coming in. Four years after it opened, a state road board member from Pinellas, Al Rogero, proposed that the Skyway be mortgaged for another thirty years and the toll retained to pay for other roads. The Chamber of Commerce, city council, county commission and Governor LeRoy Collins all endorsed the idea.

In a rare front-page editorial, the *Times* blasted the plan as a fatal blow to hopes for a toll-free bridge. It launched a public campaign against it, instigating committees that plied the streets for protest petition signatures. Within twelve days, 40,000 were gathered. Poynter was part of a delegation that took the petitions to Tallahassee and bearded the cabinet. Collins said publicly that he would have to eat crow, and the Rogero plan was rejected and the toll reduced to a dollar.

But Poynter's winning streak reached an end. In 1962 boosters asked the county to build a fifteen-mile web of causeways and bridges reaching to St. Petersburg Beach and Mullet Key. The new roads were touted as a boon to recreation, and—just incidentally—they opened up Tierra Verde Island, which promoters wanted to develop as a high-priced subdivision. To pay for the package, backers put together a bond plan that was baited to attract countywide support by dedicating much of the money to building roads elsewhere in Pinellas. Causeway tolls supposedly would pay off the bonds, but if they fell below budget, county tax money would have to plug the gap.

Poynter suspected impropriety in a deal for which private investors were so eager. He also thought the causeway revenues would fall short. Most of all, he resented the despoliation of bays and the fact that one would no longer be able to stand at the tip of the subpeninsula and look out to sea. There, from one horizon to the other, would lie a man-made barrier.

The *Times* fought the plan bitterly. A countywide referendum was held, and voters approved the project. It was cold comfort to Poynter to see his gloomy prediction come true. Revenues did not meet bond payments, and the county had to sacrifice gasoline tax money.

The Skyway issue arose again in 1966. Governor Haydon Burns, whom the *Times* had opposed for election, proposed a new roads package that would put a $25 million mortgage at high interest on the bridge. Once more the *Times* took to the ramparts, persuading 22,000 people to sign petitions of protest. A delegation to Tallahassee once more challenged the cabinet, but this time the political power was too immense. When the toll was dropped to fifty cents as part of the deal, the paper gave up its opposition.

Although the *Times*'s battle of the bays failed in the short run, it had raised the public consciousness of ecological dangers. Thus, St. Petersburg later became the first city in the state to eliminate sewage discharge in waterways, and it was one of the earliest in recycling waste water for lawn sprinkling.

Another bright spot was the matter of the Cross-Florida Barge Canal. For a century, commercial boosters had talked about cutting through the northern part of the state's peninsula, reducing the route from the Atlantic coast to the Gulf of Mexico by hundreds of miles. A serious push developed in the 1960s, and a small band of ecological defenders took up the fight. The *Times* had blown hot and cold on the concept for decades, but in 1969 it discovered the likelihood that a canal would cause incalculable harm to the water supply, agriculture, and wildlife. The paper became one of the first public voices to be raised against the project. Public opinion turned heavily anti-canal. Although much construction was completed, President Richard Nixon bowed to political pressure and stopped the undertaking in 1971.

The Limitless Sky

American newspapers were going through a change of life. Circulation growth almost stopped, and television made steady inroads on national advertising. It was a Darwinian struggle for survival: The largest and best papers continued to make good profits, and weaker ones fell by the wayside. Usually the losers were second-rate, and their death was a blessing. But sometimes a giant would fall. In 1966 one of the most admired papers in the world, the *New York Herald Tribune*, met its end after heavy losses.

Florida's newspaper industry bucked the national trend. The state was the fastest-growing in the country, gaining 37 percent in population during the 1960s. Tourism, agriculture, and business were booming, and the construction industry soon pulled out of the slump that opened the decade. Cape Canaveral's space-shot dramatics and the flight of Cubans from the Castro revolution drew the nation's attention.

No major daily capitalized on the growth more than the *St. Petersburg Times*. In the ten years ending in 1971, its circulation increased 46 percent, more than nine times the national circulation growth. It also more than doubled the percentage rise in population for St. Petersburg during the same period. Although the rate of circulation in the 1960s increase was less than a third of that of the previous decade—the postwar economic explosion—the 1971 figure of 166,513 was historic. For years Poynter had chafed at the *Times*'s stigma of being circulation runner-up to the *Tampa Tribune*, long the paper to beat. This was not just a matter of pride. With the Tampa Bay area becoming an integrated market, there was a challenge to dominate national advertising, which gravitated to the largest paper in any trading zone.

The *Times* board of directors usually consisted of working executives. In 1959 it included (*from left*) John B. Olson, general manager; Dorothy McConnie, the owner's secretary; Henrietta Poynter; Nelson Poynter; Tom C. Harris, executive editor; and Irwin Simpson, advertising director. *St. Petersburg Times.*

As the new decade opened, Joe Yauch's highly competitive circulation staff at the *Times* smelled blood, and by June 1971 the *Times* became the area's circulation leader, as unimpeachable figures from the Audit Bureau of Circulations showed. The *Times* had become the second largest paper in Florida, after the *Miami Herald*.

Advertising revenues, which allowed Poynter to build his dream newspaper, also climbed at a faster rate than elsewhere in the nation. During the Baldwin era, ad receipts increased every year except during the building slump of 1961. By 1966 the increases had risen above $1 million a year. Within five years the annual gains were almost $3 million. The advertising miracle was even more stunning in a national context. Adjusted for inflation, the U.S. increase of newspaper advertising expenditures rose 20 percent. The *Times*'s rise was 80 percent.

These numbers reflected decisive steps toward making the *Times* a finely tuned money-making machine. Alvah Chapman had set the trend in the mid-1950s, and in the 1960s and 1970s a new platoon of mostly young professionals joined the staff and expanded the systems Chapman had set up. In so doing, they put the newspaper in vastly larger buildings, invaded new territory, abandoned old ground, became the city's chief business recruiter, and overhauled the marketing strategy. Whether they increased the business side's influence at the expense of the news operation was sometimes debated among staffers.

As much as Nelson Poynter prized Chapman as general manager, they disagreed strongly on one essential—where the *Times*'s home should be. With St. Petersburg experiencing commercial flight to the suburbs like the rest of the country, Chapman thought the paper's future lay closer to shopping centers. Besides, cheaper land could be bought and better buildings erected farther from the downtown center.

But Poynter adamantly believed the downtown had to be saved and that the *Times* as the conscience of the community had to stay there. In the late 1950s the newspaper was not occupying all the upper-floor offices of the eight-story 1926 building, but it needed new presses, and installing them in the old structure plainly would be a mistake.

Jack Olson, one of Chapman's bright young men, had succeeded him as general manager. He took on the mission of dissuading Poynter from his dedication to staying exclusively in the downtown area. Olson's solution was a split plant. He lobbied Poynter to build a press building elsewhere and truck the printing plates there from the downtown building. With St. Petersburg's wide streets, driving after mid-

Nelson Poynter is hoisted to a staff member's shoulder during the celebration of its surpassing the *Tampa Tribune* as the bay area's largest newspaper in 1971. At left is Joe Yauch, circulation manager, who led the drive. *Poynter Library, University of South Florida, St. Petersburg, Florida.*

night was no problem. The paper, aided by consultants, did a massive study of the revenue growth projected for the next twenty-five years and how it would be achieved. Robust expansion was predicted, but projections later proved far too conservative.

Poynter was won over by the split plant idea, partly because it provided him room to realize his dreams of new technology. He insisted that any new building have a bold wall sign proclaiming "Color Printing Plant." Some saw it as bragging, but Poynter used it as a challenge to his staff.

Olson arranged a twenty-five-year lease on land bordering 34th Street, the city's main north-south highway. It was thirty blocks west and fourteen blocks north of the main building. The lease later was converted to a purchase, and more adjoining land was bought over the years.

A team of *Times* executives prowled the country looking for state-of-the-art ideas for such buildings. Architects designed a low, sprawling structure that could be quadrupled in modules. As a factory it was attractive, as a newspaper building it was drab. Poynter did insist on saving trees, planting shrubs, and developing an ornamental pond.

For the first time the *Times* ordered a totally new set of presses.

Poynter, obsessed with the merits of offset printing, often urged his executives to "think offset." He would conjure up the vision of two youths starting a daily newspaper exploiting offset's economies: "I'm more afraid of those two kids than I am of the *Tampa Tribune*," he would declare.

But technology had not quite caught up with Poynter's imagination. The *Times* had to continue with letterpress printing, buying ten units and soon adding four more, for a capacity of fifty-six pages.

Planners also talked of electronically transmitting the printing plates instead of trucking them out to 34th Street. The *New York Times* was to attempt that process a few years later with an abortive West Coast edition, and the *Wall Street Journal* became a national publication through satellite plants using this method. But electronic transmission did not become economical or practical in St. Petersburg for more than two decades. The 34th Street plant, completed in 1959, climaxed Olson's career at the *Times*. He moved on two years later to manage the *New York Times*'s own split plant—its experimental West Coast edition.

Although the 34th Street plant relieved some of the pressure on the downtown buildings, far more space was needed within a few years. In 1968, a gleaming new five-story addition was completed at the corner of Fifth Street and First Avenue, site of the 1920 *Times* building. Although it was difficult to mate its floor levels with the two older

The 1968 building of the *Times* (*right*) signaled the paper's commitment to downtown development. It adjoined the eight-story 1926 building. *St. Petersburg Times.*

downtown buildings, it made possible a different approach to office design. The whole complex was fitted out with carpets and attractive decor, and the new wing had conduits built in for the electronic newsroom soon to come. The new building did not solve all the space problems. And the modest lobby did not live up to dreams for a twenty-first-century newspaper plant.

A man who would have a major role in the *Times*'s development for a quarter century arrived in 1960. He was John B. ("Jack") Lake, whose flair and aggressiveness would become much talked about both in the *Times* and the community.

Irwin Simpson, who had modernized the paper's advertising department, was preparing to retire and was shopping for his successor at a national convention. He liked what he learned about Lake, then working for the *Elizabeth Journal* in New Jersey. He reported his impression to Poynter when he returned. Poynter had heard that Ralph Ingersoll, with whom he had tangled in founding *PM*, was going to buy the Elizabeth paper. He told Simpson that he knew that Lake and Ingersoll would not get along. So Poynter invited Lake to St. Petersburg for an interview.[43]

St. Petersburg was suffering an outbreak of encephalitis, a disease carried by pigeons and passed it on to humans through mosquitoes. After his interview, Lake returned to New Jersey. When Poynter called to offer him the job, his new ad director was hospitalized with the disease, a souvenir of his Florida trip. It took him a month to recover and start work.

When Jack Olson left the next year, Lake was a leading candidate to succeed him as general manager. To his chagrin, he soon learned what self-denying devotion to the newspaper Poynter demanded of his executives. Poynter called an unscheduled meeting of his top people. Lake declined to attend, as he had made commitments to join friends boating at Palm Beach. Shortly afterward, Poynter named Tom Harris general manager. A friend told Lake that Poynter passed over him because he had skipped the meeting, and Poynter had fretted at length over what trait of Lake this signified.

Harris's appointment, which would have been expected at more traditional newspapers, sharply departed from *Times* staff-building trends of the previous decade. He shared little with the new breed of scientific managers, and futuristic technology held little interest for him. But Harris was a shrewd observer of people and knew every detail of how the *Times* operated. Above all, nobody was—before or after him—so devoted to serving the paper. One could enter the newsroom long after midnight and find him working.

Despite his disappointment, Lake prided himself on becoming one of the most adept Poynter-watchers among the executives. Although Lake could be blunt and critical, he deferred to the head man's ideas, filtered out the ones he thought workable, implemented them, and persuaded Poynter against others.

The advertising people kept the money coming in. Under Lake and later Laurence T. Herman, much of the guesswork was taken out of marketing. Research, which had gotten started in the late 1950s, became a tool in all sales staffers' kits, giving them the facts to prove their claims. Lake, who had been selling to big department stores in the New York City area, knew that major advertisers were becoming more selective about media.

Shopping centers were already in place, but they needed occupants. The paper's promotion brought in the K-Mart chain three years ahead of schedule, along with others. Webb's City, gaudy as ever, continued to advertise heavily and had first call on prime space—pages four through seven in Section A. Lake reminded Poynter of how much he depended on Webb and joked that he should build a full-time fire station next to the store.

Poynter would not permit pressure from the advertising department on the editorial side, but his view of ad placement was strangely incongruous. He believed in maximum use of newsprint, and long before the Baldwin era he insisted on selling the ears—the space on each side of the page-one nameplate. To many news staffers this was a gross journalistic indignity, and although Baldwin also detested it, he got nowhere in trying to dissuade Poynter.

Another Poynter idea that would have made the paper less attractive was selling classified advertising throughout the paper—at a premium price. This was a holdover from his days at *PM*, where he failed to sell the concept to Ralph Ingersoll. It also got buried at the *Times*. Both the ear advertising and scattered classified ideas flew in the face of the policy to make the *Times* more attractive through graceful use of white space. What made these concepts more incongruous was that Poynter himself was an ardent booster of the visual upgrade.

In 1966, twilight fell on Tom Harris's prodigious career at the *Times*. Poynter took him out of the general manager position and made him associate editor, with little to do. It was a preparation for his retirement, scheduled two years later. The action erased the last vestige of the highly personal, informal management style the paper had known in its simpler days. Alvah Chapman's overhaul had doomed it, but it seemed to have an afterglow in Harris's tenure as boss of the business side.

Jack Lake stepped in as general manager and later was given the title of publisher. His appointment heralded a new wave of management staffing reminiscent of Chapman's hirings. Byron Harless, still acting as personnel consultant, had conducted a study of the paper's upper echelons and pointed out that several key people were nearing retirement. It was time to put together a new team, Harless said, and it should come from outside the city.

When retail advertising manager Chuck Frank died of a heart attack during a sales meeting in 1968, ad director Laurie Herman immediately telephoned the *Detroit News*. He told a young executive there, Leo Kubiet, about the job. Raised in West Virginia, Kubiet pursued the new academic field of advertising to the graduate level at the University of Michigan. During his eighteen years at the *Detroit News,* he seemed marked for a high position.

Three days after the call from Herman, Kubiet visited St. Petersburg to meet all the paper's top people. It was springtime, he had just left a snowstorm in Detroit, and the memory of the recent race riots there rankled him. Kubiet particularly liked the *Times*'s liberal use of color, which was limited in large cities like Detroit because of union rules. The *Times*'s rapid shift to cold type and plans for offset printing also excited Kubiet, but most of all he was impressed by Nelson Poynter's candor and sincerity. Within forty-eight hours he accepted the retail advertising spot and later became head of advertising at the paper.

A Strength Unseen

Nelson Poynter defied many stereotypes, including the one of a small man intimidated by women. All his life he had close ties to strong women, and he neither truckled to them nor seemed to feel threatened. It was of a piece with his unflagging self-confidence, which stopped short of arrogance.

No woman posed more of a potential threat to a male ego than Henrietta Malkiel Poynter. With a word or glance she could reduce a

Henrietta Poynter exerted much influence on news and editorial operations of the *Times* until her death in 1968. *Poynter Library, University of South Florida, St. Petersburg, Florida.*

man to a quivering mass. But some observers saw her, like Nelson, as a deeply caring person who was basically shy and was merely trying to cope with a world that needed mending. That she and Nelson found each other and had nearly three decades together was a miracle. Each fulfilled the other professionally. As two individuals who were extremely hard to live with, the pleasure they found in being together represented just another of their contradictions.

Certainly her looks did not bring them together. She was not careless about her face, but she knew she could do little for it, and she wore her hair pulled back like an oldtime schoolmarm. Clothes were her one vanity, and she tended toward the cutting edge of international fashion. For the office she preferred suits and simpler dresses, but in social situations there were cloaks, flowing skirts, and caftans, trimmed with an array of jangling jewelry. After the couple's 1957 trip through Asia, she took a strong turn toward Oriental designs. In conservative St. Petersburg, this heightened her mystique. Few people knew how carefully she shopped. A shrewd judge of craftsmanship, she would spot a dress in a store and wait for it to go on sale. She often bought end-of-the-season bargains.

Although she was about the same height as Nelson, as were his other two wives, she struck people as imposing. Her walk was an exaggerated stride, the result of an inner-ear balance problem.

Congressional Quarterly was both Henrietta's monument and the child she never had. She worked around the clock alongside editors and reporters in its early years. The exhaustion that followed the close of each week's edition usually made it difficult to get started on the next one, but her resilience provided the needed spur.

Like Nelson, she was known not for her writing but for her ideas, energy, and compulsion to excel. Her manner could put people off as much as her looks. She spoke in bursts, and the words came out so fast she sometimes lost track of them. The result often was tactless. Once when discussing a current topic with a reporter she confided, "I'm trying to explain this in terms *you* will understand." But people who worked closely with her invariably liked her. She made good conversation on almost anything. One friend thought of her as "an earthy highbrow . . . the most unboring person I ever knew."[44]

Although she held the title of associate editor of the *Times* from 1962 on, Henrietta never had specific duties. She had an office there and kept fairly regular working hours. Despite her brusqueness, she never tried to boss the editors. Her work took the form of advising and helping out. At one point when the opinion page staff was depleted, Stan Witwer sought her help as a writer. He would give her a subject, and she would write a thoroughly informed editorial without stopping for research, bracelets rattling away. Then she would toss Witwer the article and stride out to a department store.

Some observers believe that Henrietta had a deep impact on Nelson's political ideas, particularly in keeping him on a liberal keel. Those who observed them together overheard a nonstop conversation on politics, although they never seemed to argue. Psychologist Byron Harless divined in Nelson a deep respect for Henrietta's judgment, intellect, idealism, even her willingness to challenge him. Nelson confided to friends who watched her in action, "You know, that woman sometimes terrifies me." But he said it with pride.[45]

Although Nelson was never a thoroughgoing aesthete like his wife, she opened the world of visual art to him. When they set up housekeeping in Washington after World War II, his intimates were surprised to find their walls covered with good paintings. English friends later gave them a Picasso, which became the centerpiece of their home. Nelson also commissioned Syd Solomon, a noted Florida artist, to do a mural for the *Times* lobby.

Henrietta's skill as a hostess built for Nelson the kind of social framework he enjoyed—relaxed, tasteful, and stimulating. Her dinner parties were exquisitely planned; she would have *Times* executives come out early with their wives so they could rehearse toasts before other guests arrived.

Establishment resistance to her in St. Petersburg eroded gradually. People found that, although she held strong convictions, she never bragged of herself and could be a loyal friend. Her favorite gift to women was a gold jewelry clasp bearing hands of friendship. When she saw a situation that needed righting, she stepped in without hesitation. A local man had married a Korean woman, and St. Petersburg society shunned her. Henrietta fixed that by giving a reception for her at the Yacht Club.

As a guest, she was just as uninhibited. Once when Alicia Frazier of the DuPont family was giving a Christmas dinner party for a hundred people, the food was delayed because an important guest's plane had not arrived. Toward ten o'clock, with guests drinking too much, Henrietta sat down, banged on her glass, and sang out, "It's time to eat!" Mrs. Frazier was horrified, but she managed to produce the food. The next day, Henrietta wrote an apologetic note.[46]

The Poynters' Georgetown home became one of the best places to meet Washington people known more for brain power than for political strength. Most guests were liberals who spanned periods from the New Deal through the Johnson years, including Philip Graham, a young Floridian who made the *Washington Post* great, columnists such as Elizabeth Drew, Doris Fleeson, and Samuel Lubell, and Senators Hubert Humphrey, Paul Douglas, Claude Pepper, and Spessard Holland. The Poynters were particularly close to two young political scientists, Evron and Jeane Kirkpatrick, who later took on a conservative bent. LeRoy Collins, one of Florida's most honored governors, was keenly grateful that the Poynters had introduced him to Washingtonians.

Despite her intellect and self-confidence, Henrietta did little to seek out a public role. Aside from her position as associate editor of the *Times,* in 1966 she became vice chairman of the paper's board. And although she made public service presentations for the paper to local gatherings, she appeared in its pages mostly as coauthor with Nelson of a Sunday column. It was generally believed that, although the column was jointly thought out, she usually composed it.

As the journalistic world became interested in what was happening at the *Times*, Henrietta made linkages from which Nelson would shrink. She was the first woman to serve on the American committee of the International Press Institute and conducted seminars for the IPI, including one about a favorite project of hers, the promotion of newspaper reading among schoolchildren.

Henrietta's low profile did not keep her from gaining formal recognition. She was listed in *Who's Who in America* and in lesser such directories. Her highest honor was being chosen one of fifty distinguished alumni of the Columbia University School of Journalism for its fiftieth anniversary.

Her role as a grande dame of good works was limited mostly to art. She was a patron of the newly founded St. Petersburg Museum of Arts, and Governor Millard Caldwell named her to his committee for the Ringling Museum in Sarasota.

In November 1967 Henrietta was driving out the tree-lined road that led to their St. Petersburg home when she suffered a severe stroke. She slowly improved, although she had a horror of being incapacitated, having witnessed a friend who had been pitifully handicapped by a stroke. She never left the hospital, and on January 25, 1968, at age sixty-six, she died. By her wish, burial was immediate, with no public service and no flowers.

A short piece ran in the opinion columns pointing out that the paper rarely ran funerary editorials because "the editors . . . prefer to look ahead rather than back." It was termed "an expression of loss and a word of farewell from 727 staffers" and said Henrietta always sought not just good work, but the best, doing so with grace and understanding. It concluded: "We are a better staff because of her high standards. We shall endeavor to live up to them always."[47]

Nelson vanished from St. Petersburg as soon as he saw to the burial. Above all, he did not want to sit by a telephone taking condolences. He quickly set up living arrangements at the Georgetown house and spent time in his daughters' homes. Nancy, then living with her husband in Washington, helped him plan a domestic routine with the help of a valued housekeeper. He was proud of how much Nancy had learned from her stepmother. Friends often were invited for dinner, although he begged off invitations to go out alone.

Despite his disdain for the usual trappings that follow death, Nelson treasured the stack of condolence letters he received. They finally made him shed the tears that he had held back. Many of the tributes to Henrietta's generosity, genius for friendship, brilliance, femininity, charm, culture, unselfishness came from people he had never met. He answered each one individually.

Nelson felt a sharp pang when he wrote the first Sunday column by himself. "I loved our by-line," he wrote his mother, "and so when I had to drop Henrietta's name the total finality of that loving, working relationship jolted me more than many other more obvious things."[48] He turned to Alice, the other woman who had meant so much to him, for ultimate vindication of the marriage she never would have chosen for him: "You will be proud of her as a woman—and a newspaper woman of 'uncompromising standards and integrity.'"[49]

A difficult personal adjustment followed, and to some Nelson seemed disoriented. Then he came back stronger than ever, with a new emphasis on hard-nosed business management and less on liberalism. A close friend, Charles Donegan, the couple's physician, found him turning to a more considerate view of the political middle. Poynter, who had earlier lavished money on his dream of broadcasting in the public interest, was thinking about buying a radio station to make money.

Poynter commuted between St. Petersburg and Washington at shorter intervals. Major trouble was brewing at *Congressional Quarterly,* and he took closer control there than before Henrietta's death. He turned over the presidency of Times Publishing Company to Don Baldwin and retreated to the title of board chairman. Having vowed to take Fridays off, he kept to his plan only briefly.

South from Fairview

Poynter had dinner with Charles Donegan at least once a week. Finally Poynter asked if he could bring a date, an attractive forty-three-year-old woman named Marion Knauss. Within a few months, she and Nelson were married, with little fanfare. The house on Park Avenue had a new mistress, and Nelson had a companion who would accompany him to the end.

Just as Henrietta's background had differed sharply from that of Catherine, so Marion's was a world apart from either. She came from a family of German meat packers and grew up in a small town, Fairview, New York, in the Hudson River Valley. The Knausses had immigrated in the mid-1800s from near Stuttgart, where an ancestor had been burgomeister. Knauss Brothers' sausages became famous throughout the valley, attaining celebrity when Franklin Roosevelt had them served to King George VI and Queen Elizabeth at Hyde Park.

Cornell University was the family's favored college, but her father had died and money was short when Marion was ready. She got a scholarship to Vassar in her home city and oddly found herself having to attend the exclusive school because of economic hardship. Marion had gone to a country school with two grades per room, and she found it difficult to compete with the Vassar preppies—particularly, to her dismay, in German classes. But she graduated in three years, barely twenty years old.

Then began a phase that she and Nelson later would laughingly call her feckless career. For five years she had short stints of helping print Donald Duck comic books, selling yellow page advertising, teaching school, working in the *Time* magazine picture library, returning to school to study musicology, and plugging sheet music by playing piano in a store. She finally settled down for nine years doing research at CIA

Marion Knauss became Nelson Poynter's third wife in 1970. She took little part in the paper's management and helped her husband learn to relax. *St. Petersburg Times.*

headquarters outside Washington. Then she started wandering again, toured Europe making slides for language study materials, and ended up in St. Petersburg in 1961. Her family had connections there for decades, and cousins had built a resort hotel.

Marion got a job with the *St. Petersburg Times* library as a reference clerk. She saw Nelson first in "throne room," his office, where he always greeted new staffers at the close of orientation sessions. He was dapper and compact, but she saw in him something vital and dynamic. Marion later became a junior staffer for the editorial page. She took a leave to observe the Prague Spring in 1968, Czechoslovakia's futile rebellion against Soviet domination, and when she returned Bob Pittman asked her to do some articles. The stories caught Nelson's eye and he complimented her, but he was still mourning Henrietta.

More than a year later, friends arranged contacts and Nelson asked Marion to an art exhibit. Friends teased her because they were mentioned in a gossip column, but Nelson decided he wanted to marry her and pursued the matter briskly. Adding urgency was the fact that he had promised to go to Asia for an International Press Institute meeting.

The Asia trip was canceled, because Nelson and Marion decided to elope. His daughter Nancy got wind of it and insisted that they have a proper wedding with some relatives. They were married on a Monday morning, May 4, 1970, in Nancy's living room near Atlanta and flew off to the Virgin Islands for a honeymoon. From then on they celebrated the anniversary every month.

Best-Laid Plans

If Nelson Poynter had died while Henrietta was alive, it was understood, she would not become chief executive of the *Times*. Throughout the 1960s, it became clear that Don Baldwin would assume control of the company upon Nelson's death.

Baldwin was like Poynter in many ways—liberal, bold in ideas, generous, quick-minded. The succession seemed perfect. But their similarity held a fatal flaw. Both were dynamic men, and Baldwin could not abide playing second fiddle indefinitely. Poynter, no matter how he tried, had difficulty casting off the ties that bound him to *Times* management. Poynter's discontent surfaced in his shakeup of CQ after Henrietta's death. At the *Times* it was manifest in his feeling that the editors were getting out of touch with readers.

The paper had always—at Poynter's behest—searched out young people, many with no training in journalism, who would take a fresh, nonconformist view of the world. He favored liberal arts graduates over journalism-school products, believing the *Times* could train its recruits better than universities could. This system worked well until the generation gap widened. Poynter began to suspect that the youngsters in the newsroom were printing material that was intended to irritate conservative readers. On one occasion they ran a human interest picture of a small boy and girl walking along a path hand in hand, the kind of photo the paper thrived on. But this time one child was white, the other black.

Poynter was furious, as were many staffers to whom it was a matter of bad taste. But to the Young Turks the complaints smacked of racism. Baldwin, who never had developed sympathy for southern tradition even after a decade in Florida, was the lightning rod for Poynter's ire. Although deeply fond of the older man, Baldwin believed that Poynter was an elitist shaped by lifelong wealth and the sociology of southern Indiana, long noted for its intolerance. Baldwin noticed things like Poynter's lack of social life with black people and special favors he asked for his grandchildren.

Social critics discovered the credibility gap between mass media and their publics as the 1970s began. Poynter was quite concerned and met the issue with his usual aggressive problem-solving. The *Times* installed one of the earliest newspaper ombudsmen to respond to reader complaints. Poynter also insisted that editors take an active part in finding out what readers thought about the paper. Polls were conducted, and editors knocked on doors for interviews. Baldwin monitored the complaint phone several days to take the readers' pulse.

It seemed to Baldwin that the man at top could not be pleased. He gave Baldwin the impression of wanting to show he was in control of himself and the paper.[50]

Baldwin was nearing the boiling point. He had tried to control his quick temper over the years, but now it was becoming difficult. He would flare up over relatively minor matters, and it irritated other executives who prided themselves on keeping their cool. "Who the hell is this guy? Why is he so hard to get along with?" they muttered to Poynter, who would soothe their feelings.[51]

The matter came to a head late in 1971 over pictures of blacks in the paper. Baldwin and Lake were sitting in Poynter's office while the boss flipped through recent issues, criticizing mostly the local news section. Poynter recently had been questioning whether desk editors were going out of their way to print photos of blacks, but Baldwin believed that decisions were simply being made by color-blind young people. This time Baldwin reached the end of his fuse, particularly since Lake was siding with Poynter.[52] Baldwin stormed out of the room, shouting, "That's a bunch of horseshit!" Sound travels easily through the executive suite, and the explosion startled those in earshot.

Lake turned to Poynter and saw a terribly saddened, crestfallen man, as if there had been a death in the family. Poynter knew that Lake and Baldwin had differences, and he interpreted the outburst as directed at both Lake and himself. After a pause, he said to Lake, "Well, if you two aren't going to get along, I guess it's best that I know it now." Poynter indicated to Lake that he expected Baldwin would cool down and apologize. All through the weekend Poynter expected Baldwin to come out to his house and put the episode behind them, but there was no word.

Poynter and Baldwin had several conversations over the next few weeks to discuss their relationship. To Baldwin it seemed like a marriage gone sour because of a series of minor discords. Marion Poynter tried to heal the breach, but Nelson told her that Baldwin was becoming too partisan with his staff and making excuses for it and that the paper was becoming alienated from the community. Besides, he believed that Baldwin did not show enough devotion to the paper when he left the office to batten down his sailboat while a hurricane was approaching.[53]

Encounters between the two men increased rather than dissipated the tension. Finally, in a calm moment, Poynter told the younger man that he no longer wanted him as his successor. Baldwin called a news staff meeting and, without explanation, announced he would take early retirement. A terse news release shocked journalists throughout the state. It was years before most *Times* staffers had details of the event, but they knew Baldwin's departure was not at his initiative.

Dr. Donegan, keenly aware of Poynter's obsession with the paper, later asked him why he had let Baldwin go. His reply was, "Charles, he just was not willing to be a newspaperman twenty-four hours a day."

Chapter 8

Hope Reborn

Joseph Pulitzer, always morose and unsatisfied, often remarked that "every reporter is a hope, every editor a disappointment." Nelson Poynter adapted this to his own restless search for perfection: "Every young editor is a hope, every old editor a disappointment."[1]

The record indicated that he defined age as tenure at the *Times*. Although Tom Harris was five years younger than Poynter, he had outlived his role at the paper. Don Baldwin, still younger, had seen his star burst and crash.

Poynter showed no signs of worrying excessively about his mortality in the early 1970s, as he had good genes. When Baldwin left, Poynter was sixty-eight, and he still glowed with health and had a springy step. His mother was still alive at ninety-two, and Paul Poynter had lived to seventy-five. Nelson Poynter was determined to choose and groom his own successor as absolute ruler of the paper, but time to clone himself was running out.

Of all Poynter's hires, he was proudest of Alvah Chapman, who had come from Georgia. Now his mind went back to another Georgian, a dynamic redhead who had been making a brilliant career when they first met at newspaper conventions. Eugene Patterson had been fascinated with Poynter and sought out ideas from him when he became editor of the *Atlanta Constitution* at age thirty-seven.[2] That year they were covering the 1960 Republican National Convention in Chicago's stockyards arena. The steakhouse there was famous, and Patterson invited Poynter to dinner. They also talked over the convention issues and found that they thought much the same and liked each other.

After that they had no notable contact for eight years. Poynter knew that Patterson, protégé of famed columnist Ralph McGill, had become one of the nation's most talked-about editors. He had won the Pulitzer Prize for editorials at the height of the racial crisis. When Patterson in 1968 abruptly resigned his Atlanta job in a blowup with the company president, McGill had tried to find a new position for him. The best match McGill could think of was with the *St. Petersburg Times,* so he phoned Poynter. The answer was "Well, that's interesting," which in Poynter's language meant no interest.

Patterson went on to become managing editor of the *Washington Post.* In the bleak winter of Henrietta's death when Nelson Poynter spent much time at his Washington home, the Pattersons lived around the corner. They were part of the same circle of liberal Democratic friends such as Hubert Humphrey and Richard Scammon, and Patterson and Poynter would meet at the Metropolitan Club for lunch. During the 1969 staff upheaval at *Congressional Quarterly,* Poynter and his new *CQ* editor, Dick Billings, looked to Patterson for advice.

As number two man under *Post* editor Benjamin Bradlee, Patterson was carrying a title Bradlee had vacated when the paper's famous executive editor, J. Russell Wiggins, left to become United Nations ambassador. Bradlee continued to perform much as he had before, and Patterson found he had little mandate from above while being undercut by Howard Simons, then deputy managing editor. In Patterson's words, Bradlee needed a managing editor "like a boar needs tits." Lunching with Poynter at the Metropolitan, Patterson told him of plans to leave the *Post.*

"Well, I don't blame you," Poynter said. "You ought not be No. 2."

"I'm not really doing a very good job there and I'm not happy, so I'm going to move on."

Patterson had been pondering his future and had looked into the possibility of a job writing and teaching at the University of Florida.[3] He told Poynter he had decided that the only boss for whom he wanted to work was Nelson Poynter. If the *Times* had nothing for him, he would quit the news business and accept an offer from Duke University to teach and write books.

"Why don't you come with our company and take over *Congressional Quarterly?*" Poynter asked.

"Nels, that's not a big enough job."

"You're right."

Duke President Terry Sanford, a politician-scholar who had fought under the banner of southern liberalism like Patterson, urged the Georgian to accept the academic appointment. He styled the position "professor of the practice of political science," as Duke had no journalism department.

It was a painful transition for Patterson despite the prestige of the Duke move. Although he had no regrets about leaving the Atlanta and Washington jobs, at forty-seven he believed that the bottom had dropped out of his career. His usual self-assurance faltered. He feared that he was not as good as he had thought he was, or he would have carved out an important role for himself at the *Post*. When he arrived at Duke, he was haunted by the suspicion that he had not given his previous job his best shot.

But the thrill of teaching caught Patterson's fancy. He believed he was breaking ground with his study of how journalism interrelated with other institutions, and the chance to choose his own students from a range of disciplines intrigued him.

About a month after starting work at Duke, Patterson got a phone call from Poynter: "Come on down. I want you to run the company." He revealed Baldwin's impending departure.

Patterson considered the offer for several weeks. Dark thoughts returned. He speculated that if he stayed at Duke he always would have a slight sense of defeat, and working for Poynter held out the prospect of the greatest accomplishment of his life. Sanford tried to talk Patterson into staying. At least, the president said, he should ask Poynter for a job contract, something Patterson had never had. Patterson agreed. Two days later he received a self-typed letter from Poynter that read simply: "If you take this job you will succeed me and you can set your pay at whatever level you want. Is that a good enough contract for Terry Sandford [*sic*]?" They arrived at a salary figure, but Poynter soon called back and doubled it.

Patterson never had been to St. Petersburg, and he made no effort to do so before deciding to take the job. He believed he knew Nelson Poynter well enough, and he had read the *Times* for years. He thought that one can publish a good newspaper anywhere and learn to love one's community. Besides, he was confident that he would like the city.

A Mule, a Horse, a Tank

The Pattersons, Scotch-Irish immigrants in the early 1700s, made their way south along the Appalachian spine and staked claim on land recently extracted from the Indians. Gene's great-grandfather, along with three brothers, died in the Civil War. One of the soldier's children, John, became a lay preacher and taught in a one-room school besides farming. He read the dictionary, the Bible, and the Sears Roebuck catalog for hours on end. He spoke well and thought deeply, and he had an adoring and imitative audience in his grandson Gene.

If hard work and talent had been rewarded, John's son William would have quickly become a prosperous banker. He attended a small college for a year and married Annabel Corbett, who came from a line of country doctors in a neighboring town and became a schoolteacher.

Gene's father got his first big chance when the boy was in the first grade. It was as cashier of a big bank in Douglas, and he put all his savings into its stock. The depression came, the bank failed, and he was required by law to pay depositors an amount equal to the value of his lost stock. He refused bankruptcy and spent twenty years paying off the debt, working at small banking jobs until he died at seventy-two.

The family had just moved into a sparkling new house when the crash occurred. Gene watched his mother crying, and he wondered what a busted bank was. Within a week they had carried their furniture on a flatbed truck to a little farm near Adel which Annabel had bought from her husband's parents.

But by depression-time standards of Adel, they were fortunate because they had land to grow food and a little cash crop. Gene and his brother Bill grew up at grinding labor. They plowed with a mule, tended tobacco, chopped cotton, "stomped" peanuts, pulled corn, milked the cows, and fed the chickens. The Pattersons had to buy only salt, sugar, and coffee at the grocery store. And they felt sorry for the poor people in town who couldn't support themselves and depended on charity.

Gene's father was seldom home, losing job after job as the depression ground on. Annabel refused to uproot the family again. "I will never leave this land," she told her husband. "I left it once, and now we're going to make this our home. You go on and work wherever you can find work and come home on weekends."

And so it worked out. The father knew he was providing as well as possible, but it meant Annabel would become the dominant force in her children's upbringing. She made it clear she could not hold her head up in Adel if they got any grade below an A. Her shame when Gene made a B left a vivid mark on him.

Gene saw his father as a loser, his mother a winner. She gave him a hunger to "be somebody" and a confidence that he could. The way to do it, he learned from her, was to play to his strengths. At school, Gene learned to defend himself in playground scraps even though he was short and skinny.

Politics was something to talk about, and religion was something to be social about. Gene's father, a conservative, admired Governor Gene Talmadge, a populist demogogue whose badge was red suspenders and white supremacy. Woodrow Wilson was a hero in the home, to the father because he was a war leader and to the mother because of his idealism and erudition. The couple would debate every election, even local ones, and Annabel often settled the matter: "Pat, we just won't vote today, because I'm going to cancel out your vote."

The most magical place in Adel for Gene was a weekly newspaper shop. The earnest smell of the ink, the clatter of the flatbed press and the clink of Linotype matrices falling into place intrigued the boy. He would walk three miles on the dirt road into town on Saturdays just to watch words take shape on the lead slugs of type. "Uncle Tom" Shytle, the white-haired publisher, found out Gene was good at English and unloaded the chore of proofreading on him. Gene worked on the high school paper, the *Sparkler*. He covered basketball games he was too small to play in, and he wrote cliché-ridden copy, imitating phrases in big-city dailies.

Gene wanted to go to college as far away from the swamps of south Georgia as he could, and he heard about North Georgia College at Dahlonega, in the mountains. It was only a two-year college with 700 students, but it also was a military school for the 600 boys and the uniforms looked snappy to him.

His mother gave him a chance to earn his first year's expenses. To raise prices, the government was limiting production, and the Pattersons were allotted 3.2 acres for tobacco that year. Gene's mother let him have all of it, and he worked it by himself except for some hired help. He cleared the $300 tuition.

Even though the parents had forgone the year's tobacco income, they each scraped up spending money to send him. To pay for his laundry, he capitalized on his writing skill. Everyone had to do a weekly theme for English 101, and some boys couldn't write. Gene cranked out papers for them to turn in, payable in cash. Years later, after achieving success, he met his old professor socially and confessed that he had done his classmates' offerings at ten cents each. "As I recall," the professor said, "that's about what they were worth."

Gene took well to military discipline, but his blood ran hot with dissent when he became editor of the college paper, the *Cadet Bugler*. He wrote an angry editorial denouncing Governor Gene Talmadge's purge of academics who were calling for admission of blacks to universities. The next day Gene was taken out of class and sent to the president's office. He expected to get kicked out on the spot. President Jonathan C. Rogers was a formidable sight, with close-set eyes looking through rimless spectacles above a Roman nose. Gene was terrified.

"Sit down, Cadet Patterson."

Gene sat there while the steely gaze bore into him.

"I've read your editorial in the *Cadet Bugler* denouncing the governor."

"Yessir."

"Let me read you a sentence here: 'Governor Talmadge has placed in jeopardy the diplomas of all of us in the university system of Georgia.' Cadet Patterson, how do you spell jeopardy?"

"J-E-A-P-O-R-D-Y."

"Wrong. It's J-E-O-P-A-R-D-Y."

"Thank you, sir."

"That's all." Then he smiled.

Gene heard no more of the matter.

By that time World War II was in full swing, and Gene enrolled in journalism school at the University of Georgia after graduation from Dahlonega. He was in an advanced ROTC unit of cavalry, which allowed him to indulge in the horseback riding he had learned as a farm boy. Doubling up, he finished two years' work in twelve months. The war needed men, especially trained ones.

Six months later, the gold bars of an Armored Force second lieutenant were put on the slender shoulders of Eugene C. Patterson upon his graduation from officer school at Fort Knox. Soon he was leading his mechanized platoon across France under the command of fiery General George S. Patton, Jr., himself a cavalryman.

Patterson did not have enough service credit "points" to win him immediate discharge after the war. So he was sent to teach in the cavalry school at Fort Riley, Kansas. It was great fun, very Old West and Custerish—riding in the Sunday morning hunt, jumping in the horse shows, playing polo indoors. Patterson won a regular army commission through competitive exams. He decided reconnaissance aviation was the cavalry wave of the future and went into flight training.

Moving from base to base on the arid southwestern plains, Patterson became a fence-jumping pilot of light aircraft. He learned to land where there was no field—in cow pastures and on country roads. Ending up at what was then Camp Hood near Temple, Texas, he found an army that was being dismantled and a unit that had no mission. At twenty-three, he felt life had passed him by.

So he began to read—books, political tracts, magazines—and he saw himself as a fiction writer. In college he had written poetry. Now he spent his Sunday afternoons in the hot wooden barracks reading Hemingway, then copying it out on a portable typewriter. He started writing his own great novel about the war, but it came out hash. He realized that he knew nothing of life except the army. So he walked down the hall to the adjutant and resigned.

Patterson intended to cure his shortcomings as a novelist by working on a newspaper. He took a job on a small daily in Temple, near Camp Hood, and learned much at his assignments—ranging from city hall to armadillo festivals. He also realized he couldn't live on $28 a week.

After pawning his typewriter, trombone, and wristwatch, Patterson got a job with a daily in Macon, Georgia, paying $60 a week for sixty hours. While there he worked alongside a United Press reporter from Atlanta covering a speech. The reporter saw his story, and soon a job offer came from UP.

After learning the news agency trade in Atlanta, Patterson was sent out as bureau chief for South Carolina. It was a poor state for UP, with few clients, but it was his ticket out of the swamp. Hungry for greater thrills after eighteen months, Patterson demanded an assignment to New York or he would resign. He was sent there as a rewrite man at $80 a week. He was uneasy when he first walked into UP headquarters, but once again he rejoiced to discover he was good enough to compete. He later became New York night bureau manager.

In 1953, UP sent him to London as bureau chief. The timing was perfect, as Patterson and his wife, Sue, had just lost a baby and were told they could not have another. They were inclined to start anew somewhere else, and life in Europe fulfilled its promise. Tensions slackened between the Korean conflict and the Suez crisis of 1956. Patterson could cover the fading glory of Winston Churchill and the fairy-tale marriage of Grace Kelly to Prince Rainier.

Working for an agency was a bane and a blessing, as it was for Don Baldwin in Tokyo. Patterson strove to compress facts, use active voice, and choose words that raced across the page. It was a skill much admired in the news game, but it was not intended to be used for serious efforts.

Meanwhile he played his gift for all it was worth. He once found himself beaten by the AP on a story that Ernest Hemingway's plane had crashed in the Ugandan jungle. This was because UP's stringer—a part-time correspondent—was an expatriate Englishman named A.E. Jones who lived in a dirt-floored hut, didn't know who Hemingway was, and ignored the story.

Patterson got Jones on the radio telephone, gave him several Hemingway book titles, and told him to go to the Kampala library and learn how the author wrote. "It's essential that we find that man before AP does now that we're humiliated worldwide about missing the plane crash. And when you find him you've got to interview him and you've got to know how to talk to him."

A few days later Hemingway walked out of the jungle with his head bandaged. Into the London office poured a crystal-clear story by Jones, sent at the seventy-five-cents-a-word urgent cable rate. He apparently had read the books, because the words seemed written by Hemingway. But Patterson saw a way his wire service touch could enhance it. He pulled information out of the middle of the story and made a lead out of it: "Bulletin: Entebbe, Uganda—Ernest Hemingway came out of the jungle today carrying a bunch of bananas and a bottle of gin." The second paragraph quoted Hemingway: "My luck, she is running very good."

The story rocketed off to New York and then all over the world. It was hours ahead of AP's, and every Hemingway fan on newspaper desks loved it. Hemingway later cited it in a talk to school children: "Now that's good newspaper writing."[4]

Despite the excitement abroad, memories of home surfaced. The Supreme Court outlawed school segregation the year after Patterson arrived in London. Patterson discovered Ralph McGill was in London when the segregation story broke. He knew the great columnist had warned his readers that sooner or later they would have to face the illegality of segregation, because the court would strike it down on a Monday, its day for announcing decisions. He had headlined the column "Someday It Will Be Monday." Patterson traced McGill to his hotel and told him, "Mr. McGill, it's Monday." Then he detailed the news to him.

Two years went by, and Patterson found himself having to play London host to George Biggers, publisher of the *Atlanta Journal and Constitution* and an important UP client. Biggers was a tough advertising-oriented businessman with little editorial sensitivity. Patterson arranged the usual red carpet treatment for Biggers—a Bentley waiting at Paddington Station, a room at the Savoy, help in changing money. It was much the way Don Baldwin greeted Nelson Poynter when Don was AP editor in Tokyo.

After Biggers returned home, Patterson got a grateful letter that practically invited him to apply. He did so, and Biggers hired him immediately. By then, disproving the earlier medical verdict, he and his wife had a baby, Mary. Above all, they were going home, and Gene was entering the heart of the news business—a major daily.

Grasping the Shoe

The *Atlanta Journal and Constitution* had long been the best-known newspaper in the Southeast and still had not been eclipsed in circulation by the *Miami Herald* and the *St. Petersburg Times*. The morning *Constitution* was the region's towering conscience, having been founded three years after the Civil War. It was the vehicle of the South's premier journalist of the era, Henry W. Grady, a brilliant reporter and progressive editorialist.

Ralph McGill became editor of the *Constitution* in 1938 and exercised thought leadership perhaps as powerful as that of Grady. But an Ohio press lord, James M. Cox, had bought the *Constitution*'s evening competitor, the *Journal*, and by 1950 he had beaten the *Constitution* economically. He bought the proud old morning paper and combined its management with the *Journal*'s, although the two kept separate editorial policies.

Patterson joined the staff in 1956. Biggers had hinted that Patterson might rise fast but was cagy. He assigned Patterson to write editorials for the *Journal,* a difficult task, as he had not written an opinion piece since his university days. Three months later, in December 1956, he was appointed executive editor of both papers, over two managing editors older than he was. It was a powerful challenge to a thirty-three-year-old so new to the place.

The move was part of Biggers's plan to bring his own men into management before he retired. He had begun teaching the business side to an editorial writer named Jack Tarver so he could become publisher. But soon after Patterson's appointment, Biggers died, and Tarver took over sooner than expected. Word got around that the new boss saw his executive editor as a threat. Patterson doubted it, but he knew there could be trouble ahead because Tarver had not hired him and did not seem to like him much.

In 1960, Patterson became editor of the *Constitution,* succeeding McGill in charge of editorials. McGill took the title of the morning paper's publisher, which meant little, as his only duty was to write his column. Traditions of his new office awed Patterson as he recalled Grady, Joel Chandler Harris, McGill, and other former editors. The first column he wrote began, "The shadows on these walls are very tall."

Both men turned out columns seven days a week. Patterson approached the older man as a son, apprentice, and friend. He had much to learn and McGill had much to teach on two urgent matters—how to write well and how to deal with Georgia's searing issue of the time, the civil rights struggle.

Later McGill recalled the relationship: "Gene and I, despite the gap of years between us, had the gift of being able to talk with one another in the full meaning of the word. We could talk philosophy, ethics, morality, books, poetry, history, men and meanings. He and I would often talk about ourselves and how we had put our feet on paths that had brought us together in mutual respect."[5]

Everything about McGill fascinated Patterson. McGill was a Welshman from Tennessee with bushy hair and eyebrows, an intense face, and roller-coaster moods that would take him from scrappiness to dark introspection. Patterson loved to listen to the older man tell tales and read poetry, reflecting on the song of the language, the music and mystery of life, the cadence of passing days and seasons, the reverence for lasting things.[6]

McGill was the most visible of a small band of southern editors who took their defense of civil rights to the danger point. The others included Nelson Poynter, Harry Ashmore of Little Rock, and Hodding Carter, Jr., of Greenville, Mississippi. All got threats in the mail, and Carter packed a pistol at times.

Throughout the 1950s McGill had gone as far as he dared, although he had never been as forthright as Poynter, who lived in a city with less racial hostility. To Patterson, McGill seemed to be walking on the precipice every day. But McGill once told Patterson that he thought he had not gone far enough.

Despite his liberal sympathies, Patterson himself knew only the segregated life-style he was born into. Not until the late 1950s did he have a chance to meet blacks who were not at the lower rungs of society. He developed a close professional friendship with a young black Morehouse University instructor who invited Patterson to get to know some blacks socially. Patterson jumped at the chance, and he found that the blacks were better educated than he, and they could make friendly, excellent conversation over the punch cups. In southern parlance, he had crossed the line.

Although McGill always was the battle flag over the smoke of the field, Patterson soon made an independent name for himself with his editorials and columns on civil rights. The column that thrust him out front ran the morning after four small black girls were killed in a Birmingham church by a bomb planted by segregationists. When Patterson heard of the tragedy, he knew immediately that the murderers had given him the weapon he needed to pin the blame for injustice on respectable whites—the ones who could change things. That weapon was emotion.

Patterson believed in rational arguments, but they had been getting him nowhere, because, he thought, the belief in segregation was really a symbolic belief. It stood for the things really important to southerners—their way of life, their ancestors, their homeland, their upbringing. To attack the symbol was to attack the believer's very existence. Some politicians and preachers in the Bible Belt had long known how to get around this defense through feelings—sadness, pride, honor, and religious devotion—and Patterson had learned from their example.

Patterson's deeply emotional column started with a glimpse of the scene: "A Negro mother wept in the street Sunday morning in front of a Baptist Church in Birmingham. In her hand she held a shoe, one shoe, from the foot of her dead child. We hold that shoe with her."

Then he launched into his thesis—that the murderers would be caught, but they would serve only as the scapegoat for the southern elite that made the crime possible. "Only we can trace the truth, Southerner—you and I. We broke those children's bodies."

He knew that most of the elite were kind, decent people, the sort he had grown up around. They were the people who read editorial columns, and he shook them until their teeth rattled. In explosive bursts, he indicted them:

We—who go on electing politicians who heat the kettles of hate.

We—who raise no hand to silence the mean and little men who have their nigger jokes.

We—who stand aside in imagined rectitude and let the mad dogs that run in every society slide their leashes from our hand, and spring.

Southerners must not lay off the blame on the fool who set the bomb, he said. "We know better. We created the day. We bear the judgment. May God have mercy on the poor South that has been so led."[7]

The CBS affiliate in Atlanta sent a crew to Patterson's office and asked him to read the whole 553-word column on camera. He assumed that only excerpts would air on the local news. Then the station's news chief called to say that Walter Cronkite had requested the film, and that night Cronkite gave over a large piece of his program to air Patterson's complete reading. Nearly 2,000 letters poured in from all over the nation, compared with about twenty that Patterson was accustomed to getting for a smash column. It gave him a lifelong respect for television's power.

One night in 1964 when Patterson and his wife were visiting Washington, they attended a candlelight dinner at a friend's George-town home with about a dozen editors from around the country, plus Senator Hubert Humphrey. As dinner ended, President Lyndon Johnson strode into the room. He sat down and dominated the talk. Finally, each editor got a chance to ask a question, and Patterson was last. When he identified himself, Johnson interrupted: "I know who you are!" Then leaning over intently, he said, "I'm appointing you to my U.S. Civil Rights Commission. Will you accept?" Patterson had little idea what the commission did, but he promised to respond the next morning.

Johnson kept up the pressure by taking the Pattersons to their hotel in his car. The editor intended to make some phone calls before deciding, but at 8 A.M. he turned on the television and saw Johnson informing the White House press corps that Patterson had accepted the appointment.

The commission was becoming a vital force in shaping public opinion on the race issue. It held televised public hearings in various trouble spots, questioning local officials and often getting them to admit that they were breaking the law. Although the commission had no enforcement power, its fact-finding helped create a climate for change. Patterson felt that it was worth the monthly trip required, particularly to associate with brilliant fellow members such as Theodore Hesburgh, president of Notre Dame, and Erwin Griswold, dean of the Harvard Law School.

But there was more than enough to do at home. The civil rights conflict swirled to new climaxes in 1966, and Patterson fired off a succession of editorials backing justice for blacks. The *Times* of London commented that "Patterson enjoys serving as a lightning rod in what he regards as one of the last great revolutions in the country."

Patterson's editorials won as much national applause as his columns. A packet of them was sent to the Pulitzer Prize board, and in May 1967 it awarded him the prize for general excellence in editorial writing.

The outlook was not so bright inside the *Constitution* office. For years, tension had existed between Patterson and Tarver. Pressures in 1968 led to shouting matches.

President Johnson had put a surcharge on income taxes to pay for the Vietnam conflict, and Georgia Power Company requested a rate increase to pay its share of the increase. Tarver told Patterson that it would be a bad idea to denounce the rate increase, as the newspaper was going to raise its own subscription prices shortly. Patterson agreed to forgo editorial opposition in deference to Tarver.

But a young staff member submitted a column criticizing the Georgia Power plan, and Patterson let it run. Tarver phoned Patterson from home when he read the column. He was furious, and he cited their earlier talk. "This is not an editorial," Patterson countered. "This is a special review by a columnist, and I thought it was good judgment."

Tarver was shouting into the phone. It seemed to be the final straw. Patterson quit.

Suddenly he was without a job. Even the staff didn't know what had happened because he had left so abruptly. He felt sick, almost nauseated, when he looked in the mirror and felt the loneliness sweep over him.

But McGill saw that word got around the country quickly, and several offers came. One opportunity was to become managing editor of the *Washington Post* at double his Atlanta pay. Patterson accepted it. Unknown to him, it would be a brief detour on his route to St. Petersburg.

Sleepless Nights

St. Petersburg in late 1971 looked just as Gene Patterson had expected. Deplaning at the Tampa airport, he glimpsed the Pinellas peninsula as he traveled westward across the causeway. The road runs so low the sky and water surround one like a sphere. It seemed to Patterson one of the most stunning city entrances in the world, reminiscent of Venice.

When Patterson arrived in St. Petersburg, Poynter put him up at a beach motel. The view there, mostly uncluttered by high-rises, thrilled him, and driving into the city over wide streets through sweeping residential areas heightened the feeling. His mood fell when they reached downtown. The heart of the city looked derelict, decayed, somewhat lifeless. Patterson, full of energy at forty-eight, said to himself, "We'll fix this."

There were hopeful signs. The bayfront still was generally free from the blights of other Florida cities—commerce in Tampa, money-stuffed condos that blocked the view in Miami—thanks to Bill Straub's crusade early in the century. Patterson envisioned St. Petersburg's downtown as a jewel in Florida's coastal necklace.

Patterson commuted to St. Petersburg on weekends in the six months between his *Times* appointment and the end of Duke's school year in May 1972. After moving to Florida, Patterson got a close look at the man he had admired for decades. He began to discover the depths of Poynter's genius and character. And he learned that Poynter was so completely secure with himself—without arrogance—that he could live comfortably with his own quirks.

In some things the two men were much alike. They were both short.

They were rooted in the agricultural heartland, and both had acquired populist political sympathies growing up. Both had strong mothers, and both had fledged their professional wings in Scripps-Howard organizations.

But many things set them apart from each other. Patterson was an expert writer, and the new editor soon found that his boss's acuteness as a thinker did not transfer to the typewriter. Like Baldwin before him, he had to unscramble Poynter's written grammar and straighten his looping sentences. Although both men had an air of affability, it was second nature to Patterson. Poynter had to force himself to be outgoing, to break out of his natural privacy.

Patterson was an urbane dresser, while Poynter stuck to gray suits and bow ties. Patterson liked to drive powerful cars, but to Poynter driving was a bother. He was constantly having minor wrecks and once knocked down his garage after a party. The younger man marveled that Poynter had escaped death on the highway.

What Patterson respected most in Poynter was his independence. Poynter trusted his instincts and never was swept into popular passions or comfortable consensus. In a roomful of people who would drift into agreement, Poynter would quietly stand pat for the opposite course.

Patterson, who had brought his political beliefs along a rocky road, also admired Poynter's blend of principles and pragmatism. Poynter seemed to be a tough idealist, a two-fisted liberal. Powerful himself, Poynter knew how power could corrupt. The *New York Times* would later speak of him as tough as a railroad spike.

The memory of Baldwin's unhappy departure hung in the air when Patterson arrived, but he never asked Poynter for a full briefing and never got one. He had his hands full coping with Poynter's pressure on him, recalling that Ben Bradlee, the *Washington Post*'s editor, had once snapped at owner Katharine Graham, "Get your finger out of my eye!" Patterson was tempted to do likewise. Then to his delight and surprise, Poynter backed off after a few months, and their relationship blossomed.

It was perhaps the most wrenching change in Poynter's career at the *Times.* He was giving up control of the newspaper he had shaped, but he knew he was nearing seventy and had to give Patterson and Jack Lake a chance to learn by making ultimate decisions.

Despite Patterson's proven record, some wondered whether he

would pursue the same grail Poynter had sought. Once the two men were having lunch with lawyer Hank Baynard.

"Nelson," Baynard said with Patterson listening, "you won't be cool in the grave before Patterson will take a million dollars from one of the chains and sell out your newspaper."

Poynter grinned. "You know, Hank, I've learned in life that, if you're going to get anything done, at some point you've got to trust somebody. And I trust Gene."

Besides his titles of editor and president, Patterson, in the fashion of big business, was called chief operating officer while Poynter retreated to the role of chairman and chief executive officer. To keep the delicate experiment on course, Patterson tried to inform Poynter about everything and seek his advice often.

The new understanding almost ran aground when Patterson chose not to inform Poynter of the death of his cat while Poynter was on vacation. Poynter was angry, and he scolded Patterson: "If you wouldn't tell me about my cat, what else wouldn't you tell me about?" From then on, Patterson shielded the owner from nothing. Poynter continued to come to the office. He read the paper carefully and fired off hot memos reacting to decisions, but he did not interfere before the fact. The burden he found easiest to put down was running *Congressional Quarterly*. Patterson, with his Washington background, was eminently qualified for this task.

During the time between Baldwin's departure and Patterson's takeover, the news and editorial side of the *Times* paper had devolved to a caretaker regency. Collectively it was called "the three Bobs"— Haiman for *Times* news, Pittman for editorials, Stiff for the *Independent*. When Patterson arrived, he was appalled. Nobody seemed to be in charge. The staff looked to him like one big fraternity, with supervisors blurring the boundary with the rank and file. The job of assistant metropolitan editor was a rotating one, and today's boss was next week's subordinate.

Patterson perceived in the *Times* newsroom all the traits that had upset media managers in the social revolution of the Vietnam era— staff power, advocacy, activism, overheated democracy, adversarial belligerence. In short, he saw it as a prescription for chaos, and, he decided, some department heads were incompetent.

Staff members from Baldwin's days had their misgivings about Patterson. They stood in awe of his national reputation, his eloquence as a speaker and writer, and his well-bred politeness. But his cool reserve—interpreted by some as patronizing—was a sharp change from Baldwin's bluff directness, and his concern for lines of authority reminded them of his wartime service under Patton. At times he was spoken of privately as the "Tank Commander" or "Treads."[8]

Patterson's personnel actions did nothing to calm nerves. Within months of arriving he had changed most newsroom managers—city editor, sports editor, news features editor, telegraph editor, ombudsman, and chief photographer. The higher level—the Three Bobs and George Sweers, director of illustrations—survived the upheaval. Patterson also went hunting for people who could help build his dream of an improved paper, and he hired Andrew Barnes of the *Washington Post* to be metropolitan editor; Hubert Mizell, sports editor; Wilbur Landrey, foreign editor; and Jack Belich, chief photographer.

When one of his veteran reporters got into trouble, Patterson quickly showed he was concerned not only with new hires. Lucy Ware Morgan was a reporter in the *Times*'s Pasco County bureau, one of the branches that had stretched out to the northern edge of the Tampa Bay megalopolis. Pasco politics still tended toward a good-old-boy outlook with no tolerance for big-time journalism. Morgan, a local woman who had been a stringer before joining the regular staff, ran afoul of a Pasco judge by refusing to reveal the source of a grand jury story.

Patterson saw that Morgan was determined to stand her ground, and he dug in his heels too. Morgan was summoned to four court appearances, convicted of contempt, and sentenced to eight months in jail. Patterson made the hour-long trip to the court in Dade City with her each time and at one point he tried unsuccessfully to substitute himself for Morgan if jail time was to be served. Patterson rented a beach hotel room and ordered the Morgan family to take a weekend vacation. He told Morgan that if she had to go to jail he would hire a housekeeper to care for her children. The company spent $100,000 over three years in getting the conviction overturned on appeal, and Morgan never served a day in jail. She went on to lead a team that won a Pulitzer Prize.

Recession and Dissension

In 1973, because of the first big oil embargo, the United States sank into a recession. Wage earners were caught between prices that rose and salaries that did not. Advertising is among the first business expenses cut in a recession. This blow came as publishers were trying to cope with a newsprint shortage and rocketing prices. Newspaper revenue dipped, leading to drastic cutbacks in the news hole (space allowed for editorial material). Fewer journalists were needed, and those on the job were frustrated because their copy was trimmed or omitted.

Jack Lake and other *Times* managers faced into the wind. They decided they must deal with the income drop before they lost control. They cut profits and eliminated the extra quarterly dividend customarily given each year as a bonus to stockholders. But Poynter insisted that the company make some contribution to the staff's profit-sharing fund, even though the plan's formula did not require it because of reverses. Plummeting stock market prices had wiped out a quarter of the fund's value.

Savings also had to come from newspapers' two main costs, newsprint and personnel. To save on newsprint, an inviting target was money-losing circulation areas, places so remote that it cost more to deliver papers than was earned through subscriptions. Advertisers cared nothing about having their ads read 150 miles away, as no one there was going to buy their goods. One such luxury was home delivery in Tallahassee, the state capital and the source of much of the *Times*'s

Eugene C. Patterson (*left*) was brought in by Nelson Poynter as his successor after Don Baldwin and the owner parted ways. This 1974 picture is in the *Times* newsroom. *St. Petersburg Times*.

prestige in news coverage. To the consternation of many news staffers, it was eliminated. (See chapter 9.)

After budget-cutters had sliced newsprint expenses as thin as they could, they took on payroll. Staffing was fat because Patterson had been hiring freely before the crisis, excessively in some cases, he realized.[9] When the recession had come, attrition was counted on to lower the roster. In June of 1974, management assured staffers that no layoffs or loss of benefits were expected. But not enough people were quitting or retiring to take up the slack through attrition.

Frank Furda, recently hired from the electronic industry as the paper's treasurer, served up the bitter medicine at a Monday afternoon executive meeting: "In my experience, the only way you ever get payroll costs under control is to have a black Friday." All the others knew what he meant—a drastic all-at-once layoff. They nodded in agreement.

Management decided to cut 150 jobs. But it did not have a plan of how to break the news to the staff without throwing it into a state of shock. Poynter had always prided himself on what he called the virtue of candor, and it never occurred to him to manipulate information in his own building.

The day the layoff decision was made, Poynter had his customary get-acquainted hour with new staff members. One of them asked him if there would be layoffs. He said there would be 150.

Within hours the story hit the wires. The next morning people all over the country could read that the *St. Petersburg Times* was the first major newspaper to reduce its staff because of the recession. Other papers were planning similar moves, but they did not talk about it so bluntly or provide such a clear target for criticism. For the rest of his career, Patterson regretted that management had not handled the matter with more finesse.

At any rate, the dismissals were carried out precisely and abruptly. Haiman had the task of letting thirteen newsroom people go in one week, and all received advance notice and severance pay. When grocery prices had soared earlier, Poynter had looked for a way to slice through red tape and give staffers temporary relief. He decreed what he called the market-basket booster, a $5 weekly supplement for each employee. Then the layoffs came about, and the company decided to drop the supplement. It was another jolt for the staff.

In the midst of all this, another blow to morale came from an unlikely source—the *Times*'s own news features. Karen DeYoung, a bright, intense reporter less than two years out of college, who later became a top editor of the *Washington Post,* did a story on how the recession had touched pay scales in Pinellas County. She asked a variety of people to reveal how their annual salaries had changed in the past year and compared these with the inflation rate. Names and ages were included.

With all this frankness, DeYoung and her editor—whom Patterson later fired—felt it only fair to report her own salary, which was more than $13,000, well above a year before. That was not remarkable on a national scale, although it was more than many five-year reporters made elsewhere in the South. What caused an uproar inside the *Times* building was that it was so much higher than many top staff members earned.

Unknown to the staff, Patterson had been horrified at the low wages at the *Times* when he arrived in 1972. He created a committee to study both union and nonunion pay scales for southern newspapers, and it found that Patterson's impression was correct—salaries were far too low, as much as 50 percent.[10] Many staffers did not see the raises given certain employees in the context of the long-term effort, and it seemed to them that management was trying to buy off potential complainers one by one. Patterson tried to stem the tide of dissent by meeting with workers after the DeYoung story. When he defended her salary by saying she was a star, resentment spread even faster.

In the executive suite another shock was in the making. The company for years had shielded the staff against inflation by giving quarterly cost-of-living supplements to full-time staffers based on the consumer price index. The increases had been gradual and relatively easy for the company to swallow. But with the recession, the company could not match it.

To make up for falling revenues, Jack Lake demanded that the supplements be eliminated. Patterson argued furiously that the company must share the loss with the staff, hold the reduction to 50 percent, and take the difference out of profits, if there were any. Poynter, for the only time in his years with the two men, had to step in and halt a shouting match. He ordered the cut limited to 50 percent.

Again, communication went awry. Executives had wrestled with the need to cut the allowance for weeks, and they were thoroughly familiar with the reasons. But rumors leaked the news without explanation.

Then, after being questioned by a reporter for the staff newsletter, Poynter announced the move on bulletin boards in Patterson's absence.

Bob Haiman tried to salvage morale by drifting around the newsroom for chats.[11] He found that staffers had grown to consider the market-basket booster and the cost-of-living adjustments not as temporary injections but as normal parts of their pay and had figured them into family budgets. They saw no difference between them and what Poynter had always called earned dividends—profit sharing, pensions, insurance. He had preached that these were not charity by the company but benefits acquired through work. Despite Haiman's efforts to smooth things over, resentments had flourished too much to die easily. The newsroom always had been a happy place to work, with no sacred cows. Now something sour was in the air.

Actually the dissension had taken a purposeful bent for several months. On October 27, 1974, only a few days after the cost-of-living supplement was cut, a drive to unionize editorial employees was announced. A letter signed by eighteen employees—fifteen reporters, two assistant metropolitan editors, and a librarian—was mailed to all news staff members' homes. It proposed formation of a chapter of the Newspaper Guild, an AFL-CIO affiliate.

Most signers of the letter were young and tended to sense alienation from older staffers. They argued that the company's benefit package, by keeping up profit sharing and insurance at the expense of cost-of-living adjustments, favored veteran employees. Andy Barnes, although clearly part of management, was caught between the two forces. At age thirty-four, he was close to some of the dissidents, but to others, he represented a threat. He had recently come in from the northeastern establishment and was seen as Patterson's point man for overhauling the newsroom.

The three-page letter noted grievances—"shrinking size of the newspapers, staff layoffs, reductions in benefits, etc." Most of the letter, in a question-and-answer format, sought to allay staffers' qualms about casting their lot with organized labor. It assured them that the local chapter would have "a great deal of autonomy," that the newspaper's quality would not be diminished, and that management could not penalize them for joining.

Once the movement was in the open, a timeworn legal process began. To some oldtimers it brought to mind the futile unionizing drives at the *Times* after World War II. Above all, management had to refrain from intimidating employees. Labor lawyers were flown in from Washington, and Patterson held a series of education meetings for executives. Poynter largely kept his hands off. "Just tell them we will publish," he told Patterson.

Patterson advised the editors that they would be tempted to lose their tempers at the young dissidents. He cautioned the editors to avoid anger, to "stand firm for the company" but not use dirty tricks. Editors should not even try to find out what was going on, he told them—no listening in, not even driving past meeting sites.

Even though Patterson was president of the company and nominally Lake's superior, Poynter had fostered a feeling that Patterson was primarily responsible for news and Lake for business. That none of the trouble occurred in Lake's bailiwick gave him leverage to criticize actions on the news side. He sided with those who considered the guild organizers as incompetents and troublemakers and said they should be fired. Patterson, Haiman, and Barnes argued that the eighteen signers included some of the better writers on the staff as well as some of the more incompetent.

Patterson exerted his control. Management would tell its side of the argument, he said, but no one would be fired or threatened with firing for union activities. He noted that the paper always had supported the right to organize in its editorials and said it was not going to do otherwise in its own shop.

The company's main responses to the movement were two letters, jointly signed by Patterson and Lake, to all news staffers over three weeks in November. The first challenged advocates of the union for the high ground. It said the company was "vigorously opposed" to the organizing attempt and gave predictable reasons. The next letter dug into specifics. It compared the *Time*'s pay situation with those of other southern newspapers, not those of border state and northern companies as the guild had done. But parallels were difficult because of murky language. The *Times* cited its "goals" of paying "experienced high performers" $310 a week and "fully trained performers" $250. Figures cited for the other southern papers with guild contracts ranged from $184 to $290 for people with five to seven years' experience.

The job descriptions reflected a fundamental disagreement between the two sides. The guild insisted on raises according to seniority, whereas editors preferred to decide each case on merit when a worker displayed journeyman competence.

The company boasted of its benefits package, defying the guild to show that it had won one as good as anywhere. Included were nine days off a year besides vacation, company-funded pensions, half-free medical insurance, fully free life insurance, and, before they were suspended, cost-of-living supplements and profit sharing.

Even while tension mounted in the newsroom, the union group kept a mostly low-key tone in a letter sent to staffers November 10. The list of signers had grown to twenty-two. The new letter cited what the dissidents saw as breach of faith by supervisors who allegedly went back on their word not to lay off staff or cut benefits. It held up the "earned dividends" label the company had used and said reductions in the market-basket booster and cost-of-living supplement represented a pay cut of about 8 percent. "How did we 'unearn' such substantial parts of our incomes?" it asked.

Other exchanges between the sides were more bitter. Poynter faced the staff at a general meeting and responded to written questions. One person asked the paper to advise staffers on how to get food stamps because they would need them to feed their families. Another critic asked whether, on the same day the layoffs were announced, the newspaper had offered to buy a Picasso painting from the University of South Florida and give it to the City of St. Petersburg. Poynter denied the accusation, then explained that he and his wife and the Poynter Fund were interested in contributing to mounting a heroic sculpture by Picasso on the waterfront.

The paper's announcement that its executives had forgone a raise that year brought ridicule at the meeting. Poynter agreed that it was a mistake to brag about the decision, but he went to lengths to praise the quality of his managers.

Much of the discord revolved around Jeff Bruce, a twenty-five-year-old assistant metropolitan editor hired by Patterson. Although Bruce was uncertain whether his job made him legally a part of management and thus ineligible to join the union, he signed the original document. Soon Patterson transferred Bruce to the reporting staff, declaring his former job a management spot. "I must have supervisors through whom I can communicate my management policies to the staff," he announced. Peggy Vlerebome, the other assistant metro editor who signed the letter, also changed to a nonsupervisory job when Patterson requested it.

The guild promptly filed a complaint with the federal government

claiming that Bruce's transfer was an unfair and illegal labor practice. The complaint said Bruce had in effect been fired by being moved
to another position. It also charged that Patterson had announced
that employees would be terminated for union activities, although
he flatly denied it. The government investigated and dismissed the
complaint.

The *Times* covered the organizing drive and the legal case with
several stories in its own columns and the staff publication, all giving
both sides of the dispute. Angel Castillo, Jr., one of the chief guild
organizers, wrote the *Times* story about the complaint over Bruce.

The twenty-two signers fell far short of a majority of news employees. To enlist more—and to allay fears and doubts of the signers—
organizers scheduled a meeting for Saturday, November 23. They
billed it as a family affair, with babysitters.

Just before that meeting, two things happened that changed the
course of events. First, one of the positions vacated by Bruce and
Vlerebome was filled by Mike Foley, from the same job on the *Independent*. It was a routine move, but it symbolized that management
was acting aggressively. Next, staffers received another mailing, not
from the contending sides but from fellow employees opposing the
union. Two women who had never identified with critics of management, Bette Orsini and Lucy Morgan, originated the letter.

Orsini had grown up with the *Times* and had liked the three
generations of its top editors she had known. She realized that its
financial health was threatened, and she believed the executives had a
much better record of concern for the paper than the dissidents did.
Mostly she worried that no voice for long-term considerations was
coming from the staff.[12]

Moreover, Orsini felt that organizers were using steamroller tactics.
They had gone from desk to desk collecting paycheck stubs, which
bore no names, so they could make a rough analysis of comparative
pay, tacking the list on the bulletin board. One salary was much higher
than others, and rumor identified it as Orsini's. One staffer complained
loudly that she deserved as much as Orsini, who had actually refused to
hand over her stub.

Orsini started drafting a statement of her views. Fellow workers
stopped by, asking to sign it. Morgan heard about the project and
suggested that they collaborate. She shared Orsini's feelings about
management and had a southerner's skepticism about unions. She

thought that the guild, aside from being disruptive, simply was not needed by the staff.[13]

In one night the two women edited Orsini's version into one page. They floated it in the main office and bureaus, not expecting a huge response, but fifty-seven people quickly signed. The letter, avoiding details and harsh words, declared that the signers would refuse to sign union authorization cards. They predicted that the union would jeopardize the *Times*'s security, expressed confidence in management, rejected salary comparisons with papers in the Northeast, and urged the guild group not to hold ill feelings.

The November 23 meeting went ahead in a hotel room, with visiting guild officers talking about how shutdowns and strikes could be set up. Many listeners were disappointed; they were not interested in hurting the paper they cared about.

The drive clearly was doomed for lack of support, and it died quietly. The staff underwent a time of healing. Executives had said there would be no retributions, no long memories of vengeance. Snide remarks in the newsroom finally turned into banter. Haiman knew the tension was gone when he was briefing some reporters on a difficult assignment. One of them joked, "You know, we'll organize on you again." The episode of dissent had no visible harm on the careers of the twenty-two union signers. Four stayed on at the *Times* and were promoted. The others drifted away, some to better jobs.

As the recession began to ease in 1975, the *Times* put first priority on salaries to attract and keep valued employees. It made a survey of newspaper pay scales in the South and Southeast, which showed the *Times* was not out of line with papers its size but said that the paper planned to compete nationally it would have to pay more, even though its benefits package was superior. The *Times* did so.

Despite the recovery, the period would remain a dark shadow in the minds of those involved. It had cost Patterson the most sleepless nights he would ever know at the paper, even though he had emerged from it having earned the Poynter mantle.

For the future of the newspaper it would have a profound effect. Poynter had been keeping his options open to leave the company to the staff after his death. The guild effort, which he saw as an immature reaction to a recession, persuaded him to scrap any such idea.[14]

In a Strange Land

For all his roots in the Midwest, Nelson Poynter's soul was in the Northeast. He had gone through undergraduate economics at Indiana University, but his intellectual Eden had been Yale, where he earned a master's in the same field. Having learned the newspaper business in his father's offices, he took a reserved view of collegiate journalism education.

To Poynter, the ideal journalist grazed liberally in academia, preferably the Ivy League, and then picked up professional lore on the job. This was the norm in Washington and northeastward, but it had not always worked out at the *St. Petersburg Times*. Poynter's earlier editors, such as Tom Harris, Stan Witwer, and Sandy Stiles, had little or no college, and Don Baldwin did not graduate. Later ones—Bob Haiman, Bob Stiff, Mike Foley, and Gene Patterson—all were journalism school products. The few Ivy Leaguers who flitted down to St. Petersburg usually cashed in on the training they got there and went on to better-paid jobs in the Northeast.

If anyone seemed an unlikely candidate for a long term in St. Petersburg, it was Andrew Barnes, whom Patterson brought in as metropolitan editor the year after his own arrival. Barnes was so thoroughly a New Englander that he considered it an intrinsic personal element, like his spectacled blue eyes and unruly brown curls.

Andy Barnes came from several generations of intellectuals on his father's side. The family had commuted from rural northwest Connecticut to Manhattan townhouses, moving easily among the famous and brilliant. His father and an uncle had gone to Harvard, another uncle to Yale. One uncle was drama critic for the *New York Herald Tribune;* the other, an advertising specialist, was vice president of Time, Inc.[15]

Andy's father, Joseph, was correspondent for the *New York Herald Tribune* in the Soviet Union the spring of 1939 when Hitler rolled across central Europe and prepared to invade Poland. His wife, Elizabeth, decided to go back to Connecticut to have her baby, and Andy was born in Torrington, a machine parts manufacturing center. The couple had bought a house for $2,000 from a bootlegger.

Elizabeth Brown Barnes was brilliant like her husband but had grown up differently. Her father was a classic entrepreneur, always promoting some money-making venture. She was born in Duluth, Minnesota, pursued liberal arts studies at Bryn Mawr, got a master's in psychology at Columbia, and taught at Sarah Lawrence. After a marriage to Vanderbilt heir Frederick Field and a trip around the world, she divorced him and married Joseph Barnes. She devoted much of her career to freelance editing and writing.

Andy's parents came through the depression comfortably. They had a four-story row house on New York's West 22nd Street and went to the country for weekends—bearing the dual "Connecticut and New York" address that gave cachet to social announcements.

Andy looked on his father as deeply intelligent, charismatic, and scholarly, a robust man who gardened and cut wood. When Joseph Barnes became foreign editor of the *Herald Tribune,* he crossed paths with Nelson Poynter when both worked for the Office of War Information. After World War II he was the last editor to try to breathe life into *PM,* Ralph Ingersoll's experimental daily, with which Poynter also had an ill-fated involvement. *PM,* rechristened *The Star,* died in 1949, six months after Barnes took over.

Joseph Barnes was an admirer of Wendell Willkie, the liberal Republican from Indiana who failed to stop Franklin Roosevelt from a third term in 1940. He accompanied Willkie on a global trip and helped him produce his visionary book, *One World.* He wrote a biography of Willkie, then spent the rest of his life as a book editor for Simon & Schuster. He supervised such noted books as William L. Shirer's *The Rise and Fall of the Third Reich* and Leo Rosten's *The Religions of the World.*

Barnes's heavy smoking brought him years of struggle with emphysema and cancer. He persuaded his employers to let him come to the office only a day and a half each week, then worked at the farm by his telephone the rest of the time—long before computer commuting became common. Because his reputation brought in lucrative books, the company bowed to his wishes. He also pursued his passion, translating novels from French and Russian. His son enjoyed being around him as his life wound down and he worked to the limit, writing or puttering at farm chores.

The Barnes children—Andy had a sister and two stepsisters—grew up mostly in Manhattan. Andy attended a progressive school based on John Dewey's ideas and later New York's High School of Music and Arts, where he played clarinet. Then he went to Harvard, where he majored in history and continued his music. Andy's father and uncle had been presidents of the *Crimson,* the campus newspaper, but he decided not to compete with their record. It was the Kennedy era, but Andy, like his family a supporter of Adlai Stevenson, was not enthusiastic about the newcomer.

Andy did not make remarkable grades. He always wanted to argue with economics teachers because he could not accept their neatly theoretical world view. A few notable professors, such as historians Oscar Handlin and Arthur Schlesinger, Jr., left an impact on him. The summer before his senior year, Andy married Molly Otis, a student at Pembroke. That year he commuted by train to Harvard.

Barnes caught the job-hunting fever rather late. About ten days before he graduated he visited the *Providence Journal* in Rhode Island, which had a distinguished record for news and editorials going back to 1829. Sevellon Brown, known as the conscience of his state, had recently retired as editor. Not having had a vocation for journalism, Barnes decided on impulse to ask the *Journal* editors for a job. They said yes. When he broke the news to his father, surprise and pleasure lit up Joseph Barnes's face. He gave his son some rare advice—never to go to work without having read the paper closely.

Uncertain as he had been, Barnes was fascinated by journalism. He covered Bristol, fifteen miles from Providence. It was a former slave-trading port, peopled by heirs to fortunes and by Portuguese rubber workers. He felt liberated to be out of school and intended never to go back. It was a thrill to have found a role in life. During two years with the *Journal*, Barnes became bureau chief in Woonsocket. His father decided he was too parochial, so he sent the couple to England for the summer.

When he was twenty-four, the draft caught up with Barnes. He endured the heat and sand of Fort Dix, New Jersey, for basic training. A colonel at West Point wanted someone to put out the student newspaper and recruited Barnes straight out of basic. Just as he was sorting that assignment out, a staff cutback reassigned him as a dental supply worker to Fort Hamilton in Brooklyn, where he encountered all the faces of society. This work took little time, and he volunteered to spend his afternoons teaching remedial English, mostly to illiterate mess sergeants who had to pass a high school equivalency test to reenlist. When Barnes was released in 1965, it seemed time to seek a larger arena, although he received an offer to return to his old job.

For once he called on his father to help. Through his father's connections, he was able to talk with people at the *New York Times*, the *Washington Post,* and NBC. He wrote off NBC because he found himself in rooms full of men with pancake makeup. To him it symbolized a cosmetic approach to news. The *Times* offered him work as a copyboy, a well-worn path of entry for would-be reporters, many with master's degrees. The *Post* said it would take him on as a reporter at less pay than he could get at the *Journal,* but his wife felt that Providence was too boring, so he accepted. He had no idea that thousands of journalists would have killed for a chance with the *Post;* he just thought reporting there might be interesting.

Assigned at first as a reporter in a prosperous Maryland suburb, Barnes was called to the *Post*'s main office to fill in for three months as an assignment editor, quickly earning him a reputation as an organizer. Barnes also became a swing man—someone with has the ability and resilience to shift rapidly from one line of work to another. During elections, when the *Post* coordinated an information pool for local media, he would supervise an army of part-timers who counted votes manually. He also alternated turns as day city editor with reporting stints.

Then came a year in Paris with his family, supported by the prestigious Alicia Patterson Fellowship. He studied urban affairs, probing the relationship between how a place is organized and what it is like to live in. By that time Gene Patterson had become managing editor of the *Post,* and when the Paris year ended Barnes wrote him saying he would work at anything but preferred writing. Patterson agreed with all his arguments but appointed him deputy metropolitan editor. He was able to get back to reporting assignments but often had to return to the desk. When the job of education editor became open, he jumped at it as a way out of instability. He had writers reporting to him, and he was relatively autonomous.

Despite his earlier devotion to writing, Barnes could see that it was not his strongest point. He considered his stories straightforward and clear but not brilliant. Instead, Barnes grew to like management. Whereas others saw it as drudgery, he thought a supervisor could be creative, and he liked being involved with ideas and important projects.

Barnes also found a challenge in helping people do their best work. He would focus on people's careers—where they had been and where they might go—and listened to what they said. He discovered that few managers were able to find pleasure in such things.

Eugene C. Patterson (*left*) hired Andrew Barnes from the *Washington Post* in 1973 as metropolitan editor. After two promotions, Barnes became the *Times*'s chief executive upon Patterson's retirement. *St. Petersburg Times.*

The *Post* newsroom exposed Barnes to management by flair. He felt a kinship with editors there who dealt in witty repartee, as he had something of a sharp tongue himself. Perhaps Barnes's most valuable management skill was his bent for preparation. He would read and question and ponder, and by the time of an important meeting he would be primed—even more than he acknowledged to others.

Covering education proved absorbing for Barnes—so much so that he became jaundiced by its failings. His own children were in school by then, and it was increasingly difficult to send them off to classes. He steadily wrote more critically, and he fell into bitter arguments with his supervisor, who didn't want such material. One day in October 1973, when Barnes was pondering how he could publish his observations that a Virginia high school was failing in its work, Gene Patterson called from St. Petersburg. He said he was looking for someone to run the local staff and he thought highly of Barnes's record. Patterson wanted him to come down for a visit.

Barnes's first impulse was to stay home. He had never gone to Florida and did not want to. Patterson's presence made a difference; Barnes liked and trusted him, and during difficult days for Barnes at the *Post,* Patterson's moral, human approach had appealed to him. He decided to go.

Patterson met him at the Tampa airport and pulled Poynter's old trick of circling to the beaches and into the downtown area, seemingly without having been out of sight of water. At the *Times* office, everything appeared less impressive than at the *Post.* A meeting of the news staff added to the feeling of small-town journalism.

Barnes went home with an offer to become assistant managing editor and metropolitan editor. He hated to leave the *Post.* His wife was running a private school, and they didn't want to uproot the children. They went through a difficult weekend at their country cabin, entertaining guests while deciding what to do.

When they said yes, Barnes knew the problem would be more than just a trauma of resettling. He was a fully formed adult, and he was from New York. Far more than 1,200 miles separated it from St. Petersburg.

Chapter 9

The Three-Ring Circus

The week W. L. Straub took over the *St. Petersburg Times* in 1901, its news columns revealed that a Mr. Adams was substituting as barber while the regular one took a northern trip. Also in the news was an ice cream social that netted $12 for a church guild. A man named Lew King had created a stir when he rode a bicycle on Central Avenue with a gigantic kingfish across his shoulder.

As for the nation and the world, readers learned that a new torpedo boat had broken all speed records at New London, Connecticut. In Chartres, France, a drunken father murdered his five children. But anything outside Pinellas County was far down Straub's list of concerns unless it had a special local effect.

Advertising was highlighted by the announcement that the City Drug Store was selling Smith's Tonic, guaranteed to cure intermittent, continuous, bilious, and every other kind of fever and chill—or your money back.

Over the next seven decades St. Petersburg and its morning newspaper would gradually become big, prosperous, sophisticated, and complex. The paper reaped prizes for stories that took reporters far afield, even to other countries. Ice cream socials and rotating barbers disappeared from journalistic view in the second half of the century. No one earned Pulitzer Prizes for reporting them.

Still another change was under way in the years after Nelson Poynter's death. Once again there was a headline on a church fundraiser, this time for a synagogue auction.[1] The same day, a parent could learn the school cafeterias were offering plump chicken nuggets with honey mustard sauce next Tuesday.[2] At the Largo work-release jail, someone had stolen a trap used to catch stray cats.[3] And in the ad columns Arthur's Hair Goods was offering to "restore your present hair unit to like-new condition." For those with no such worries, the Village Barber provided a $1 coupon for any service.[4]

But three *Times* reporters also were writing about a summit conference in Washington. Effects of the partial missile ban signed at that meeting were assessed in Magna, Utah, population 17,000, by a writer for the paper's national staff. Another staffer covered election violence in Haiti.

On the feature section's front page, a color photograph showed dancers embracing in skin-colored tights. Nearby was a staff-written study of a nationwide trend toward a new form of criminal psychology.[5] An investigation ranging halfway around the world turned up charges of irregularity in the operation of a local art museum.

As the *Times* approached the end of the century it found its reputation on the line in at least three distinct news areas. It was competing toe-to-toe with parochial shopping guides for neighborhood news. It continued nurturing its renown for sophisticated community analysis. And it was setting out to cover the whole country, even the world, with its own reporters. In that area it would see its accomplishments measured in a class that included the *Washington Post,* the *Los Angeles Times,* and the *Boston Globe.* Perhaps the newspaper was facing an even greater challenge—to clone itself into ten regional editions, most of which had the earmarks of a separate newspaper: their own staffs, editorials, and sales operations.

Waves of improvement had swept the *Times* news operation forward for decades, particularly in the 1960s after Don Baldwin and later Bob Haiman became managing editor. But the force that carried the paper toward the 1980s took its direction from the ideas of Gene Patterson and his appointee, Andy Barnes.

The 1964 probe of the Florida Turnpike that won the paper's first Pulitzer still was remembered as the pinnacle of special projects (investigative stories) when Barnes arrived as metropolitan editor in 1973. Since 1964, prize-winning exposés had spurted profusely out of the pipeline, and the staff prided itself on them.

Barnes knew that such feats, despite their flashiness, were easier than across-the-board improvement of news coverage, which in the long run was the paper's most urgent need. Special projects required only one or two hotshot reporters and as little as a couple of months to complete. But they often got quick results in terms of reform, and they were exciting to do.[6]

So Barnes moved quickly to encourage and support staffers who came up with such ideas. A strange episode that culminated in a *Times* investigation had its beginnings soon after World War II, when a reform-minded young man named Floyd Christian became Pinellas County school superintendent. The paper repeatedly supported him for reelection and later endorsed him as the first appointive superintendent.

Reporter Bette Orsini, working the education beat, wrote a story revealing that Christian had used students and school system materials to build an ornate bar in his home. He heard about the story before it was printed and weepingly appealed to *Times* editors for leniency. The editors decided to kill the story.

In part as a result of his favorable publicity in St. Petersburg, Christian went on to win election as state commissioner of education. The *Times* backed his efforts, made more difficult by the fact that he was a Democrat serving with Claude Kirk, an eccentric Republican governor who vetoed educational appropriations.

Orsini continued winning prizes for her educational coverage, making a reputation for extracting pungent information from abstruse public documents. One day in 1972, as she pored over data about standardized tests given Florida students, she wondered how the state bought such materials. She soon ran into a swirling mass of unexplained facts. Working over the records for weeks, she traced the corporations that had sold materials to the Education Department back to one address in St. Petersburg. The companies had interlocking boards of directors, and all the top figures refused to talk. One of them was Floyd Christian.

Orsini put together enough facts to show that a friend of Christian's had constructed the maze of corporations that had profited from business with Christian's department. Pieces of the puzzle ranged from a meeting in Luxembourg to a Bahamas bank account in the name of "Zera R. Tom," which she deciphered as a composite of the names of Christian's three children. Christian again approached *Times* editors, claiming Orsini was carrying out a personal vendetta. This time they stood firm. Christian publicly denounced the paper, claiming that he had been its favorite target for much of his professional life.

A legislative committee investigated Orsini's allegations. Indictments of Christian on nineteen counts of bribery, conspiracy, and perjury followed. Christian plea-bargained and admitted taking unauthorized compensation and committing perjury. He paid a $43,000 fine and served several months in prison on a federal charge of income tax evasion.

Nelson Poynter, late in his life, expressed regret that the *Times* did not print Orsini's story about construction of Christian's bar, as he believed the county superintendent would have been fired: "Pinellas might have gotten a less able superintendent, but the state of Florida would have been saved the disgrace that it endured when he was a cabinet official. . . . I'm confident that he would never have reached the cabinet if that small story had been printed."[7]

As enthusiasm for such stories as the Christian episode bubbled higher, internal problems made such exploits painfully difficult. It was the time of labor unrest in the newsroom, shortages of newsprint, the strain of converting to computer operation and offset printing, and a temporary drop in profits. Meanwhile a new management team came together in the newsroom. Patterson chose three strong-minded men who differed greatly, and problems resulted: In 1976 Bob Haiman became executive editor, Barnes managing editor, and Ray Herndon metropolitan editor.

Old-timers around the newspaper did not know what to make of Barnes and his Ivy League ways. He had a penchant for dropping unfamiliar words into casual conversation. Cliff Camp joked that after a talk with Barnes he sometimes would have to consult the dictionary to know what he said. Once during a staff conference, Barnes said a lead (first paragraph) on a story he disapproved of was "egregiously mis-led." Amid puzzled looks, managing editor Mike Foley explained, "That means it's a shitty lead." But Barnes had come through the guild crisis with wide respect. He showed that he managed well, delegating authority and giving staffers his loyalty and praise.[8] Like Baldwin when he arrived, he knew little about business and production matters but worked hard to inform himself.

Although Haiman and Barnes tried to be considerate of each other, the line between their duties never was clear. For the record they stated the norm—that Haiman as senior executive was in charge of long-term matters and Barnes dealt with daily concerns. This policy clashed with their natural inclinations, and reality often reflected that fact. But through it all they managed to avoid open conflict.

Herndon was another matter. He had worked for United Press International in Paris and was UPI bureau chief in Saigon during the Vietnam conflict. He came to the *Times* from the *Miami Herald* city desk when Haiman and Barnes moved up and soon showed a talent for ideas and words. But some staffers complained about their dealings with him, particularly alleging that he used sexist language. Some people resigned, but Barnes felt Herndon was Patterson's man and hesitated to make an issue of the matter. Within three years Herndon was gone.[9]

With regional editions proliferating, demands of staffing them had to be balanced with the desire for big story projects. Sometimes the result was more noise than substance. Patterson would chide Barnes for running a "three yards and a cloud of dust" newsroom.

Doing It the Hard Way

Before his paper had won any Pulitzer prizes, Nelson Poynter confided to an associate that he did not expect ever to enter the charmed circle. Pulitzers are won by exposing corruption, which means a newspaper has a vested interest in having enough corruption around to expose, he said. The *St. Petersburg Times* would never reach that point, he added, because it was committed to making local government so good that it would avoid such baseness. He intended to achieve that goal by dissecting the community's problems and explaining them—and giving solutions—so clearly and vividly that the people would find the higher path themselves. In essence, he was a teacher. In some ways this coincided with avant-garde newspaper ideas, but it was a more difficult approach than most editors had the patience or resources to try. Besides, it became confused with the argument over objectivity.

Around the turn of the century the Associated Press had emerged as a common supplier of national and international news to papers of all political colors. Because it had to avoid offending any customers, it put out stories so sanitized of viewpoint that they usually emerged as vapid collections of unexplained, often meaningless facts. But they did set the ethical norm for fairness and impartiality, and the AP style of writing became the touchstone even for reporters who never worked for the agency. Until the 1960s the most daring suggestions were made by two noted journalism professors—Curtis D. MacDougall with his concept of "interpretation," and Neale Copple with his "depth reporting."[10]

The social revolution of the 1960s and early 1970s brought innovative ways to write about public affairs. "New Journalism" was the general label, and at its highest level it graced stories with a touch of literary elegance and the insight of social research. But there were spinoffs such as "advocacy journalism," in which facts were manipulated to serve prejudices. Worst of all, in the view of establishment editors, most practitioners of these occult arts looked like hippies—long hair, beards, no bras, and the like.

The upheavals left some raw feelings in the *Times* newsroom, but experimentation had always come more easily there than was the norm for newspapers. Don Baldwin, despite his AP background, had encouraged virtuosity while he was editor. Competition among staffers crackled in the air, and weekly writing contests put extra dollars in pockets of those who tried hardest. The New Journalists, admired by many recruits to the *Times* staff, had basically the same goals that Poynter had long preached, despite the difference in personal trappings. Like him they wanted to achieve a more humane society through journalism.

No one was better able to take up the cudgel for good writing than Gene Patterson. His own skill with words inclined him to do so, but his constant study of many newspapers impelled him into the battle. He realized that readership of newspapers was declining because they were unreadable. The writing was bilge, he mused, and editors were underestimating readers' intelligence. His assessment of the typical American was that "he has a sense of taste and language and literacy, and he understands why he follows a well-written story and . . . why he throws down a paper that leads him off into blind alleys of bad writing causing him to work too hard to learn what was in the lazy writer's mind."[11]

So when Gene Patterson made better writing one of his first objectives, the timing was right. Once he got past the purgatory of the oil crisis, guild conflict, and staff cutbacks, he could pursue his dream. As 1977–78 president of the American Society of Newspaper Editors (ASNE), he took advantage of the *Times*'s year-long experiment with a writing coach, Roy Peter Clark, to get the attention of his colleagues around the country.

Patterson induced the editors' group to join publishers in a massive three-year study to find how to make newspapers more readable. In his farewell address as president, he heralded what he called a new dimension in the profession—explanatory journalism: "In that new dimension we would commit to the goal of telling an issue whole—taking greater responsibility for bringing clarity to the pros and cons of it—with simplicity which can only spring from a writer's comprehension."[12]

Poynter's idea—that the highest calling of a newspaper was to spread light, not fire—was catching on. The ultimate acceptance came eight years after Patterson raised the cry at the ASNE convention. A new category for the Pulitzer Prizes was created. It was called explanatory journalism.

A Prize with a Price

The Fort Harrison Hotel was a stately if not handsome landmark in downtown Clearwater. It was named after a log stronghold which, during the Seminole wars a century and a half before, had been a place of healing for wounded soldiers. In a more graceful era the eleven-story hotel, covered with buff-colored stucco, had been the local version of a downtown fixture found in practically every Florida resort city—the elegant address for wealthy winter visitors. But now that Clearwater's central area was losing tourists to sassy beachfront palaces, the 272-room hotel was for sale.

L. Ron Hubbard, a paunchy sixty-four-year-old science fiction writer who favored military jumpsuits, was cruising the world in a 3,280-ton yacht. He claimed to have visited heaven several times, according to an Australian government report. On the second visit, 42 trillion years ago, he found paradise to have fallen on evil days like the Fort Harrison Hotel: "The place is shabby. The vegetation is gone. The pillars are scruffy. The saints have vanished. So have the angels."

If Hubbard could not save heaven, he could resurrect the Fort Harrison. In late 1975 his organization, under the name of United Churches of Florida, announced in January 1976 that it was moving its worldwide headquarters there. A secretive Delaware corporation related to the group set about buying a half-dozen buildings, mostly in the downtown area.

One United Churches official, who also wore a jumpsuit, put a smiling face on public dealings. He said that his was "a new organization dedicated to relating religious thought to a changing modern world" and would operate the hotel as "a facility for seminars involving groups of all denominations." He predicted that within weeks the hotel would be half-full of such groups from all over the nation, perhaps the world.[13] For the downtown that meant trade, which the city government and Chamber of Commerce so urgently wanted. A massive public relations campaign followed. The organization offered its help to civic and church groups and sought membership in the chamber. It never mentioned Hubbard, who stayed out of sight.

United Churches asked Clearwater Mayor Gabriel Cazares for help in getting the federal government to sell it a fifteen-story waterfront condominium. But Cazares had been hearing some strange reports about the group. He had noticed more and more security personnel at the hotel armed with billy clubs and Mace. He replied that he would like to see corporate and financial data about the organization before he did anything.

Reporters, particularly Bette Orsini of the *Times,* also were seeking answers. They found that the group hated publicity. What they did not know then was that some United Churches officials were listing their enemies and planning to punish them. An internal directive labeled a "power project" called for an investigation to "distinguish our friends from our enemies and handle as needed."[14] One official devised a hoax—never carried out—to get *Clearwater Sun* reporter Mark Sableman fired. An elderly woman was to go to Sableman's superior, screaming that he had sexually assaulted her son (or grandson) and threaten to tell police.[15] Another message, unsigned, passed through the organization's channels. It referred to the *Times* chairman: "Poynter is a millionaire. Does he have a butler, maid, cook, shofer, gardener, etc. Put an FSM onto one of these things and get the low down on he and his wife." (An FSM was a spy.)

The newcomers had reason to worry. They learned that Orsini had cracked their most guarded secret—that United Churches was a front for the Church of Scientology. The latter group had been involved in legal difficulties with the federal government for more than a decade, particularly over whether it deserved tax-exempt status. Before Orsini could publish her exclusive, the organization rushed in a public relations team from California and in a bold stroke canceled her advantage by publicly announcing its Scientologist identity.

But Orsini's stories about other matters had stung the Scientology leaders. One article was about the "E-meter," an electrical device the church used in initiating new members. Scientologists believed that evil originated 75 million years ago when a tyrant named Xemu had exterminated the people of ninety planets, including Earth, with thermonuclear bombs. Modern mankind had thus been contaminated in spirit.[16]

To become cleansed of past traumas, initiates underwent counseling ("auditing") by a church agent using an E-meter, which supposedly would identify stresses. The meter was never wrong, Hubbard had said: "It sees all, knows all. It tells everything."[17] An initial auditing session could cost as little as $25. But, church dogma stated, the process was like climbing stairs to the desired condition of "clear"—"a state of supra-human awareness and ability."[18] A convert who reached the top would have paid the church $10,000 to $12,000. The church reportedly was taking in $100 million a year.

Tax collectors at various levels had long contended that Scientology was a business enterprise masquerading as a church and should be taxed as such. Officials of the group had fought back in the courts, and, as was learned later, a secret agent had been planted inside IRS and had taken thousands of documents from it.

Orsini's revelations about the E-meter brought a quick response. Scientology formally threatened to file a libel suit against the *Times* and Orsini. The *Clearwater Sun* got a similar warning.

Thus, Pinellas County began to experience what had happened in other parts of the country: Persons or institutions that incurred the anger of the church could expect an unrelenting campaign to discredit or intimidate them. Eight years before, Hubbard had issued an order that anyone whom the church declared was fair game could be "deprived of property, or injured by any means by any Scientologist without any discipline of the Scientologist. May be tricked, sued or lied to or destroyed."[19]

The *Times* reported that the group itself had boasted of suing the U.S. Army, Interpol, the Los Angeles Police Department, the Central Intelligence Agency, the Internal Revenue Service, the Treasury Department, and many other federal, state, and local agencies. One of several suits against the State Department asked $48 million for allegedly spreading false reports about Scientology around the world.

Although the organization did not follow through on its threat to sue the newspapers, the *Times* filed its own suit asking for an injunction against harassment. Scientology did sue Mayor Cazares for $1 million, claiming libel, slander, and violation of civil rights. The city commission voted to pay his legal costs, and Cazares filed a libel suit against the church for $8 million.

Within days Clearwater was abuzz with the controversy. The local League of Women Voters and the Pinellas County Democratic Committee publicly supported Cazares. Some clergymen had welcomed United Churches warmly, but they were furious when they found they had been deceived. The Clearwater Ministerial Association refused to listen to a Scientologist speaker and voted support for the mayor. A radio talk show host who had raised questions about Scientology was fired after the church threatened to sue the station. The manager said the station could not have survived the litigation. The employee later was rehired.

Meanwhile, business was booming at the Fort Harrison. About 500 persons, a press release said, were staying at the hotel and donating as much as $10,000 each. Pinellas County denied the Scientologists' request for tax exemption.

The *Times* continued its revelations about the group. Orsini pieced together evidence that indicated that funds were moving from its tax-exempt units to the Church of Scientology of California, which had lost its tax exemption. An IRS memorandum had contended that tithes had gone to trust accounts in Swiss banks to which Hubbard and his wife, Mary Sue, were the sole signatories. Later, under legal pressure, Hubbard was replaced as a signatory by two other persons chosen by his wife.

But Scientology was fighting back. In a March 1976 letter marked secret, one official reported to another that a "chart of enemy lines" had been drawn up with the purpose of infiltrating agents into their offices. The *Times* topped the list, followed by Cazares, two broadcasters, and the state and district prosecutors. Other memos noted that Scientology agents were trying to get jobs with the newspaper and the St. Petersburg law firm that represented it. Offices of the paper's Washington attorney were burglarized and its file there was ransacked. Information from both law firms soon circulated in Scientology interoffice messages.

One Scientology official proposed a scheme to have a woman agent telephone Patterson's wife and fake an interview. A tape was to be made that could be distorted to portray Sue Patterson as criticizing Poynter. The tape was to be publicized with the object of making Patterson and Poynter "the laughing stocks of the newspaper world." The official's superior vetoed the plan on the grounds that it would not work.[20]

A Scientology publication asserted that Poynter was "allegedly an employee of the Central Intelligence Agency." This may have been a twist on the fact that during World War II, Poynter had worked for William Donovan, who went on to head the Office of Strategic Services, predecessor of the CIA. At any rate, George Bush, CIA director in the mid-1970s, refuted the Scientology claim in a letter to Patterson.

Orsini and her family took the brunt of the Scientology attack. Leaders of the group learned that she was onto something more damaging when one of them found mention of her in IRS files he was copying secretly on weekends. She was inquiring about legal moves against the group in preparation for her stories on its tax problems.

Two days before United Churches was revealed to be Scientology, the "assistant guardian for information" at the Fort Harrison sent an associate a proposal "to get Bette Orsini removed from a position of power and attack" at the *Times*. His idea was to send a Scientologist to the *Times* office posing as a messenger from a Mafia boss; the caller would leave $100 with an editor and ask him to pass it on to Orsini as pay for her supposedly supplying the Mafia with *Times* files. Apparently the plan was never carried out.

The *Times*'s lawsuit against harassment by Scientologists was dropped before coming to trial, not because there had been any settlement, Patterson announced, but to avoid the risk of "bringing harm to a completely innocent organization that might have lacked the means to defend itself against the Scientologists."[21] That cryptic reference was not publicly explained for more than two years, but a drama that was painfully wrenching to the Orsinis was unfolding. Scientology leaders had uncovered the fact that Bette Orsini's husband, Andrew, was director of the Easter Seal Society of Pinellas County. As a physical therapist, his career was devoted to helping crippled children.

Twelve months after the Scientologists arrived in the county, an anonymous letter was received by area newspapers, the city consumer affairs office, the local board of charities, and the state attorney. It purported to be from someone who was a rich businessman and portrayed the writer as a longtime contributor to various local charities. Now, he said, his attorney had told him that his Easter Seal donations might not be deductible because the society's director was guilty of criminal misconduct. He said Andy Orsini should be arrested, and he enclosed copies of official documents.

Times reporter Chris Cubbison was sent by editors to check out the claim. It turned out to be a distortion of an actual event. Every year the State of Florida sends a form to corporations so it can levy a franchise tax. In the case of nonprofit groups such as the Easter Seal Society, the tax is token. But if it is not paid, the charter is revoked. One year the state had sent the Easter Seal form to a wrong address. Having submitted no tax, the society lost its right to operate, but the error soon was discovered and the revocation canceled.

Once Cubbison had reported his findings, Bette Orsini was put on the story. She tracked down a man named Ben Shaw, who had legally bought copies of the entire Pinellas Easter Seal file but had given a false identification as a reporter. Shaw was subpoenaed and testified that he had spent Scientology funds to buy the file but denied writing the anonymous letter. He refused to name the one other person to whom he said he gave copies of the file.

Bette Orsini never was able to prove who had sent the letter and tried to wreck her husband's career, but she did learn the name put on the campaign against her. It was Operation Bunny Bust.

The apparatus of Scientology dirty tricks finally flew apart in Washington, not Clearwater. Soon after the Fort Harrison purchase, two Scientologists forged identification cards to enter IRS offices in the capital. They secretly copied documents there for several months until a suspicious librarian called in FBI agents. Their questioning later led to the two Scientologists' arrest, and one of them cooperated with investigators.

At 6 o'clock one July morning in 1977, FBI agents battered through doors of Scientology offices in Los Angeles and Washington, seizing 48,169 documents. What they found led a grand jury in the capital to indict Mary Sue Hubbard and ten other Scientology "guardians" on twenty-eight counts of conspiracy, theft, and burglary. Nine were convicted of one count each, and two remained fugitives. L. Ron Hubbard was listed in the documents as an unindicted co-conspirator.

After the convictions, the judge opened the seized documents to the public. *Times* Washington correspondent Charles Stafford feverishly plowed through them, fearing that the Scientologists might succeed in legal moves to reclose the files. The newspaper sent two reporters from St. Petersburg to help, and they selected handfuls of sheets for photo-copying.

The files disclosed a panorama of Scientologists' intrigues to wreck reputations and intimidate those who displeased them, as well as years of taking files, giving false testimony, and other illegal acts. For the first time all the plotting and spying against the *Times* and other institutions came to light, along with the private files taken from so-called enemies. Stafford was embarrassed when he found thirteen close-typed pages with summaries of memos, letters, and reporters' notes from the *Times*. "Suddenly you feel that you are peering over the shoulder of a fellow reporter, tiptoeing into the big boss' office while he is at dinner and rummaging through his desk," he wrote.[22]

Stafford got a terse message from Patterson to fly to St. Petersburg immediately for a conference. The chairman told him he should pull out all the stops and weave from the court documents a coherent account of the entire bizarre story—particularly the Pinellas part.

"Charlie, I want you to go back and tell the story *whole,*" Patterson said. "If you do a good job, we'll win the Pulitzer Prize." His hunch was well founded. He had served on the Pulitzer selection board for six years.

Stafford returned to Washington and spent five weeks producing a fourteen-part series. His biggest job was imposing some order on the mountain of documents. The FBI had kept them in the order of file cabinets in which they were found, but the reporter had to trace a narrative path through the maze.

Making no attempt to conceal his moral outrage, Stafford wrote the series in terms of Greek tragedy and biblical rectitude. Contrasting the Scientologists' deeds with religious norms, he intoned: "This is the law of the God of Israel: Thou shalt not steal" and "This is the com-mandment of Jesus: Thou shalt love thy neighbor as thyself."[23]

It had been a good year for the newsroom, and the *Times* submitted four entries for the 1980 Pulitzer. One was a Scientology package—Orsini's probes over four years and Stafford's wrap-up series. When a selection board member's entry is being considered, he or she must wait outside the jury room. As he had done often before, Patterson paced the halls. Then word came: The Scientology entry had not won the public service prize for which it had been submitted. It had been shifted to the national reporting category and had won it. Now the

Bette Orsini, who be-
came a *Times* reporter
during World War II,
exclaims at learning that
coverage she initiated
had won a Pulitzer Prize
in 1980. *St. Petersburg
Times.*

Times was recognized not only as an elite newspaper but as one that
operated at the national level.

When she got the news at home, Orsini lay down on the floor and
kicked her legs in the air. Although he shared the $1,000 prize with her,
Stafford gave her the credit for the major role. After the series was
published, Stafford was approached through a private detective by a
man who identified himself as a wealthy European who wanted to get
his daughter back from under the Scientologists' influence. Stafford
was very careful about what he said to the man.

Months later, a court case revealed the caller was a Scientology
representative. "Why did you lie to me?" Stafford demanded of him.
"Oh, we all do that" was the reply.[24]

Abroad in St. Petersburg

The column, spread across the top of page two, started off telling about
an Argentine teenager named Dagmar. Soldiers had raided her home,
gunned her down, and dragged her off to a torture chamber. The
incident, which had happened ten years earlier, was used to explain

how Argentina had arrived at its military atrocity trials. Besides human interest, the article had a dash of history going back 400 years, a comparison with how other governments were handling the problem, even a critique of U.S. policy. Tacked below the Argentine discussion was a four-inch commentary on civil strife in Fiji that gave background never touched on spot news stories. The column was written in St. Petersburg, in a tiny office jammed with files and two desks. Its author was Wilbur Landrey, a balding man with horn-rimmed glasses who could pass as a bank president. Within two weeks he would be in London covering the British parliamentary election.

To gather the material, Landrey had telephoned several journalist friends in Argentina and dipped into resource material. But the most important ingredient was nearly forty years as a foreign correspondent.

Landrey came from Kansas City, always a synonym for America's heartland. An axiom in the United Press news agency was that reporters should tell a story so a milkman in Kansas City could understand it. Bill Landrey's father had been a reporter, his grandfather the owner of a weekly. Going to work for United Press, Landrey served in the New York world headquarters and went to Columbia University on the side. He graduated in political science. In 1948 he was sent to the Paris UP bureau, and his passport was in his pocket from then on.

When Gene Patterson took over the London UP bureau, Landrey was there as a reporter. As UP bought out International News Service and became UPI, Landry acquired administrative duties for one region after another—the Middle East, Africa, the Caribbean, Latin America. In 1970 he became UPI foreign editor.

Financial problems were closing in on UPI, and Landrey could see little hope for expanding the foreign service. One day in 1975, as he was puzzling over how to cover political warfare in Portugal, he received a letter from Patterson, with whom he had lost contact for almost twenty years. Patterson invited Landrey to join the *Times* staff because "we want to have the best foreign news report in the country."

It was not a sudden whim. Patterson had long wanted to do something with the *Times*'s foreign coverage. He had no hopes of setting up a network of foreign bureaus, but he believed that his readers—more cosmopolitan than most—deserved something better than gleanings from wire services. AP and UPI provided a wealth of information, and that was the problem. Readers were so inundated with international data that it became confusing. Someone was needed to digest it, put it into perspective and make it readable. Patterson told Landrey he could travel whenever and wherever he wanted, all expenses paid. He would be his own editor and could write as he pleased.

Landrey at fifty-one had enormous energy and lust for breaking events, and he clearly was not going to be an ivory tower foreign editor. It soon became apparent, however, that Landry was spread too thin. Processing copy was the least valuable thing he could do, so another former UPI foreign editor, Jack Payton, was brought in with the title of foreign news editor.

Landrey's highest priority became making the foreign news comprehensible. His main vehicle was his bylined column. He realized that his readers did not include as many government junkies as in Washington or New York, but he avoided being as simplistic as *USA Today* was to be later. One tactic he used was to put headline events into local perspective. When Israelis waged tank battles in Lebanon, Landrey showed how close they were to Israeli towns by imagining the fighting going on in Largo, an exurb of St. Petersburg. He superimposed maps of news areas over local geography and often devised color graphics. The effort paid off in reader response: One survey showed that Landrey's column ranked with that of the sports editor for the highest readership.

Foreign travel steadily absorbed more of Landrey's time. Rapidly improving technology such as satellite transmission and laptop computers simplified sending his material back to the *Times* newsroom. Short of overseas bureaus, Landrey figured, the next best resource was stringers—part-time correspondents. He steadily worked up a team of nearly twenty, closely supervised by telephone.

The Business of Covering Business

An ill-founded myth about Nelson Poynter was that, as a New Dealing Yale economist who stood for the little man, he was anti-business. On the contrary, he fiercely believed in making a profit and keeping clear-cut lines of authority. His closest friends in St. Petersburg came from the financial and legal establishment, and he enjoyed such comforts of wealth as travel, dinner parties, and art collecting.

Nevertheless, St. Petersburg seemed to offer poor prospects for mainstream business journalism when Poynter moved there. It could not hold a candle to neighboring Tampa as a commercial center. The typical reader of its business pages was interested in about half a dozen agate-sized lines of type each day—stock quotations. Even the wildest forecasts would not have predicted that the *Times*, as it approached its second century, would have business—along with politics and sports— as its strongest field.

For decades, real estate coverage was the closest the paper had come to emphasizing business. As a tidal wave of new homes rolled farther into the Pinellas countryside after World War II, the *Times* rode the crest with both penetrating news and tempting displays of residential luxury. And millions of dollars worth of advertising swirled in with it.

Douglas Doubleday had garnered many state and national prizes for his work on real estate and architecture in the late 1950s and early 1960s. He had risen so far above the boosterism common among home-section editors that he became known as real estate and economics analyst.

Doubleday was fired from the *Times* in 1967 after being accused of involvement in a real estate deal called Bayfront Plaza. Visions of a high-rise skyline replacing the decayed downtown section were being dangled before the city in efforts to put over a $50 million redevelopment package. The *Times* gave it forceful support on the editorial page, and Doubleday followed it in the news columns.

A group of prominent downtown merchants opposed the plan and claimed that Doubleday's coverage was slanted in line with the editorial policy. They did some digging in official records and submitted a paid advertisement to the *Times* that mentioned "big profits" made on the Bayfront Plaza and suggested wryly, "Have the *St. Petersburg Times* tout your speculation."[25] The ad cited what it claimed was evidence that Doubleday was a director of a company that made 63 percent profit in one year by buying property and then selling it to the city for the plaza.

The *Times* ad department brought the ad copy on a Friday to Don Baldwin, then executive editor. He felt that it showed conflict of interest, and his anger ignited. The next morning he took it to Poynter's home, and the owner was incensed. They agreed that Doubleday had to go. A brief story on Monday's front page—unusual emphasis for such a matter—announced that Doubleday had chosen "early retirement." It made no mention of the accusation against the journalist, but the opponents' ad ran on page three of the same issue.

Business pages continued to cater to retirees who had their fortunes, large or small, on Wall Street, giving a wide range of investment information. This policy changed late in Baldwin's era, when editors saw local commerce becoming important news. The city was booming on a broad front, not just from the capricious prosperity of real estate sales. Buyouts—a breeze that would billow in the 1980s—were connecting Pinellas companies to big money elsewhere.

It was time, the editors decided, to find a journalist with the sophistication to talk with local business leaders on their own terms. They found such a man at the *Wall Street Journal*. He was Clayton Reed, who had learned his trade during twenty years there. As a sign of the *Times*'s commitment, Reed was made a senior editor, with more prestige than his predecessors. They had reported to the city editor, but he went directly to the managing editor. Bob Haiman told him, "Clay, you're the expert. You tell us what you think ought to be done."

Reed submitted a wish list, which management set about fulfilling. Among other matters, he brought his knowledge gained at the *Journal* to improving the stock listings. Realizing that stock ownership had spread to a vastly broader population, Reed set out to remove the mystery from it. His application of consumerism to Wall Street caused some stockbrokers to complain. Reed humanized the market by buying a portfolio of stocks for his young son. He chronicled the boy's dealings with his stockbroker and his decisions to buy or sell, keeping track of his earnings. It proved so educational that the son later won simultaneous scholarships at Harvard and MIT.

The spotlight moved from New York to St. Petersburg. Reed was the first *Times* business editor to become a high-profile columnist, and *Times* editors caught on to the economic revolution. When Reed would develop a hot story about business they frequently would snatch it away for display on the front of sections A or B, leaving Reed with a hole at the top of his own section.

Reed developed terminal cancer in 1979. Replacing him posed a problem. The *Times* had embraced high-level business journalism a decade before, and now the concept was growing exponentially among other newspapers. This made for a shortage of qualified personnel. Management turned to its own staff and chose Elizabeth Whitney, the real estate editor. She had turned out a succession of prize-winning stories embarrassing to the land sales industry. A national trade publication referred to her as the real estate editor who had won the most awards in the country. Whitney's promotion to business editor also marked a large expansion of women's role in the newsroom.

A New Day

"Day," the brave new feature section launched during Baldwin's editorship, sailed into the Patterson period with all flags flying. *Times* people were testing flashlights to see which worked best, critiquing restaurants, and panning musical performances with expert aplomb.

Among readers, conservative opposition to the change died slowly. Haiman had an almost evangelistic zeal for sweeping away the sexism of old concepts that features were for women as sports were for men. (Later he reflected that change may have come too far, too fast.) To send a clear signal, Haiman appointed a man as "Day" editor when Anne Rowe Goldman took extended leave in 1972 to have a baby. He lasted only a year before being replaced by one of Patterson's earliest stars, Buddy Martin.

Martin had no pretensions in the arts, but he had a flair for editing. He immediately brought in innovative young writers. The most talked-about feature probably was consumer news, which fitted in both with the "me" orientation and the economic crisis.

The *Times* became the first newspaper in the country with a staff column testing advertising claims for products. Titled "Watch This Space" and written by Carolyn Nolte, it was syndicated nationally and ran in as many as 145 newspapers. Nolte wrote the column in a spare, uncolored tone to avoid unfairness to business. She would cite the claim, give comments from the manufacturer, then tell how the product was tested and the outcome.

Many projects went beyond the column and bloomed into major spreads. Anything to do with automobiles was a thumping success with readers. Long before such stories became a cliché with news media, dishonest auto tune-up shops were spotlighted by the *Times*. Staffers would have a car tuned to perfection, then insert one defect that caused a malfunction. They would take it to another shop and see what repairs were prescribed at what price. The process would be repeated for many shops. It was a slow, expensive process, but the published results caused a sensation.

No less popular were exposés of car-selling scams. A reporter would go around to various dealers in the fevered Pinellas auto market area and compare prices, sales practices, and hidden charges. A shady practice treated separately was invasion of car buyers' privacy. The *Times* discovered that some dealers maneuvered pairs of customers, usually married couples, into discussing their bargaining strategy when the salesman left the office. The seller would eavesdrop electronically and discover their top price, then persuade them to pay it.

Taste tests on food and drink items also went over well. Donut shops, ice cream counters, and pizza parlors were ranked for all imaginable qualities—flavor, crispness, freshness, and the like. The *Times* also assembled a panel of drinkers for a blind test of various brands of whiskey. It turned out that most could tell no difference between expensive brands and cheaper ones.

All the consumer exposés gave the *Times* advertising department a running case of jitters, as it had to face a barrage of complaints from advertisers. But advertising director Laurie Herman and his successor, Leo Kubiet, resisted the temptation to interfere. Lawsuits also were a danger. The staff brought in company lawyers when planning sensitive stories. The caution paid off; no suits were filed.

Toys Discontinued

For decades the operation of the *Times* sports department sounded like a good news/bad news joke. The good news was that management did little to interfere; the bad news was that it cared too little to make the department outstanding.

Anomalies plagued the paper's sports coverage. Big national and world events were displayed lavishly, but there was little money to cover them except by wire service copy. St. Petersburg was moving up toward the top twenty metropolitan areas in population, but it had no major university or professional teams. Bright young people flocked to work for *Times* sports, but once they got their training and the respect for having worked there they cashed it in for jobs with bigger papers.

Then, in 1978, *Time* magazine named the *St. Petersburg Times* sports department one of the six best in the country. The others were in New York, Washington, Los Angeles, and Boston. The magazine judged that "reader for reader and pound for pound, few U.S. papers can match" the *Times*'s commitment to sports—or to local and national news. Running thirty-six columns of sports per day and seventy-eight on Sunday, the *Times* sent staffers on many out-of-town assignments and served well its retired northern readers interested in their hometowns, the article added.[26]

The change, of course, had not happened overnight. Don Baldwin sent young Tom Kelly in as sports editor during his push for excellence in the 1960s. When Gene Patterson arrived as *Times* editor in 1972, word got around that reforming the sports department was his top priority. His big move was to hire Buddy Martin away from the Gannett News Service to be sports editor. Then he brought in Van McKenzie from a Gannett paper to assist Martin.

Martin aggressively expanded coverage, strong on innovative reader appeals. McKenzie's long suit was planning team reportage of major events and assembling it into flashily designed packages. One result was that the *Times* won first place two years running in the Associated Press Managing Editors competition for sports sections. Martin and McKenzie devised a daily page that reported a vast range of sports results in small type. It soon became widely imitated.

Sharing the Reins

Patterson had been editor and president of the *Times* only four months when Nelson Poynter set out for a convention in Buenos Aires in 1972. The editorial board still had not decided what to do about an endorsement in that fall's Nixon-McGovern presidential election. Most members had little enthusiasm for McGovern, and polls showed the Pinellas electorate backing Nixon seven to one. There was always the option of no endorsement at all.

The choice was not so difficult for Poynter. He had lost any regard for Nixon when, as a young politician, the Californian had conducted a smear campaign to defeat Congresswoman Helen Gahagan Douglas. The Checkers speech in 1952 convinced him even more that Nixon lacked the minimal integrity that should be expected of a president.

Patterson caught Poynter on the elevator as the boss was leaving for the airport. "Hey, Nelson, this is your bat, your ball, and your playing field here," he said, "and I haven't had a chance to talk to you about whom we're going to endorse for president." Poynter turned to him and grinned. "You're not going to endorse Nixon, are you?"

So the *Times* became one of the lonely band of papers backing McGovern. Patterson had not been tempted to do otherwise, but the fact that Poynter had not made a point of settling the matter before his departure drove home to the editor the trust that the owner placed in his executives.[27]

This was the keynote throughout the last six years of Poynter's life. By the time Bob Pittman arrived and took charge of the editorial page in 1963, Poynter had developed a way of guiding editorial policy without crudely interfering with his deputies' work. But he clearly could yank the reins when he felt strongly about it, as occurred in the 1973 St. Petersburg mayoral election.

The *Times* tends to influence voting more in city elections, which are nonpartisan, than in national races. So the editorial board debated for weeks over whether to endorse C. Randolph Wedding, a successful businessman who was weak on environmental protection, or Barbara Gammon, a much-publicized gadfly who had darted from one issue to another without notable effectiveness. Although Pittman as chairman of the editorial board normally preferred to reach consensus, in this case he brought it to a vote. By a split decision, Gammon was chosen.

Poynter heard about the choice before an editorial was run. He overruled the board and ordered an endorsement of Wedding. The action shocked the majority board members, not because they were angry—they too had doubts about Gammon—but because it was so unexpected. Neither before nor after was this Poynter's normal practice. Patterson, who had concurred in the choice of Gammon, later declared himself wrong: "I didn't do my job as editor that day, so Nelson did it for me."[28]

Just as in the days when Straub continually raised readers' eyebrows, the Patterson-era *Times* earned its state and national reputation not so much because of the causes it endorsed but rather because of the way it did so. Most notably, the paper set the agenda. Its prestige primarily was based not on how many readers answered a call for action but rather on how often it started them to thinking about some proposal.

Furthermore, with investigative news-page series keyed to the editorials, it would provide factual ammunition for action-oriented readers. This typically took the form of a tabloid special section that would probe a subject to depths never plumbed by lawmakers or their staff. When such a tabloid landed on every legislator's desk, it sent waves throughout the capitol.

The other earmark of the *Times*'s approach was that it was, as Poynter liked to describe himself, "butt-headed." Once the paper took

The *Times* editorial board became well known in the 1950s for its grilling of political candidates before deciding on endorsements. Here the board interviews Governor Bob Graham in 1980. *St. Petersburg Times.*

up a cause, it stood firm, even though it might be in a minority position a long time. In most fields, though, it eventually prevailed.

Because of this persistence, the Patterson era showed no sharp editorial break with the past. The paper never wavered from its long-standing commitments to better education, ecological protection, openness in government, good social services, gun control, an end to capital punishment, and prison and court reform.

Although taking unpopular stands won applause from observers around the country, it made for tough going at home. The *Times*'s stands on gun control and capital punishment always went down poorly with the majority in its conservative constituency, but Republican legislators from Pinellas tended to respect the paper. Not only did they see the regard their colleagues in Tallahassee held for it, but it also dealt with them fairly on issues and their own careers.

A Place to Stay

When, in the 1880s, Peter Demens cast his lot with the fishing camp that would become St. Petersburg, he faced competition from other settlements around the tip of the subpeninsula that wanted to lead development in the area. Over the next century, St. Petersburg's downtown had soared into position as lodestar of the Pinellas firmament, but decay set in during the 1960s. Hotels and stores closed, and sidewalks no longer were thronged with winter visitors. Pigeons no longer flocked to Williams Park, as there were few people to feed them. History had come full circle. Now the outlying communities were asking why their taxes should support downtown redevelopment, which they saw as just another shopping center—a dying one at that.

Nelson Poynter never had doubts about the matter. Although he conceded the loss of retirees who got richer and moved to the suburbs, he had visions of gleaming palaces of finance, professions, and recreation rising on the bayfront. The *Times* failed to win voter support to build Pier Park, a chichi place to spend money, but it kept the faith.

Ever since the *Times* completed its eight-story building in 1926, its physical presence had been easy on the eye. As buildings in its block slowly became seedier, it had kept up appearances. In 1952 the paper built a four-story wing primarily for presses, only to move them later to a satellite plant. Then in 1968, on a corner where it had demolished two decrepit hotels, it doubled its space with a spiffy five-story building topped by a penthouse auditorium. Visually, the result was three buildings going in opposite directions, but space needs were relieved for a while.

Patterson had set the paper's editorial course when he decided his first day in St. Petersburg that downtown renewal should get first priority for editorial fervor. It was to be the monolithic issue on which the *Times* both broke its lance and climbed to glory. Ironically, its failures would come partly because of its successes.

The *Times* had a special attachment to downtown survival because it was proud that former editor Bill Straub had saved the waterfront from commercial exploitation. But when retirees largely abandoned the center of the city and bought homes in the suburbs, traditional sources of investment dried up.

Bold new ideas obviously were required. Some came from entrepreneurs who wanted to turn downtown into a professional and entertainment center. A fifteen-story tower holding offices and shops opened in 1979. Appealing to young sophisticates who had just acquired the class label of yuppies, a dingy downtown block was reborn with elegant boutiques and eating nooks.

But public money was another matter. When city government tried to get involved in some projects, it faced a rebellion from the suburbs. Voters soundly rejected a $60 million stadium to be built near the waterfront. The biggest fight was over a glittering pleasure palace that its promoters wanted to build and name Pier Park. The site was to be the Vinoy Mole, a thumb of land that had been dredged from the bay decades before. It was near the defunct Vinoy Park, once dowager queen of downtown resort hotels. Promoter of the idea was James Rouse, who had rejuvenated downtown areas of Baltimore and Norfolk with similar projects. They were multistory galleries of shops and restaurants—shopping centers long on glitter if not on value.

Civic leaders flocked to support the proposal. The *Times* waged a major campaign for it, citing the economic benefits that might accrue to the whole community. City Hall would be a partner in the plan, providing free land and some of the construction cost. This stirred up the same forces that had beaten the stadium. They argued that Pier Park would be just another shopping center, and the city had no business getting involved with private enterprise.

This project went down in defeat at the polls also. Much blame was laid at the *Times*'s doorstep. Some critics said that the paper had pushed so hard that it had provoked a backlash. Others said that, although the editorial page had been steadfast, reporters covering the campaign had wounded it fatally with skeptical pinpricks.

But the most severe handicaps the *Times* may have imposed on Pier Park and other such efforts were the outgrowth of crusades that the paper never expected would have such an effect. One was the city manager system, a concept adopted by the city at Bill Straub's urging when he was editor. For decades Poynter had fought to build professional management into the city government, taking it out of the tangles of personal politics, but this also weakened political leadership. Unlike Tampa, which always had been ruled by one populist baron or another, the St. Petersburg City Council usually was a revolving door of faceless lawmakers who had brief moments of power. When a great cause needed someone well known to lead it, the supply was short.

The other trap in which the *Times* caught itself was Poynter's continual preaching that, above all, St. Petersburg should be the best place in the world to live. This credo meant that commercialism and industrial growth should take second place to what Poynter called "residentialism." People deserved to be snug and secure in their suburban enclaves, he seemed to say. Although Poynter never used this doctrine as a weapon against downtown development, others were tempted to do so. And the Pier Park advocacy left the paper vulnerable to charges of inconsistency by seeming to abandon residential values.

Except for Pier Park, the *Times*'s record clearly was one of protecting the waterfront's serenity. The paper brought out its guns against a tacky "Olde English Village" proposed for the area, as well as against a glass bubble to be built over the Municipal Pier. It also staunchly resisted developers' semantic gambit of disparaging "passive use" of the park for family outings, jogging, games, and sunbathing.

In one stand against exploitation the paper faced both tradition and public apathy. Poynter had always opposed the use of sixty-two acres of prime waterfront property for the downtown airport. This was the place from which early-day daredevils had operated, and it served the Coast Guard for several decades in its forays against bootlegging during Prohibition and against German submarines in World War II.

The city acquired ownership of the property, and the field reverted to general aviation—small private craft. So short were the runways that planes were continually crashing into the bay, and hotels and offices across the street stood in constant danger. The paper's stand was always unpopular, as pilots formed a potent lobby and could always stir up a romantic appeal for keeping the field. Also working against the move was the fact that both international airports in the area were getting overcrowded, and there would be no place for the private fliers to go.

On statewide issues, the *Times* kept up its stubborn fight against whatever it thought would pollute either the physical or moral environment. It was one of the first to call for a brake on Florida's sacrosanct growth by inflow from other states. "Growth management" became the euphemism for making sure there were enough room and services before allowing more houses to be built.

Bob Graham, a politician who set out to improve the state's lagging educational system, got the *Times*'s hearty support. When he ran for governor, the paper backed him from the point when he had only 5 percent public favor in polls. He went on to win. The paper scolded him for hesitancy at first, dubbing him "Governor Jello," but it gave him much political muscle throughout his eight years in office.

The *Times* also defended virtues such as official honesty in a state where old ways were going out of fashion. One such high-minded sortie brought widespread criticism of the paper, even from some of its own staffers and other supporters. In 1978 backers of a proposed law permitting gambling casinos succeeded in getting a statewide referendum on the ballot. In Patterson's absence in Europe, Jack Lake led the Times Publishing Company to join other major Florida newspapers in contributing money to a successful campaign to defeat the proposal.

When critics accused the paper of getting involved in power politics, Patterson responded that its $25,000 gift was justified because the question was one of societal values and standards, not politics. In later years he said he would refrain from doing so again, not because he thought it was a conflict but because some perceived it as such. During a subsequent casino effort the paper kept its opposition on the editorial page.

The Red Ball

In the days of hot metal, when newspapers were set into type made from molten lead, typographical errors were pervasive. No matter how diligent the proofreading, they cropped up even in headlines and advertisements. They became part of the folklore, and collections of funny ones were published as books.

Typos infuriated Nelson Poynter. To him, the presence of even one proclaimed the newspaper had failed to reach perfection that day. He considered it a mockery of the *Times*'s claim to be Florida's best newspaper, and he wanted the staff to know it.

One morning, reading a rash of such errors soured his breakfast. On the way to his office, he passed Jack Lake's. He bustled in and told Lake what he wanted—a red ball on top of the *Times* building that would light up anytime there was a single typo. Staffers could see it when they came to work.

"Goddammit, Nelson," said Lake, "we're not going to do something like that."

Poynter snapped back: "That's the way we're going to make the staff aware that, by God, we didn't do the best we could yesterday."

Lake managed to talk him out of the idea, but the story spread among staffers.[29] They also were obsessive about accuracy, and the threat made them even more careful. But they were manacled by outmoded technology. As America put satellites into space, its newspapers were burdened with production methods almost unchanged from the 1890s.

Clanging iron monsters set type at a speed that rarely exceeded ten lines per minute. These were assembled laboriously into iron frames along with metal photoengravings. From the raised surface a cardboard mold (matrix) was made. Molten metal was poured over the curved surface to produce a rotary press plate. Muscular pressmen hefted the forty-two-pound plates onto temperamental presses, and finally the printed product could emerge.

Although the process drew on the main idea of twentieth-century production—the assembly line—it differed in one essential: It did not move forward in an unbroken line. If a typo occurred, the process stood still while operators went back to typesetting and repeated the sequence step by step. Ironically, mistakes were as likely to occur during the correction phase as in the original.

Poynter had been trying to yank newspaper production out of the nineteenth century ever since he showed in the 1945 printers' strike that he could publish the *Times* with cold type. This photographic process eliminated the debris, fumes, weight, and delay of hot metal. Poynter also was an apostle of offset printing, a form of lithography that produced far better results than letterpress, the old standard. The technology had been available since before World War II, but more development was needed to make it feasible for large-volume dailies.

Although cold type and offset brought out the best in each other, pioneers could use one without the other, thereby encouraging parallel paths of experimentation. Poynter grasped at advances in both fields as soon as he could coax them out of equipment manufacturers. The first breakthroughs came with type; the *Times* pioneered with several innovations to make Linotypes more efficient.

But Poynter knew the answer lay in computers. They were being used in commercial printing plants, and he was determined to bring them into newspapers. In 1967, he found the man to do it: V. Donald Rebholz, an energetic, outgoing young man who had graduated from Carnegie Tech in printing management. He had managed Bethlehem Steel's in-house printing plant, the first one in the country to use a computer. Poynter took Rebholz on in 1967 as assistant to Jack Lake, then general manager. Lake quickly turned the typesetting problem over to Rebholz.

The printing equipment industry was edging toward the computer age with some harebrained ideas and little courage, Rebholz believed. This attitude jibed well with Poynter's outlook. For one thing, the industry was bound up in a technology called optical character recognition (OCR). Venturesome newspapers all over the country were buying these devices, electronic eyes that would read stories that had come out of reporters' typewriters and turn them into a signal that would set cold type. Rebholz saw OCR as a flawed technology because it did not allow journalists and proofreaders to make changes easily once the copy was keyboarded. He saw that the future of word processors was in such file maintenance. The only way to do this was to bring the copy onto a display screen (VDT) where it could be viewed while keyboarding and editing.

Florida newspapers were setting the nation's pace in technology, and the *Times* generally led them. Rebholz made a deal with the Harris company, an old-line typesetting manufacturer that had just opened a Florida branch oriented to space-age projects. The *Times* offered a $50,000 advance purchase for Harris to develop newspaper VDTs of the kind Rebholz wanted.

Times managers drew up a modernization plan with a $19 million price tag for conversion to cold type and offset. The *Evening Independent,* a simpler operation, would precede the morning newspaper in the changeover. The whole process was complete by mid-1975.

Meanwhile, development of offset presses went ahead. In the 1930s Poynter had addressed a publishers' meeting and extolled the promise of offset, but it was 1966 before Poynter could find an offset press in some degree practical for large papers. He bought a Goss Suburban, designed for commercial printing, and used it for sections printed in advance, such as the Sunday magazine. Reproduction, particularly of photographs, fairly sparkled, but its main purpose was to teach pressmen how to use offset. The *Times* and several other middle-sized dailies banded together to pressure manufacturers to provide larger offset presses. Goss was persuaded to take the plunge. In 1968, the *Times* bought the new Goss press, the Metro, becoming the largest paper to do so. It would be eight years longer any daily had more offset units than the *Times* did.

The struggles to get adequate presses and train people to use them went on until June 25, 1975. On that day a retired stereotyper made a sentimental return to the plant to cast the last hot metal plate. After 1975, reporters wrote their stories on terminals, ultimately setting type as they did it. Editors massaged the product and wrote headlines the same way. Press capacity increased in regular surges.

The need for Poynter's twinkling red ball atop the building had long disappeared. And the lists of newspaper boners grew yellow with age.

Reaching Less, Grasping More

Some executives on the *Times* hungered for a relatively new kind of growth—geographic. After having captured the *Independent* and, in effect, overcome the *Clearwater Sun*'s competition, it was nearing saturation density of circulation in Pinellas County. But the *Times*'s splendid isolation on the subpeninsula now worked against it. Even though it passed the *Tampa Tribune* in total circulation in 1971, the *Tribune* dominated the rural areas and small cities in an arc-like embrace both up and down the west coast and inland.

Certainly the *Times* could not challenge its old rival in all three directions at once, so it had to choose one. The northward coast beyond Pinellas County seemed doomed to remain sparsely populated cattle ranches, woodlands, and swamps. Going inland would mean leaping over Tampa into the dense corridor stretching toward Orlando. The paper appeared to have the best chance southward toward Sarasota.

By the late 1960s, southwest Florida possessed teeming markets of sun-seekers. They soon would build an urban strip from Bradenton, just across the bay from St. Petersburg, through Sarasota and Fort Myers, nearly a hundred miles away, down to Naples. Along the highways it was the quintessential roadside glitz—endless minor commercial attractions ranging from the National Police Museum to the Waltzing Waters musical fountains, plus more traditional places such as the Ringling Museum of Art and the circus's winter quarters. Substantial communities such as Sarasota, Bradenton, and Port Charlotte were building up. A few miles inland was still the preserve of cowboys and alligators, but metropolitan sprawl was pushing subdivisions toward them.

So the *Times* made a big push southward in 1973. It started printing a special edition called the *Manatee Times,* named for the county containing Bradenton. It opened bureaus as far south as Punta Gorda, twenty-two miles north of Fort Myers. In effect it competed not only with the hometown dailies in Sarasota and Bradenton for local news and advertising but also with the *Tampa Tribune* as the metropolitan publication that many people bought as a second paper.

The effort was to be Joe Yauch's final thrust as circulation director. He retired in 1973 and was succeeded by David Fluker, who like Yauch had come up through the sweaty ranks of newspaper deliverymen. But unlike Yauch he was a homegrown talent, not an import from up north.

When Fluker stepped into the top job, he had a tremendous advantage. Newspapers elsewhere were having trouble selling subscriptions to a new generation uninterested in the mainstream community represented by the press. Besides, the new adults had been brought up on television. But retirees still flowed to Florida's Gulf coast to establish new homes, and they were more affluent than incoming pensioners of earlier decades. They had grown up reading several newspapers daily and could easily afford a subscription. To get their business all a circulation department had to do was toss the paper on the lawn on time.

Another factor in Fluker's favor was that once readers got used to reading the *Times,* they were not inclined to give it up. Subscribers of some newspapers dropped out so rapidly the subscription departments had to replace 125 percent of the total annually just to stay even. The *Times* had an annual dropout rate of only 17 percent, and any sales over that increased the total.

The circulation empire that Fluker inherited stretched nearly 600 miles from rack sales in Pensacola, the state's Panhandle gateway, to home delivery in Naples, where the Everglades began. It was longer than the distance between New York City and Cincinnati.

Even the home delivery area was enormous. Fluker boasted that, in a sense, the sun set on it no more than it did on the Union Jack. Speaking to a club in Tallahassee, he said, "I can get up in the morning here and read a copy of the *Times* that has been delivered to my door. Then I can get in my car, drive all day to Naples and pick up a copy that was delivered there the same morning."

The *Times* had built statewide prestige because of its news coverage and editorials about state government. Nearly 5,000 subscribers in Tallahassee could read the paper over their morning coffee, a quality big-city companion to their small local daily. Thus, the *Times* had access not only to the powerful in state government but also to thousands whose permanent homes were elsewhere in the state. The paper's reform-minded staff, particularly the Tallahassee bureau, felt their professional lifeblood depended on the governor's being able to get the paper on his doorstep. But it was vanity circulation. Distribution costs far exceeded income from subscriptions and ad sales. Jack

Lake came up with an analysis that showed each subscriber in Tallahassee represented a $100 annual loss to the paper.

Poynter could shrug off the loss until the 1973 oil embargo led the *Times* to tighten belts. Interdepartmental spats were rife. Circulation said it could sell more papers in the outlying zones if the people could read more local ads, but advertising claimed that it could sell more space if merchants could count on more circulation. Jack Lake believed that the news operation was not covering subjects of interest to the south coast such as citrus and cattle. Nor did rival newspapers in those areas prove to be pushovers.

Joe Yauch had always fiercely championed expansion. But when he retired and the emergency hit, Lake prevailed with the argument that remote circulation was draining off nearly a million dollars a year that should be spent on improving the paper. He decided that a phased pullout from the entire south coast and remote northern points—notably Tallahassee and Gainesville—was necessary, but Fluker convinced the leadership that it should be done all at once. Withdrawing in pieces would be like chopping off one's fingers a joint at a time, he argued. The pullout cost the *Times* 7,500 daily sales and 10,000 on Sundays. Aggressive selling in the remaining area made up the loss, even in the depths of the economic crisis, and total circulation at the end of 1974 was several thousand ahead of the year before.

Having largely abandoned the south coast, the *Times* concentrated its expansion northward—not to the ego-boosting glamor of Tallahassee and Gainesville, but to St. Petersburg's own backyard. Aside from Clearwater and Tarpon Springs in northern Pinellas County, the *Times* had never paid much attention to the scattered towns reaching up the coastal highway. Decades before, the *Times* had fought to get the highway built as a way to bring midwestern tourists south without going through Tampa. The corridor had remained a haven of cattle ranchers and small farmers.

But in the 1970s the seventy-five-mile strip of U.S. 19 became a Cinderella of exurban development. The roadway finally became crowded with commuters. Three counties formed layers northward from Pinellas. They tended to divide into rival factions—the west sides dominated by St. Petersburg because of the U.S. 19 funnel, the east sides drawn to Tampa via routes leading there.

In the 1940s the *Times* began what forty years later would become a major dimension—separate content for different communities in the circulation area. Instead of mingling all Clearwater stories with local ones, it began adding extra pages in the local section that were distributed only to upper Pinellas. The paper remained that way until 1968, when seemingly endless amoeba-like divisions began. Each spun-off edition bore the name *Times* but with some local name coming first. The usual practice was to produce a section full of news and advertising for a particular community, put a localized name-plate on the front page, and insert the regular *St. Petersburg Times* in it. Thus the reader in an outlying community could have the best of two worlds—a hometown paper produced by *Times* staffers working in that neighborhood plus a metropolitan, globally oriented major daily.

In 1978 the *Times* opened an avant garde $1.4 million news, advertising, and circulation building in Clearwater to house the edition there and give the final push that would bypass the local daily, the *Clearwater Sun*. Other regional editions soon gained their own new buildings. After experiments with decentralized printing, all production returned to the St. Petersburg plant.

Unlike the abortive drive to the south, the *Times*'s turn northward proved profitable. It became the basis for a circulation gold mine. Over the fifteen years after Gene Patterson came to the *Times,* daily circulation nearly doubled, to more than 300,000, and Sunday sales reached nearly 400,000. The *Times* had moved into the class of the country's major newspapers and was the largest between Washington and Miami.

Branching Out

"What's a Zippy Newspaper Like the *Times* Doing in a Town Like St. Petersburg?" asked the title of a national magazine article in 1981. Snobbish observers, in the Northeast and elsewhere, had been asking the question for almost a quarter of a century. When *Times* people replied, they were hard-put if they tried to present their hometown as the Boston of the South, but they could boast their operations were not confined to St. Petersburg.

Since 1945 the *Times* had supported *Congressional Quarterly,* an elegant offspring in Washington that spoke to a national audience. For more than a decade the newspaper had kept it in a style beyond its means until it began earning its keep. Actually *CQ* had a family of its own—a newspaper depth feature service, a thriving book publisher, a newsletter, and a broadcast service. Almost every year CQ spawned some new enterprise.

Critics often asserted that the CQ connection violated Poynter's rule against chain operations. But his Standards of Ownership referred to local newspapers that owed loyalty to their communities, not to national information agencies like CQ. The Washington operation was born two years before Poynter wrote the Standards, so he clearly did not include it in the ban.

Nor did he exclude magazines. Almost as early as his move to St. Petersburg, he showed interest in that field. He bought the title of a defunct labor publication called *The Floridian* and experimented with a projected state news magazine, but it was only after his death that his idea engendered a steadily growing circle of publications. They would include a chain that brought new standards of sophistication to state business magazines.

In the two decades after World War II, Nelson and Henrietta Poynter often disappeared from St. Petersburg for months. Most likely they could be found in Washington, where they had met and fallen in love while working for the government early in the war. They were in their element there, surrounded by stimulating people and events.

They spent most of their working hours on *Congressional Quarterly,* which embodied their concept that journalism needed an impartial provider of data that would go beneath the surface. Despite the name, CQ was a weekly newsletter whose early subscribers were mainly newspapers that paid fees based on circulation. As its main function was to give reporters and editorial writers information on which to build their articles, it remained out of the public eye for decades, but it made many journalists look good.

CQ's proudest boast was its rock-steady accuracy. Its initials were the newspaper copyediting symbol for correct. Although some papers thought the service invaluable, not enough bought it. Nelson and Henrietta covered losses of *Press Research,* its predecessor, and CQ for four years. *Times* directors voted them a $30,000 bonus to make up the losses, although it did not pay for their labor. Then the Poynters deeded CQ to the newspaper for $1, and the *Times* carried the losses until the break-even point was reached.

The Poynters built CQ frugally. Nelson believed in hiring a few seasoned editors to supervise young professionals who would settle for low pay because the work was good training for later jobs. Employees were not expected to analyze the data they gathered, and they seldom went to Capitol Hill. Even so *CQ* became known as a seedbed for journalists. One who became a *Washington Post* editor recalled, "I wore glasses permanently after four years there, but it was a hell of an education."[30]

Although Nelson apparently controlled *CQ* operations, Henrietta was the hot wire of editorial ideas. Often working in Washington even when Nelson was in St. Petersburg, she would swing into town with a burst of energy, talking with congressional insiders about the latest trends. Then she would scatter memos with story tips all over the *CQ* office.

Henrietta rarely worked a regular eight-hour day, but her influence was constant in the office. Her deft phrasing and immense charm were legendary. Although *CQ* staffers saw her role as a leading Washington hostess from a distance, she could be surprisingly solicitous of their needs. She came to the rescue of one woman staffer beleaguered with babysitting problems by sending her housekeeper over to help once a week.

It took a decade for the Poynters to find *CQ* leadership they could rely on. Buel Weare, a Princeton Phi Beta Kappa who had been an executive of the *New York Herald Tribune* for nine years, received a block of shares as a lure to become publisher in 1954. A year later the Poynters found the editor who would guide the publication for thirteen years in Thomas N. Schroth, last managing editor of the defunct *Brooklyn Eagle* and a former reporter for United Press and *Time* magazine.

The new management combination began paying off. In 1957, for the first time, *CQ* turned a profit, about $16,000, or 8 percent of revenues. This occurred soon after purchase of *Editorial Research Reports,* founded in 1923 to produce several long articles on all fields of news, not just Congress. Unlike *CQ* material, which almost always was used for background, *ERR* pieces often ran verbatim in subscribing newspapers, much like syndicated material. At the same time, *CQ* was incorporated as a subsidiary of Times Publishing Company, whose board would annually elect a *CQ* board, invariably made up of *Times* executives and a few top people in the subsidiary.

Weare knew what large newspapers usually paid for material, and he knew that *CQ* was vastly underpriced. He boosted its prices, revenues rose sharply, and few subscribers canceled. Ledgers stayed in the black until 1970. Profits passed the $1 million mark the first time in 1966.

The enterprise was finally getting national attention. The American Heritage Foundation chose *CQ* over more than 15,000 entries in a contest to stimulate public voting. Admirers had nominated *CQ*, as it did not submit an entry.[31]

Time magazine also ran a twelve-inch story extolling *CQ*'s virtues and noting its "gold-plated" subscriber list included more than half the members of Congress, 282 top newspapers, and more than 300 organizations. For up to $1,000 yearly they got "the only authoritative weekly condensation of how every member of Congress voted, what congressional committees are up to, how lobbies are faring—everything, in fact, that has to do with Congress." Feats that were almost impossible without *CQ* were cited. Young war veteran George Smathers won election to the Senate by repeatedly reading his opponent's voting record from its pages. Reporters exposed Senator Joseph McCarthy's lies by using *CQ* figures.[32]

Newsweek covered nearly a page with a 1965 feature about *CQ*, including a picture of Poynter. The occasion was publication of a 2,040-page reference work called *Congress and the Nation*, which was published every four years afterward. *Newsweek* used words like "indispensable," "painstaking," and "tireless" to describe the weekly service. Although *CQ* held to its rigid nonpartisanship, the article ascribed to it a role rarely mentioned before—watchdog.[33] "The federal government will never set up an adequate agency to check on itself, and a foundation is too timid for that," Nelson Poynter was quoted as saying. "So it had to be a private enterprise beholden to its clients."

Clients by then numbered 4,000. It was going to the White House, embassies, the FBI and CIA, and even government offices in communist countries.

When Henrietta Poynter died in January 1968, Nelson's grief drove him to near-seclusion in Washington. Once his energy recovered, he turned to *CQ*. After a year of internal conflict, he fired Schroth at Christmastime. Poynter publicly expressed dissatisfaction with "the degree of progress and the quality of our service." Although Poynter said he was taking full charge himself, he brought along a replacement for Schroth as editor—Richard Billings, thirty-eight, another Princeton graduate who had been an editor at *Life* magazine and was writing editorials for the *St. Petersburg Times*. Poynter pledged that the *CQ* formula would remain the same, "but I think we will become more responsive and move faster."[34]

The immediate outcome of Poynter's thrust was troubling. Schroth took several top editors, even a copyboy, along with him to found a competing report, the *National Journal*. The *Journal* quickly gained ground, and in 1970 *CQ* marked its first annual loss since 1956. After the initial walkouts in sympathy with Schroth, several other valuable staffers left. The product worsened even as Billings tried to rebuild the staff. One *CQ* executive conceded that in the early 1970s the *Journal* was as good or better than *CQ*.[35]

CQ's fortunes began to turn around in 1972 after Poynter replaced Billings with William B. Dickinson, Jr., a forty-one-year-old professional journalist from Kansas City who had worked for United Press International before joining *CQ*'s affiliate, *ERR,* in 1959. He had supervised two major *CQ* books—the second edition of *Congress and the Nation* and its new *Guide to the Congress of the United States.* He also had developed *News Check,* a news digest for high school classes. Dickinson stayed as editor only two years, until the *Washington Post* hired him away to head its new Writers Group syndicate.

When Gene Patterson began work as *Times* president in 1972, Poynter gleefully dropped *CQ* in his lap, so the decision on Dickinson's replacement largely devolved on him. Dickinson recommended Wayne Kelley, who had grown up in Miami, worked on Georgia newspapers, and served as the *Atlanta Journal*'s Washington correspondent before joining the *CQ* staff in 1969. Patterson wanted to seek someone with a nationally known name, but he agreed to try Kelley as managing editor. After a year's probation, Kelley was named *CQ* executive editor and Hoyt Gimlin, another experienced staffer, became *ERR*'s editor. Both men would be key figures in a growing stability for the storm-tossed company.

The business side was healing its wounds also. The *Times*'s long-established profit-sharing plan was duplicated for *CQ* employees in 1972, when profits got big enough to share. A golden touch recalling that of Weare's in the 1950s came with the 1973 appointment of Paul Massa as general manager. Massa, with a background in educational publishing, launched into an aggressive marketing strategy.

Nothing symbolized the upturn more than *CQ*'s new quarters, occupied in 1974. The rented five-story building had a spectacular view overlooking Rock Creek Park, where Poynter had always loved to take walks. A decade later the company bought the building for $4.7 million, beginning of a period of restless expansion and profit margins ranging generally between 10 and 15 percent. The revenue total in 1987, at $15.5 million, was nearly nine times that of 1969.

New products and services spun off older ones at a dizzying rate. Books were one of the fastest growth areas as management began to understand the enormous market for educational materials. Lyndon Johnson's administration had funded school libraries heavily, and the momentum took on a life of its own. The books also were aimed at an audience within arm's reach of anyone involved with government— bureaucrats, politicians, journalists, and business people.

Electronic journalism proved less successful. The first big thrust in this direction was a twenty-two-part public television series, *Congressional Outlook*. It was the fruition of Poynter's dream of using TV for public education that went back to his failed attempt to get a commercial channel in the 1950s. Each program explored one issue coming up in Congress for decision, and the concept was that viewers would form opinions in time to let their representatives know. It aimed at complete impartiality. Funding came from Corporation for Public Broadcasting and the Cities Service petroleum company.

The series started weekly, airing on more than 100 public stations in September 1978. By the next winter a national magazine said it had a "tacky, underfinanced look that CQ's editors were unhappy with" and it was being wound down. Soon it was abandoned. A five-minute daily radio show originating in the CQ offices and broadcast by a Washington public station proved a modest but continuing success.

CQ, like all the components of Poynter's journalistic apparatus, was finally running well after the mid-1970s, with no need for his close watch. Although there is little evidence that he considered himself expendable, his mortality clearly was becoming more of a factor in his planning.

Chapter 10

In Pursuit of Forever

Nelson Poynter once told his lawyer, Hank Baynard, that he refused to bequeath the *Times* to his family because "I've never met my great-grandchildren, and I might not like them."[1] It was a figure of speech, meaning that he refused to turn over the paper to anyone he was not sure was willing and able to carry on his principles.

American journalism in the twentieth century evolved as it did at least partly because of publishers' genes. Earlier newspaper builders like Pulitzer, Ochs, and Scripps gave their character, good or bad, to their creations. They spoke with the authority of ownership—untrammeled, in most cases, by boards of directors. But when they looked beyond the grave, they could see only two ways to keep their creations on a steady path. They sold them to people they trusted, or, with the vanity of fatherhood, they willed them to their children.

The results generally were dismal. Most painful to watch was the failure of heirs. Pulitzer's sons and grandsons were good-spirited men, but they could not keep the empire from slowly crumbling. The nearest approach to success among major papers was that of the *New York Times*. Although Adolph Ochs could not assure that his heirs would be as effective as he had been, the old man built an institution that reproduced itself regardless of his family's genetic roulette.

Poynter boasted he had bought control of the *Times* from his father. But he had no intention of selling it, because he lacked confidence in any likely buyer. His closest friend among big-city publishers, John S.

Knight, once suggested over dinner in Washington that Poynter sell him the paper. Poynter was so furious that he turned cool toward Knight from then on.[2]

Ironically, his reluctance to have the *Times* sold was another reason for not wanting to bequeath it to his family. Inheritance taxes were so high that heirs often had to sell a company just to pay them. In earlier decades the *Times*'s market value was so low that taxes would have been little problem. After World War II, however, newspapers throughout Florida became hot investment properties, and their prices—along with potential inheritance taxes—soared. No one was sure what the *Times* was worth as Poynter grew older. Some said $200 million, and that would have meant a tax bill of about $70 million. Other price estimates ran as high as $400 million. Certainly no Poynter heirs could cope with that level of taxes.

In the 1950s a new alternative emerged: Turn over some or all of a company to a foundation, thereby allowing an owner to perpetuate his ideas. So the Poynter Fund, a foundation named in honor of Nelson's parents, was set up in 1953. It consisted at first of a board of directors (including people from outside the company), a few hundred thousand dollars, and a slim brochure offering college fellowships up to $1,000. Henrietta Poynter left her stock in the company to the fund, raising its assets to more than $5 million by 1969.

Nelson Poynter had a far greater vision for the foundation. He wanted to will it the entire newspaper and associated properties, averting the evils he saw in other disposition methods. Best of all, this would allow him to advance a radical new idea—perpetual control of the company by one person at a time, a logical step from his Standards of Ownership.

Although Poynter used the foundation concept to build his dream of a newspaper that would never be corrupted by greed, existing law opened the door for gross abuses by others. Some owners kept their huge incomes while using their foundations as tax shelters for company profits. Others indulged their taste for political power by diverting tax-exempt revenues to support campaigns and propaganda.

Over the years, favorable laws catapulted foundations into prominence, until activists like Ralph Nader began to lobby for them, angering representatives. Many pushed liberal causes that were not popular on Capitol Hill.

Of the 22,000 foundations in the country, only about twenty

brought objections among members of Congress. But in 1969, after President Nixon's election, the time was politically ripe to strike down the abuses. New rules were passed, notably controls on "self-dealing"—using foundations for their owners' enrichment—and lobbying. Buried in the code was a provision that threatened to shatter Poynter's dream of protecting the future of his newspaper: A private foundation could not own more than 20 percent of a profit-making enterprise.

So it was back to the drawing board for the *Times*'s financial expert, Cliff Camp. He and general manager Jack Lake huddled endlessly with Washington lawyers. As usual, Poynter asked the impossible—how to deliver the paper into one superbly qualified person's hands yet not pass ownership to money grubbers. And, as usual, his helpers set out to meet his demands.

Forging a Key

When Cliff Camp undertook the puzzle, he was grateful in a way for his dilemma. He had never liked the idea of giving the company to the Poynter Fund. Although he knew that it was not a tax dodge, it looked like one. The foundation had little reason for existence other than owning a newspaper. Using one of his favorite words, he insisted that it had no *mission*.[3] He would tell Poynter that, and the owner would launch into a long lecture on how Camp did not understand the concept. Camp knew he did not understand, but he believed that neither did Poynter, so he was happy to discard the Poynter Fund proposal.

Throughout the early 1970s, idea after idea was explored, picked apart, and usually shelved or flatly rejected. Among them were ownership by the pension and profit-sharing fund, by Yale University or some other educational institution, even by a sole proprietor to whom it would be given. One recourse never taken seriously was public commercial ownership, to which many newspapers—the *New York Times,* the *Washington Post,* and the *Miami Herald*—were turning. Poynter was dead set against it. He was terrified that stockholders might try to shape editorial decisions. In fact, he already had a minority owner, his sister, with about 6 percent of the shares. He always feared that she might seek editorial influence, but she did not.

Pension fund ownership looked ideal on the surface. Camp opposed it, and Poynter was doubtful also, but they and other planners talked about it at length.

Some newspaper owners had bequeathed or sold the stock to their employees. Newspapers in Kansas City and Milwaukee had been handled this way. One problem was that employees would have to run the pension fund, and that meant running the paper. Camp argued that the genius of American business was the healthy interplay among owner, managers, and employees. If employees filled the owner role, the balance was lost and a conflict of interest would result.

Besides, Camp maintained, the prospect that the pension fund would have stock in the company as its major resource was dangerous to the employees. Every staff member's future was staked on the financial health of the fund, and the company had always been careful to invest the fund's assets in properties totally divorced from the newspaper. Thus, no matter what happened to the *Times,* the fund was as safe as the American economy.

The idea of passing the paper's control to a single individual got to the heart of Poynter's desire to replicate his authority. But the actual value of the company could not be left in such a person's hands, as that might tempt corruption. If the individual were given control but not the assets, Camp feared, this person might change the arrangement after getting control. The person chosen would not be the kind to do that, Poynter protested. After all, he held that power himself and had not abused it. But attorneys vetoed this proposal because there was no legal way to give away only part of the company. If the control went, the asset went.

Amid the thrusts and parries, Poynter kept edging back to his passion for education. He was a close friend of Montgomery Curtis, director of the American Press Institute (API), which ran refresher seminars for practicing journalists. Poynter liked to talk about his yearning to set up a "junior API" in St. Petersburg.[4] He used the diminutive because he was sour on contributing to what he called "bricks and mortar" projects rather than to the learning that went on inside buildings. Philanthropists usually liked to see their gifts—and often their names—enshrined in soaring edifices. Fund-raisers knew how to cater to this vanity, but Poynter had no taste for it. He was skeptical even of grandiose, expensive training programs. A great believer in seed money, he wanted to spread his money around, nurturing new or unpopular ideas that might sprout and attract funds from other donors.

Poynter had a great fondness for Yale and Indiana, his alma maters, and had committed himself to giving $1 million to each. Yale had its Poynter Fellows program with its own director and a media design studio Poynter underwrote. Indiana, with one of the best journalism schools in the country, had the Poynter Center for the Study of Ethics and American Institutions. But he doubted that Yale or Indiana could achieve his goals, and despite his "junior API" references, Poynter preferred not to imitate the older program. Instead, he wanted to take up where it left off, to do what no other institution in the country was doing. He would introduce relatively untouched subjects like writing styles, newspaper management, design, and ethics.

Fortunately Poynter's Washington lawyers had a creative bent. The more the people from the *Times* talked with them about education, the more they warmed to it. They decided that Poynter could legally found an educational institution himself and give the company to it.

Still, Poynter was not sure that he wanted to burden the paper with the cumbersome bureaucracy and lack of direction that schools usually entail. As the brainstormers explored the concept, though, it began to excite him. He turned to Camp and said, "You know, this is something we can focus on, because we'll be improving the breed—journalism, all media."[5]

Then started the phase, familiar to all Poynter watchers, in which he became euphoric about an idea and demanded that his lieutenants figure out how to implement it. The others caught his enthusiasm. The lawyers did the heavy work of sculpting a plan. Camp would take a proposal from them, add his analysis, and carry it to Poynter, who would usually tear it apart. After a seemingly endless stretch, a solution that everyone could agree on emerged.

The capstone of the plan was a training school to be called Modern Media Institute (MMI). To assure that the government would not view the school as a tax dodge, it would have the necessary educational trappings—a faculty, a student body, and a curriculum. To meet Poynter's demands, it would remain flexible and relatively unburdened. Most instructors and students would be short-termers, and the output would be highly focused training stints, not degree programs.

Most important, the institute would be a separate, not-for-profit corporation at arm's length from the *Times*. It would not provide a training unit for the newspaper but would serve all of American journalism, and it would have its own building and staff. The Poynter Fund would continue as a minor foundation and would deed its scanty stock in the *Times* company to MMI, keeping about a million dollars to produce income for scholarships.

But of all the ideas in the plan, two were destined to become radically new ways to structure a newspaper. These had to do with ownership and control of the company.

Back in place was Poynter's dream of giving away his company—the newspaper, *Congressional Quarterly,* and a commercial printing house. His will bequeathed 74 percent of the stock to MMI, 11 percent to his wife, and 9 percent to his children. (The children later sold their stock to MMI, and Marion Poynter designated hers as a bequest.) His sister held the rest. MMI's share of distributed profits would go for its educational programs. The company could reduce distributions by plowing back the bulk of its profits into improving its position, as it always had under Poynter. Even so, the plan held out the likelihood of making MMI very rich.

The control solution was perhaps even more audacious. It also salvaged Poynter's hopes for one-person control and answered nagging questions.

How would the person be chosen? Poynter would choose his own successor. The successor would do the same, and so on in perpetuity.

How would the asset be divorced from control? MMI would have the asset—company shares—but not control of it. Poynter's successor would have control as holder of the proxy to vote the shares. The new chief would get no financial benefit other than the right to set his or her own salary. MMI would have a board of trustees, but the one who was chief executive officer of the *Times* would have the deciding word, because that person held the proxy.

Would the plan pass muster with the government? Poynter's lawyers obtained informal clearance from the Internal Revenue Service in the form of a determination letter. Of course, the whole structure might collapse if the IRS should decide to attack it after Poynter's death, which seemed well in the future.

Sunset on the Bay

When Nelson and Marion Poynter returned from a Caribbean honeymoon in 1970, he set about in his brisk way to make 900 Park Street her home rather than Henrietta's. "I know it's hard for you," he told Marion. "If you don't like this house, we don't have to stay here. Let's burn it down."[6]

At first the constant furniture moving seemed awkward to Marion. Nelson wavered between aggressive change and reluctance to give up old patterns. Marion knew that she wanted to change the room arrangement. Henrietta and Nelson had maintained separate bedrooms and studies in different wings; Marion consolidated them.

She chose to go slowly in matters such as art. Nelson and Henrietta had collected paintings together over twenty-five years, and he continued after her death. His tastes were a result of coaching by Henrietta, his own impulses, and his penchant for patronizing artists whom he knew and liked, such as Syd Solomon of Sarasota.

The devotion that many friends had for Henrietta was legendary, and Nelson steered Marion toward those he felt would be open and support her. Richard Harkness, a noted former radio journalist, and his wife particularly welcomed her in their Washington home. Marion applied herself to carrying on with the dinner parties at which Henrietta had been adept. Nelson usually initiated and scheduled them, but she learned to take over planning. Her small-town background did little to orient her to high society.

The quiet life, with just the two of them or with Nelson's family, worked better. He was immensely pleased, almost like a new father, the day a new Steinway grand piano arrived. Guests would ask Marion to play after dinner and would sing around the piano. It was mostly light music, with a few classics. Nelson's grandchildren loved to romp and dance as she played, although Marion was not ready to be a complete grandmother. She had the children call her "Grandmari," using part of her name.

Marion had no special talent as a cook, but Nelson's eating habits put no demand on her. He had a delicate digestion and preferred a simple diet. Besides, he thought driving miles for a meal or spending more than five minutes in the kitchen was a waste of time. Their cook prepared most of the food, and Marion was equally happy with

Nelson Poynter, shown
here in 1974 four years
before his death,
gradually turned over
control of the paper to
Eugene Patterson. *St.
Petersburg Times.*

macaroni and cheese at home or frog legs at La Grenouille. Nelson left
the choice of wines to Marion, but he was particularly fond of martinis. He had a low tolerance for alcohol, and Marion resented the gusto
of some hosts in pushing drinks on him.

It seemed to Marion that Nelson had unconsciously sought a third
wife who would be a replacement for Henrietta. He began preparing
her to take over some of her predecessor's duties at *Congressional
Quarterly* and wanted her to help continue the *Times* column he and
Henrietta had coauthored. But he soon realized that her background
did not fit her for such a life. Besides, Marion disdained imitation.

Marion consented to take some role at the *Times.* A management
job was not appropriate. Nelson offered to break his severe antinepo-
tism rule to make a place for her as a writer, but she preferred to avoid
a special dispensation. Marion devised the title "contributing editor,"
which meant that she was available for special tasks if needed. One, a
pet project of Nelson's, was a plan to encourage children's reading by
linking quality television programs with newspapers in the classroom.

Nelson seemed proud of Marion's education and intelligence, and
when they went to Vassar for a class reunion he beamed at the respect
that her classmates showed her. He discussed business problems with
her at length.

Although her husband's old-fashioned courtliness charmed Marion, his toleration of some forms of sexism angered her. She resented the exclusion of women from the National Press Club, a favorite Washington haunt of Nelson's, and particularly from its annual Gridiron Dinner, when political celebrities were skewered in song and dance. When she rebuked him, he would counter that having women there would "gum things up." What he meant, she knew, was that he liked to swing around the room having quick chats with the members, and if women were along his courtesy would constrain him to move slowly.

Mostly Marion was content to contribute to her husband's happiness. She liked to think of his three wives as filling complementary roles in his life. To her, Catherine was the bride of his youth, Henrietta was the partner, and she was the fun one.

Nelson seemed almost boyish in his outlook and appearance, at least until the summer of 1976. The only serious worry Marion had about his health was his apnea, which caused him to stop breathing for startling periods in his sleep. His life had always followed a quadrennial rhythm because of his lust for presidential elections. He was attending the 1976 Democratic convention in New York City when he fell in a hotel bathtub and cracked a vertebra. It was very painful and marked the point when his liveliness began to fade. An earlier family doctor had always told Nelson he had a sound heart, so it came as a shock to him when in 1977 he had an atrial fibrillation. By then under the care of Dr. Charles Donegan, he took blood thinner.

Poynter's appearance worsened slowly but steadily. Those who had not seen him in some time were shocked. When Virginia Frankel, a cousin of Henrietta's who had been like a sister, saw him on a 1978 visit to New York, his physical decline startled her.

On June 11, 1978, the University of South Florida in Tampa gave Poynter an honorary doctorate in recognition of how he had inspired his staff members toward excellence. He smiled broadly as the USF president draped a hood on him, but he looked tired.

Four days later he died.

The vicious gossip that had plagued Poynter all his career in St. Petersburg rose to haunt his memory. Donegan got permission from Marion to have an autopsy done, and the hospital pathologist performed it the morning after the death. It showed a massive cerebral hemorrhage. There was arteriosclerosis but relatively little heart disease. Later that morning, Donegan received a phone call from the coroner, who told him the body could not be cremated for forty-eight hours. The coroner explained that he had been phoned by authorities in Tallahassee and was told that someone purporting to be from a newspaper had come into a state office that morning and had said Poynter died under very mysterious circumstances. When the coroner found there had been an autopsy, he dropped the matter. As time passed, Donegan mused about what stories would have circulated if he had not been cautious.[7]

Nelson's longest-lasting bond—with his mother—remained in place when he died. But less than five months later, two days before her ninety-ninth birthday, she quietly died at the Brightwaters home.

Life after Death

Bob Haiman stood in his office and looked eastward over Tampa Bay. As an executive lair, the office was elegant but modest. Rising a few feet above adjacent rooms, it glowed with lustrous woods and tasteful abstract art. It covered only 198 square feet, smaller by a third than the nearby men's room.

But the view outside was the thing. Haiman could watch white yachts bobbing in Bayboro Harbor and sun sparkling the waves. Framing the picture to the left were the tranquil beige lines of a university branch campus, with its Nelson Poynter Memorial Library in the foreground. Stretching across the scene were the three acres of Nelson Poynter Park, a green swath that anchored the city's seven-mile chain of waterfront parks, one of them named for Poynter's great predecessor, Bill Straub. Facing the park on the right was the Salvador Dali Museum, a graceful modern structure housing the world's largest nongovernmental collection of the eccentric painter's work. Its existence owed much to *Times* support. Beyond all this was the horizon, where sky met bay. The scene tugged at the imagination. Gazing out there where gulls wheeled and skimmed, one could find an idea.

Turning his back to the waterfront, Haiman could peer down into the quiet spaces of the building's Great Hall, filled with meditative light and defined by expanses of glass and a grove of mahogany-faced pillars, panels, and stairs. Carpets muffled footfalls, and marble cooled the senses. A benign pool reached across the entire facade.

The Poynter Institute's building was less than two years old, and already it already sheltered thirty-four seminars. The increase in activity was smooth as the revving of a Rolls-Royce engine. Each seminar

The Poynter Institute for Media Studies occupied its new building facing Tampa Bay in 1985. *Poynter Institute.*

had only fifteen students and five teachers. Gathered around a conference table or chatting in pairs in placid nooks, the scholars did little to break the monastic calm.

The institute had good reason to present a serene countenance. It probably was the only educational institution in the country without money problems. Though it was not a large one, Haiman could count on enough income to do whatever he had in mind and tuck away a million a year in endowment. Heading an operation with money-earning assets worth perhaps $500 million, according to a broker's estimate, he could be sanguine about the future. Past growth also was a comforting indicator. The institute's budget was almost ten times its first one a decade before, and its floor space was seven times the earliest quarters.

Unlike college presidents, Haiman had no ongoing commitments like degree plans and long-term student bodies. Each year he could increase, decrease, or change the institute's teaching program without apology. His everyday responsibility was to oversee a full-time staff of seventeen and maintain the building. But always before him was the challenge of cultivating the institute's reputation as the world's most forward-looking training center for journalism.

The institute had its origins at a time of stress in the Poynter enterprises, with change of leadership and a national financial crisis. It also revived Don Baldwin's journalistic career after his painful departure from the *Times* presidency. Leaving was no easy matter for Baldwin, even in practical matters. It took him several months to disengage himself from official positions with Poynter's several companies.[8] Payouts had to be arranged to repurchase stock Baldwin owned. Throughout the paper's life, various top executives had owned small blocks of shares, usually paid for through dividends. But as Poynter set about planning his estate he started buying it back, and Baldwin was the last such stockholder.

Baldwin stayed on into the spring of 1972 when Gene Patterson was commuting from Duke to take over the editorship. Then Baldwin accepted a teaching and consulting job with the University of South Florida in Tampa. Baldwin remained on good terms with Poynter and had dinner in his home about twice a year. They talked about plans for an enterprise that would achieve the owner's long-standing goals of avoiding inheritance taxes and begetting a totally unique training center.

Modern Media Institute's name implied that its mission was to serve all mass media, although Poynter still thought of it as an effort largely benefiting newspapers. He hosted a meeting of journalism deans from over the country to suggest plans. They had to work within parameters that Poynter set. Major expenditures had to be on people, not buildings, and undertakings must not duplicate those of any other institution. "Don't waste my time or yours re-inventing wheels that are running nicely elsewhere," he would say.

One Sunday evening in 1975 the Baldwins were having dinner with Nelson and Marion at the Poynter home. Nelson had mixed his fabled martinis, and the talk got around to the institute. "Why don't you come over and run it?" he asked Baldwin.

Baldwin liked the idea. He was getting bored with the USF journalism department, and the idea of starting something new intrigued him. He was in excellent health at age fifty-eight, and the idea of coming back to Poynter operations at a lower level did not disturb him. He and Gene Patterson were good friends.

Within two days Baldwin accepted the offer. He moved into an office on the seventh floor of the *Times,* took on a temporary secretary, and dug out files on the years of planning. Despite the early appearance of being under the newspaper's wing, Baldwin had to build a not-for-profit corporation from scratch. This meant complete arm's-length dealings with the *Times*—separate pension systems, office supplies, telephones. The operation had to meet federal law to be eligible to inherit Poynter's holdings in the newspaper.

Absurd problems arose because of the strict separation. MMI had no established credit to buy basic goods and services, and Baldwin could not point out the obvious—Poynter's money was available for any debt. For a while suppliers treated the institute like a fly-by-night interloper. On one occasion, a locksmith demanded cash on the spot for repairing the door.

By December, MMI had moved into its own quarters. For $1,000 a month it rented a former bank building on Central Avenue two blocks from the *Times*. Although the structure measured only 4,500 square feet, it had an imposing art deco facade with the solid look of a huge office safe.

It was not ideal. The air conditioning did not work well, offices spilled into each other, and patrons of an inelegant bar next door wandered in off the street. A bank vault gaped open between the coffee bar and the restroom, inspiring jokes. There was space for only one conference, and when two were held the students had to use chairs in alternate hours.

More important was the challenge to set up an educational program. Besides meeting Poynter's criteria, Baldwin had to comply with the government's demand that the institute have a curriculum, a student body, and a faculty.

Baldwin traveled about the country visiting other training centers, particularly the American Press Institute and newspapers' in-house training institutes. Poynter's rule against duplication made it difficult to borrow curriculum ideas from other places. MMI's planners paid close attention to Northwestern University's widely discussed urban journalism program, which gave students much field experience, but they concluded that it was so good that MMI should do something else. Several journalism schools, including the universities of Indiana, Kansas, Nebraska and Florida, were studied. The idea that schools should teach newspaper management—that they should prepare students not just to be editorial workers but also leaders—was emerging around the country. Baldwin decided that no school had exploited the area enough to bar it as a subject for MMI.

So the institute found its first mission—and also a guinea pig. In fall of 1975, MMI offered a six-week management program for young people from the Tampa Bay area, particularly university students and *Times* staffers. Local professors of fields such as marketing and accounting were brought in for brief stints. Enrollees took time off from other obligations to spend a few hours a week at the institute. They paid no tuition. The experiment taught the planners much, including how easy it would be to become a training arm of the *Times,* which would violate the arm's-length requirement.

Hard truths about finances also were learned. Poynter had insisted that training programs ought to be so good that anyone would pay fees. MMI leaders found that most high school and college students had no funds to pay tuition or even room and board. In fact, many needed summertime jobs to earn money for regular school expenses. So Poynter came around to providing fellowships for students, although mass media that sent employees were expected to pay the full tab.

The first effort also gave the institute confidence to try other things. Baldwin started bringing in school newspaper staffs for training exercises in production. Summer programs were offered, particularly in photography. Early years saw another experiment that flourished later—making films and videotapes about professional matters. To show differences among news media, the institute portrayed how a newspaper and a TV station varied in covering a Ku Klux Klan rally.

A bold step forward was taken in 1976 with the institute's first newspaper-management program for graduate students. Full expenses and tuition were offered to all fifteen persons admitted. They studied full-time for about three months, and many got academic credit from their universities. This action marked a breakthrough in getting the quality of students the institute wanted. Announcements were sent around the country, and competition for admission was stiff. Applicants had to have top grades, proven interest in management, and some professional experience.

Teachers were carefully chosen. They came from as far as Chicago and Boston and stayed a week or two for lectures and informal contacts with students. Ideas such as case studies were drawn from the best MBA centers.

Students sensed the program's quality and an opportunity for career success. They developed camaraderie and usually lived and ate together at places on the beach. Having the *Times* close at hand provided a chance for students to see firsthand one of the nation's most professionally managed papers. Executives came to classes and told about their own experiences. Students shadowed them in the *Times* building, sitting in on conferences and asking questions.

More than before, MMI had to keep a strict guard against being tied too closely to the paper. Students could do almost anything at the *Times* office except provide services. The newspaper had to pay normal fees to enroll its employees in classes. Any institute student not already on the *Times* staff had to wait three years to be considered for a job there.

The institute existed largely on donations from the *Times* and its Poynter Fund. It got all the money it asked for, but the allotment was relatively small because it was groping to find its mission. The budget ranged from $210,399 to $288,826 during the first four years.

With Poynter's death and the settlement of his estate, the roles were reversed. In a legal sense, the newspaper became a dependency of the institute because it was an owned property. Executives of the *Times* continued to make up most of the institute's board of trustees. As Baldwin expanded the MMI programs, ample funds were available. In 1980 the budget level surged by 35 percent.

A crucial decision set MMI on a trajectory of its own, independent of the newspaper. Cliff Camp devised a plan to invest about $1 million a year as an endowment so that within a decade or two the fund's income would make the institute permanent regardless of what happened to *Times* properties.

The new money launched a program to improve writing skills of young journalists. This became a hallmark of the institute over the years after 1979, when Baldwin hired a young Ph.D. named Roy Peter Clark. He had grown up on Long Island and graduated in English from Providence, a Catholic college. Graduate work in medieval literature led to a teaching job at Auburn University's Montgomery campus. While there he became fascinated with the challenge of explaining the South to northerners like himself. His writing skills developed so well he sold pieces to the *New York Times* and other major papers on such subjects as Civil War monuments and southern dialects and religions.

Clark also became a successful teacher of writing. He was sensitive to faults that afflicted most newspaper writing—gracelessness, dullness, lack of clarity. Gaining the attention of Edwin Newman, then the nation's leading critic of bad writing, he was invited to appear on NBC's "Today Show."

Then Clark heard a strong voice for reform coming out of the

American Society of Newspaper Editors. At the ASNE's meeting in Hawaii, the main subject was the economic woes of the press in the wake of the world oil crisis. Several editors maintained that newspapers could make more money if they stressed good reportage and writing. The group's president, Eugene Patterson, took up the cause. He led in getting the ASNE to set up a system of annual awards, and he advanced the idea that each newspaper should have its own training program.

Patterson decided to start a project at the *Times* that could serve as a model. He had heard of Clark's work and invited him down to talk about heading it. Even though Clark, by his own later admission, acted like a "smartass young English teacher," he impressed the paper's executives enough to be hired.[9]

The newsroom potentially represented a den of lions for Clark. Some reporters resented having to listen to a man who had never worked a news beat. Even the sophisticated Andy Barnes, by then managing editor, disagreed with Clark about some of the writers that he held out as paragons of style, such as Jimmy Breslin. Barnes preferred conventional practices like attributing most facts to sources and including all data, even if it was untidy and got in the way of telling a good yarn. As time went on, the gap between the two men's ideas narrowed.

Clark worked hard at winning over *Times* people. They had expected a tweedy professorial type. Clark, a slight, balding man, identified with younger staffers through his age (twenty-nine), enthusiasm, and quick wit. For four months Clark studied the newsroom and its output. He pored over each reporter's clippings, asked them questions, and edged into low-key advice. He used praise as much as criticism and discovered that reporters were hungry for recognition of their good work. Weekly newsletters were issued and luncheon meetings were held to talk about writing.

The best writers tended to be the most receptive. Howell Raines, a star reporter, took Clark along on assignments, and popular columnist Dick Bothwell welcomed his curiosity, saying, "You're the first person who's ever asked questions about my writing." Clark's initial public commentary on a *Times* writer's work was put on a bulletin board. It took apart a column by Gene Patterson, who set the pattern for others by posting a self-denigrating response.

At the end of the year-long experiment, Clark reported to the next

ASNE convention, setting off an explosion of favorable comment. He found himself being embraced by a proud Nelson Poynter, who, never a good writer himself, had been skeptical but supported Patterson's efforts. Clark had taken a year's leave from Auburn, but he asked the *Times* to keep him on as a staff writer. The editors agreed and did not cut his salary. He worked primarily as a film critic.

Poynter's death only two months later and the increase in funds for MMI gave Clark an idea. He proposed a joint appointment for himself to the institute staff. He wanted to conduct national seminars on writing while continuing to write for the *Times,* but this idea was vetoed because it violated the separation between the institute and the newspaper. Clark was offered a one-third salary increase to join the MMI staff completely. He was reluctant to leave writing, but his bosses persuaded him with the prospect that MMI could become a national center for writing education.

A few months after he joined the institute in February 1980, Clark found that the prediction might come true. Because of interest caused by the ASNE report, MMI was swamped with applications for its first writing seminar. Within three months the institute had sponsored two more such seminars. Clark described his work as that of a coach, a word that he had been hesitant to use at first. The idea that each paper should use a writing coach quickly spread around the country.

Clark's work led MMI into book publishing. He started by editing the winning entries in ASNE's annual writing competition. He interviewed each writer, explained how the story was put together, and analyzed the result as an introduction to the work itself. MMI published each year's winners under the title *Best Newspaper Writing* and marketed the book nationally. It also published speeches made at its conferences.

Now that the institute had management and writing as fields for study—it called them centers—the search went on for more. The next center, ethics, emerged in 1981. Ethics always had been a touchy subject because most editors resented anyone's telling them what was professionally right or wrong, so journalism schools had dealt gently with the matter. Besides, professors had only a small body of knowledge to teach, as newspaper leaders rarely provided information.

Watergate changed this, and newspaper executives became accustomed to spilling their self-doubts at conventions. These panel discussions lacked continuity, and MMI decided to fill the void. It held a seminar for newspaper publishers on the topic "Power and Morality." Those attending devoted a weekend to comparing great works of philosophy, religion, politics, and literature with their own outlooks. The ethics center moved toward controversies of the day, first examining whether the press had become too adversarial with the government. Editors met philosophers and media critics for a conference in 1982, and the findings came out in a book called *The Adversary Press.* A similar group gathered a month later to debate the question of whether the Washington press was telling readers what they needed to know. One of the seminar's leaders was Harold Evans, former editor of the *Times* of London and an internationally respected journalist who had moved to the United States.

Also in 1981, the fourth center, graphics and design, was born. Like ethics, this subject had been poorly served by schools. Breakthroughs in bright, modern design had been pioneered by a few small and medium-sized dailies like the *Times,* but little organized teaching material existed. The institute sponsored two highly successful seminars for newspaper design people, led by Mario Garcia, who taught at the University of South Florida. They proved highly successful. Garcia joined the institute staff and visited more than seventy newspapers around the world as a consultant. He also wrote a standard textbook.

By 1983, MMI had built the four pillars on which its educational canopy would rest—the centers for management, writing, design and graphics, and ethics. Students and visiting teachers were interacting smoothly, a permanent faculty had begun forming, and word was spreading about the programs.

Everything was poised for a wave of expansion. Bob Haiman was at the peak of his professional career as executive editor of the *Times.* He could get things done, he thought big and had boundless enthusiasm, and although he was still only forty-seven his concept of Poynter's philosophy went back nearly a quarter of a century. So Patterson made him president of MMI.

Baldwin again stepped aside to make room for a younger man, although there was none of the tension that marked his 1972 departure from the *Times.* Haiman welcomed the chance to keep Baldwin on the staff. As a consultant, he eased the transition by advising Haiman, and much of his time in succeeding years was devoted to heading special projects.

With the luxury of having had the basic structure built by Baldwin,

Haiman could take the long view. He drew up a five-year plan, pledging himself to erect a new building, double the faculty, expand the curriculum, go beyond training for print media (particularly into television), expand services to other countries, and raise the institute's image nationally. All this would take more money, and the *Times*'s mounting profits filled the need. In Haiman's first year the operating budget soared 74 percent, topping $2 million by 1986. All the goals depended heavily on the new building. Baldwin had bought a half-acre lot at the north edge of the St. Petersburg's waterfront branch campus of the University of South Florida. Architects had drawn plans for a modest training center.

Haiman spent hours on the lot musing on how it could be used. Finally he decided that it was inadequate for the building needed, much less for later expansion. Besides, he thought, the institute ought to overlook the harbor, not be separated from it by the campus. The institute board agreed. The perfect location was found, lying eight blocks from the *Times* and fronting on a major street, but sprawling across its 1.8 acres were an auto body shop, a machine shop, and abandoned houses frequented by vagrants. Nearly a year went by while a realtor put together the purchase. The previous site went to the university, sold at its purchase price, well below market value.

To Haiman, the building project became a search for a grail. It not only had to serve the institute's needs, but it had to be an architectural jewel. Most important, Haiman demanded an artistic symbol of MMI's ideals and values. Probably no journalist had ever dreamed so lavishly about a building since William Randolph Hearst planned his castle at San Simeon. Haiman drew up a seven-page, single-spaced prescription for a building adequate for a "100-year institution." It must "signal solidity, permanence and enduring strength," he declared, and "should say quality, dignity, elegance, class" but not sacrifice "warmth, beauty or grace." Closer to the point, he demanded that the building inspire learning—not only in seminar rooms, classrooms, and laboratories but in nooks where scholars might have "serendipitous encounters" and ignite new ideas.

Aside from meeting internal needs, Haiman wrote, the building should harmonize with nearby university buildings and "acknowledge and embrace" the park and harbor across the street. He became lyrical about how the structure must adapt to the Florida sun, providing "an oasis of shade and coolness" that did not look like "a concrete bunker which shuts out the natural environment." And, more pragmatically, he noted that the building must "protect itself" from its neighborhood on three sides.

The resulting design evoked ideas from Spain, China, and Frank Lloyd Wright, with a touch of Pompeii. Airy views were everywhere. To the front, a wall of glass peered out across a reflecting pool, a patio with a trellised colonnade, then to the park and boat basin beyond. On the other three sides were leaf-perfect gardens embraced by the building, the patio in back serving as an outdoor classroom. The red-tiled roof lapped out into wide overhangs. The building left room on the lot for more than forty varieties of plants. Six towering phoenix palms stood guard across the front. Tucked away in the entrance court was a forty-foot laurel oak moved at a cost of $10,000 from the lot that the institute previously owned.

The Great Hall doubled as an entrance lounge and a banquet pavilion. Fifty-five feet above marble floors was a 2,500-square-foot skylight over a web of wooden beams. Classrooms, offices, and a library overlooked the hall. Mahogany veneers covered walls and pillars. Woodworking went on for nine months, and four men toiled for a month on a railing and staircase. A local supplier went to Italy to choose red, tan, and white marble. Some walls were faced in polished, fossilized limestone from the Florida Keys. Hidden behind the glossy surfaces were miles of conduits for any future computer, audiovisual, and power needs. An amphitheater included three types of projection equipment and could record and transmit live television signals. Any event in one classroom could be televised in another.

When staff members moved into the building in October 1985, the institute bore a new name. Even before the ground breaking the year before, trustees had decided that it was time to do something they could never have done while Nelson Poynter was alive—name it after him. He had always resisted attempts to set his name in stone over programs he had funded at Indiana, Yale, and St. Petersburg.

But it was time to end the ambiguities of the name Modern Media Institute. Marion Poynter, speaker at the ground breaking, said, "What makes me certain that Nelson will not come back to haunt us . . . is that we have recognized that the private dreams of his lifetime must ultimately take a public shape if they are to become visible." So the sign over the door read "The Poynter Institute for Media Studies."

The new building's 31,000 square feet averaged out as space for two large suburban houses for each faculty member. With furnishings it had cost $6 million, nearly $200 a square foot. Haiman clearly had room not only to house his burgeoning programs but also to expand the institute's role.

The Last Act

In 1988, ten years after Nelson's death and a year after Eleanor's, the Poynter drama still had not played itself out. Conflicts had recurred across sixty-two years, since that rancorous family dinner in 1926. Then, what seemed the final scenes began to unfold with bitter fatefulness.

After Nelson withdrew his lawsuit to repurchase Eleanor's 200 shares of *Times* voting stock (out of 500 total) in the 1950s, surface peace returned to the family. Nels and Bugsie, as the siblings called each other, entertained each other socially, exchanged gifts, jointly cared for their mother, and talked about politics and family news. Nelson helped his sister gain admission to the exclusive St. Petersburg Yacht Club. Eleanor addressed a thank-you for a Thanksgiving dinner to Nelson and Marion as "Sweet Things."[10] Another such holiday feast brought a note that Eleanor's husband had deemed it "the most perfect Christmas ever."[11]

Every year Nelson asked Eleanor to sell him her stock.[12] Once the company's board set aside a fund for that purpose, and Nelson always insisted that board meetings not start before the appointed hour in case Eleanor should attend. In 1972 Nelson made an elaborate proposal to give her $2,000 a week if she would arrange for her shares to be returned to the company for $3 million after her death, thereby avoiding inheritance taxes.[13] But Eleanor's two daughters, Mary Alice and Anne, were starting families of their own by then. Eleanor felt that, contrary to her father's wish, her offspring would benefit far less than Nelson's, and she saw his repurchase attempts as intended to take advantage of her.[14] Nevertheless, she shrank from turning the quarrel into a public brawl.[15]

A few months later Nelson wrote a memo noting that he had heard that Eleanor was shopping her stock in New York, seeking $8–$11 million: "The price would be determined by the buyer successfully bringing a suit, and upsetting the present distribution of dividends. Presumably the only way such suit could be successful would be to force the Times Publishing Company to call its present participating preferred stock."[16] Eerily, that was what exactly what happened later.

When Nelson died in 1978, he owned 300 voting shares and 3,000 preferred shares in the enterprise, having recalled Eleanor's 1,500 preferred shares in the 1950s. That left her with only the 200 voting shares, which received 5.7 percent of dividends.

After Gene Patterson succeeded Nelson in control, he inherited the task of buying Eleanor's 200 voting shares. The two sides differ on how resolute he was. Patterson said he persisted for ten years, but Eleanor would not negotiate. Her lawyer said Patterson's only offer occurred in 1979. Its terms resembled those of Nelson's 1972 offer except that the value was raised to $5.4 million, and Eleanor declined.[17]

Patterson and Eleanor continued to have occasional friendly chats, without result. Nelson had maintained a no-nepotism policy in staffing, although two of his wives had worked for the paper. Patterson sensed resentment from Eleanor because he applied the policy to members of her family. She accused him of letting "the dead hand" run the paper—something that Nelson had always told Patterson he was not to do after taking over.[18]

Quite to the contrary, Patterson was making major changes in the company's structure. In 1986 he folded the money-losing *Evening Independent,* and the next year he launched a massive and expensive attempt to become the dominant newspaper of the Tampa Bay area by trying to beat the *Tampa Tribune* in its home county. (The effort still had not succeeded six years later.)

Upon Eleanor's death in August 1987, her stock went to her daughters, along with the burden of paying an estate tax. Unlike their mother, they had to raise money, so the following December they hired Henry Ansbacher Inc., a New York media broker known for handling cases similar to that in St. Petersburg. The firm had represented Sallie Bingham in a much-publicized family dispute that led to the sale of the historic *Courier Journal* company in Louisville. Ansbacher's president, Hylton Philipson, first tried to make a deal with the *Times.* He set up a meeting in Patterson's office and offered to sell for $120 million. Patterson refused and left the meeting, putting it in the hands of his attorney. The daughters interpreted this as a signal that "he could not have cared less."[19]

Philipson negotiated with some Tampa business people, but they decided the profits were too low. Major newspaper chains in Washington, Miami, Los Angeles, and Chicago also shrank from the deal because of uncertain profits. Besides, a clubbish fraternalism that prevailed among newspaper owners inhibited hostile takeovers.

Patterson apparently expected Philipson to come back, chastened by the rebuffs, with a lower price. Philipson, seeing Patterson's action as a "refusal to go down either of the straightforward roads," felt he had no option other than turning to "nontraditional" investors.[20] Even at that point, he offered the *Times* managers another chance, telling them: "Look, you guys probably thought I was bluffing you when I told you I thought I could get a reasonable valuation for the stock. For heaven's sake, believe me that I have a deal lined up now." Patterson read it as just another threat, and Philipson said he got no reply.[21]

Just how nontraditional Philipson was prepared to be soon became apparent. Although television and magazines had become fair game for free-lance corporate buccaneers, newspapers up for sale nearly always attracted only people specializing in that field. Philipson found a buyer for the *Times* stock with one foot in the Texas oil fields and another in cutthroat finance.

He was Robert Muse Bass, third of four brothers who inherited the fortune of legendary wildcatter Sid Richardson and ballooned it to $6 billion. Shy, blond, and wispy, he embodied his New England schooldays more than his two-fisted ancestry. He went to a Massachusetts prep school, graduated from Yale, and earned an MBA from Stanford. At age forty he still was described as boyish, but he labeled himself as "an economic animal." Splitting off from his brothers, he had amassed a $2 billion war chest mostly by corporate takeovers and breakups. Normally he operated through partners.

Bass paid Eleanor Jamison's daughters $28 million for their stock and took them into a partnership that assured them 40 percent of any gains in the *Times* venture. Patterson later said that if the brokers had let him bid against the Bass offer he would have readily topped it.[22]

The Bass deal was signed in August 1988, but not until the last week of October did Andy Barnes receive a call from the Texas: "I'm Robert Bass. I've purchased the minority stock from the Jamison daughters and I wanted you to hear it from me first."

Barnes was caught in several binds. Besides the obvious threat to the company's stability, there was a sentimental problem. The newspaper was dedicating its new building and holding parties marking Patterson's retirement at the month's end. Barnes told Patterson about the call, and they agreed to keep it quiet until Barnes had taken over on November 1. They still had not revealed the news when the rival *Tampa Tribune* broke the story on November 3. Many *Times* staffers were stunned, not only at the news but at the fact that the management had allowed them to be beaten on it.

Barnes was quoted as saying that he was not concerned about the purchase and that it would not affect operation of the paper.[23] A spokesman for Bass also denied any plans for a challenge, praised the management, and said that Bass planned to be "a long-term shareholder." Bass did ask Barnes to withhold dividend payments from the Poynter Institute until they could meet, but the money had already been paid.

Bass arrived by private jet for a three-hour meeting in January. He and his aide had lunch in the staff cafeteria, exchanged pleasantries, and asked questions. Then, deflecting questions by *Times* reporters, they left.

Bass made his first move early in February. He demanded that the company call (buy out) the 3,000 shares of preferred stock under their original terms—$106 each, for a total of $318,000. This expense would be nothing to the company, but it would mean that the Bass stock would be converted instantly from a 5.7 percent share to 40 percent. With the preferred shares eliminated, only the 500 common (voting) shares would remain.

The year before, the company had paid about $3 million in dividends, with $2.6 million going to the institute and the rest to Marion Poynter. Under Bass's formula, he would have gotten $1.2 million and the institute $1.8 million. As expected, Barnes refused. He said it would not be in the interest of the majority stockholder, the institute.

After nearly a year of quiet, the Bass forces brought up their big guns. On January 30, 1990, they offered $270 million for all the stock they did not own. They even argued that management would be acting against the institute's best interests if it turned down the offer, because the institute could invest its $234 million share and earn far more than the $2.6 million it was getting from the newspaper.

A word that had almost never been heard at the *Times* offices— fiduciary—suddenly became painfully familiar. It refers to holding something in trust for others. In this case, it was the legal responsibility of a company's managers to protect the interest of all stockholders, majority and minority, and Bass argued that management had not done so. With the assurance of power and sanctity of a noble cause, the managers had been able to brush off the Jamisons' claim that refusing to recall the preferred stock damaged them.

It was no secret among lawyers that Bass could support his argument with legal precedents. The *Tampa Tribune*, which was reporting the events with embarrassing intensity, quoted such lawyers as saying Barnes and his staff were "no business match" for the Bass group. "They may know newspapers but they don't know anything about business," according to one *Tribune* source.[24] Of course, *Times* managers had built one of the nation's fabled money-makers, but they did it outside the precincts of high finance.

Predictably, Barnes rejected the offer, saying, "I see no reason to dismantle Nelson Poynter's legacy . . . merely to enrich private investor interests."[25] The institute's board concurred two weeks later, approving unanimously a motion by Marion Poynter, who could have walked away from the sale with $36 million. By then largely removed from the decision-making process, she explained her action in terms of her memory of Poynter and her reliance on the managers: "Nelson spent the better part of a lifetime assembling defenses against such assaults as these. . . . Fortunately, there are enough people still who are able to read between the top and bottom lines."[26] But even before the board could add its blessing to Barnes's decision, Bass made it clear he had not expected the buyout offer to be accepted. Only a week after making it, he filed suit in Tampa federal court, seeking to force the recall of the institute's preferred stock.

The most novel thing about the suit was the motives that it ascribed to the people who had run the *Times*. It claimed that Patterson's buyout offer to the daughters was less than the company's officers had "granted themselves" in profit sharing and incentives that year. It also said the institute "purports to be a tax-exempt institution" dedicated to training journalists but that Poynter had created it for the "primary purpose of perpetuating absolute control of [Times] Publishing by its management, free of any oversight."[27]

If Barnes miscalculated the law and the financial power that faced him, Bass seemed oblivious of how the newspaper's own staff, the legal profession, and the political establishment would react. At any rate, he had faced a massive wave of condemnation. Barnes, who had avoided publicity almost as much as Bass, began firing off salvoes couched in terms of bumper stickers and obviously intended to be published. He told the newspaper's staff, "Our challenger sees things only in terms of dollars, and I find that if I'm speaking to be understood by the readers and viewers of America, I need to put that into quotable, pithy terms. You call it 'the bashful billionaire corporate raider,' and it gets into print. And you call him a 'vandal,' and it gets into print. And I think that's the appropriate thing for me to be doing in the role I play now. But I guess I'm just enough embarrassed to be using those impolite elocutions to feel a little sensitive."[28]

This avowal of Bass-bashing, as the *Miami Herald* called it, marked open season on hostile words and grand gestures. Loyalist reporters organized a group called STOP—Save the *Times* from Outside Profiteers. They wore buttons showing a large-mouth bass with a red slash, and they raised a collection from 1,371 staffers to pay for a full-page ad in the *Times* and a smaller one in the Dallas–Fort Worth edition of the *Wall Street Journal*. The ads were headed "Times Staff to Bass: Go Fish" and warned him, "Don't expect our support, Mr. Bass. Expect a fight."[29]

Barnes compared the Bass initiative to someone's "being permitted to throw paint at a beautiful painting." He also sounded a combative note: "We are not going to lose the fight. We will be extremely aggressive, and the cost to them will be very high. We would do everything we have to do, legally. . . . Once the other side called it a fight, we wanted to show ourselves as the good guys and them as the bad guys."[30] He predicted that the legal battle could go on for five to ten years.

Leading main-line liberal lawyers also rallied to the cause. Florida Attorney General Bob Butterworth identified himself with it. Talbot (Sandy) D'Alemberte, a member of a noted Miami law firm and soon to become president of the American Bar Association, signed on as special counsel for the Poynter Institute. At his request, Butterworth persuaded Griffin Bell, former U.S. attorney general, to become his special assistant in the case, along with DuBose Ausley, an old pro in Tallahassee. These moves appeared to indicate courtroom fireworks, but a legal publication noted prophetically that Bell had a reputation for "not carrying litigation to a rancorous, bitter end," describing him as "a facilitator."[31]

Even before the lawsuit, the newspaper, with Butterworth's help, had steered through the Florida legislature a bill to make it easier for closely held corporations such as the *Times* to resist hostile takeovers.

The measure permitted company directors to consider factors such as charitable contributions, employees, and customers in deciding on an offer. The *Times* hired two lobbyists to shepherd the bill, explaining that it was "trying to hire advocacy when under attack." They went to work the same day the paper ran an editorial criticizing certain types of lobbying.[32]

Opinion writers across the country raised a chorus of censure against the Bass move. Eleanor Randolph, a former *Times* staffer who became a syndicated *Washington Post* columnist, compared it to a shark's attack on a bleeding swimmer, who in this case emitted the smell of big profits. She called the *Times* "something of a news shrine."[33] John Morton, a columnist for the *Washington Journalism Review,* asked rhetorically, "Can a newspaper owner's dream to bequeath his assets for a laudable public purpose be thwarted by an outsider's pursuit of cash?"[34]

The *Times* management also did not hesitate to use its own columns to protect its interests. In the lull between Bass's purchase of the stock and his filing a suit, Barnes halted in-depth reporting about Bass by the business news desk.[35] The newspaper had assigned a top reporter to gather a massive exposition of the dispute. Two months in the making, the article was somewhat distanced from the company line but generally sympathetic. The *Times* killed it because, as Barnes explained, "When Bob Bass purchased the stock we saw no reason to take an adversarial position or risk irritating him." But after the court action, it was run as a three-part, page-one series. Barnes noted, "Now that [he] has sued the *Times,* I'm not worried if I make him angry."[36]

When the Bass forces tried to buy an advertisement in the *Times* to present their arguments, the paper turned them down, using the rationale that the ad accused management of a "breach of fiduciary duty" and that this was not true. The *Times* would reject other ads that were not proven to be true, Barnes said, adding, "To let Bass attack us in our own pages seemed foolish."[37] The ad ran instead in the *Tampa Tribune,* easily obtainable in St. Petersburg.

David Bonderman, Bass's top assistant, rejected Barnes's implications that they wanted only maximum profits, at the expense of editorial quality if necessary. He pointed out that papers like the *New York Times* and the *Washington Post* were traded on the stock market, adding, "The St. Pete *Times* is the only newspaper that has all the economic decisions made by someone with no economic interest in the newspaper. Andy acts like that's the holy grail, but no one is like that but the St. Pete *Times* and *Pravda*."[38]

The public bickering subsided during the spring and early summer of 1990. Then on August 17, with no warning, the two sides issued a starchily written joint press release. It announced the dispute had been settled out of court.

Details were hazy and incomplete at best. There were indications that, although the agreement may have been forged by lawyers, the key decision on whether to accept it was made by a special advisory board made up of two journalism deans, a law school dean, a political scientist, and a newspaper columnist. In turn they had been advised by a retired business school dean.

The picture that emerged from other newspapers' coverage was that (1) the *Times* would call all the preferred stock at the original price, as requested by Bass; (2) Bass would sell the *Times* an undisclosed part of the 40 percent common shares immediately, and the *New York Times* quoted insiders as saying this was most of the total;[39] the rest would be sold the same way after three years under "certain circumstances"; (3) Barnes would vote all the common stock; (4) dividends on common stock would rise "substantially" in the next five years; and (5) the *Times* bowed to Bass's demand that details of the settlement be kept secret for three years.

Perhaps the greatest irony of the settlement was that each side would donate $300,000 to set up a chair in media ethics at the University of South Florida in the name of Eleanor Jamison. For decades Nelson had chided her for what he saw as her elevation of profits over principle. When the Bass people had complained of their ad's being rejected, Barnes had retorted, "Who are they, to give us journalism lessons?"[40] Now, the *Times* would help make it possible for the last word in ethics to be spoken in the name of the person who had originated the conflict.

What did the settlement cost the *Times*? The paper would not say, and estimates varied widely. The *Wall Street Journal* said $50–$75 million. The *New York Times* said $100–$150 million.

What did the *Times* get, other than escape from the lawsuit? Barnes said the agreement assured "the long-term independence, journalistic control and competitive vigor" of the paper, as well as "significant support" for the Poynter Institute. When Attorney General Butterworth investigated to make sure that the institute did not suffer, institute president Robert Haiman told him that over twelve years the income would be $17 million above what would have been likely under the old arrangement.

At any rate, it appeared that the *Times* would ride out the storm. The same week that it announced the settlement, it revealed that profits were running 3 percent ahead of the year before. The *New York Times* said that revenues in 1989 had been $231 million, and it estimated the company's worth at $500–$700 million.

The first two years of Barnes's presidency had been absorbed in the dispute. Now he could return to normal with his usual good humor. He wrote in a New Year's column, "We end the year strong and ready to go. What then of '91?"[41] The next day he found out. A letter came from Yale University, where Nelson Poynter had earned his master's. It said Yale was looking into the possibility of claiming ownership of the *Times*.

Poynter's will had named Yale as contingent beneficiary if the plan to give his stock to the Poynter Institute failed to get the approval of the Internal Revenue Service. But the IRS went along with the plan, and Yale had received $1.3 million in gifts at various times. Now the university was asking for financial records that would help it to decide whether it would challenge the institute's tax-exempt status. If successful, it would revive the contingency and receive a $500 million windfall.

Once again, invective poured from people at the *Times*. "A new low in education funding," said Andrew Corty, marketing director. "Pure greed," said George Rahdert, a *Times* lawyer. Buttons sprouted on staffers' lapels: "SAY: Stop the A——from Yale." Yale's general counsel, Dorothy Robinson, responded with Ivy League gentility, "I have no response to those kinds of words, but to say that we attempted to make a polite and businesslike request, and I'm surprised they seem to be trying to sensationalize it."[42]

What had led Yale to think it could seize the prize became a subject of speculation. Bass was a loyal Yale alumnus and may have initiated the action. Robinson said she was alerted by Bass's Washington lawyer. And, the year before, a magazine about tax matters raised a question about the institute's tax-exempt status and said it was not organized exclusively for charitable purposes as the law required.

Once again Barnes vowed to fight the issue out in the courts and win, but this time it was not necessary. Four months later, Yale quietly dropped its "study."

So it appeared that the last fright had emerged from the *Times*'s closet of ghosts. The battle with Bass and the skirmish with Yale had been fought ostensibly to vindicate Nelson Poynter's ideals. At a heavy price that would no doubt mortgage the paper's future, the framework of these ideals—independent ownership, one-person control, viability of the Poynter Institute—remained in place. But the substance of the newspaper, which had been such a quintessence of Nelson Poynter during his lifetime, now had become, in the turmoil of the two years, a reflection of Andy Barnes. Ironically, this was inevitable under the plan Poynter devised. If he was to claim the right to be a loner, he must be succeeded by loners.

Chapter 11

━━━

The Long View

When Nelson Poynter died, the *Times* of London described him as "one of the most remarkable of American newspaper proprietors" even though he lived in "an unremarkable town."[1] Many journalists on Poynter's own paper today share this view—particularly those who had migrated from points north in the late twentieth century. Even high-level editors let it be known that they consider their service akin to that of Peace Corps volunteers in a Third World country.

If pressed to explain how the newspaper in which they take pride reached so lofty a status, considering that Poynter did not join it permanently until it was a half-century old, they explain that the paper was a small rag until he arrived.[2] He could make such an improvement, according to this theory, because he grew up in the relatively enlightened latitudes of Indiana.

This was a strange turn of events. Until recent times, a steady flow of refugees from the bitter winters and industrial grime of the North had seen the entry to Pinellas County as a golden door. "People who had lived lives of dull glumness in distant places come here and immediately burst into song and other unusual things," wrote Michigan-born Bill Straub, the great early editor of the *Times*.[3]

There was less enthusiasm for the newspaper itself, although it was good enough to attain the nation's second largest advertising linage in 1925 and to outpace two rivals—the older *Evening Independent* (in the days when afternoon papers had a natural advantage) and a tabloid that flourished briefly in the 1920s. The same year as the *Times*'s advertising peak, a Chicago financial publication cited the paper for a "superb news service" larger than any other outside Florida and editors who were "the ablest that can be found."[4] As for editorial influence, it would be difficult to match the range and extent of Straub's impact on his community in the decade after he took over the paper in 1901.

But the notion that the *Times*'s greatness and uniqueness were achieved in spite of its location rather than because of it defies historical evidence. St. Petersburg's path of development differed from those of other Florida cities—much more so from cities in other states. The Pinellas County subpeninsula was almost isolated from the main body of the state until the mid-1950s, and the very act of entering it thrilled newcomers. Dick Bothwell, who escaped the wintry rigors of South Dakota to make a career as a *Times* humor columnist, recalled rolling across the bay causeway one night in 1939 on a Greyhound bus: "It seemed to me we were approaching a bright, glowing island out in the middle of the sea."[5]

St. Petersburg did not experience the frenzied north-south land traffic that spawned gaudy resorts and thriving trade centers elsewhere in Florida. When a narrow-gauge railroad snaked through the subpeninsula's neck and arrived in 1888, the year the city was born, it stopped there. A bay stood in the way on three sides, meaning that most people who went to St. Petersburg made a point of doing so rather than stopping off on their way elsewhere. Although this is largely true also of Miami, the fact that a major railroad went there gave it a more feverish growth and a more diverse population than St. Petersburg, and Miami's linkages with Latin America made it much more of a multiethnic melting pot.

Thus, while St. Petersburg missed much of the ferment that might have made it more newsworthy, it also escaped the turbulence of other Florida cities—Latins versus Anglos first in Tampa and then in Miami, Deep South crackers versus worldly transplants in Jacksonville, quick-buck invaders versus agricultural gentry in Orlando, and the seething resentment of blacks in all of them. The only massive invasions St. Petersburg ever had were by middle- and upper-middle-class settlers before and after World War I and after World War II. These immigrants typically wanted suburban homes and conventional jobs, preferably in the smokeless electronics plants.

Certainly there was the Green Bench syndrome—the annual migration of elderly visitors who perplexed the city's image peddlers. Thousands of them lounged about in the city's center, but they did not dominate St. Petersburg's public life, and in the 1950s they settled in the suburbs and became nearly invisible.

The *Times* felt little pressure from overheated crime and scandal news. Time magazine, explaining why it chose the *St. Petersburg Times* as one of the nation's ten best dailies in 1984, noted that life there was so sleepy that the newspaper "sometimes has to fill its local news pages with reports of kindly neighbors and lost dogs."[6] Poynter, with his Christian Science upbringing, actually preferred a constructive world view. He would not have embraced the "good news" fad that afflicted the 1980s, but he believed that a newspaper's highest calling was to instruct and inspire, not titillate.

Poynter was truly a man of the world. In his college days he drifted around the globe, trying to become a foreign correspondent. He later sought doggedly to buy a major daily in New York and to found one in Chicago. He shared in the creation of an innovative New York newspaper, *PM*, until he fell out with its founder, Ralph Ingersoll. He did make his mark in his beloved Washington, along with his brilliant wife, Henrietta, when he founded a high-minded periodical that fulfilled his schoolmasterish dreams, *Congressional Quarterly*. And he spent World War II in high-level propaganda jobs.

But when he acquired control of the *Times* and finally settled into St. Petersburg at age forty-five, Poynter's professed goal was to make the city the best place in the world to live. His quiet self-confidence was unshakable, and it is unlikely that he would have wasted his efforts if he did not think St. Petersburg could rise to his challenge. Not until two decades later did he shift primarily from this civic challenge to a professional one—to make the *Times* the best newspaper in Florida.

Despite his flings at national journalism, Poynter came to recognize that the real genius of American political and journalistic life lay in its localism, somewhat as Frederick Jackson Turner maintained in his frontier thesis. Poynter loathed the passivity and elitism of European publics, and he pursued a Jeffersonian vision that grass-roots citizen-statesmen were better equipped to direct civic life than bureaucrats in Washington, even though Poynter was a liberal Democrat in an age when his party was centralizing power at the federal level. In this view, the news medium that guides its public toward progress, no matter how small the community, serves better than one that focuses on global affairs.

A look at journalism history makes this clear. Far more editorial distinction has been won in the interior than in New York. William Allen White made a monumental reputation in a small Kansas town. Joseph Pulitzer did his finest work in St. Louis, and history has raised few New Yorkers to the status of Henry Grady of Atlanta, Henry Watterson and Barry Bingham of Louisville, and William Rockhill Nelson of Kansas City.

But to say that St. Petersburg's unique nature helped make the *Times* distinctive is not to maintain that the metamorphosis would have occurred without Nelson Poynter. The *Independent* was amply endowed with talented editors and managers in its first half-century, but it began its decline even before the national tide turned against afternoon papers. And the *Times* itself did not start approaching its present level until after Poynter had been firmly in control more than a decade.

What, then, were the essential qualities that Poynter added?

They did not include brilliance at the daily tasks of journalism—writing, copyediting, and designing—although he performed these tasks often enough to understand them. Poynter had the judgment to choose men and women who could do these things exceedingly well, and he maximized the conditions under which they performed. Even the broad editorial strategies for which the *Times* became famous—the massive series of depth reporting, the glittering graphics, the powerful editorial campaigns—were developed by his lieutenants.

Nor was Poynter a good manager in the conventional sense. Certainly he was responsible for innovations at the *Times* long before their general adoption—goal-oriented management, personnel development, profit sharing, and technological pioneering. But he drove his staffers mercilessly, maddened them with unclear instructions, paid too little to keep the best of them, and sometimes brushed aside astute and devoted aides. He kept profits somewhat low for the sake of reinvestment and refused to diversify holdings. He blithely antagonized subscribers and advertisers with his editorial stands. Most hurtfully, in the long run, he let family jealousies prevent him from solving a problem he knew would fester and burst—the ownership of *Times* stock by relatives with whom he disagreed.

So what was left? Without a doubt, Poynter's essential contribution was his obsessiveness and his singularity—his "butt-headedness," as he called it. The *New York Times* likened his toughness to that of a railroad spike. His addiction to work drove him to wake executives after midnight to brainstorm with them, and it cost him his first marriage and, for many years, closeness with his children.

He was obsessed with professional progress on both editorial and business sides. His volcanic production of ideas both inspired and perplexed those around him. If they said something could not be done, he would slam a dime down on the desk and demand to know why not: "I'm the reader. I've just paid to buy your paper. And you tell me it can't be done?"

He was obsessed with civic virtue. Although the *Times* under his leadership was one of the most consistently liberal papers in the country, ideology always ranked below character in public people and long-term sensibility in government programs; if anything, Poynter edged rightward late in his life. He went beyond mere approval of bipartisanship and actively promoted it in his county with a robust relish for competitiveness.

And he was obsessed with solvency. He obviously enjoyed making money with a newspaper, as this talent distinguished him in his youth before taking over the *Times*. There was no personal greed or inflated devotion to stockholders, but making the *Times* prosperous meant independence from his parents and sister and proof to them that he could excel at the family business. It also meant that he could make the *Times* as good as he wanted to and thumb his nose at bankers in the process.

Poynter's singular nature could be read simply as the streak of narcissism that is essential to leadership. His self-confidence did not manifest itself as egotism but rather in his style of management. He had mixed results working for others in his youth, including some severe failures. Only by wresting control of the *Times* from his family could he perform at his best. His individuality engendered his fetish for one-person command at the paper, even perpetuating it after his death. It sustained his lonely battles against perceived evils such as handgun trafficking, tax favors for newspapers, and legalized gambling. No doubt his reluctance to share control caused some stumbles in converting the *Times* into an institution that would survive him.

The complex and often thorny relationships within the Poynter family had much to do with Nelson's choice of the path less taken. Two women—his mother, Alice, and his second wife, Henrietta—had enormous influence on him. Alice both bolstered his confidence with unfailing love and infected him with a fixation for excellence. Henrietta offered him a partnership of the mind. The father, Paul, was a foil who gave Nelson a model of what he did not want to be. And his sister, Eleanor, goaded him into mulishness just by opposing him.

This very aloneness calls into question Nelson Poynter's lasting effects on his newspaper. His true humility prevented a cult worship of him, to the extent that fifteen years after his death probably a majority of *Times* staffers had never seen him nor knew much about him. How could it remain Poynter's paper when he went to such lengths to ensure it became Gene Patterson's paper and later Andy Barnes's and so on? The only stricture he put on his successors was that they honor his cherished Standards of Ownership, and Patterson promptly rewrote them after taking over (although with little change).

Poynter's memory must rest not on the fact that he operated and expanded an outstanding newspaper, as Patterson and Barnes have, but that he created one—and made it possible to remain so. Many standards of excellence the *Times* set have become almost commonplace across the country. There is a great irony in the fact that the *Times* is a better "product" than it was even under Poynter, but observers marvel at it far less than before.

If a vehicle for Poynter's feistiness and idealism exists anywhere, it probably is the Poynter Institute. It can try out ideas for their own sake, think the unthinkable, distill the wisdom of the nation's best minds and call up unsettling agendas—all in the freedom that only ample funding can give. It was to create this paradise of the mind that Poynter dared to stand alone.

━━━━━━━━

The Standards of Ownership by Nelson Poynter, August 6, 1947

This is a guide for my heirs, trustees, executors, advisors who have any responsibilities in disposing of any of my newspaper properties and equities. These standards shall be used as a yardstick in choosing the purchaser of The St. Petersburg Times, or any other properties which I own. A fair and equitable price must be realized from my properties but my executors shall be under no obligation to sell my interests to the highest bidder, but they may accept any offer from any bidder for any amount deemed by them to be fair and reasonable, and upon any terms deemed by them to be acceptable in view of the following:

1. Ownership or participation in ownership of a publication or broadcasting property is a sacred trust and a great privilege.

2. Any publication or broadcasting property has unusual obligations to the community in which it operates, and any new owner must be sensitive to this.

3. The owners of a publication or broadcasting station cannot compromise with the integrity of the news and information that is sold or given to the public.

4. A publication or broadcasting station must be aggressive in its service to the community and not wait to be prodded into rendering that service. A publisher or broadcaster must share the zeal and enthusiasm for what is new each day. He does not belong as an owner unless he has such enthusiasm.

5. Adequate and modern equipment is vital for successful publishing or broadcasting, but it is secondary to staff.

6. A "chain" owner cannot do justice to local publications or radio stations. His devotion and loyalty to any one area is bound to be diluted or divided if he has other ownerships and interests.

7. I expect every member of any staff to be above average in his respective job. I expect my successor to demand standards of his staff as high or higher than mine. A concern that expects its staff to be above average must be willing to pay staffers above average.

8. Any modern capitalistic institution must expect to provide pensions that promise honest and dignified retirement to members of the staff who have devoted their lives to the institution.

9. Mere ownership in a paper or broadcasting station does not entitle an individual to a salary. All salaries should be commensurate with the services rendered to the institution.

10. A publication or broadcasting station cannot best serve its community if it is encumbered with outside interests. Its editorial policy should not be tinctured with ownership in enterprises not related to newspapering or broadcasting.

11. To maintain a strong editorial policy, a newspaper or broadcasting concern must be in a sound financial condition. Reserves must be built. Debts must be reduced and extinguished.

12. To qualify as an owner of a newspaper or broadcasting station, a prospect should have a well-rounded appreciation of the contribution that is made by all departments in publishing or broadcasting—the technical—sales—distribution departments—and above all, the creative or editorial departments.

13. A payment of not more than six per cent dividends on the present capitalization should be considered fair until debts are discharged, reserves built and technical equipment brought up to a position of second to none on the West Coast of Florida.

14. Dividends beyond six per cent should be equalized with bonuses to employes on a formula which I expect to perfect in the coming several years, a formula that recognizes length of service and contribution to the enterprise.

15. A publication is so individualistic in nature that complete control should be concentrated in an individual. Voting stock should never be permitted to scatter.

Sources and Notes

This book is largely based on primary sources, as little research had been done on Nelson Poynter or the *St. Petersburg Times*. The principal types of primary material are correspondence, personal documentary collections, company records, microfilms, and interviews, conducted by the author and by others. Most interviews were audiotaped, and some were videotaped; manuscripts or typescripts of the dialogues were preserved in all cases.

A major repository of valuable materials was the Nelson Poynter Collection of the Poynter Library, University of South Florida, St. Petersburg campus. It has benefited from a masterful job of organization and cataloging by David Shedden. Some materials have been placed there in earlier years and later withdrawn, and others were added long after Poynter's death.

Another indispensable asset was the content notes amassed by Tom Harris. These were abstracts of items in the *Times* from 1901 through 1975. He also partially completed a first draft of what was to have been a history of the newspaper before his health failed. Works noted by Robert Hooker and David C. Coulson were useful, as were transcripts and tapes of interviews by Hooker.

Times files of Poynter's papers that had not been placed in the archives, including copies of Federal Bureau of Investigation files on Poynter, also were opened to me. Usefulness of the Poynter papers was limited somewhat by their massiveness and the fact that they had not been catalogued.

Although nearly all the events and interpretations contained in the book were generated by citable sources, the author's own experiences have made an indelible mark on the writing. As a journalist during much of the time when Poynter owned the *Times*, I observed its work for three decades, partly through the eyes of my friends and former students there. I worked for the company for a year and benefited from a Poynter Fund Fellowship.

Unless otherwise indicated, interviews were by the author and letters and other unpublished documents are from the Poynter Collection, Nelson Poynter Library, University of South Florida, St. Petersburg campus. Where no page numbers are given for items in the *Times*, citations are from content notes made by Tom C. Harris and held by the Harris family.

Abbreviations

AP	Alice Poynter
Chronology	Nelson Poynter, "Chronology of Poynter Family Finances and Transactions Since 1927," July 26, 1965, in files of the *Times*.
EJ	Eleanor Jamison
Fuller	Walter P. Fuller. *St. Petersburg and Its People*. St. Petersburg: Great Outdoors Publishing Co. 1972.
Grismer	Karl H. Grismer. *The Story of St. Petersburg*. St. Petersburg: P. K. Smith and Company, 1948.
Harris	Tom C. Harris, unpublished history of the *St. Petersburg Times*, in the files of the *Times*.
Hooker	Robert Hooker, "The Times and Its Times," supplement to the *St. Petersburg Times*, July 25, 1984.
NP	Nelson Poynter
PC	Poynter Collection
PP	Paul Poynter
SPT	*St. Petersburg Times*

Prologue

1. H.G. Davis, Jr., to Robert N. Pierce, July 7, 1988, in the files of the author.

Chapter 1

Interviews with Robert Haiman, Andrew Barnes, Eugene Patterson, John B. Lake, Donald K. Baldwin, Marion Poynter, and Robert Pittman provided the bulk of material for this chapter. In several cases, I asked persons to write their recollections of the day Nelson Poynter died, telling them I would partially quote them without attribution. Haiman and Patterson were particularly helpful in this respect.

1. Andrew Barnes, interview with Robert Hooker, June 19, 1984.

2. Nelson Poynter to Eugene Patterson, April 4, 1975, in the files of the *Times*.

Chapter 2

Secondary materials were used in this chapter more than any other. Although a wide range of histories of Florida and Pinellas County were consulted, the Grismer, Fuller, and Tebeau books noted below were especially useful. The archives of the Pinellas County Historical Museum produced many helpful documents, and Dr. Bob Harris assisted in making them available. Robert Hooker's files also provided essential elements.

Copies of the *Times*, either in paper or microfilm, are woefully scarce for its first seventeen years of existence, and even beginning in 1901 there are gaps as long as a year. Unfortunately, no entity with necessary resources has shown any interest in trying to locate missing numbers.

For information on 1900–1930, the unpublished memoirs of W. L. Straub and Ralph Reed were of great service, as were the personal papers of C. C. Carr, graciously loaned by his daughter, Mrs. James Fausch. Jay B. Starkey and his wife, Blanche Straub Starkey, daughter of W. L. Straub, were generous with their memories.

1. "Excursion to Tarpon Springs," *West Hillsborough Times*, May 12, 1887, p. 2.

2. Charlton W. Tebeau, *A History of Florida* (Miami: University of Miami Press, 1971), p. 292.

3. J. Pendleton Gaines, Jr.,"A Century in Florida Journalism" (thesis, University of Florida, 1949, p. 57).

4. Ralph Reed, "Reverend Reynolds Was First Editor," *SPT*, June 3, 1959, p. 10B.

5. James Scott Hanna, "The Brandon Family of Southwest Florida," Pinellas County Historical Museum, p. 98.

6. Ibid., p. 99; notes in the files of Robert Hooker, *SPT*.

7. *Clear Water Times*, July 12, 1873, p. 2.

8. Hanna, "The Brandon Family of Southwest Florida," p. 101.

9. Ibid., p. 1.

10. *Clear Water Times*, Oct. 6, 1877.

11. Grismer, p. 52.

12. Frank Luther Mott, *American Journalism*, 3d ed. (New York: Macmillan Company, 1962), pp. 478–79.

13. *West Hillsborough Times*, July 22, 1886, p. 4.

14. Ibid.

15. Ibid.

16. Harris, chap. 1, p. 11.

17. *West Hillsborough Times*, Aug, 1, 1884. p. 1.

18. Ibid., April 14, 1887, p. 2.

19. Ibid., Dec. 16, 1886, p. 3.

20. Hooker, p. 10.

21. Notes by Richard J. Morgan's daughter and granddaughter in Hooker files.

22. Hooker, p. 10.

23. Interview with J. J. Lassiter, *SPT*, Oct. 10, 1954, p. 2B.

24. Harris, chap. 1, p. 15.

25. Dick Bothwell, "Of All Things," *SPT*, Aug. 30, 1979, p. 1B.

26. Publication by *SPT* dated 1897, p. 1.

27. Ibid.

28. Ibid., p. 17.

29. *SPT*, Nov. 6, 1932 (clipping in PC).

30. Ibid., p. 60.

31. The younger Gore went on to become editor of the opposition newspaper, the *Sub-Peninsula Sun*. Later he worked for the *Florida Times-Union* at Jacksonville before becoming managing editor of the *Atlanta Constitution*. He turned to selling a patent medicine called Tanalac and moved to Miami as a real estate investor. Dick Bothwell, "Of All Things," *SPT*, Aug. 30, 1979, p. 1B.

32. Harris, chap. 2, p. 4.

33. *SPT*, April 4, 1901.

34. Paul Poynter was born in Eminence, Indiana, in 1875 to Jesse A. and Letitia Bennett Poynter.

35. PP to AP, Sept. 4, 1912.

36. PP to AP, undated.

37. PP to AP, Sept. 4, 1912.

38. *SPT*, Jan. 10, 1917.

39. Ibid., Jan. 16, 1919.

40. Ibid., Sept. 21, 1928.

41. Hooker, p. 29.

42. *SPT*, Feb. 18, 1925.

43. Ibid., July 3, 1916.

44. Ibid., Feb. 28, 1924.

Chapter 3

The Poynter family scrapbooks and correspondence, along with Nelson Poynter's chronology noted below and the FBI files on Poynter, which he obtained late in his life, were crucial in this chapter. The Coulson dissertation and videotapes in the Governor's Project on Oral History were also useful.

1. NP to AP, May 6, 1926, and Jan. 3, 1966.

2. Poynter family scrapbook, PC.

3. Ibid.

4. Chronology, p. 1.

5. NP to AP, June 18, 1936.

6. Poynter family scrapbook, PC.

7. Poynter served as national treasurer of Sigma Delta Chi for a short time after his graduation.

8. NP to AP, June 24, 1923.

9. NP to AP, June 7, 1923.

10. NP to AP, June 24, 1923.

11. Ibid.

12. NP to AP, June 1924.

13. AP to NP, Oct. 20, 1924.

14. Internal memorandum, FBI, Feb. 25, 1941.

15. Chronology, p. 2.

16. Ibid., p. 3.

17. Ibid.

18. In a videotaped interview May 22, 1977, by Don Baldwin and Marion Poynter, Nelson Poynter spoke of a $25,000 profit in Clearwater. However, in his chronology he set the profit at about $20,000 in notes.

19. Internal memorandum from the Miami bureau to Washington headquarters, FBI, Feb. 28, l941.

20. Chronology, p. 4.

21. David C. Coulson, "Nelson Poynter: Study of an Independent Publisher and His Standards of Ownership" (dissertation, University of Minnesota, 1982), p. 18.

22. NP to AP, Dec. 26, 1931.

23. NP to AP, May 12, 1933.

24. Memorandum by NP, Sept. 16, 1939, apparently sent to Ralph Ingersoll and to others, PC.

25. Ibid.

26. NP to AP, April 17, 1926; internal memorandum from Cincinnati bureau to Washington headquarters, FBI, Feb. 25, 1941.

27. NP to AP, Dec. 5, 1935,

28. Internal memorandum from Cincinnati bureau to Washington headquarters, FBI, Feb. 26, 1941.

29. "Nation's Press Can Save Democracy," 69:24, June 13, 1936, p. 7.

30. Memorandum from NP, not addressed, Sept. 16, 1939, PC.

31. NP to Roy W. Howard, Sept. 16, 1939.

32. Ibid., Sept. 18, 1939.

33. Internal memorandum from Cincinnati bureau to Washington headquarters, FBI, Feb. 25, 1941.

34. Internal memorandum from St. Paul bureau to Washington headquarters, FBI, Feb. 25, 1941.

35. Ibid.

36. John Cowles to NP, Sept. 28, 1939.

37. Gardner Cowles, Jr., to NP (telegram), Sept. 29, 1939.

38. *SPT,* Oct. 14, 1928.

39. Ibid., March 6, 1929.

40. Ibid., June 19, 1929.

41. The full leadership in 1928 was listed as Paul Poynter, president; F. R. Francke, secretary and treasurer, W. L. Straub, editor; C. C. Carr, vice-president and general manager; John W. Falconnier, managing editor; Max Ulrich, circulation manager; H. A. Orrell, mechanical superintendent; and Joe Plaskett, classified manager.

42. E. J. Ottaway to C. C. Carr, June 6, 1931.

43. Hooker, p. 36.

44. C. C. Carr to PP, June 11, 1934.

45. NP to PP, April 29, 1935.

46. Hooker, p. 37.

47. Ibid.

48. Chronology, p. 6.

49. *SPT,* Aug. 4, 1935.

50. Hooker, p. 36.

51. Chronology, p. 7.

52. Ibid.

53. NP to AP, July 27, 1935.

54. Ibid., June 15, 1936.

55. Hooker, p. 36.

Chapter 4

In addition to the sources noted for chapter 3, chapter 4 was aided by Roy Hoopes's book *Ralph Ingersoll: A Biography,* Burt Garnett's unpublished memoirs (in the author's files), and the divorce petition of Catherine F. Poynter.

1. *SPT,* Jan. 16, 1938.

2. Ibid., March 25, 1938.

3. Ibid., April 13, 1938.

4. Ibid., Aug. 6, 1938.

5. Ibid., Sept. 14, 1938.

6. Ibid., Oct. 8, 1939.

7. Grismer, p. 191.

8. *SPT,* March 8, 1939.

9. NP to John Cowles, Sept. 30, 1939.

10. Roy Hoopes, *Ralph Ingersoll: A Biography* (New York: Atheneum, 1985), p. 192.

11. Ibid., p. 401.

12. Videotaped interview with NP by Eugene Patterson, Robert Pittman, and Donald K. Baldwin, Jan. 12, 1977.

13. Hoopes, *Ralph Ingersoll,* pp. 398-403.

14. NP to AP, Aug. 19, 1939.

15. NP to AP, Sept.19, 1939.

16. NP to Ralph Ingersoll, memorandum, Aug. 12, 1939.

17. Ibid.

18. NP to Ingersoll, memorandum, Aug. 25, 1939.

19. Hoopes, pp. 193-95.

20. NP to Ingersoll, undated memorandum.

21. Ingersoll to NP, Sept. 15, 1939.

22. Ibid.

23. NP to Ingersoll, Sept. 16, 1939.

24. Ibid., Sept. 23, 1939.

25. Ingersoll to NP, Feb. 28, 1940.

26. Documents in PC.

27. NP to Ingersoll, April 6, 1940.

28. NP, "A Proposition to Create a New Newspaper," ca. August 1939, PC.

29. NP to PP and AP, April 3, 1942.

30. *SPT,* Jan. 23, 1940.

31. Fuller, p. 310.

32. NP to Charles Stuart Guthrie, July 26, 1940.

33. NP to James W. Young, memorandum, Feb. 13, 1941.

34. J. Edgar Hoover to D. M. Ladd, memorandum, Dec. 8, 1941.

35. M.A. Jones to "Mr. Nichols," memorandum, April 21, 1954.

36. J. Edgar Hoover to D. M. Ladd, memorandum, Dec. 8, 1941.

37. Most details about circumstances of the divorce come from the petition filed by Catherine F. Poynter in the Sixth Circuit Court of Florida, Clearwater, and associated documents. Consequently they present only one side of the matter. See vol. 073, pp. 1585–1669, of the court records.

38. Burt Garnett, untitled and undated manuscript of memoirs about the *SPT;* copy in the author's files.

39. NP to PP and AP, April 3, 1942.

40. NP to AP, April 16, 1942.

41. Untitled document in Poynter Collection.

42. *New Masses,* June 30, 1942.

43. *Variety,* June 17, 1942, p. 1.

44. *New Masses,* June 30, 1942.

45. Ibid.

46. Roy Hoopes, *Americans Remember* (New York: Hawthorn Books, 1977), p. 169.

47. Ibid., pp. 167-68.

48. Document in PC.

49. Banquet program in Nelson Poynter scrapbook, in files of author.

50. Uncited clipping in Nelson Poynter scrapbook.

51. Henrietta Poynter to AP, April 1943.

52. Hoopes, *Americans Remember,* p. 389.

Chapter 5

The files of the *Times,* both as an indicator of the paper's development and as a place to find reminiscent articles about it, were the principal source for material in this chapter. Taped interviews with Stan Witwer and the Hooker work also were utilized.

1. Interview with Stan Witwer by Robert Hooker, May 9, 1984.

2. *SPT,* May 5, 1940.

3. Ibid., May 16, 1941.

4. Ibid., June 22, 1941.

5. Ibid., Aug. 8, 1942.

6. Ibid., April 10, 1942.

7. Ibid., Dec. 13, 1941.

8. Ibid., Jan. 31, 1942.

9. Robert Stiff, *Floridian* supplement to *SPT,* May 3, 1981, pp. 10-16.

10. *SPT,* Dec. 5, 1944.

11. Ibid., Sept. 1, 1944.

12. Ibid., March 22, 1945.

13. Ibid., Oct. 13, Nov. 2, 1945.

14. Ibid., Dec. 22, 1946.

15. Ibid., May 16, 1949.

16. Ibid., Sept. 3, 1952.

17. Ibid., May 17, 1953.

18. Ibid., June 9, 1953.

19. Ibid., Aug. 21, 1954.

20. Ibid., Nov. 6, 1954.

21. Ibid., Dec. 20, 1954.

22. Ibid., July 30, 1955.

23. Ibid., Nov. 8, 1955.

24. Ibid., Sept. 5, 19, 1957.

25. Videotaped interview with Martha Rudy Wallace by Robert Pittmann, Sept. 25, 1984, PC.

26. *SPT,* Oct. 24, 1948.

Chapter 6

Aside from the Poynter family correspondence and the files of the paper, the source most consulted was the chronicle of the 1945–46 strike, *Newspaper Printing in St. Petersburg* edited by Burt Garnett. The FBI files and the

Coulson dissertation also helped, along with interviews with John Olson, Alvah Shortell, Don Shortell, Glenn Dill, Clifton Camp, John Parker, Joan Alexander, Rae Weimer, and Tom Harris (taped by Robert Pittman).

1. AP to Henrietta Poynter, Jan. 4, 1954.
2. AP to NP, July 7, 1943.
3. Ibid., July 8, 1946.
4. NP to AP, Dec. 20, 1944.
5. Ibid., Aug. 17, 1946.
6. Ibid., Oct. 19, 1943.
7. PC.
8. Chronology, p. 7.
9. Ibid., p. 8.
10. Ibid., p. 10.
11. Ibid., p. 11.
12. AP to NP, Aug. 21, 1939.
13. NP to AP, Sept. 20, 1940.
14. AP to NP, October (undated) 1940.
15. Ibid., Nov. 28, 1940.
16. Ibid.
17. Ibid., Dec. 21, 1941.
18. Ibid.
19. Ibid., Nov. 27, 1941.
20. AP to PP, Sept. 1, 1942.
21. Ibid.
22. NP to AP, Sept. 9, 1941.
23. AP to NP, Dec. 22, 1941.
24. Ibid., Oct. 24, 1943.
25. NP to PP, AP and EJ, June 6, 1942.
26. NP To Hubert Thompson, memorandum, June 6, 1942.
27. NP to PP, AP and EJ, June 6, 1942.
28. Ibid., June 10, 1942.
29. NP to AP, June 1, 1943.
30. Eugene Patterson, "William Allen White Is Calling Us Home Again," *Quill,* April 1980, p. 21.
31. NP to AP, Oct. 26, 1943.
32. *SPT,* July 15, 1984.
33. Ibid., Nov. 21, 1945, p. 1.
34. Burt Garnett, ed., *Newspaper Printing in St. Petersburg* (St. Petersburg: Times Publishing Company, 1946), p. 21.
35. Ibid., p. 23.
36. *SPT,* June 25, 1946.
37. Ibid., Oct. 20, 1946.

38. NP to AP, Oct. 21, 1946.

39. Ibid., Dec. 27, 1946.

40. *SPT,* Feb. 23, 1947.

41. "Times Pressmen," *SPT,* Aug. 18, 1949, p. 1A; "Press Strike Negotiations Break Down," *SPT,* Aug. 21, 1949.

42. "Times Pressmen Walk Out, Then Set Up Picket Line," *SPT,* Nov. 15, 1952, p. 15; "Times Pressmen Still Picketing," *SPT,* Nov. 16, 1952, p. 1B.

43. NP to AP, July 14, 1945.

44. AP to NP, July 8, 1946.

45. AP to Henrietta Poynter, April 7, 1954.

46. Chronology, p. 12.

47. NP to PP, Aug. 3, 1947.

48. Ibid.

49. Videotaped interview with Nelson Poynter by Eugene Patterson, Robert Pittman and Donald K. Baldwin, Jan. 12, 1977.

50. Ibid.

51. Ibid.

52. Ibid.

53. Ibid.

54. Ibid.

55. NP to AP, Sept. 14, 1949.

56. Interview with Irwin Simpson, April 27, 1986.

57. Hooker, p. 56.

58. Interview with Byron Harless, Oct. 18, 1985.

59. NP to AP, Aug. 7, 1962.

60. Ibid., June 9, 1953.

61. Ibid., Sept. 9, 1953.

62. *SPT,* Jan. 6, 1951.

63. Ibid., Oct. 24, 1952, p. 25.

64. Intraoffice memorandum, FBI, May 7, 1954.

65. Ibid.

66. Ibid.

67. *SPT,* Jan. 12, 1955, p. 6.

68. Ibid., May 5, 1956, p. 1B.

69. Chronology, p. 13.

70. AP to NP, Dec. 26, 1955.

71. Chronology, p. 14.

72. Ibid., p. 15.

73. AP to NP, Dec. 31, 1955.

74. Ibid., Jan. 10, 1956.

75. NP to AP, Jan. 14, 1956.

76. David W. Dyer to NP, March 3, 1956.

77. Chronology, p. 15.

78. Ibid.

79. NP to AP, Dec. 31, 1956.

Chapter 7

Most of the sources noted above were used in this chapter. Robert Haiman's recollections were an important factor, as were talks with Donald Baldwin and Byron Harless. Also significant were interviews with George Sweers, Robert Pittman, Bette Orsini, Robert Stiff, David Laventhol, David Lawrence, Frank Peters, Anne Rowe Goldman, John B. Lake, Irwin Simpson, Laurence T. Herman, Leo Kubiet, Katharine Graham, Richard Scammon, Marion Poynter, Clifton Camp, Martin Dyckman, Sanford Stiles, and James Scofield. Letters from Leon H. Keyserling and Max M. Kampelman were informative. The FBI files on Poynter were drawn on extensively.

1. *Time,* Oct. 20, 1959, p. 80.

2. *Newsweek,* July 16, 1962, p. 75.

3. Hooker, p. 13.

4. Harris, chap. 11, p. 6.

5. Videotaped interview with NP by Eugene Patterson, Robert Pittman, and Donald K. Baldwin, Jan. 12, 1977.

6. Ibid.

7. Hooker, p. 13.

8. Donna M. Peltier, "The 'Standards for Ownership': Nelson Poynter's Manifesto" (thesis, University of Florida, 1975), p. 85.

9. Hooker, p. 20.

10. *SPT,* Sept. 14, 1958.

11. Ibid., March 29, 1957.

12. Hooker, p. 66.

13. *SPT,* April 8, 1967.

14. Ibid., March 24, 1967.

15. Hooker, p. 66.

16. HP to AP, Nov. 2, 1957.

17. NP to AP, Aug. 9, 1956.

18. Ibid., April 13, 1955.

19. Ibid., Feb. 15, 1960.

20. Ibid., Jan. 4, 1966.

21. Ibid., April 23, 1962.

22. Ibid., May 15, 1956.

23. Ibid., Aug. 10, 1958.

24. Ibid., July 9, 1964.

25. Ibid., Jan. 9, 1961.

26. Ibid., July 7, 1958.

27. Ibid., Jan. 3, 1957.

28. Ibid., Aug. 13, 1961.

29. *SPT,* May 25, 1951.

30. NP to Mrs. Lyle L. Chaffee, March 3, 1960.

31. *SPT,* March 10, 1960, p. 7A.

32. Shortly before his death, acting under provisions of the Freedom of Information Act, NP obtained censored copies of documents in his FBI file.

33. Undated clipping, PC.

34. Name-check report on NP by FBI furnished to U.S. Information Agency, Nov. 7, 1956.

35. *Congressional Record,* 106:38, March 2, 1960.

36. Intraoffice memorandum, FBI, April 21, 1954.

37. *New York Times,* Oct. 5, 1944, p. 11.

38. Ibid.

39. J. Edgar Hoover to NP, April 8, 1952.

40. Ibid., April 15, 1952.

41. Los Angeles FBI bureau to Washington headquarters, telegram, May 16, 1963.

42. *SPT,* Jan. 27, 1939.

43. Interview with Irwin Simpson, May 30, 1984.

44. Mary V. Thayer, quoted in a draft sketch of Henrietta Poynter by Helene Monberg (1968).

45. Interview with Byron Harless, Oct. 18, 1985.

46. Interview with Donald K. Baldwin by Robert Hooker, May 31, 1984.

47. *SPT,* Jan. 26, 1968.

48. NP to AP, Feb. 15, 1968.

49. Ibid., Feb. 5, 1968.

50. Interview with Donald K. Baldwin by Robert Hooker, May 31, 1984.

51. Interview with Clifton D. Camp by Robert Hooker, June 6, 1984.

52. Interview with Donald K. Baldwin by Robert Hooker, May 31, 1984.

53. Interview with Marion Poynter, July 30, 1987.

Chapter 8

Various interviews of Eugene Patterson and Andrew Barnes conducted over several years provided the bulk of the material for this chapter. Also of value were interviews with John B. Lake, Robert Haiman, Bette Orsini, Lucy Morgan, and Martin Dyckman. A paper by E. Mayer Maloney Jr., "Unions in the Newsroom," also was of benefit.

1. Interview of Robert Pittman, April 6, 1987.

2. Interview of Eugene Patterson by David Shedden, Sept. 8, 1984.

3. Interview of Rae O. Weimer, Jan. 31, 1992.

4. Interview of Eugene Patterson by Robert Hooker, May 28, 1984.

5. Interview of Eugene Patterson by David Shedden, Sept. 8, 1984.

6. Ibid.

7. *Atlanta Constitution,* Sept. 16, 1963.

8. Hooker, 70.

9. Interview with Eugene Patterson by Robert Hooker, May 28, 1984.

10. E. Mayer Maloney, Jr., "Unions in the Newsroom: The *St. Petersburg Times*" (unpublished paper for the Poynter Institute, November 1980).

11. Interview with Robert Haiman, April 16, 1987.

12. Interview with Bette Orsini, May 19, 1987.

13. Interview with Lucy Morgan, May 27, 1987.

14. Letter from Eugene Patterson to Robert N. Pierce, May 28, 1987.

15. Interview of Andrew Barnes by Robert Hooker, June 19, 1984.

Chapter 9

Files of the *Times* and various national magazines were instrumental here, particularly in the case of the newspaper's collected stories on the Scientology episode, issued as a reprint. Bette Orsini was very helpful on this subject. Other interviews included those with Michael Foley, Eugene Patterson, Andrew Barnes, Charles Stafford, Wilbur Landrey, Elizabeth Whitney, Douglas Doubleday, Robert Haiman, Elizabeth Whitney, Helen Huntley, Hubert Mizell, Jack Ellison, Robert Pittman, John B. Lake, V. Donald Rebholz, David Fluker, Robert Althaus, John Irwin, Richard Edmonds, Neville Green, Paul Tash, John Costa, Wayne Kelley, Hoyt Gimlin, Neil Skene, and John O'Hearn.

1. *SPT, City Times and Independent* section, Dec. 10, 1987, p. 6.

2. Ibid., p. 12.

3. Ibid., p. 1.

4. Ibid., p. 10.

5. *SPT,* Dec. 1, 1987, p. 1D.

6. Interview with Andrew Barnes, Dec. 4, 1987.

7. Coulson, "Nelson Poynter," p. 150.

8. Hooker, p. 78.

9. Interview with Andrew Barnes, April 21, 1987.

10. Curtis D. MacDougall, *Interpretative Reporting,* 7th ed. (New York: Macmillan, 1977); Neale Copple, *Depth Reporting* (Englewood Cliffs, N. J.: Prentice-Hall, 1964).

11. *Problems of Journalism* (Washington, D.C.: American Society of Newspaper Editors, 1978), p. 85.

12. Ibid.

13. *SPT, Floridian* section, June 5, 1978, p. 5.

14. Charles Stafford, special report on Scientology, *SPT,* Jan. 9, 1980 (republished as booklet), p. 3.

15. Ibid.

16. Larry King, "L. Ron Hubbard: The Wizard of Scientology," *SPT*, Feb. 2, l986, p. 1B.

17. Ibid.

18. Stafford, special report, p. 4.

19. *SPT, Floridian* section, June 5, 1978, p. 5.

20. Stafford, special report, p. 11.

21. Ibid.

22. *SPT*, Nov. 10, 1979, P. 1A.

23. Stafford, special report, p. 3.

24. Interview with Charles Stafford, Jan. 20, 1988.

25. *SPT*, March 6, 1967, p. 3.

26. Ibid., Aug. 28, 1978, p. 5B.

27. Interview of Eugene Patterson by David Shedden, Sept. 8, 1984.

28. Interview of Eugene Patterson by Robert Hooker, May 18, 1984; interview of Robert Pittman by author, Feb. 12, 1987.

29. Interview with John B. Lake by Robert Hooker, May 30, 1984.

30. "Instant Encyclopedia," *Newsweek*, Sept. 13, 1965, p. 78.

31. *SPT*, April 11, 1953.

32. "Calling CQ," *Time*, Sept. 6, 1954, pp. 66, 68.

33. "Instant Encyclopedia."

34. "Battle of Capitol Hill," *Newsweek*, April 14, 1969, p. 100.

35. "All in the Family," *Washington Journalism Review*, January/February 1979, p. 48.

Chapter 10

Interviews, both in person and through videotapes, were a principal source. Among the most useful were those with Eugene Patterson, Clifton Camp, Marion Poynter, Charles Donegan, Robert Haiman, Roy Peter Clark, and Donald K. Baldwin. The files of various newspapers and magazines over the nation were elements in material about the Bass and Yale episodes.

1. Interview with Eugene Patterson by Robert Hooker, May 18, 1984.

2. Hooker, pp. 48-49.

3. Interview with Clifton D. Camp by Robert Hooker, June 6, 1984.

4. Interview with Clifton D. Camp, April 6, 1987.

5. Interview with Clifton D. Camp by Robert Hooker, June 6, 1984.

6. Interview with Marion Poynter, July 30, 1987.

7. Videotaped interview with Charles Donegan by Donald K. Baldwin, Sept. 19, 1984, in PC.

8. Interview with Donald Baldwin, July 14, 1987.

9. Interview with Roy Peter Clark, Aug. 3, 1987.

10. EJ to NP and Marion Poynter, undated.

11. Ibid., Dec. 29, 1975.

12. Robert Pittman, "Nelson Poynter Would Be Proud," *SPT*, Aug. 19, 1990, p. 1D.

13. EJ to NP, March 20, 1972.

14. Jeff Smith, "Fighting over Paper Continues," *Tampa Tribune*, Feb. 13, 1990, p. 1B.

15. Ibid., p. 3B.

16. Unaddressed memo in Poynter family papers.

17. Smith, "Fighting over Paper Continues."

18. Susan Taylor Martin, "A Great Grudge," *SPT*, Feb. 25, 1990, p. 14A.

19. Smith, "Fighting over Paper Continues."

20. Martin, "A Great Grudge."

21. Ibid.

22. Eugene Patterson, letter to the *Times* staff.

23. Jeff Smith, "Times, Bass Group at Odds over Stock," *Tampa Tribune*, Nov. 4, 1988, p. 1D.

24. Jeff Smith, "Times Spurns Buyout Offer," *Tampa Tribune*, Feb. 1, 1990, pp. 1D, 5D.

25. Ibid.

26. Stephen Koff, "Trustees Reject Offer to Sell Times," *SPT*, Feb. 17, 1990, pp. 1A, 4A.

27. Jeff Smith, "Bass Group Sues Times Publishing," *Tampa Tribune*, Feb. 7, 1990, p. 1D.

28. Andy Barnes, "In All This Distraction, We Must Not Lose Our Focus," *Times Line*, March 1, 1990, p. 1.

29. "Times Seeks Dismissal of Bass Suit," *Times Line*, May 10, 1990, p. 3; John Donnelly, "For the St. Pete Times, a Patch of Poison Ivy," *Miami Herald*, Jan. 20, 1991, p. 3G.

30. Jeff Smith, "Battle for the St. Petersburg Times," *Tampa Tribune*, Feb. 25, 1990, p. 1E.

31. Tim O'Reiley, "Big Guns Rally 'Round St. Pete Times," *Miami Review*, April 4, 1990, p. 3.

32. Debra Gersh, "St. Pete Times Hires Lobbyists to Help Pass Anti-Takeover Bill," *Editor & Publisher*, June 17, 1989, p. 24.

33. "Newspapers, Bass and Sharks," *Washington Post*, Feb. 22, 1990, p. A23.

34. "Bass Strikes in St. Petersburg," *Washington Journalism Review*, March 1989, p. 10.

35. Celia W. Dugger, "News Executive, Texas Billionaire Fight for Soul of St. Pete Times," *Miami Herald*, Feb. 12, pp. 1A, 18A.

36. Carl Goldfarb, "Times Runs Article on Feud over Paper," *Miami Herald*, Feb. 26, 1990, p. 5B.

37. Andy Barnes, "We Have No Obligation to Print Untruths," *Times Line,* March 15, 1990, p. 1.

38. Dugger, "News Executive, Texas Billionaire Fight for Soul of St. Pete Times."

39. Alex S. Jones, "St. Petersburg Times Agrees to Buy Out Bass Investors," *New York Times,* Aug. 18, 1990, p. 33.

40. Barnes, "We Have No Obligation to Print Untruths."

41. Andrew Barnes, "Taking Stock of the Newspaper and Looking Ahead to Its Future," *SPT,* Jan. 6, 1991, p. 2D.

42. Donnelly, "For the St. Pete Times, a Patch of Poison Ivy."

Chapter 11

1. "US Loses Outstanding Press Leader in Nelson Poynter," June 17, 1978, *Times* (London), p. 4.

2. Susan Taylor Martin, "A Great Grudge," *SPT,* Feb. 25, 1990, p. 1.

3. *SPT,* Oct. 14, 1928.

4. Quoted in *SPT,* Feb. 18, 1925.

5. Biographical material in the files of the *Times,* dated March 13, 1974.

6. *Time,* April 30, 1984, p. 61.

Thanks

This book exists because Tom Harris started the task of portraying the *Times*. Tom, who played a monumental role in the *Times*'s development, undertook to write a centennial history of the newspaper in his last years. He summarized the major items in every extant issue of the *Times* from 1901 through June 1975. Besides being an enormous asset for historians, his notes took him on a sentimental odyssey, as he had worked on most of the stories he sketched. There were even the proud little mentions of his children's school honors here and there.

Tom also wrote twelve chapters of a draft history of the *Times*, carrying the account into the 1920s. But his final illness clearly was hampering his work, so he turned over his materials to Robert Hooker, a *Times* staffer who benefited from them in writing a history of the first hundred years, *The Times and Its Times*. This eighty-page work appeared as a supplement to the newspaper's centennial edition, July 25, 1984. Its dry-eyed approach absorbed some of the querulous reactions that must befall any work of this sort.

Many people wanted to see this book written, and that placed a heavy responsibility on me. That they trusted me enough to help me added to my sense of duty. Much to my regret, I had to relearn a truth that every reporter encounters: Few people can be dispassionate and thus consistently candid about things closest to their hearts. Certainly this applies to journalists who love a newspaper as much as many of my sources have loved the *Times*.

If I had not had the professional companionship of Buddy Davis, I could not have finished. He was critic, confessor, and anchor to reality. Ralph Lowenstein was the matchmaker who brought me to the task, and he helped me unsnarl tangled chapters.

Gene Patterson asked me to write the book and gave his time and thoughts. Sandy Stiles was there at every step, opening doors, pointing out glitches, and doctoring words. Andy Barnes shared my excitement, and Tom Rawlins and Eddie Moran made problems disappear. David Shedden put the Poynter archives in usable form and helped me through the maze. Bob Haiman placed his remarkable memory at my disposal, as well as facilities of the Poynter Institute. Marion Poynter cared deeply about historical validity and literally went out of her way to help.

For fear of omitting some of the present and former *Times* staffers who enhanced the book, I will not try to name more. But among people outside the paper, I want to thank Dwight Teeter, Walda Metcalf, Ray Washington, Pat and Peg Harris, Jean Chance, Marge Fausch, Dolores Jenkins of the University of Florida Libraries, and Mr. and Mrs. Jay Starkey.

Index

Library of Congress Cataloging-in-Publication Data

Pierce, Robert N. (Robert Nash), 1931–
      A sacred trust: Nelson Poynter and the St. Petersburg times /
      Robert N. Pierce.
           p.   cm.
      Includes bibliographical references and index.
      ISBN 0-8130-1234-1
      1. St. Petersburg times.   2. Poynter, Nelson, 1903–1978.
      3. Newspaper publishing—United States—History—20th century.
      I. Title.
      PN4899.S875S836   1993   93-1392
      071'.5963—dc20   CIP